D0947535

Building Sisterhood

Women and Gender in North American Religions
Amanda Porterfield and Mary Farrell Bednarowski, *Series Editors*

*Theresa Maxis, The Holder of the Fire*, Nancy Lee Smith, I.H.M., iconographer.
William Glaab, photographer. Copyright © 1995 SSIHM.

# Building Sisterhood

*A Feminist History of the Sisters,*
*Servants of the Immaculate Heart of Mary*

◆　◆　◆

Sisters, Servants of the Immaculate Heart of Mary
Monroe, Michigan

Syracuse University Press

First Edition 1997
97  98  99  00  01  02       6  5  4  3  2

All photographs are courtesy of the SSIHM Monroe Archives.

Permission to reprint from the following sources is gratefully acknowledged:

*Composing a Life* by Mary Catherine Bateson. By permission of Penguin USA.

*From Framework to Freedom: A History of the Sister Formation Conference* by Marjorie Noterman Beane. By permission of the author and the Univ. Press of America.

*Surpassing the Love of Men: Romantic Friendship and Love Between Women from the Renaissance to the Present* by Lillian Faderman. By permission of William Morrow.

*Mother Clotilda and Early Companions of the Sisters, Servants of the Immaculate Heart of Mary* by Xaveria McHugh, I.H.M. By permission of Reed Reference.

"Impression of Stately Beauty Surrounds St. Mary Buildings" (10 May 1932). By permission of the *Monroe Evening News.*

"A Scrap of Romantic History" (July 1885) by John H. Greene, S.S.J., in *St. Joseph's Advocate.* By permission of the Josephite Fathers (Mill Hill Fathers).

*Constitution and Directory of the Institute of the Sisters of Divine Providence Established at Saint-Jean-de-Bassel, Diocese of Metz.* By permission of the Sisters of Divine Providence, Melbourne, Ky.

*Constitutions of the Sisters of Charity Established in the State of Kentucky.* By permission of the Sisters of Charity of Nazareth, Ky.

Application form of the Sisters of the Holy Cross of Notre Dame, Ind. By permission of the Sisters of the Holy Cross of Notre Dame, Ind.

Directory for Novices (1865) of the Sisters, Servants of the Immaculate Heart of Mary. By permission of the Sisters, Servants of the Immaculate Heart of Mary of Scranton, Pa.

The paper used in this publication meets the minimum requirements of American National Standard for Information Sciences—Permanence of Paper for Printed Library Materials, ANSI Z39.48-1984. ∞™

### Library of Congress Cataloging-in-Publication Data

Building sisterhood : a feminist history of the Sisters, Servants of
the Immaculate Heart of Mary / [compiled by] Sisters, Servants of
the Immaculate Heart of Mary, Monroe, Michigan.—1st ed.
p.  cm.—(Women and gender in North American religions)
Includes bibliographical references and index.
ISBN 0-8156-2737-8 (cloth : alk. paper).—ISBN 0-8156-2741-6 (pbk. : alk. paper)
1. Sisters, Servants of the Immaculate Heart of Mary—History.
I. Sisters, Servants of the Immaculate Heart of Mary.   II. Series.
BX4522.B85   1997
271'.97—DC21        96-46580

*Manufactured in the United States of America*

*"Tell . . . all my beloved Sisters, those who know
me and those I never saw, that I gather up all that my
heart can contain of happy desires, wishes and hopes for them."*
Mother Theresa Maxis to Sister Genevieve Morrissey,
29 January 1883

◆    ◆    ◆

This book of essays is dedicated to all Sisters,
Servants of the Immaculate Heart of Mary, living and
deceased, and to all sisters with whom we share
values, gifts, and solidarity.

# Contents

# Illustrations

# Foreword

Dorothy McDaniel, I.H.M.

In these pages is a story for everyone: IHM sisters, sisters in other religious communities, and readers of every persuasion who love to discover humanity's story as told through diverse lifestyles. This is a book for women—and for men as well—who seek common ground in the search for life's deepest values.

This collection of essays is based on the history of the Sisters, Servants of the Immaculate Heart of Mary (IHM), founded in Monroe, Michigan, in 1845. Two independent sister congregations in Pennsylvania, one in Scranton and another in Immaculata, also trace their roots to this beginning. Thus, the volume lends a perspective to a heritage cherished today by almost 3,000 women who call themselves IHM, and by the hundreds more who preceded them.

In November 1988, the IHM Central administration took up a 1987 proposal by eighteen sisters and associates suggesting a feminist, interdisciplinary, collaborative approach to IHM history. The elected congregational leadership recognized the initiative not as a call for a comprehensive history (such as our Sister Rosalita Kelly wrote fifty years earlier) but rather for a new way of approaching the IHM story. In March 1990, Joan Glisky, I.H.M., the congregation's general secretary and the appointed coordinator of the project, invited potential participants to a weekend gathering to discuss how the work might be accomplished.

During the next four years and beyond, the IHM congregation witnessed the overflowing enthusiasm and remarkable energy of the women who, under the aegis of Claiming Our Roots (COR), invested themselves in the enterprise as COR members. *Cor* is the Latin word meaning "heart." It is an appropriate choice for two reasons (beyond its symbolism in the acronym): "Heart" is part of the name of the congregation, and much love has gone into this work.

For the COR members, and for the congregation itself, the collaboration became something of a preparation for the IHM sesquicentennial in

1995. As highly conscious carriers of the community history, these women offered memory as the nutriment that poet Adrienne Rich has claimed it to be (see Rich 1986).

They embodied in the process itself something of the content of the IHM story underlying their essays: women collaborating, empowering, befriending, mentoring, supporting, and listening deeply to one another. The congregation is enriched by these women; IHMs and all readers are indebted to them for illustrating—in their words and in their actions— some of the controlling paradigms in the stories that empower us.

Although each essay has been researched thoroughly, the writer's conclusions do not necessarily represent a congregational position. They do, however, invite compelling discussion among members and other readers as well.

No book is ever a single-handed production and certainly not one written in a consciously collaborative mode. In the name of the IHM congregation, we thank the writers whose work appears on these pages. Special appreciation is due to Joan Glisky, who as COR coordinator gave hours and days of every month to this project. Particular appreciation goes also to Celeste Rabaut, I.H.M., archivist emeritus and COR member, who unstintingly contributed her assistance and the resources of the IHM archives; to Julie Wortman, whose genuine zest for the work of editing guided COR writers in shaping and honing their essays; to Margaret Susan Thompson, Ph.D., history professor and author of numerous articles on women's history, whose mentoring and enthusiasm persisted even to the honoring of this volume with an introductory essay and an introduction to each section; and to the sponsors of the History of Women Religious Conference who twice—in 1992 and in 1995—included panels of COR members who reported on the work in process.

Many others made this collaboration genuine and far-reaching. They include Rose Matthew Mangini, I.H.M., who succeeded Celeste as archivist for the congregation, and the archives staff, particularly Imelda Neaton, I.H.M., who with her coworkers accessed materials readily and efficiently; Suzanne Fleming, I.H.M., who transcribed and edited the Mary Joseph Walker papers; Judy Gilleran, whose painstaking transcription of verbatim material helped make the story come alive; and to Patricia Aseltyne, I.H.M., who cheerfully and skillfully transcribed numerous interviews. Appreciation extends to Wilma Rooney, I.H.M., and Genevieve Mary Simon, I.H.M., the archivists of our sister communities in Pennsylvania, and to Mary Reparata Clarke, O.S.P., in the Baltimore motherhouse of the Oblate Sisters of Providence, for their invaluable assistance and for the use of their resources; to Dr. Carol Coburn of Avila College in Kansas City, Missouri, for her generous advice to COR writers during the History of Women Religious Conference in Tarrytown, New York, in 1992; and to Elizabeth Mary Larson, I.H.M., chair of the sociology department at Marygrove College in Detroit, for her consultation on a questionnaire developed by Barbara Johns, I.H.M., to explore an important story about the evolution of the teaching mission in urban America. Warm gratitude goes to Marguerite Daly, I.H.M., whose unfailing hospitality provided a welcoming ambience for committee meetings and on research days in Monroe; to the IHM sisters whose stories inspire and energize this volume; and to friends everywhere who kept anticipation alive by their support and encouragement. Special thanks go to Nancy Sylvester, I.H.M., who with the assistance of Beth Laura coordinated the publication process with Syracuse University Press; to Nancy Dunn for her editing skills; to Barbara Johns, I.H.M., for her computer assistance at the final stage of preparation; and to Nila Neill, I.H.M., Trudy Baltes, I.H.M., and Carolyn Kerwin, I.H.M., for assisting in the final manuscript edit. Special appreciation is due to Suzanne Fleming, I.H.M., and to Celeste Rabaut, I.H.M., for handling the final editing and research for the preparation of the manuscript for publication. Their untiring dedication and countless hours ensured the excellence of the volume to which so many other contributed so much. Finally, our deep appreciation goes to William Kevin Cawley and Roman Godzak, archivists respectively for the University of Notre Dame and the Detroit Archdiocese, for their tireless assistance and patient understanding.

This story is feminist in the noblest sense. It is about the power of individual women and the strength of their collective energies. It is about building and sustaining a community.

You may find in the IHM story some of the roots of your own story. Perhaps you will discover a fresh hope for just and compassionate outcomes as you engage in life's struggles against the horizon of your own deepest beliefs.

# Contributors

MARYFRAN BARBER, I.H.M., served from 1990 until 1993 on an IHM committee charged with proposing ways of restructuring and simplifying the congregation's government. She holds a doctorate in chemistry from Wayne State University, is former associate professor of chemistry at Marygrove College in Detroit, and serves on the board of Detroit's Core City Neighborhoods.

MARGARET BRENNAN, I.H.M., is professor emerita of pastoral theology at Regis College of the Toronto School of Theology. She holds a doctorate in theology and served as general superior of the IHM congregation and as president of the Leadership Conference of Women Religious during the Vatican II period. She has lectured and conducted workshops in the areas of ministry, spirituality, and the role of women in the church. She is currently coordinator of the six-year theological education process undertaken by the IHM congregation.

ELLEN CLANON, I.H.M., was for forty-seven years a teacher of English, from elementary grades through graduate school. She holds a master's degree in education from Wayne State University and did additional graduate work at the following universities: Toronto, St. Louis, Loyola, Iowa, Minnesota, North Carolina Central (Durham), and Sydney. She is currently in retirement but remains actively involved in research, writing, editing, and consultation.

SUZANNE M. FLEMING, I.H.M., is a visiting scholar at the University of Michigan and holds a doctorate in inorganic chemistry from the University of Michigan. From 1986 until 1989 she served as vice chancellor and professor of chemistry at the University of Wisconsin-Eau Claire and from 1983 until 1986 she was provost and academic vice president at Western Illinois University. She has also been an academic administrator at Eastern Michigan University. At Detroit's Marygrove College she was academic vice president for five years following an extended tenure as professor of chemistry and chair of the Division of Natural Science. Fleming has published in professional chemical journals and has been active and held office in numerous scientific and professional organizations.

JOAN GLISKY, I.H.M., served as general secretary and as secretary to the president of the IHM congregation from 1988 through June 1994. She holds a master's degree in theology from Marquette University and pursued doctoral work in religious studies at the Catholic University of America. She has been an educator at elementary, secondary, and undergraduate levels and has served as a parish director of religious education. Currently, she works in adult education.

MARY ANN HINSDALE, I.H.M., is associate professor and chair of the religious studies department at the College of the Holy Cross in Worcester, Massachusetts, where she has been on the faculty since 1987. She holds a doctorate in systematic theology from the University of St. Michael's College, Toronto. In her teaching and research, she has focused on ecclesiology, Christian anthropology, hermeneutics, and feminist theory. She is the author of the forthcoming *Power and Participation in the U.S. Catholic Church: Ecclesiology from the Margins* and coauthor of *It Comes from the People: Community Development and Local Theology.*

BARBARA JOHNS, I.H.M., is associate professor of English and chair of the department at Detroit's Marygrove College, where she has both directed publications and been editor and principal writer for the Marygrove College alumni magazine. She holds a doctorate in American literature from the University of Detroit and has published several articles on the spinster figure in nineteenth-century American literature.

MARY MCCANN, I.H.M., is president of the IHM congregation. From 1982 until 1994, she was associate director of spirituality and ministry programs at Regis College of the Toronto School of Theology. From 1990 to 1993, she chaired an IHM committee charged with proposing ways of restructuring and simplifying the congregation's government. McCann holds a doctorate in educational administration from the University of Notre Dame and is also an experienced spiritual director.

DOROTHY MCDANIEL, I.H.M., teaches at Ladywood High School in Livonia, Michigan (and in adult education in Southgate, Michigan) in her chosen fields of physics and mathematics. She holds a master's degree with a physics major from St. Louis University. During twenty years of teaching physics and mathematics at the secondary and college levels, she developed specialty courses in those disciplines for the nonmathematically gifted. From 1979–94 she served in congregational leadership as province treasurer, provincial, and from 1988–94, as president.

AMATA MILLER, I.H.M., is chief financial officer at Detroit's Marygrove College and is the former economist and education coordinator for NET-WORK, a national Catholic social justice lobby based in Washington, D.C. She has lectured and written widely on economic justice issues, economic literacy, social analysis, socially responsible investing, and other strategies for social transformation. She serves on the board of directors of several national organizations, such as Mercy Housing, Inc., and Shorebank Corporation. She holds a doctorate in economics from the University of California at Berkeley and has taught economics at Marygrove College and at St. Edward's University in Austin, Texas. She was financial vice-president of the IHM congregation from 1976 until 1988.

CAROL QUIGLEY, I.H.M., worked in grassroots community organizing in Detroit for five years, prior to being named vice-president for development for Detroit's Marygrove College in 1994. From 1982–88, she was president of the Sisters, Servants of the Immaculate Heart of Mary. While serving in that capacity, she was elected president of the Leadership Conference of Women Religious and was on its national board for five years. Quigley has served on several boards at the national, state, and local levels. She holds a master of arts in theology from the Toronto School of Theology.

CELESTE RABAUT, I.H.M., joined the COR project as archivist of the IHM congregation (now archivist emerita). She holds a master's degree in library science from the Catholic University of America. She served as general secretary of the IHM congregation for six years and was a member of the library staff at Marygrove College for thirty years.

JOSPHINE SFERRELLA, I.H.M., is data/research director for the Archdiocese of Chicago's Office of Catholic Education, which serves the largest parochial school system in the country. She holds a master's degree from Fordham University and a doctoral degree in sociology from Wayne State University, Detroit. An educator for fifty years, she has served as teacher, supervisor, dean, and principal at all levels: diocesan, university, college, secondary, and elementary and has served on many civic and community organization boards. She is currently a member of the governing board for Immaculate Heart of Mary High School in Westchester, Illinois.

JANE SHEA, I.H.M., serves as an archivist and oral historian for the IHM congregation. She holds a master's degree in administration from the University of Michigan, and she served as a school administrator for nineteen years. She also served for four years as administrator of the St. Mary's Health Care Center at the IHM motherhouse in Monroe, Michigan. Recently, Shea coauthored a pictorial history of the three IHM congregations.

MARITA-CONSTANCE SUPAN, I.H.M., is a Ph.D. candidate and a practicing clinical psychologist with specialities in trauma and dissociative disorders, women's issues, and child play therapy. Supan keeps her hand in the related areas of spirituality, feminist literary studies, ecojustice, and education. A longtime member of the Immaculata congregation before she incorporated into the Monroe community, Supan calls herself a "bicultural IHM."

NANCY SYLVESTER, I.H.M., is vice-president of the IHM congregation. She was on staff with NETWORK, a national Catholic social justice lobby in Washington, D.C., from 1977 to 1992, serving as National Coordinator during 1982–92. She is a published author and lectures widely on a variety of topics including feminism, economic justice, political responsibility, ecofeminism, and Catholic social teaching. She serves on a number of national boards including Common Cause, Mary's Pence, and the National Interfaith Committee for Worker Justice. She received her undergraduate degree from St. Louis University and her master's from St. Mary's College, Winona, Minnesota.

MARGARET SUSAN THOMPSON is associate professor of history, political science, and women's studies at Syracuse University. She received her bachelor's degree from Smith College and her master's degree and doctorate from the University of Wisconsin-Madison. She has written and lectured extensively on the history of Catholic women religious in the United States, and is the author of a forthcoming book on the subject, *The Yoke of Grace: American Nuns and Social Change, 1808–1917.* She is also the author of *The "Spider Web": Congress and Lobbying in the Age of Grant.*

JULIE A. WORTMAN served as editor for the Claiming Our Roots project. Formerly on the communications staff at the Episcopal Church's national headquarters in New York, she is managing editor of the Detroit-based *Witness Magazine,* a journal that examines church and society in the light of faith and conscience. She is a trustee of the Episcopal Diocese of Michigan and a rubber stamp fanatic.

# Abbreviations

| | |
|---|---|
| AC | Acts of Chapter |
| ACz | Alexander Czvitkovicz, C.SS.R. |
| AD | Amadeus Dowd, I.H.M. |
| AF | Application form, IHM |
| A of A | Affirmations of Assembly, MS |
| AgC | Agenda Committee |
| AGR | Archivium Generale Redemptoristarum, Rome |
| AGS | Alphonsine Godfroy-Smyth, I.H.M. |
| AIC | "Reasons to Weigh Against Immaculata Closing," MS |
| AMG | Anna Marie Grix, I.H.M. |
| AR | Angela Rees, I.H.M. |
| ARBEI | Annual Report to Bureau of Educational Institutions, University of Michigan |
| Art. | Article of the Constitutions of SSIHM, Monroe, Michigan |
| AsP | IHM Assembly '87 Proceedings |
| AW | Annette Walters, C.S.J. |
| BC | "[Book of Customs] Instructions for Superiors" 1863, MS |
| BCZ | B. C. Ziegler Co. |
| BH | Bernard Hafkenscheid, C.SS.R. |
| BJ | Barbara Johns, I.H.M. |
| BS | Bridget Smith, I.H.M. |
| B.V.M. | Sisters of Charity of Blessed Virgin Mary |
| BW | Bijou Whipple, granddaughter of Roderick O'Connor |
| CB | Catherine Biry, I.H.M. |
| CBM | Corporation Board Minutes |
| CC | Customs of the Congregation |

| | |
|---|---|
| CCDP | Constitutions of the Sisters of Divine Providence of Melbourne, Kentucky (1883) |
| CD | Celesta Duffy, I.H.M. |
| C.D.P. | Congregation of Divine Providence |
| CDPA | Sisters of Divine Providence Archives |
| CF | Caritas Ferguson, I.H.M. |
| CFR | Caritas Ferguson Recollections |
| CH | Clotilda Hoskyns, I.H.M. |
| C.H.M. | Congregation of the Humility of Mary |
| CL | Circular letter |
| Cloth. L | Clothing list |
| CM | Council Minutes |
| CMSW | Conference of Major Superiors of Women |
| CMy | Colette Myers, I.H.M. |
| Com. Con. | Comments on the Constitutions, MS |
| Conf. | Conference |
| Con. Rep. | Confidential Report of IHMs |
| Const. | Constitutions of the Congregation of the Sisters, Servants of the Immaculate Heart of Mary, Monroe |
| COR | Claiming Our Roots |
| CRHC | Celestine Renauld's "Historical Cronology [sic]," MS |
| C.S.C. | Congregation of the Sisters of the Holy Cross |
| CSCA | Sisters of the Holy Cross Archives |
| CSCN | Constitutions of the Sisters of Charity of Nazareth, Kentucky |
| C.S.J. | Sisters of Saint Joseph |
| C.SS.R. | Redemptorist Fathers and Brothers |
| CWSED | Congregational Withdrawal Summary by Earned Degree, MS SSIHM, Monroe |
| CXR | Celestine Xavier Renauld, I.H.M. |
| DAA | Detroit Archdiocesan Archives |
| D.C. | Daughters of Charity of Saint Vincent de Paul |
| DCr | Davidica Cronin, I.H.M. |
| DeCH | DeChantel Hayes, I.H.M. (Immaculata) |
| DD | Domitilla Donohue, I.H.M. |
| DDP | Domitilla Donohue Papers |
| DG | Discussion group |
| DH | Doris Henn, I.H.M. |

| | |
|---|---|
| DHOA | Diocese of Hamilton, Ontario, Archives |
| DJD | Dennis James Dougherty, Bishop of Philadelphia |
| DJK | D. J. Kenny (of B. C. Ziegler Co.) |
| DLHR | "Design for Living: History of the Rule," MS (Kelly) |
| DMcC | Diane McCormick, I.H.M. |
| DMcD | Dorothy McDaniel, I.H.M. |
| EBM | Executive Board member |
| EBMin. | Executive Board minutes |
| EBSM | Executive Board staff members |
| EC | Ellen Clanon, I.H.M. |
| EF | Egidius Flanagan, I.H.M. |
| EJ | Father Edward Joos |
| EJC | Edward Joos conference |
| EO | Education Office, SSIHM, Monroe |
| ER | Entrance records, SSIHM, Monroe |
| FACI | "Some Reasons For and Against the Continuance of Immaculata," MS |
| FAL | Ferdinand A. Litz, C.SS.R. |
| FDeH | Frederick DeHeld, C.SS.R. |
| FM | Frances Manor, I.H.M. |
| FXS | Francis Xavier Schnüttgen, C.SS.R. |
| GES | Giles Eguidius Smulders, C.SS.R. |
| GG | Gertrude Gerretsen, I.H.M. |
| GI | Group interview |
| GLS | Guide for Local Superiors, MS |
| GM | Genevieve Morrissey, I.H.M. (Scranton) |
| GMS | Genevieve Mary Simon, I.H.M., archivist of Immaculata IHM Congregation |
| GP | Government Plan |
| GPa | George Paré, historian of Archdiocese of Detroit |
| GR | George Ruland, C.SS.R. |
| GSR | General Superiors Report: 1966–71; 1972–76 1982–88 |
| HB | Henry Brennan |
| HD | Hugh Duffy, S.S.J., historian of Oblate Sisters of Providence |
| HFG | Henry F. Giesen, C.SS.R. |
| HMg | History of Marygrove College, MS (Kelly) |
| H of C | "A History of the Constitutions," MS (Maher) |

| | |
|---|---|
| HTC | Holy Trinity Chronicles, MS Detroit, Michigan |
| HV | Helen Vivian |
| IA | SSIHM Immaculata Archives |
| ID | Ignatia Doyle, I.H.M. |
| IFS | Instructions for Superiors, MS |
| IHM | Congregation of the Sisters, Servants of the Immaculate Heart of Mary |
| IHMC | Immaculate Heart of Mary chronicles, MS Minnetonka, Minnesota |
| IHM H/H | "IHM History/Heritage: A Mosaic of Strong Traditions," MS |
| IHS | Immaculata High School |
| IHSAS | IHS Alumnae Survey |
| IHSCL | IHS Class Lists, MS |
| IHSF | IHS Files |
| IHSMC | IHS Mission Chronicles, MS |
| IHSNCRM | IHS North Central report materials |
| IHSPPS | IHS Parent to Parent Survey |
| IHS Prosp. | "Immaculata High School for Girls," [Detroit, Michigan], MS |
| IHSSG | IHS Student Guide |
| IHSYB | IHS Yearbook |
| IMN | Instructions for Mistresses of Novices, MS |
| IN | Instructions for Novices, MS |
| INe | Imelda Neaton, I.H.M. |
| Info. | Information Handbook (updated periodically) |
| Inst. | Instruction |
| ITM | Ida Therese McGinty, I.H.M. |
| IW | Ignatius Walker, I.H.M. |
| JDeN | Father John DeNève |
| JF | Bishop John Farrell of Hamilton, Ontario |
| JGil | Father John Gillard |
| JG | Joan Glisky, I.H.M. |
| JMB | John Mary Baker, I.H.M. |
| JMJ | Joseph Mary Jacobs, C.SS.R. |
| JNN | John Nepomucene Neumann, C.SS.R., Bishop of Philadelphia |
| JP | James Poirier, C.SS.R. |

| | |
|---|---|
| JR | Jamesetta Rhoads, I.H.M. |
| JRi | Justina Reilly, I.H.M. |
| JS | Josephine Sferrella, I.H.M. |
| JSh | Jane Shea, I.H.M. |
| JVG | Father John Van Gennip |
| JVOR | Father John Vincent O'Reilly |
| JW | James Wood, Bishop of Philadelphia |
| KF | Kenneth Foyster, archivist of the Hamilton, Ontario, diocese |
| KIO | "Reasons Why It Seems Feasible to Keep Immaculata Open," MS |
| KWL | Kent W. Leach |
| LAG | Local assembly group |
| LD | Leocadia Delanty, I.H.M. |
| LFG | Louis Florent Gillet, C.SS.R. |
| Life | Biography of Mary Joseph Walker, MS |
| LP | List for Postulants, MS |
| LS | Ludwina Schulte, I.H.M. |
| LW | Listing of Withdrawals from Monroe SSIHM, MS |
| MA | SSIHM Monroe Archives |
| MAH | Mary Ann Hinsdale, I.H.M. |
| MAR | Maria Alma Ryan, I.H.M., historian of Immaculata Congregation |
| *Marq.* | *Marquee,* IHS student newspaper |
| MAW | Marie Andre Walsh, I.H.M. |
| MB | Margaret Brennan, I.H.M. |
| MC | Margaret Cutcher, I.H.M. |
| MCM | Mount Carmel Mission, Wyandotte, Michigan (Superiors Guides), MS |
| MCon | Mother Consuella, O.S.P. |
| MCS | Marie Chantal Sipes, I.H.M. |
| MCSu | Marita-Constance Supan, I.H.M. |
| MD | Marguerite Daly, I.H.M. |
| MDeD | M. Deloul Diary |
| MDI | Management Design Incorporated |
| MDIR | Management Design Incorporated Report |
| Mem. Stat. | Membership Statistics, MS SSIHM Monroe |

| | |
|---|---|
| Mengy. | Menology: A remembering written after a sister's death and arranged by date of death, MS |
| MEP | Mary Emil Penet, I.H.M. |
| MfB | Maryfran Barber, I.H.M. |
| Mg | Marygrove College, Detroit |
| MgC | Marygrove College chronicles, MS |
| MgCC | Marygrove College *Contact,* Alumnae Publication |
| MgNCSS | "Marygrove College North Central Association Institutional Self-Study Report," MS |
| MJC | Mary Judith Connelly, I.H.M. |
| MJG | Michael James Gallagher, Bishop of Detroit |
| MJM | Mary Jo Maher, I.H.M. |
| MJS | Mary Jerome Sanford, I.H.M. |
| MJW | Mary Joseph Walker, I.H.M. |
| MJWP | Mary Joseph Walker Papers |
| MK | Mary Kinney, I.H.M. |
| MM | Monroe Motherhouse |
| MMC | Monroe Motherhouse chronicles, MS |
| MMcC | Mary McCann, I.H.M. |
| MMcD | Mrs. McDermott |
| MMcK | Margaret McKoan, I.H.M. |
| M of MR | "Memories of Sister Miriam Raymo" |
| MPR | Mary Patrick Riley, I.H.M. |
| MPRy | Mary Philip Ryan, O.P., historian of Adrian Dominican Congregation |
| MR | Miriam Raymo, I.H.M. |
| MRC | M. Reparata Clarke, O.S.P. |
| MRO | Membership Record, Official SSIHM Monroe |
| MST | Margaret Susan Thompson |
| MVG | Mary VanGilder, I.H.M. |
| MW | Mary Whipple, I.H.M. |
| MWJ | Mother Wilhelmina's journal (Sisters of Saint Mary of Oregon) |
| NC | Novitiate Collection |
| NCE | *New Catholic Encyclopedia* |
| NCEA | National Catholic Educational Association |
| NCWC | National Catholic Welfare Conference |
| ND | Novitiate Directory (1903, 1957) |

| | |
|---|---|
| NF | Nicholas Firle, C.SS.R. |
| NFM | *New Family Manual* |
| OAD | Office of the Academic Dean, Mg |
| OCD | *Official Catholic Directory* |
| O.F.M. | Franciscan Friars |
| OG | Oliver Golden, lawyer for SSIHM, Monroe |
| OGCR | Operational Guidelines Committee Report, MS |
| OHC | "Outline of History of the Constitutions," MS (Kelly) |
| O.M.I. | Oblates of Mary Immaculate |
| O.P. | Dominican Sisters |
| O.S.B. | Benedictines |
| O.S.P. | Oblate Sisters of Providence |
| OSPA | OSP Archives |
| OSPAn | OSP Motherhouse Annals |
| OSPR | OSP Rule |
| OSPRe | OSP Report |
| PA | Patricia Aseltyne, I.H.M. |
| PB | Prudentia Brand, I.H.M. |
| PC | Peter Chakert, C.SS.R. |
| PDOD | Personnel Diagram and Operational Description, MS |
| PGRL | Principles of Government in Religious Life, MS |
| PJW | P. Joseph Wissel, C.SS.R. |
| PPL | Peter Paul Lefevere, Bishop of Detroit |
| PRAL | Primitive Rule of Saint Alphonsus |
| Pr. Bk. | Profession Book |
| Prosp. | Prospectus |
| Quest. | Questionnaire |
| RA | Representative Asssembly |
| RAD | RA delegate |
| RAF | RA facilitator |
| RAM | RA Minutes |
| RAO | RA observer |
| RAR | RA Report |
| RDC | Residence Directory Compilation, MS SSIHM, Monroe |
| RECW | Report of the Everett Curriculum Workshop |
| R from A | "Rebuilding from Ashes" |
| RH | Ruth Hankerd, I.H.M. |

| | |
|---|---|
| RHN | Ruth Hankerd notes, MS |
| RK | Rosalita Kelly, I.H.M. |
| RMcD | Ruth McDonell, I.H.M. |
| RMM | Rose Matthew Mangini, I.H.M., archivist of Monroe IHM Congregation |
| RN | Robert Nessler |
| RSSC | Regulations for the Society of the Sisters of Charity |
| SA | SSIHM Scranton Archives |
| SAP | Study Abroad Program |
| SCNA | Sisters of Charity of Nazareth Archives, Kentucky |
| SCT | S. C. Turner |
| SF | Suzanne Fleming, I.H.M. |
| SFAATY | "Still Finer after All These Years" |
| SFC | Sister Formation Conference |
| SFM | Saint Francis Mission (Superiors Guide), MS |
| SGG | Superiors Guide/Gleanings, MS |
| S.J. | Jesuit Fathers and Brothers |
| SJD | Saint Joseph, Detroit |
| SLWY | "Statistical Listing of Withdrawal by Years," MS SSIHM, Monroe |
| SM | Spiro Micallef |
| SMA | Saint Mary, Adrian, Michigan |
| SMHCCB | Saint Mary Health Care Center brochure, MS |
| SMP | Saint Mary, Painesville, Ohio |
| SN | "Separation Notes," MS (Kelly) |
| S.N.D.deN. | Sisters of Notre Dame de Namur |
| S of F | "Story of the Fire" |
| S.P. | Sisters of Providence |
| SPCC | Saint Peter Claver chronicles, Mobile, Alabama |
| SS | Summer School |
| SSIHM | Sisters, Servants of the Immaculate Heart of Mary |
| S.S.J. | St. Joseph's Society of the Sacred Heart (Josephite Fathers) |
| S.S.J. | Sisters of Saint Joseph |
| SSMOA | Sisters of Saint Mary of Oregon Archives, Beaverton, Oregon |
| TM | Theresa Maxis, I.H.M. |
| TMcG | Teresa McGivney, I.H.M. |
| TMN | "Notes Regarding the Foundation," MS |

| | |
|---|---|
| T of E | "A Tradition of Excellence: The IHM Educational Ministry," MS |
| UNDA | University of Notre Dame Archives |
| WC | West Chester (motherhouse moved to Immaculata, Pa. in 1930s) |
| WCN | "West Chester Notes," MS (Mary James Sweeney, I.H.M.) |
| WR | Wilma Rooney, I.H.M., archivist of Scranton IHM Congregation |
| XB | Xaveria Barton, I.H.M. |
| XE | Xavier Eagan, I.H.M. |

Building Sisterhood

# Introduction

## Concentric Circles of Sisterhood

### Margaret Susan Thompson

The seed for *Building Sisterhood* was planted in 1988, when the central administration of the religious community known as the Sisters, Servants of the Immaculate Heart of Mary of Monroe, Michigan (or, more familiarly, the IHMs) authorized creation of a task force to "set up a process for examining the history of the Congregation from an interdisciplinary, feminist perspective." In so doing, the leadership was responding to a proposal that was submitted to the 1988 chapter (constituent governing body) calling for the creation of a task force to implement feminist research into IHM history. The small group that submitted what became Proposal 14 understood this as one way to implement what the entire congregation pledged itself to in their 1987 Assembly, to "consciously choose to educate [o]urselves to the feminist perspective . . . and to operate from our understandings as they develop." Although the chapter did not deliberate on this proposal, the leadership's subsequent action can be credited directly to this grassroots initiative (COR doc., Feb. 1991, MA).

The task force, comprised of volunteers from among the IHM sisters, met for the first time in March 1990 and was named Claiming Our Roots, or COR. That meeting began a process that lasted for more than a year and that resulted in a set of seventeen working assumptions about the nature of history, about feminist scholarship, and about the group's own mandate from the community. (See the Appendix for the text of the working assumptions). Since then, additional women have joined COR as consultants, observers, researchers, and writers; still others—most but not all of them IHMs—have supported various aspects of the endeavor.

My own connection with COR began in April 1991. As a historian of American sisters and a feminist, I was invited to serve as a consultant who could bring context to the final stages of the project. After reading the early COR documents as well as minutes of its first year's meetings,

1

I became both excited about what had started to emerge and rather skeptical about what I might be able to add. It was clear that COR was a remarkable group of women: bright, rigorous, articulate, prayerful, willing to take risks—and to laugh a lot along the way. Who would not want to spend time with such women, superfluous as my participation might be? Thus, I traveled to Monroe, Michigan, where the IHMs have their deepest roots, for my first face-to-face contact with COR members.

Since that weekend, I have been kept informed about the group's evolution and efforts through frequent written and verbal communication. Also, several COR members attended the second History of Women Religious conference in 1992, where we resumed face-to-face dialogue. Then, early in 1993, I was asked to write the introduction to COR's proposed book—an invitation that I had hoped would come and that took me about seven-and-a-half seconds to accept. Thus, I have had the chance to read one or more versions of most of the essays that appear in this volume, appropriately entitled *Building Sisterhood*—a book that grew into being during more than four years of intensive and innovative activity.

There, in bare-boned terms, is the story of COR's origins and of my involvement with it. However, like a chronology or an organization chart, such a summary conveys little of the reality that is COR or of my response to the undeniably limited role I have played.

Historians are causal creatures, obsessed with motivation and grounding for whatever phenomena we try to explain. Despite assertions to the contrary from generations of scholars, however, we are not wholly objective; like all inquirers, we inevitably bring our own pasts and preconceptions to the subjects we explore. Therefore, it seems appropriate to preface my assertions with a brief explanation of my perspective on the history of American sisters generally and of the IHMs in particular.

I grew up in near ignorance of nuns. My non-Catholic childhood was spent in a university town of the Deep South, with one Catholic church and no school or other institution where sisters might have been found. Only two images—distinct but not inconsistent—interrupted my obliviousness to nuns. The first appeared when I attended the original Broadway production of *The Sound of Music*, in which Mary Martin portrayed the world's oldest (failed) postulant and the cloistered religious seemed to spend most of their time singing. The second was a fascination with the books of Maryknoll's Sister Maria del Rey, which I discovered in the public library and which chronicled the adventures of her order's missionaries in Asia, Latin America, and the Pacific. From the former encounter, I determined that nuns were unusually happy creatures who nonetheless did their part to subvert the Nazis; from the latter, I became convinced that sisters were among the most adventurous and daring of women, highly accomplished professionals who lived far more exciting lives than most of the other role models presented to me as a preteen.

As I got older, sisters made only sporadic incursions into my consciousness—as participants in civil rights demonstrations or antiwar rallies, as tutors of inner-city youth, and as occasional guests on television programs. They wore modified habits and spoke articulately about issues of social justice. Such was the state of my (un)awareness until autumn 1982, when a faculty colleague at Syracuse University told me one day at lunch that she had taught a sister in a graduate seminar the previous semester and that she had had a few conversations with her about religious life. "It was fascinating," my colleague declared. "Sisters really are very interesting people." Then, she asked a question whose effect neither of us could possibly have understood at the time: "Why don't you think about including a lecture about sisters in your History of American Women course next term?"[1] The result was not only a lecture but a fascination with what I discovered about the remarkable and generally unknown record of sisters' contributions both to U.S. history and to American Catholicism. Long after that first lecture was researched and delivered, I found myself poring eagerly over whatever books I could find about these women. Within a year, I decided that their story had to be told and that I might as well be the one to tell it.

Thus, my own understanding of sisters evolved not within a religious framework but within the context of women's history and feminist studies, not from personal experience with the "good sisters" at some vaguely remembered parochial school but from research and personal acquaintances that date back only to the mid-1980s. Since beginning my exploration into what has evolved into a book-length feminist analysis of the Americanization of the lives of women religious, I have read hundreds of books, visited more than six dozen congregational archives (including those both of the Monroe and of the Scranton, Pennsylvania, IHMs), and come into contact with countless sisters who continue the traditions of community, spirituality, and service that their foremothers initiated in the United States nearly two centuries ago.[2]

This, then, is the vantage point from which I shall attempt to put *Building Sisterhood* in context, as my mandate from COR asked. Like the essays that follow, this contextual analysis is both intellectual and affective, objective and subjective, communal and highly personal. *Building Sisterhood* is all these things because it is preeminently a story of sisterhood.

One of the most prominent metaphors in feminist discourse is the

1. The colleague was Amanda Porterfield, formerly of Syracuse University and later professor of religious studies at Indiana University/Purdue University-Indianapolis, who has continued to provide valued personal and intellectual support for my research.
2. See Thompson (forthcoming). Some of my preliminary findings, upon which I draw extensively in this essay, are contained in Thompson 1986a, 1987a, 1989b, 1991, 1992, 1994.

circle, something that has neither beginning nor end and that challenges presumptions of hierarchy because all of the circle is equidistant from the center. I have come to see COR as a set of concentric circles, each representing a dimension of the sisterhood that both initiated and continues to inform its analysis.

Near the center is the organized sisterhood of the IHM congregation, the group of women religious whose past and present brought focus to the essays in this volume.

The IHMs are not unique, however. As a canonical community of apostolic sisters—that is, an uncloistered congregation, approved by the church hierarchy and formed to undertake active ministry—the IHMs were among more than 420 such groups that had established themselves in the United States by 1917.[3] Thus, another of the concentric circles of sisterhood is that which unites the experiences of hundreds of thousands of women who have taken religious vows as have the IHMs. A broad look at religious sisterhood in America helps determine where the IHMs fit into the picture. Further, the deliberately feminist approach that COR has taken from the outset suggests the largest of the concentric circles: the sisterhood that feminists perceive among all women, regardless of their experiences or states of life. Most of the contributors to this book make the feminist dimensions of their analyses explicit, and I will try (here and in my introductions to each part of the book) to suggest some of the broad implications that emerge from the overall work.

Finally, turning back to the very center, there is the special sisterhood of COR itself. Although all of the task force members as well as the writers of each chapter are members of the IHM congregation, the particular experiences they shared in COR for more than four years created bonds of sisterhood that are theirs alone. It is this heart of COR—the *cor* of COR—that is most difficult to convey in words and yet so important to understand, for the deliberation, collaboration, ritual, rigor, humor, tears, struggles, celebrations, and emerging awareness of COR are characteristic of the circles of sisterhood that comprised its context and informed its vision.

◆   ◆   ◆

The history of the IHMs, including the community's founding and early experiences, provides most of the substance of the essays that follow. The IHM community, like nearly all of the twenty-seven apostolic congregations that preceded it, was born more out of practical necessity

3. I have identified 422 such communities; a list will appear as an appendix to Thompson (forthcoming). Principal sources I consulted in compiling this list were Dehey 1930, Lexau 1964, Thomas 1983, and Curry 1989. Additionally, I have incorporated individual references encountered in the course of my research.

than out of spiritual impulse.[4] Teachers were needed to serve a growing population, and—like the majority of Catholics at the time—clerics on the Michigan frontier believed that religious could more effectively assume the responsibilities of forming the young than men or women who were not committed permanently by vow to such ministry.[5]

Indeed, the birth of the IHMs did not represent the first effort to provide sister-teachers to instruct the area's young women. Some itinerant French Poor Clares, as well as a briefly extant group under the direction of pioneer missionary Father Gabriel Richard, had conducted short-lived schools in Detroit during the first decade of the nineteenth century. In Monroe, there had even been a previous attempt to begin a religious order: Father Samuel Smith, pastor of St. Anthony's Church, created what he designated a "monastery" in 1829 to take charge of a school in his parish. Although he did this without authorization, the house was said to contain both sisters and novices when Bishop Edward Fenwick of Cincinnati (who at that time had jurisdiction over Michigan) granted it tentative approval in early 1830. However, when Father Smith left St. Anthony's and Monroe later that year, both school and community were disbanded (Tentler 1990, 83–97; see also Koester 1980 and Sullivan 1940). Thus, the IHMs would constitute the first women's religious order to establish itself permanently in Michigan.

The IHMs owe their existence to both female and male founders. For many years—in fact, until after Vatican II—primacy in this respect was given to the young Redemptorist missionary Father Louis Florent Gillet. It was he, after all, who presented to both his bishop and his religious superiors the case that sisters were desirable and necessary; it was he who invited Sister Marie Therese of Baltimore's Oblate Sisters of Providence to leave her community and help to birth a new one on the banks of the River Raisin. However, three factors make a persuasive case for the co-equality of Sister Marie Therese (later, Mother Theresa Maxis) in the endeavor.[6] First, it is clear from her writings (some unavailable to earlier IHM historians) that she was desirous of leaving the Oblates even before Gillet's formal invitation and that, in all likelihood, she had offered to follow him west during a visit he had made to Baltimore in the months before her departure. Second, Gillet remained in Michigan for less than two years after the IHM community was formed in 1845; thus, Maxis's

4. This figure is derived from "Table of US Founding Dates" in Thomas 1983, 169–76; generalization is based on my research, some of which is included in the works listed in note 2.

5. This notion of the spiritual superiority of sisters is discussed extensively in Thompson 1989b, 1991.

6. I base this discussion on the work of Margaret Gannon (1992) and, especially, Marita-Constance Supan (see chap. 1 in the present volume), along with that of Suzanne Fleming, (see chap. 2 in the present volume).

influence was much more extensive than his. Indeed, it was she rather than Father Gillet or his confreres—all of whom had left Monroe by 1855 —who was determined to preserve Alphonsian practices as the basis for IHM spirituality. Even today, that spirituality (based firmly on theological and devotional traditions developed by St. Alphonsus Liguori) is recognizable as an essential part of the IHM charism and tradition (see chapter 3 of the volume). Finally, the attribution of primacy to Gillet is consistent with Catholic tradition, which historically has given clerics credit for all that occurs within their pastoral jurisdictions.[7] Thus, the emerging truth is that although Gillet was a significant factor in the establishment of the IHMs, at least as much credit is due to the woman who collaborated with him.

Still, it was difficult for COR to determine and spell out exactly what roles Gillet and Maxis played in laying the foundation for the community. In deliberations and in actual research, agonizing questions arose: To what extent would feminist intentionality lead to a distorted emphasis on the woman's contribution? On the other hand, to what extent had patriarchal assumptions resulted in a diminution of her significance, and what was the responsibility of feminist scholars to acknowledge and remedy that situation? It is clear, from the minutes of COR meetings and from several of the accounts presented in this volume, that celebrating the formative influence of Maxis is important—if not fundamental —to understanding the meaning of IHM sisterhood. All IHMs share her legacy and are the spiritual beneficiaries of her gifts and of her suffering.

In dealing with the circumstances of their founding, COR and the IHMs had to confront a number of factors that, superficially at least, seemed unique. Theresa Maxis Duchemin was a woman of color, the daughter of an unmarried San Domingan (now Haitian) woman; however, after her departure from the Oblate Sisters of Providence, she spent the rest of her life passing as white. Given that the IHM order was for most of its history deliberately and exclusively a white congregation, and that until recently illegitimacy required special dispensation under canon law before a prospective member could be admitted, these matters traditionally had been regarded as problematic and embarrassing, easier to obscure or ignore than to acknowledge. As some of the essays in this book suggest, Maxis's racial identity continued to complicate her own life and the lives of subsequent generations of IHMs in communities both in Michigan and in Pennsylvania.[8]

In what ways did the fact that Maxis was a woman of color exacer-

---

7. See, for example, almost every entry in Dehey 1930 for the most telling evidence of this.

8. See, in particular, chaps. 1 and 2 in the present volume. See also Gannon 1992 and Shea and Supan 1983. I have addressed these issues in Thompson 1985, 1989a.

bate the tensions that emerged between her and various clerics who sought hegemony over the IHMs? To what extent was her eighteen-year exile from the congregation of her founding and even from the country of her birth (she left the United States for Canada) attributable to her status as a person of mixed race? Even today, answers to such questions may be impossible to discern definitively, but it became clear to COR that the integrity of IHM sisterhood demanded that such issues be confronted with honesty and rigor.

Thus, the circles of sisterhood encompassing the Monroe IHMs are in turn circumscribed by factors unique to these women's history. Even—or perhaps especially—as they have been obscured over the years, the controversies surrounding Maxis have had pronounced effects on what it has meant to be a Monroe IHM. For example, would Father Edward Joos have been able to exercise the extent and duration of authority over the IHMs that he enjoyed for forty-four years had not Maxis been who she was? Would submission to clericalism have become so characteristic of the congregation during its first century and beyond had not most of its senior members followed Maxis to Pennsylvania in the 1850s, thereby leaving the young, inexperienced, sickly, and scrupulous convert Mary Joseph Walker to become, in effect, "true foundress" in the minds of those who stayed behind in Monroe? Would a founder less concerned than Maxis about maintaining secrecy regarding her background have been more capable of preventing the division of her sisters into distinct communities that were officially forbidden for years from communicating with each other? Would today's IHM sisterhood, then, incorporate all of Maxis's daughters into a single and unbroken circle instead of the three more or less cousinly bodies that pledge separate loyalties to Monroe, Michigan, to Immaculata, Pennsylvania, and to Scranton, Pennsylvania?

A volume such as *Building Sisterhood* cannot answer all of these questions, but it can at least ask them—explicitly, forthrightly, and in some cases for the first time. What has emerged is a powerful historical subtext that records the survival of an underground IHM charism, a personally empowering spirituality that is the legacy both of Maxis and of St. Alphonsus. This subterranean charism represents an ongoing (although neither consistent nor wholesale)[9] challenge to what several of the authors describe as the authoritarian and Jansenistic[10] framework

9. See, for example, chaps. 5 and 10 in the present volume.

10. Officially, Jansenism was a deterministic theology that grew out of reformist inclinations but was ultimately condemned by the Catholic Church because it disregarded free will and depended on predestination; its narrow definition of morality downplayed personal responsibility and initiative. Unofficially, it is often seen as having tainted the thinking and behavior of many Catholics (including many clerics) through excessive reliance on rules and on legalistic structures to define spirituality and morality in religious communities and in secular life.

imposed on the congregation by Detroit Bishop Peter Paul Lefevere and Father Joos during the nearly half-century of Joos's reign as ecclesiastical superior to the IHMs. It is impossible to determine the extent to which the charism was deliberately maintained as a form of resistance and the extent to which it was unintended and unconscious. What is clear, however, is that underneath the formalism and legalism that defined so much of the congregation's outer framework for more than a century after Mother Theresa's departure there was a definite persistence of the flexibility, personalism, and pioneer creativity that were characteristic of the community's first decade (explored in detail in the essay by Marita-Constance Supan).

The particular ways in which these traits manifested themselves are valued components of IHM folklore and tradition. Joan Glisky's essay catalogs the many proscriptions against "particular friendships" in IHM Constitutions and practice, but her research and that of Nancy Sylvester make it evident that sisters in every period of IHM history have found ways to circumvent such restrictions. Similarly, Amata Miller's analysis of the extraordinary building program undertaken during the Great Depression reflects the "providential"—and practical—spirituality that Mother Theresa brought with her from the Oblates; the delightful aside concerning Mother Ruth Hankerd and Sister Miriam Raymo's surreptitious stops for fast food is a richly human example of subversive yet pervasive playfulness. Both Carol Quigley and Jane Shea, in their treatments of mental and of physical illness, record a legacy of loving and sisterly care that survived despite a distorted religious notion of "death to self" that encouraged disregard for the well-being of others and indifference to their suffering. Finally, as Barbara Johns recalls in her account of Immaculata High School, underneath the facade of Marian meekness and gentility that the faculty members worked so diligently to model in themselves and to instill in the "young ladies" under their tutelage was a respect for rigor, for intellectual curiosity, and for womanly accomplishment that was constitutive of IHM education.

Ultimately, however, the power and pervasiveness of personalism is recorded most movingly in Margaret Brennan's essay on IHM spirituality. Even as regular religious observance came to be defined as the saying of prayers uniformly and in unison, the Monroe tradition of poverty books —in effect, compilations of favorite prayers, psalms, devotions, and quotations for reflection—encouraged each sister to develop and express her own special and distinct relationship to God. At its most profound level, therefore, and even when it appeared to reflect standardization, the circle of sisterhood that collectively defined and embraced IHMs was composed of individuals.

◆　　◆　　◆

Even as particular attributes of the Monroe sisterhood are acknowledged, attributes that shaped a unique IHM identity, the group's kinship with the larger community of America's women religious must be recognized and affirmed. Others besides the IHMs trace their origins to founders as unlike the supposedly traditional model as was Mother Theresa Maxis of Monroe. Odilia Berger, for example, founder of the Franciscan Sisters of Mary, was an unwed mother (see Henninger 1979)—as was Sister Anthony Duchemin, O.S.P., Maxis Duchemin's own mother! The women who began orders such as the Hawthorne Dominicans, the Religious of the Holy Child Jesus, the Sisters of Divine Compassion, and the Franciscans of Perpetual Adoration (La Crosse) were separated from spouses or divorced.[11] Like Mother Theresa, Mother St. Andrew Feltin of the Sisters of Divine Providence (in Texas) was forced into exile from her community (ironically, for an identical eighteen years); her congregation too was eventually divided, by a bishop's determination and not hers.[12] Similarly, a number of other American founders were women who belonged to a succession of congregations; among these were Mothers Alfred Moes, Stanislaus Leary, and Scholastica Kerst.[13] Moreover, like the IHMs in Monroe, other religious "families" have had to confront the trauma of founders' departures as well as separations both temporary and permanent—frequently prompted by clerics rather than sisters. Add to these experiences those of temporary excommunication and interdict, corporate relocation to escape abusive prelates, and clerical interference in juridical and administrative processes (for admission or dismissal of members, handling of finances, and selection of leaders)—not to mention frustration in defining or pursuing spiritual goals—and it is evident how typical the IHM atypicality really is (see Thompson 1991; also 1987b).

Readers with some knowledge of pre–Vatican II religious life, for example, will recognize much that is familiar in Mary Ann Hinsdale's insightful account of IHM novitiate formation, although her essay is rich with detail particular to this congregation. Similarly, people who remember women's secondary schools will recognize in Barbara Johns's piece the similarities the IHMs' Immaculata High School shared with dozens of such schools throughout the country. On the other hand, Josephine M.

---

11. See the biographies of Rose Hawthorne Lathrop (Maynard 1948; Valenti 1991), Cornelia Connelly (Flaxman 1991), and Mary Veronica Starr (Brady 1962), along with the discussion of Mother M. Antonia Herb of the LaCrosse Franciscans in Ludwig 1950, 415–20.

12. See several of my articles (1987a,1989b,1991) for treatment of Mother St. Andrew Feltin; also Callahan 1954 and Murphy 1980 (a biography of Mother St. Andrew's successor, with extensive coverage of the latter's exile).

13. On Moes, see Kraman 1990. Sister Peg Brennan of the Rochester Sisters of St. Joseph has written an unpublished biography of Leary, *Persistence of Vision*; see also Thomas 1948. For Kerst, see Boo 1991.

Sferrella's essay on the education of the IHM sisters themselves describes a phenomenon that has parallels in other American congregations but that here—in its relatively early emphasis on professionalism and advanced studies—was precedent-setting. The pathbreaking role of the IHMs in what became known as the Sister Formation Movement, which Sferrella also discusses, introduced much of what had originated in Monroe to sisters across the country, thereby enabling others to share in the fruits of this truly atypical development.[14]

In the years since Vatican II, contact and cooperation among religious communities has become the norm. No longer is it remarkable that women from various orders routinely work, live, and pray together; no longer are they separated by barriers of habit, constitutional minutiae, or rigidly enforced custom. However, sisters' general lack of familiarity with the entirety of their own—much less others'—congregational histories has resulted in a tendency to underestimate the common bonds they share with others. Lacking a perspective about shared experiences, communities have been led by some sort of imposed decorum of piety to obscure and even deny what they believe must be aberrant or disedifying pieces of their traditions. Such distorted notions of religious propriety have had consequences, both for contemporary praxis and for the construction of a relevant past.

A single example will serve to illustrate the dangers. Various of the COR scholars note, correctly, that before Vatican II, strictness of observance and an exaggerated rigor were characteristic of life in the Monroe congregation. For decades, this was a source of community pride and of individual salvific reassurance, because any sister who was obedient according to these precepts was well on her way to what was deemed as perfection and, presumably, to heaven. Unquestionably, hundreds of women were able to adjust to the expected standards—and doubtless achieved both temporal fulfillment and eternal reward for their efforts. Still, Carol Quigley suggests in her essay that at least some of the mental illness that has been diagnosed in IHMs of every generation can be attributed to the inability of certain individuals to fit into a standardized, rigid, and perhaps unhealthy mold. Marita-Constance Supan and Suzanne Fleming, meanwhile, reveal that this mold derives more from the legacies of the scrupulous and deferential Mother Mary Joseph Walker and the Jansenistic Father Joos than it does from the intentions and charism of Maxis, Gillet, and the earliest pioneer sisters. Meanwhile, subsequent generations of congregational leaders denigrated and minimized the formative roles of Maxis and of Gillet or stigmatized them as unfortunate deviations from which the community later needed to be saved by its

---

14. Additional information on Sister Formation can be found in chapter 12 of the present volume.

"true" founders, Walker and Joos. Under the circumstances, who is aberrant, and what really are the community's most fundamental values and behavioral norms? What adjustments in self-understanding are required of a group that comes to recognize that its earliest roots have been depreciated and that some of the most basic values it has espoused derive not from its original charism but from reaction against that charism?

Attempts such as COR's at uncovering the realities beneath the layers of pious myth are both difficult and painful—even if, in the end, they are liberating. Sisters who make the effort must not only do the nitty-gritty of research that is integral to all historical inquiry, they must also be prepared to discard the hagiographic baggage accumulated through several generations of synthetic (and frequently quite reassuring) tradition-building. Even so, the pain and difficulty can be assuaged to the degree that they are understood as part of a process that engages an even wider circle of sisterhood than any single community can contain. In the aftermath of Vatican II, such processes have been entered into by dozens of groups, with frequently unexpected results. The fact that so many of these inquiries have been done—and that they have been done independently of one another—is due to the remaining (although lesser) barriers that separate congregations because of persistent assumptions about perceived uniqueness and because of practices that value the solitary scholarly inquiry over the collaborative one. Perhaps what is required here is a new component to the spirituality of poverty—a recognition that congregations do not own their pasts exclusively but, rather, share them with a larger community.

Thus, it is important to realize that the IHMs are not alone in needing to uncover the truth of their past and in needing to reinterpret what has been handed down. Nor are they the only ones to have started to do so. Even as the IHMs struggle to acknowledge Maxis as a founder in whom they can take pride and as one who had a vision very different from that which has been long accepted as quintessentially IHM, the Sisters of St. Joseph of Peace have begun to reidentify themselves gratefully as daughters of the apostate Margaret Anna Cusack, who left the Catholic Church after persistent clashes with prelates and who spent much of the last decade of her life writing harsh critiques of Roman clerical authoritarianism.[15] Similarly, only for the past decade or so have the Sisters of St. Mary of Oregon faced openly their origins in what must be recognized as a schismatic cult, not to mention the demotion and humiliation of their Mother Wilhelmina, the woman who preserved their story in her diary and memoirs, saw to their rescue and rehabilitation, and served as their first (if demoted) superior (see MWJ, SSMOA; Schoenberg 1986). Groups whose founders or former leaders spent their final years in obscurity or

15. See McQuaide 1992; Cusack 1891; Eagar 1979; Vidulich 1975; O'Neill 1990.

exile are too numerous to recount; only now are at least some of these congregations looking frankly at the stultifying factors of institutional life that led to the suppression or censure of the prophetic and free spirits among them.[16] As a result, and contrary to earlier notions of proper and edifying piety, it appears that deviation from some ahistorical and mythical norm is in reality an essential element of life in a religious congregation!

Therefore, as they have struggled to confront their own heritage with honesty and intellectual rigor, the Monroe IHMs are assuming their place within a larger circle of sisterhood that includes all women religious who have taken seriously the call of Vatican II to explore and claim identification with the truth of their pasts. Another task remains, even as the IHMs complete their research and publish their findings: The product of their labors—like similar endeavors by other sisters—must rightfully be placed into a context that transcends specificity and exclusivity and that celebrates a sisterhood broader and deeper than one bounded either by community membership or by canonical status.[17]

◆   ◆   ◆

Underlying the COR project and fundamental to the impetus that gave it birth was the commitment made by a group of women at the 1987 IHM Assembly to the process of "reflecting on our experience *as women*" and their consequent choice "to educate [o]urselves to the feminist perspective . . . and to operate from our understandings as they develop." Thus, from the outset, COR members joined a circle of sisterhood in which IHM history became linked with women's history. This may seem unremarkable; after all, sisters are female before they are nuns, and they retain their gender after taking vows. However, the bonds of womanhood uniting sisters and other women has been obscured, and occasionally overtly denied, in what has evolved into traditional religious life. Femaleness has been given a distinct—and confusing—significance.

Traditionally, religious were told they had to die to self in order to pursue the perfection of the evangelical counsels. Literally and figura-

---

16. In addition to many of the accounts already cited, see in particular Bogel and Brach 1983, and my discussions of Mother Catherine O'Connor, S.L., found in Thompson, 1986a, 1986b, 1987a, 1991, 1994.

17. There are ironies here, for the call to rediscover founders' charisms came directly from the hierarchy; thus, in responding to it (initially, at least), sisters—including the IHMs —were acting out of precisely the sort of daughterly obedience that was fundamental to the history that they were revising. It is difficult to imagine that the prelates who called for the rediscovery of founders' charisms expected what has been uncovered. They could not have guessed that underneath the pious rhetoric there would be strong, assertive, and controversial women who challenged not only the comfort of their own times but that of the present as well.

tively, the old self was buried: religious clothing concealed the female anatomy and religious names were assigned without regard to gender. From their entry into a community, sisters typically were told they were living in a higher state of grace than people not gifted with this vocation; thus, distinctiveness from rather than similarity to those outside was evidence of cooperation with that grace. Sisters were to avoid discussing (and, ideally, thinking about) their lives prior to entering the convent; references to old friendships, or even to friendships with women in the community, were considered part of the old "man" that was to be cast off. There was strict regulation of contacts outside the community, including personal conversations that might have encouraged discovery of kinship and of common interests with women still "in the world."[18] Meanwhile, pious readings written by men—or, at least, granted the imprimatur of male clerical authorities—stressed the value of virtues described as "manly" and decried any vestiges of the "spiritually effeminate." Thus, in multiple dimensions, sisters were encouraged to ignore or repudiate female aspects of their identity, especially their similarities to or prior existence as laywomen.[19]

This message was strangely mixed, however. The same spirituality that stressed manly virtues and equated chastity with denial of sexuality also designated sisters as spiritual mothers of those to whom they ministered—and as brides of Christ. Indeed, religious life seemed to grant the force of natural law to some so-called feminine characteristics and behaviors. This was most evident in the contrast between women religious and clerics. The priest, upon whom sisters were dependent for most of their spiritual nourishment (and for all the sacraments), was designated an *alter Christus* to whom the "spousal" sister owed deference, submission, and gratitude (see Thompson 1989b, 1991). Consider, for instance, this admonition from the Rule of a women's order quite similar to the IHMs:

> Distrust your knowledge and be set on nothing whatsoever. Hold to nothing against the decision of a priest, though it might seem to you that you have read or heard that which you have in mind. I have known people who thought they had heard me say things that I never said, and others who have misunderstood what I did say. With all the more reason should you distrust your intelligence and your memory if there be a

18. This kind of personal interaction was, of course, forbidden among sisters as well; see chaps. 5 and 6 of the present volume, which explain that the principal rationale for such intracommunity prohibitions was fear of "particular friendships." Nevertheless, such prohibitions restricted bonding among the sisters as women.

19. Sisters, like all women, are precluded from ordination in the Catholic Church and are therefore members of the laity. In popular usage, however, the term "laywomen" is used only to refer to women not under religious vows.

question of a passage from Holy Scripture, or some similar difficulty, always submitting your judgment to that of priests; but if exceptionally and for good reasons, you should think some one of them evidently wrong, you may certainly consult others. However, generally speaking, be assured that in spite of all you may know or remember, it is far more probable that it is you who are in error.[20] (CCDP 1883, art. XX, 80, CDPA)

Such assumptions about the appropriateness of women's deference were not confined to the spiritual or the sacramental realms. For instance, women were considered incapable of governing themselves independent of male leadership. Until the twentieth century, no woman could serve as the final superior of a woman's congregation in juridical matters; the men who filled such roles wielded enormous power, as this passage from a representative women's Constitution reveals:

The Superior General, being the head of the whole Company throughout Kentucky, and other places whither it may be extended, nothing can be done in it, no resolution can be carried into effect, without his concurrence or approbation; and, in all cases, if the vote be equally divided in the Council, he has the casting vote. In matters of importance, such as making improvements on the property belonging to the Sisters; receiving new foundations, legacies, donations; buying or leasing real property; borrowing money to an account heretofore specified; dispensing for a time with any point of the Rules; admitting Candidates or Novices; or dismissing them either; removing Sisters from one place to another; he must be consulted in person. To him it belongs to examine the affairs of the Company and its accounts; to confirm the resolutions taken; to approve of the new Establishments. To him also belongs to permit any of the Sisters to add corporal austerities to those already allowed by the Rules; to appoint ordinary or extraordinary Confessors, with the approbation of the diocesan Bishop, out of the priests already approved by him, unless he should receive from him certain restrictions concerning individuals.

Although the Bishop has an unalienable right to appoint any priest he may think proper in his respective Diocese as Confessor, nevertheless, it is humbly presumed he will permit the Superior General to make any representation to him respecting those appointments, which he will weigh in his wisdom.[21] (CSCN 1878, 8–9, SCNA)

---

20. This section is appropriately called "On Distrust of One's Own Light."

21 Should these sisters have forgotten the alleged virtue of submitting to such clerical authority, they needed only to turn to their Customary, published the preceding year: "They shall, for the love of God, suffer cheerfully inconveniences, contradictions, scoffings, calumnies, and other mortifications, which they may have to endure, even for their good actions; remembering that our Savior, who was innocence itself, endured far greater sufferings, and even prayed for those who crucified him; and that, in all their pains, they have but a small share in the cross, which he was pleased to carry, in order to merit for them the happiness of beholding him for ever in heaven" (RSSC 1877, 5, SCNA). This type of deference to clerics was meant to be practiced at various organizational levels of religious life;

The result of such precepts, particularly when reinforced by ecclesiastical approbation and by codification into the Holy Rule of a congregation, was total dependency and, most likely, tacit acceptance of the notion that women have limited potential.

Eventually, of course, Catholic sisters came to rediscover—or discover—their identity as women, with feminist theory playing a role in this awakening. The IHMs are not alone in their realization that the apparatus that enclosed them within the state of perfection also separated them from other women. Since Vatican II, Catholic women, lay as well as religious, have discovered that what they have in common is vastly more significant than what differentiates them. Both groups had been constrained by remarkably similar assumptions about what is natural or inherent to women; both are discovering that most of these assumptions are man-made rather than of divine origin. The "spousal" subordination of nuns, for instance, is akin to that of women in traditional marriages. Its design is directly traceable to male clerics' determination to find a safe and familiar way to handle women who, in their religious fervor, had managed to remove themselves from the jurisdiction of fathers or of husbands. The restrictions that nuns themselves placed on their own education and ministries, the feminine gentility that came to characterize their demeanor, their presumed revulsion against worldly prominence and power—all these and more applied equally to their sisters outside the convent. As COR's working assumption no. 7 declares: "[P]atriarchy exists in society and its institutions, including [but not solely] the church" (See appendix); all women, therefore, have experienced it and must cope with its consequences.

The process of developing and claiming a feminist awareness—that is, an energizing realization of the full and complete power and humanness of women—has come easily for no one, within or outside religious life. Indeed, some women of great intelligence, creativity, and insight have been unable to complete the journey and have experienced substantial pain and even alienation as a result. Ellen Clanon's essay in this volume tells the story of such an individual. Sister Mary Patrick Riley was a pioneer educator, an innovator of national renown who for years played a major role in the advancement of IHM professionalism. However, she could not embrace the sweeping changes that ensued in the aftermath of Vatican II, and her life ended sadly, in largely self-imposed isolation from many in the very community to which she had devoted her life. Clanon's sympathetic account is in this respect the story of a representative woman, one whose life sheds light on the experiences of those who felt left behind (or swept aside) in the wake of feminism.

---

just as a reverend mother was subordinate to the bishop or to his designated ecclesiastical superior, female local superiors of residences away from the motherhouse were subordinate to pastors—and, indeed, to all parish priests.

As communication between nuns and laywomen progresses, the circle of sisterhood that includes both will become larger and more fully realized. Research of the sort represented in this book will facilitate this growth in at least two ways. First, throughout these essays, feminist insights from a variety of disciplines—sociology, psychology, literature, and history—have been incorporated deliberately and effectively. By delineating a religious subject in terms congruent with secular scholarship, the COR writers have made their work both palatable and accessible to general feminist scholars. Second, and equally important, *Building Sisterhood* can introduce secular scholars to feminist spirituality and theology. This is a field that has remained relatively unknown to many feminists, who mistakenly equate religion with the patriarchal structures that have surrounded it and therefore dismiss religion as at best a topic of marginal (and usually negative) significance to them. COR—not to mention the IHM history that is its focus—demonstrates convincingly that a life of faith is not incompatible either with intellectual rigor or with a feminist perspective. Even if theology and spirituality are overtly treated in only a few of the essays in this volume, their implicit role—and the evident experience of faith manifest both in the writers and in the women who are their subjects—should help to dispel many feminists' misconceptions about religion.

◆  ◆  ◆

One of the essays in which spirituality figures most prominently is that by Maryfran Barber and Mary M. McCann, on a post–Vatican II IHM experiment in collegial governance known as the representative assembly (RA). Barber and McCann discuss the brief lifespan (1972–75) of what they call the "RA of less-than-happy memory" and, more important, suggest some of the reasons for its failure. "Perhaps the most commonly accepted analysis," they write, "is the one voiced by many members of the RA: 'We simply weren't ready.'" Barber and McCann continue: "Given the IHMs' long history of hierarchy, the change to collegial governance was too abrupt. . . . The delegates lacked adequate communication skills; they had not yet learned to be in touch with and express their feelings, particularly anger; they did not know how to deal constructively with conflict. In summary, they were expecting too much of themselves."

Nonetheless, in the end, the authors do not dismiss the RA as a failure. Rather, they interpret it in the light of John of the Cross's concept of the "dark night of the soul" and Sister Constance FitzGerald's understanding of "impasse" situations, both of which are attempts to describe those times in which "what looks and feels like disintegration, meaninglessness, and even death at one's present level of perception and affectivity is, at a more profound but hidden level of faith, a process of purification leading to a resurrection experience." The problem, they declare, was that "the congregation was unable to see and to choose the creative, spiritual potential of the impasse it experienced." However, the lessons of the experience may be powerful: "[I]mpasse is a place in and through which the Spirit hovers over the chaos, breathing life into being where previously there was no life. The RA is history, but its legacy lives on. We believe that the RA 'of less-than-happy memory' challenges us to contemplate and to discern our experience's of communal darkness and struggle, knowing that the darkness may contain the new and authentic life for which our hearts long."

I would argue that the "new and authentic life for which our hearts long" has manifested itself, to a very great extent, in the circle of sisterhood that is COR. Indeed, the very aptness of considering COR as a circle of sisterhood reveals how much growth has occurred among IHMs since the days of the RA. Barber and McCann tell of one RA delegate's recollection of her reaction to the logistics of representative assembly meetings: " 'It was like in a circle and then there was a stagelike space where the altar was in the novitiate. That's where some of the action was going on.' When asked 'Did the circle "speak" to you?' the delegate answered: 'Well, yes, the whole idea was that we all had some authority; that we were all in a decision-making mode.' However, she then corrected her image: 'It was like a half-circle, not a complete circle.' " My observations, reading of the minutes of meetings I did not attend, and discussions with participants all suggest the extent to which the COR process was different from that of the RA.

From the beginning, members of the COR task force acted on the premise that how they worked was as important as—and, moreover, constituent of—what they produced.[22] Perusal of the group's minutes reveals that part of every meeting, sometimes the greater part, was devoted to discernment regarding process; additionally, to prepare for these discussions, the group read extensively in the literature of feminist theory, process, and organization theory Reflecting these concerns in action, COR sessions regularly began with prayer, new members were incorporated into the body with ritual, and facilitators were drawn from among COR itself and varied from occasion to occasion. Because the women were expected to do their homework before the gatherings, it could be assumed that everyone present was prepared for active involvement in the group's work; the minutes indicate that most of those present usually participated in discussions and that all contributions were taken seri-

22. An early memorandum by Maryfran Barber, in fact, cites Judy Chicago's *The Birthing Project* as a work offering potential insight as the group developed a process that would allow "decentralized work while maintaining central focus and artistic control," a process that would be "participatory," "collaborative," and "collegial" (MfB to COR, COR Doc., 1991, MA).

ously. I attended two COR meetings, which I have no reason to believe were unrepresentative. Everyone sat in a circle—absent the "stagelike space" that had intruded into the RA—occupying comfortable chairs and partaking freely of readily available refreshments. Business came first; when the group was in session, attention was focused completely on the tasks at hand and conversation was largely substantive. Despite the relaxed atmosphere, a great deal was accomplished in a relatively short period of time.

To some extent, the sisterhood among COR members can be explained by two group characteristics. First, all belong to the same religious congregation and therefore can draw upon a common tradition, shared prior experience, and at least some previous acquaintance with each other.[23] Second, COR is an intentional group; everyone in it chose to participate and, implicitly at least, was favorably disposed from the outset towards the body's rationale and purpose. However, these factors alone are not sufficient to explain COR's success in developing its own sisterhood; if they were, the RA would have become a circle of collegial creativity. I believe it was the group's overtly feminist approach, its persistent nurturing of congenial process, and its members' prior involvement in circles with similar dynamics that contributed substantially to its achievement. None of this is provable in the literal sense, of course. Still, collegiality does not just happen; it depends mightily upon the commitment of persons working to ensure that it does happen. As COR's working assumptions no. 11 states, the group has believed from the outset that "the *way* we do feminist history is crucial to *what* we discover as our history" and therefore it made a wise and ongoing investment of time and energy in the "design [of] a feminist process for the history project that includes active participation, collaboration, and consciousness of our own biases" (see appendix).

It would be misleading to suggest that COR represents some sort of utopian community—that it has remained untouched by tension, pain, controversy, or disruption. A couple of people have left the group. Some of the women who are still involved maintain reservations about the degree of overt feminism in COR's operating assumptions and procedures; although their opinions are respected, they have not substantively altered how COR has proceeded. Especially in the early stages of COR's work, there was disagreement over issues in IHM history: whether The-

23. However, as of May 1994, the Michigan IHM congregation had 822 members (JG, congregational secretary, telephone conversation with author, 2 May 1994) and had many more in the past. Further, especially in recent years, IHM sisters live and work throughout the United States and abroad (two writers for *Building Sisterhood* lived in Canada, for example). Thus, it would be a mistake to exaggerate the extent to which COR members knew each other prior to their service on this task force.

resa Maxis Duchemin should be identified as founder (or cofounder, along with Father Gillet);[24] how relations between Monroe and the two Pennsylvania IHM communities should be treated, or if those communities should be included at all; the awkwardness of discussing or identifying difficult personalities (especially those who are still alive); and so on.

A difficult issue that remained troublesome to the very end of the writing process was how to present names. Specifically, were all persons to be referred to by last names only, or were sisters—especially those from the first century of IHM history—to be called by their religious titles and names?[25] Some believed that a feminist approach required uniform usage for all women and men and that references to women by first names and religious titles (e.g., Mother Ruth, Sister Mary Patrick) were sexist and subordinating. Others, however, argued that women who during their lifetimes were never called by their last names should not be so designated in this volume, asserting that ahistorical usage was anachronistic as well as destructive of sisterly respect among companions in community. In the end, the COR group decided that, as a general rule, last names were preferable—a decision that left room for appropriate exceptions. In addition, one writer who felt strongly that this approach would obscure both her and her subjects' voices was affirmed in her decision to use religious first names.

Another persistent problem was even more difficult and delicate. There was some hesitancy to offer necessary criticism of what members had written; despite a group commitment to honesty, members tended to shy away from the inevitable confrontations. The need to affirm each member's integrity and worth was undeniably important, but occasionally it threatened to supersede the equally important value of ensuring the quality of the book being produced. As sometimes is the case in

24. The Constitutions approved by the 1988 General Chapter (and privately published that year) contains the following reference to the IHMs' origins: "We cherish and are inspired by the lives of those who founded our Congregation, Louis Florent Gillet, Marie Therese Maxis, our pioneer Sisters, and by the lives of all our Sisters who have gone before us" (11). As discussion at the final COR Writers Group meeting (4 June 1994) underscored, however, this phrasing does as much to obscure as to resolve the founder/cofounders debate.

25. In the IHMs, as in most religious congregations prior to Vatican II, women received new names (usually those of saints) when they entered the novitiate. This was symbolic of their taking on a new life. Additionally, they were referred to by the title "Sister," although those in leadership used "Mother" as their title. (The usage varied among congregations; in some—although not among the IHMs—all finally professed members, or all those who had been professed for a certain number of years or who had ever held high office, were called "Mother.") In the majority of congregations, including the IHMs, sisters no longer used their family surnames; instead, they appended the initials of their congregations to their religious names, e.g., "Sister Mary Patrick, I.H.M."

feminist circles, the group seemed to fear that criticism was inherently destructive rather than potentially constructive. To put this into colloquial (but under the circumstances quite appropriate) language, COR members were loathe to trash their sisters. In the end, however, the tough discussions occurred, and the resulting volume is better for them.

To acknowledge difficulties does not undermine the premise that a circle of sisterhood was created and maintained within COR and that it is real, strong, and likely to outlive the task force and its work. No family —and sisters, whether in a religious congregation or not, are by definition family—is without disputes or tensions. What is crucial is that problems are confronted and resolved rather than evaded or buried. COR's members consistently have tried resolution. As a result, its circle and its sisterhood have been forged solidly.

◆     ◆     ◆

As IHMs, as sisters, as women, and as members of COR, the writers whose efforts are contained in this volume bring the various circles of which they are parts into the context and substance of their work. It is tempting, therefore, to forget that the writers and collaborators represented here are, before all else, very distinct and fully formed individuals. To the common task, each woman brought the full range of her unique gifts; as the essays that follow reveal unmistakably, the collegial and cooperative was not intended to obscure the particular and personal. Individuality manifests itself clearly and deliberately throughout the book. After all the writing and revision, each author's distinctive voice, interpretive insights, and individual expertise have been respected and preserved (as the above discussion about names suggests). The result is a collection that may be less uniform than many anthologies but that thereby conveys the diversity of COR's members and of their historical perspectives.

Such individuality, ultimately, is as essential to what COR is all about as is the degree of collegiality and synergy that the group was able to develop. Moreover, as Margaret Brennan reminds us in her chapter of this volume, a creative tension between individuality and common purpose is the very spiritual foundation of the IHM congregation, and this spirituality is fundamental to *Building Sisterhood* as well. Despite Maxis's profound commitment to the spiritual legacy of Gillet and the Redemptorists, she had a concomitant appreciation for each sister's need to develop and express a personal relationship with God. Brennan places this charism within an explicitly feminist context: "Feminist thought is grounded in an ecological ethic that sees the relationship of all reality in an interconnected web of diversity, subjectivity, interdependence, and community. At the same time, however, it prizes autonomy, self-actualization, and the individual and unique way in which each person approaches the transcendent God who is also immanently present in all created reality."

Citing the work of Elizabeth A. Johnson, Brennan goes on to describe "this cosmic reality as a circle of mutuality grounded and sustained by the Spirit who, as the great creative Matrix, attracts it toward the future." Thus, Brennan concludes, the tension is resolved in "sustained interaction around the foundational issues of faith and of life that form the basis for our belonging to one another and for our common dedication to the mission of Jesus in a contemporary church and world that is dramatically different from that which gave us birth and growth." In other words, it is resolved through active awareness of and engagement in individual and collective history.

This awareness and engagement is, in the end, what has impelled the COR project and its participants. It is an ongoing process, one that will not end with the publication of this book. Nonetheless, the IHMs who have begun the journey here have taken a very important first step—one, it is hoped, that will be followed by those of other women, in their own circles of sisterhood.

# PART ONE

# Groundings

# The Context

Margaret Susan Thompson

Until relatively recently, historical writing about communities of women religious tended to be more reassuring and affective than analytical. Accuracy, in many cases, was secondary to pious edification; facts were less significant than inspirational myths. Statements of faith— "the extraordinary growth of the community was witness to God's grace" —were asserted as fact, while incidents or personalities that did not fit stereotypic understandings of what nuns supposedly were all about were downplayed, obscured, or eliminated from the official record. According to historian Barbara Misner, these traditional accounts, written mainly by nuns, either constituted mere factual "annals" or were "characterized chiefly by a desire to edify and inspire, and there is often more hagiography than apologetics. (One might suspect there were vocation directors behind the projects)" (Misner 1982, 2).

Such an approach would be problematic in dealing with any historical subject, but it has especially serious consequences for both the study and the living out of religious life. This is because a community's charism —that is, the spiritual impetus that impelled it into existence and thereby enables it to make a unique contribution both to Catholicism and to the wider religious culture—presumably derives from the actual inspiration or gift of its founder(s). Thus, distortion of the historical record, and most significantly of founders' legacies, makes it impossible for members to respond validly to that charismatic impulse, to embrace it fully, and to reflect it clearly in their own lives. They may be devout, hardworking, and accomplished; they may be happy, ministerially fruitful, and acclaimed by those inside and outside their church. Regardless, their collective legitimacy as a religious congregation is compromised in a very basic way, because the charism that justifies the body's existence is fundamentally compromised. That is why, to facilitate the renewal that vowed women and men were called to undergo in the aftermath of Vatican II, Pope Paul VI charged them to begin with a "return . . . to the original

25

inspiration behind [each] given community . . . loyal recognition and safekeeping should be accorded to the spirit of founders, as also to all the particular goals and wholesome traditions which constitute the heritage of each community" (*Perfectae Caritatis*, par. 2, quoted in Abbott 1966, 468).

As is clear in all the essays of this volume (particularly the first three), the IHMs encountered a number of sticky situations in responding to that charge, for their charism derives from individuals whose stories are hardly the stuff of which pious myths are made. Theresa Maxis Duchemin was a woman of color, born out of wedlock to a woman of San Domingan (now Haitian) descent. In 1845, she left the Oblate Sisters of Providence, in which she first had taken vows—indeed, she abandoned her responsibilities as its assistant superior—and fled with another member of that order to Monroe, Michigan, to start a new community that would be wholly and uncompromisingly white. Moreover, she did so at the behest of a Redemptorist missionary priest whose behavior at times prompted concerns about his own stability, particularly among some members of his religious congregation. Within two years—under charges of various improprieties and indiscretions that were later proven without foundation but that left him temporarily broken and embittered—Father Louis Florent Gillet left Monroe and then his religious order, wandered for several years over three continents, and finally returned to his native France, where he entered a Trappist monastery. A decade later, Theresa Maxis Duchemin—known as Mother Theresa Maxis among the IHMs— was deposed as the sisters' superior and herself departed from the scene. She went first to Pennsylvania, where she led half her community in establishing a foundation that soon was forcibly separated from its Michigan motherhouse. Then, after becoming embroiled in disputes and being accused of alleged disobedience to prelates both in Detroit and in Philadelphia, she endured eighteen years of exile in Canada. Meanwhile, until after the turn of the twentieth century (in other words, for nearly one-third of its history), the congregation in Monroe was under the jurisdiction of a rigoristic and legalistic ecclesiastical superior, Father Edward Joos, who decided that part of his mission was to mold the sisters into the icons that nuns were supposed to be.

Consequently, an official record began to be composed that bore little resemblance to what actually had happened during the IHMs' first years of existence but which was soon transformed into community tradition and became accepted as fact. Maxis's persona and role were veiled; Gillet was remembered fondly but only vaguely, as having little apparent influence on the direction that the community took. Instead, Joos was regarded as the "beloved father," while Maxis's successor, the frail and more submissive Mary Joseph Walker, became identified as the community's "true foundress." Slowly but inexorably, the official IHM story became indistinguishable from those of congregations whose origins presented none of its idiosyncrasies and problems.[1]

However, the accounts by Marita-Constance Supan, Suzanne Fleming, and Margaret Brennan make it clear that the foundational contributions of Maxis and of Gillet were not eradicated. In particular, Brennan's analysis of IHM spirituality demonstrates powerfully that a unique devotional life—rooted in Gillet's Redemptorist experience but transformed into something new by Maxis's creative personalism—has been an important dimension of what historically has defined the IHMs, even if it has not been identified as such. In this and in other powerful if frequently unacknowledged ways, the Maxis/Gillet charism consistently shaped the memory and experience of Monroe's IHMs, even as the legacies of Walker and Joos also exerted their own determinative influences upon the congregation. Thus, to understand fully the "particular goals and wholesome traditions" that constitute the IHM heritage, the work of these three authors, who collectively delineate and weigh the contributions of *all* the persons who defined the congregation's identity, is invaluable.

Such efforts should be of interest to large numbers of persons outside the circle of IHM sisterhood. In piecing together factual and analytic accounts of what really happened, these essays provide case studies in feminist historical recovery and reconstruction. What happened to Maxis is representative of the experience of thousands of women of the past, obscure as well as notable. Vilified and banished for her assertiveness, for her lack of social respectability, and for her determination to remain faithful to what she believed was a mandate given to her by God, she saw her intentions and her community coopted by men who thought they knew better than she what that community should be all about. For her part, Walker, less original than Maxis, largely acquiesced in that clerical cooptation—accepting, as have so many women throughout history, that by virtue of his gender and his ordination, father really did know best.

The essays by Supan and Fleming are also feminist in their insistence upon letting the two women who are their subjects speak for themselves. Because the authors wish to convey not only the experiences but also the perspectives of Maxis and Walker, their pieces present two very different takes on many of the same events and circumstances. They are not incompatible but they are distinct, and after reading them it is evident that only through both these lenses can anything approaching a focused picture of

1. See, for example, the treatment of the IHMs contained in Dehey 1930 (386–91). This volume, a nearly complete compendium of brief accounts of every Catholic women's community still extant at the time of its publication, presented chronologically in order of founding, is a classic example of the hagiographic school of historical commemoration, and what it says about the sisters in Monroe is no exception to this general rule.

early IHM history become clear. In this, the stories of these two women and their successors in religious life demonstrate kinship with the historical experience of women generally. As anthropologist Mary Catherine Bateson has put it, constancy is an illusion:

> Fluidity and discontinuity are central to the reality in which we live. Women have always lived discontinuous and contingent lives.... As a result, the ability to shift from one preoccupation to another, to divide one's attention, to improvise in new circumstances, has always been important to women.
>
> Once you begin to see these lives of multiple commitments and multiple beginnings as an emerging pattern rather than an aberration, it takes no more than a second look to discover the models for that reinvention on every side, to look for the followers of visions that are not fixed but that evolve from day to day. Each such model, like each individual work of art, is a comment about the world outside the frame. Just as change stimulates us to look for more abstract constancies, so the individual effort to compose a life, framed by birth and death and carefully pieced together from disparate elements, becomes a statement on the unity of living. These works of art, still incomplete, are parables in process, the living metaphors with which we describe the world. (1990, 13, 17–18)

Mother Theresa Maxis, I.H.M.

# 1

# Dangerous Memory

## Mother M. Theresa Maxis Duchemin and the Michigan Congregation of the Sisters, IHM

### Marita-Constance Supan, I.H.M.

Three years after its targeted release for the congregation's 1945 centennial, Sister M. Rosalita Kelly's *No Greater Service*—an exhaustively researched and fully referenced and indexed history of the Sisters, Servants of the Immaculate Heart of Mary, of Monroe, Michigan—finally appeared in print. To historian-friend Monsignor John Tracy Ellis, Kelly had reflected on her uncompromising thoroughness and had voiced her frustration with still-unanswered questions: "If I could only go along and let the unravelled events remain unravelled! But it seems God and my teachers didn't make me that way. Even at that, there are a few gaps that remain stubbornly wide, despite the research of a dozen years" (Mengy. of RK, 26 Jan. 1964, MA).

In her history, Kelly highlighted Father Louis Florent Gillet, C.SS.R., a Belgian missionary, and Mother M. Theresa Maxis Duchemin, I.H.M., a woman of color who passed for white in pioneer Michigan, as pivotal in the congregation's founding, alloting to each a full chapter. Kelly demonstrated that Maxis had exerted so profound and so controversial an influence on IHM identity that by 1859, hierarchical response to her had precipitated her forced exile from Michigan and the congregation's formal division.

For sisters who had entered the community after the early 1940s, Kelly's work supplied welcome detail about a figure with whom they were vaguely but favorably acquainted; for the majority of IHMs, however, Maxis's story came as completely new information. Until that juncture, core perceptions of foundation events in Monroe had come to be embodied in a yearly Founder's Day celebration, when log cabins wobbled up from cardboard and crayon in IHM classrooms and students vied

31

for the privilege of posing as Gillet or as one of the three "first sisters" to dramatize a treasured tradition: "[S]he that had a cup had no saucer and she that had a spoon had no fork" ([Shanley] 1916, 34). However, had any generation of IHMs been asked whose influence dominated congregational life, most would have pointed not to the voiceless tableau figures but to Monsignor Edward Joos, the congregation's director and superior from his appointment twelve years after the founding until his death 44 years later.[1]

Joos's memory forked lightning. Many IHMs mythologized him as a near-savior to whom, "after God, the community owes its preservation and the formation of its religious and educational ideals" (Marygrove 1927, 17); conferences read during annual retreats perpetuated his voice, and emerging questions of values and behavior faced the standard of "our dear Father's" canonized wisdom. Less publicly, other sisters decried Joos as a picayune autocrat, "a real czar" from whom "no superior was safe" and who controlled everything, from the spiritual writers IHMs read to whether they wore corsets (CF, interviewed by RK, 1934, notes in MA). However divergent their personal responses to him, few IHMs denied that Joos's tenure had profoundly affected the shape of the congregation. He had revised the Rule and had solidified customs in clear, written form; he had also maintained influential ties with a succession of Detroit prelates who lauded the educational excellence of "Joos's proud ladies" (MMcK to author, 8 Nov. 1992, MA) and who assigned them choice schools in the diocese.[2] Controversial and omnipresent, Joos was a stabilizing if constricting force during years in which the congregation developed from a frontier missionary band of eighteen to a highly respected teaching corps 155 strong.[3]

Kelly's history, new in emphasis and content, sent tremors through IHM self-perception. The book heightened the gratitude and awe with which IHMs recalled their founding, but it also made clear that their ritual Founder's Day tableau ironically depicted a discomfiting historical subtext: the congregation's earliest voices had, in fact, been silenced.[4]

---

1. These assessments were borne out in all of eight interviews by the author in 1992–93 with sisters who entered in 1920, 1921, 1922, 1925, 1926, 1929, and 1945. Audiotapes of interviews were stolen. References are from notes taken during interviews, MA.

2. Adrian Dominican sisters recall their experience of being "blue lined," as IHMs (who wore blue habits) were given the more prestigious schools (MPRy, interviewed by MST, May 1986, quoted in Thompson 1989a, 153–54).

3. Calculation of sisters on mission in 1900 by Celeste Rabaut, I.H.M., and Rose Matthew Mangini, I.H.M., archivists (Monroe).

4. For example: "There *wasn't* any talk. No one knew anything about her [Theresa] until now (IHM sister [entrance 1921], interviewed by author, 31 Oct. 1992); "It wasn't just the silence. It was SILENCE in capital letters. It was great big capitals" (IHM sister [entrance 1922], interviewed by author, 31 Oct. 1992).

With Kelly's choice to present the truth, Theresa Maxis Duchemin raised her face to the light and stepped center stage in congregational history.

The catalyst for telling Maxis's story seems to have been Kelly's 1934 visit to the Oblate Sisters of Providence in Baltimore.[5] A smudged correspondence card preserves her consternation: "Didn't see any other Oblate except Portress. Told Mother was ill. Kept waiting a half hour or more. Father [John] Gillard walked in at last. What he didn't say about IHMs and their treatment of Oblates. I saw a few things myself. The meeting was *hot* at points. We parted Christians—if not friends. He gave me the Scranton *Sisters IHM*[6] all duly marked with his comments" (RK, reverse side of correspondence card to MCon, May 1934, draft, MA). A resolute Kelly—unaware until then that existing histories had reworked Maxis's background, formative role, and painful exile—underscored the words with a force that threatened to slice the page.

Within a month of that heated encounter, Kelly had hand copied Gillard's glosses into her own volume of *The Sisters of the I.H.M.*, had set before Mother Ruth Hankerd her conditions for continued research, and had returned the Oblate chaplain's book to Baltimore with a terse pledge: "I think I can give you assurance now that when our Community history is told a decade hence it will stand by the facts. This is the desire of those who now govern our Congregation" (RK to JGil, 11 June 1934, MA). Recollections survive of Kelly's anger at "what had been done to the history," and a trail of straightforward correspondence and feisty glosses on original documents witnesses to her determination to unearth the long-buried memory of Maxis. Kelly did not chronicle the burial itself nor explore its significance for the congregation, though her "Separation Notes" (draft MS, 19–20, MA) document her awareness of the strategic suppression of Maxis's legacy. Perhaps she believed such considerations lay outside the scope of her work; perhaps she (or her superiors) decided a longer view was needed, time for the graveyard guardians themselves to be laid to rest.[7] Whatever her reasons, Kelly consciously laid aside a set of questions about IHM history that have persisted into the present.

Some of these questions can be answered through a new look at Maxis's personal history and at her formative role in the community. Grounding my work in primary sources and in the intimations of subtexts, I rely on the hermeneutics of feminist theory and feminist literary

5. The Oblate Sisters of Providence, founded in Baltimore, Maryland, in 1829, were the first congregation of black women religious in the United States.

6. [Gillespie] 1921, which presented Maxis as a (presumably white) Baltimore laywoman.

7. Margaret McKoan, I.H.M., who as a novice translated French passages for Kelly's volume, reflected: "I realize that Sr. Rosalita knew much, much more than she was *allowed* to write in her scholarly book . . . I do know that her book was carefully edited, page by page" (MMcK to DMcD, 27 July 1992, copy in MA).

criticism and on psychological insights related to women's development and socialization to contend that, in the face of conflicting pressures from both outside and within the congregation, IHMs experienced Maxis's memory as so dangerous that they "split her off" from corporate awareness by first suppressing, then strategically reinventing, the primitive congregational history.[8] Splitting off Maxis and the qualities that she embodied facilitated congregational survival and development in the midst of female double binds—"damned if you do, damned if you don't" situations with two added twists: denial that the dilemma exists and behavior by others that fosters the illusion of support while it perpetuates the conditions that produce the double binds (Waites 1993, 43–59)—into which women were socialized in the nineteenth-and early twentieth-century American culture and Catholic church. The same splitting precipitated a crisis of integrity for the IHM congregation.

### Theresa Maxis Duchemin: Woman of Color, 1810–45

Bright-skinned and blue-eyed, Marie Almaide Maxis Duchemin (later Mother Theresa Maxis)[9] was the illegitimate child of a white British father and a biracial San Domingan (Haitian) mother (WCN, 1–2, IA).[10] She grew up in pre–Civil War Baltimore, where the settings she called home placed her in two distinct racial/cultural circles. Her place in the Duchemin family (whose name her mother had adopted) exposed her to the world of monied, influential whites, including those who spoke English,[11] while her faith development and schooling immersed her in the French-

8. "Splitting off" refers here to a psychological process in which aspects of the self that are experienced as dangerous are split off, or dissociated, from awareness and a partial or pseudo-self, deemed more acceptable by external standards, is fostered. Maintaining this dissociation over time requires immense energy; hypervigilance and tight controls on perceptions and on experience are necessary, in order to prevent inner stirrings that might prompt the "remembering" of the exiled self, with its anxiety-producing possibilities. For the "split self" as an experience of creative and/or socially powerful nineteenth-century women, see Rigney 1978, 3–12, and Rich 1979, 33–49.

9. In this section, I refer to Mother Theresa by her adopted French surname, Duchemin, which she used at the time; after 1845, I will refer to her (as she did to herself) as Maxis.

10. Historically, great attention has been paid to whether Duchemin was an octaroon or a quadroon, signaling the immense significance given her degree of blackness. During and well after her time, African ancestry in any degree confined one to the "colored" stratum of American society, with the strictures imposed on it by the white majority. Mary James Sweeney's "West Chester Notes" (2–3, IA) do not settle the question, because they contain references in which the antecedents are not altogether clear. No record has been found of Duchemin's birth or baptism (likely because "colored" records were unofficial).

11. The *Baltimore Town and Fells Point Directory* (first edition, 1796), 43, held by the Maryland Historical Society, lists Francois Duchemin as white and a "gentleman," i.e., wealthy enough not to have an occupation.

speaking refugee community of color that was encapsulated within an otherwise white, English city.

The Duchemins had fled the 1793 slave uprisings in St. Domingo and had brought with them to the port of Baltimore a ten-year-old girl of color, Marie Annette ("Betsy") Maxis, whose parents had perished in the carnage (WCN, 1, IA). The Duchemins raised her, benefitted from her work in their home, and provided for her training as a nurse. In spring 1810, Betsy bore a daughter, Marie Almaide Maxis Duchemin, by a visiting cousin of the Baltimore Howards (WCN, 1; MAR to RK, 2 Nov. 1943, IA). (The nature of the couple's relationship is unknown, but given the customs of the day and Betsy Duchemin's unexplained presence at the Howard Estate at this and other junctures, it is possible that sexual availability was an expected service.) Reared by her mother in the Duchemin household, the child claimed neither the Howard name nor the considerable privilege attached to it. In her last years, she recounted a single, poignant experience of her father to Mary James Sweeney, I.H.M., who wrote that at the age of eight or nine, "She was taken to the door of the drawing room in the Howard home outside of Baltimore and told that the visiting English major was her father. It seems she did not speak to him, but went back again and again to look at him. She never mentioned whether he saw her or not, or even whether he knew of her existence" (WCN, 2, IA).

While the elder Duchemin spent considerable time in nursing duties, the child boarded in a free school for San Domingan refugees, conducted in the home of Elizabeth Lange and Marie Magdalen Balas, both of San Domingan descent (Sherwood 1931, 11–12). Thus, in a period when women of color were notoriously undereducated, Duchemin became fluent in French and English, skilled in disciplines from mathematics to fine needlework, and grounded in a lively devotional life. She quoted Latin phrases and displayed a marked literary excellence, patent in her later letters. In 1829, Duchemin joined Lange, Balas, and Ros(in)e Boegue, to found the Oblate Sisters of Providence and to "consecrate themselves to God, and to the Christian education of young girls of colour" as Oblate Sisters of Providence (OSPR, 1829, quoted in Posey 1994, 18).[12] James Marie Hector Nicholas Joubert de La Muraille, a Sulpician and the Oblate cofounder and director, on 1 June 1829 noted in his *Diary* that Duchemin was "nineteen years of age . . . very pious and also very capable of rendering great services to the institution" (cited in Sherwood 1931, 21).

Though the women were French-speaking and free, thus more likely

12. Though Maryland law did not forbid the education of free black children, public sentiment made it impossible for them to attend school with whites; Baltimore made no provision for black children's (separate) public education until 1867 (Sherwood 1929, 14–15, 17–19, 21).

to be perceived as European, their racial heritage sparked intense ambivalence among Catholics in a slaveholding state thirty-two years before the
Civil War (Sherwood 1931, vii). Nonetheless, the future Oblates found
strong advocates in Joubert and in Archbishop James Whitfield, and they
spent the "novitiate" year developing a Rule by which to live as professional religious women in a context fundamentally hostile to persons of
color.[13] Lange noted that being "persons of color and religious at the same
time" necessitated proceeding "in such a manner as not to appear too
arrogant on the one hand and on the other, not to miss the respect which
is due to the state we have embraced and the holy habit which we have
the honor to wear" (OSPAn I, 38–39, quoted in Posey 1994, 28).

The resulting Rule did not rely on classical models (Franciscan, Dominican, Ignatian, Benedictine, etc.) but instead blended the sisters' West
African spiritual heritage and Joubert's French Sulpician spirituality. West
African spirituality centered on a trio of core values: reliance on the
Providence of God; a vision of life and service based on the paradigm of
the extended family; and a profound awareness of concrete daily events
of individual and communal life as the locus of God's revelation. Similarly, French Sulpician asceticism "emphasized the manifestation of the
divine life within as opposed to the 'Rigorism' of those influenced by the
Jansenists" (Posey 1994, 26).[14] In practice, these tenets enabled a community whose fate was contingent on the responses of an ambivalent hierarchy and population to fashion a life based on the convictions that God
was ultimately in charge, that the personal call and mutual equality of
the members required decision-making processes rooted in prayer and
open exchange, and that transformation of day-to-day practicalities was
the yardstick of authentic piety.

On the surface, the Oblates' work appeared typical for New World
congregations, focusing on preserving immigrants' religious-cultural heritage while integrating them into the evolving American mainstream.
However, for French-speaking, free women of color and their students,
racial prejudice redefined the task. Ultimately, the Oblates created a
unique institution, which adapted the traditional French convent school

13. The Oblates' consultative style is well-documented in the congregation's first sixty
years. For example, "15 September 35 [1835] the director assembled the Sisters today to
make known to them the proposition . . . by the Superior of the Seminary, to have two of
the Sisters of Providence manage that house. He said that this unexpected request worried
and troubled him and that he wished to remain neutral in the affair, which concerned all at
one time . . . He said that they should by the following Sunday make known, by writing,
their intention to the Superior of the Seminary. He also said that the Sisters should have no
fear of making the conditions which they judged agreeable" (OSPAn I, 38, 96, cited in Posey
1994, 28n. 50).

14. For a description of Jansenism in the IHM context, see chap. 2 of the present
volume.

to address the faith-formation and educational needs of the black Catholic community in the United States (cited in Posey 1994, 22).

During the relatively quiet, formative years of the sisterhood, Duchemin—then Sister Marie Therese—honed her teaching and administrative skills and benefited from Joubert's spiritual guidance. In 1832, she welcomed her mother into the community. That year, cholera raged through Baltimore, and the new Sister Anthony Duchemin first volunteered nursing skills at the almshouse, then was summoned to care for the Archbishop, and days later, his housekeeper. On the second day of this last mission, Duchemin's mother contracted the disease and died by nightfall, her daughter kept away by threat of contagion (Sherwood 1931, 60–61). The young Duchemin, her spirituality and worldview already profoundly imprinted by illegitimacy and by racial marginalization, was left without family at age twenty-three.[15]

A decade later, the Oblates elected Duchemin general superior at a critical juncture in congregational history. Joubert had grown so ill that his duties—even the writing of his *Diary*—had fallen to Duchemin (Sherwood 1931, 93); when the Sulpicians' European superior, alarmed at the fragmentation of missionaries to America in a multiplying set of works, prohibited all activities but their stated mission of training priests, the weakened Joubert could find no successor to direct the Oblates. Moreover, Baltimoreans and their new Archbishop, Samuel Eccleston, had lost sympathy for the sisterhood. The wave of French immigration having subsided, new entrants were increasingly African American—some of them former slaves (manumission papers, OSPA, cited in Posey 1994, 25n. 41)—rather than French mulatto, and students were poor African American children, less acceptable to the white population and less likely to pay needed tuition than the monied immigrants of earlier years. Finally, a virulent anti-Catholicism had gained a stronghold in the city. By 1843, the Oblate Sisters huddled in the convent parlor while hecklers lobbed rocks through windows and threatened physical violence. Friends avoided them, and frightened parents withdrew children from the school. With neither director nor advocate, the sisters turned to Redemptorist parishes for Mass and sacraments, even as the archbishop forbade them to accept new entrants and urged professed sisters to return to the world as pious servants.[16]

In the desperate hope of attracting financial support from the descen-

15. I rely here on the assumption from the behavioral sciences that early life experience determines the cognitive-affective schema from which an individual interprets subsequent events. On the implications of this assumption for the development of one's God-image and spirituality, see Rizzuto 1979.

16. An undated document signed by Thaddeus Anwander, C.SS.R., Oblate director from 1847 to 1855, notes: "After the death of Rev. James Joubert they were forbidden to receive any more Candidates, but that prohibition was cancelled in 1850 or so" (OSPA).

dants of Charles Carroll, Duchemin set out to revise the Rule and to rename the congregation the Sisters of St. Charles (WCN, 3, IA). When her plan faltered, the Oblates were reduced to taking in wash and mending to feed themselves and the few orphans left in the house (Sherwood 1931, 108–9). Duchemin read the signs of impending death for the congregation. Moreover, she understood the implications of finding herself—a woman whose education and proven leadership could never outweigh the liabilities of race—alone in the world. She did not have a single blood relative, nor is there evidence to suggest that the Duchemins played a role in her adult life.[17]

Two images—the biracial child half-hidden at the drawing room door of a mansion she could never inhabit, and the young religious teaching as her mother died—illumine Duchemin's worldview. Experience had confirmed the terrifying and ever present possibility of loss over which she felt little control, and in the absence of human protectors, Duchemin had developed a strong reliance on God's Providence and a parallel inclination to clutch life's reins in her own hands through decisive action. These intertwined tendencies made her charismatic and daring, able to trust and to act from her own ground of reference. They also made her controlling, naïvely impetuous, and frequently out of touch with the potential consequences of her choices. Both sets of qualities were patent as the Oblates faced likely dissolution.

Duchemin chose nearby parish priest Peter Chakert, C.SS.R., as spiritual director while she begged God and scanned the horizon for a providential opportunity for "regular" religious life.[18] According to Duchemin's faith perspective, God sent it rapping at her door in the form of two Belgian visitors: Detroit bishop Peter Paul Lefevere and Redemptorist missionary Louis Florent Gillet. The two arrived separately in Baltimore in late spring 1843, Lefevere for the Fifth Provincial Council of American Bishops and Gillet to begin his work in America. During episcopal deliberations, the "colored" sisters created something of a curiosity for the prelates, and Lefevere "was kind enough to say Mass in our Chapel" (OSPAn, 19 May 1843, OSPA). Gillet, newly arrived at St. James

17. The precariousness of even a free biracial woman's future during the 1840s became clear to me when I heard an interview with a 94-year-old Oblate sister, taped in 1962 by Brooklyn diocesan priest Leonard DiFalco. At the mention of the archbishop's edict urging the Oblates to "return to the world," the interviewee, remembering Maxis's lack of family, became agitated. Her voice rose as she declared that if the community had dissolved, "Why, Father, Theresa would have to be a *slave!*" See also Wilson 1859; Russell 1990, 1–19.

18. Joubert had strategically avoided equating the Oblates with white religious of perpetual vows by providing instead for annual "promises," which had not been formally renewed since Joubert's death in 1843. Entries in MDeD (trans. in OSPA) for 13 Oct. and for 22 Nov. 1844 verify that Maxis had been seeking a community of strict observance well before she left the Oblates. (See also MMC, 1845, MA).

Church, sought out the French-speaking Oblates both as a refuge from German confreres and parishioners who irritated him and as an audience hungry for his eloquent preaching on religious life (TMN, 3–4, MA; OSPAn, 14 and 21 July 1843, OSPA). Lefevere saw in his fellow Belgian an answer to his own concerns and by summer's end, he had invited Gillet to preach missions to scattered French congregations in the then wilderness of southeast Michigan. Though chronologies of precise inter-actions differ, it is clear that between the summers of 1843 and 1845, Gillet and Duchemin planned a frontier school and a foundation of religious women to sustain it. As Duchemin later recalled, "Before leaving Balti-more he asked me if I would like to go too as there were no catholic [sic] schools in the place, a need which must be supplied. I answered 'yes,' but left him to go first to prepare the way; he promised to let me know when to come" (TMN, 4–5, MA). Her descriptions of the preaching mis-sions that Gillet conducted in Michigan carry the energy and detail of firsthand exchanges, probably during Gillet's return visits to Baltimore during summer and autumn 1844 (MDeD, 22 Nov. 1844, trans. in OSPA).

Gillet's fervor, his penchant for action, and the prospect that he "would be able to train both professed and novice" in Redemptorist spirituality captured Duchemin's imagination (TMN, 11, MA). With a pair of sister-companions she had drawn into her plan, Duchemin envi-sioned both the adventure she relished and the stable religious entity for which she longed (OSPAn, 9 Sept. 1845, OSPA), and she gambled that in pioneer territory ten days from Baltimore her light skin and intellectual and administrative gifts would gain her entry to a world otherwise closed to persons of color.[19] Once in Michigan, Duchemin would send for Sister Ann Constance Shaaff, a light-skinned Baltimorean, but would advise Sister Stanislaus "not to come, as her color was too dark" (OSPRe, 3, OSPA). Duchemin seems not to have taken into account that the prelates she had met during Council days in Baltimore might themselves sub-scribe to the racism of the era.

On 9 September 1845, after "the necessary trials to find the will of God in regard to my leaving" (TMN, 3, MA), Duchemin shocked the unsuspecting Oblate community by departing for Michigan (OSPAn, 9 Sept. 1845, OSPA). Chakert sent her to Lefevere with his blessing and with a letter of introduction that identified her Oblate connections and gave Chakert's assessment of their situation: "The bearer of this [sic] few lines is Sister Theresia [sic] formerly Superior of an [sic] comunity [sic]

19. Duchemin is described by Sweeney: "She must have been a beautiful child for she was a strikingly beautiful woman even in her later years . . . if she had any early pictures, she never showed them, but she said only that she had very light hair. She had blue eyes. . . . Unless you knew her background, you would never suspect that she was an octaroon" (WCN, 2–3, IA).

instituted for the education of coloured childern [*sic*]. . . . As she speaks french [*sic*] and english [*sic*] and [is] otherwise well instructed, I have ventured to send her to him [Gillet] seeing that she can do very little good in Baltimore." He added a comment that foreshadowed future conflict: "I hope fath. Gillet will or has already made his agreement, with you. I do not suspect that he might any way undertake some thing [*sic*] of this kind without consulting his Bishop" (PC to PPL, 9 Sept. 1845, UNDA).

## "Some Thing of this Kind," 1845–55

The ten-day journey to Monroe marked a radical transition during which Marie Therese Duchemin, French religious woman of color acquainted with a sophisticated eastern city's drawing rooms and basement chapels, stepped into the persona of Mary Theresa Maxis, white, bilingual fashioner of a congregation in frontier Michigan. The identity she left behind would be known only to her Oblate companion Ann Shaaff, who would follow; to Gillet and his successor, Giles Egidius Smulders, C.SS.R.; and to the bishops she had met in Baltimore, Lefevere and (probably) John Nepomucene Neumann, C.SS.R.[20]

The diocese Maxis entered had been established only twelve years earlier, at which time it included not only the upper and lower peninsulas of what is now Michigan but also the territory of Wisconsin and part of Minnesota (Tentler 1990, 13). It had remained "a mostly impenetrable wilderness," with the "frontier trading post" of Detroit as its center, for the whole episcopate of German ordinary Frederic Rese (Tentler 1990, 15). Rese began well, but he shortly managed to accrue sizable debts and to antagonize both influential laymen and some of his own clergy, who at that time numbered "something like 22," five of whom he had recruited himself (Tentler 1990, 15–16). The financial panics of 1837 and 1839, the deep economic depression of the early 1840s, and the slow rate of Catholic immigration during his tenure militated against significant growth of the diocese. Rese's episcopate sank quickly; by 1840, Rome had accepted his resignation from an active role in Michigan but not from the office of bishop, which he retained until his death in Germany in 1871. When Rese's successor, Peter Paul Lefevere, arrived in Detroit shortly before Christmas 1841, clergy—reduced by attrition to "perhaps 15" (Tentler 1990, 20)—and faithful had been without a bishop for nearly two years. The limited educational and charitable works begun under Rese had been virtually abandoned, and debts and taxes incurred from property purchases had mounted unaddressed.

20. From Dec. 1841 to Mar. 1844—the period of Joubert's illness and of Maxis's contact with C.SS.R.s—Neumann served as assistant at St. James, Baltimore, and as a circuit missionary to German congregations from New York to Richmond, Virginia. He became bishop of Philadelphia in 1852 (Curley 1952, 92–98, 179).

Lefevere's experience as frontier missionary in the Missouri/Illinois wilderness from 1833 to 1838 afforded him both insight into the physical and emotional hardships his priests faced and a compassion for their struggle to maintain the stamina, personal discipline, and pastoral dedication their labors required. At the same time, his temperament, ethnic background, and spirituality inclined him to a pessimistic view of human nature and a fierce asceticism that strove to eradicate pride, self-indulgence, and, among other social evils, dancing and "pic-nics." "The world is hastening to its perdition," he cautioned in his 1850 pastoral letter, and "the greater part even of Christians will be lost" unless they conform their lives to "that Gospel . . . which promises the Kingdom of Heaven only to those who do themselves violence" (cited in Tentler 1990, 18). Lefevere's "essentially monarchical vision of the Church" informed his primary episcopal goal—to rein in the territory's considerable clerical autonomy in the service of a strong centralized authority (Tentler 1990, 19). Lefevere saw deference to the hierarchy as integral to Catholic piety and relied on a revival of popular devotion to consolidate his control with a minimum of open confrontation. His sensitivity to the least challenge to his authority was likely exacerbated by the fact that he conducted his entire episcopate as coadjutor to the phantom Rese.

To understand his expectations, it must be noted that religious women in Lefevere's native Belgium tended to be from the peasant class, traditionally subservient to clerics and accustomed to domestic labors. Lefevere combined such assumptions about religious women with the pervasive racism of the time;[21] he would later warn Philadelphia's coadjutor, James Wood, that Duchemin displayed "all the softness, slyness, and low cunning of the mulatto" (PPL to JW, 2 Aug. 1859, DAA).

During the first ten years of the Monroe foundation, Lefevere was stretched thin addressing inherited difficulties throughout the diocese and was probably grateful for Monroe's relative stability. Parish, rectory, and convent felt little direct impact from the bishop's efforts at consolidating his authority. St. Mary (formerly St. Antoine) parish community included French, German, and English "congregations," which gathered separately for preaching in their native tongues. Gillet, temperamentally irked by Germans (perhaps the more so due to the French-German rift within the Redemptorists (Hoegerl [1979]), recruited Simon Sanderl, C.SS.R., to minister to that sector of his congregation; while the less robust Francis Poilvache, C.SS.R., held down the fort for the French at Monroe, Gillet traveled on horseback within a 60-mile radius to a string of French settlements along the Detroit River and Lake Erie as far south as the Ohio border, and to Irish congregations in the western woods (LFG to FDeH, 13 Apr. 1845, MA).

Gillet brimmed with expansive dreams and with the energy and

21. For an exploration of nineteenth-century Catholic attitudes toward African Americans, see Thompson 1985.

decisive organizing ability to achieve them. Within two years of coming to America, he had pioneered preaching missions to established parishes and begun French Temperance Societies whose members numbered in the thousands. He selected the port of Monroe, "the most important place after Detroit" (PPL to ACz, 6 Mar. 1844, DAA), for the establishment of the first French-speaking Redemptorist house in America, from which he envisioned missionaries radiating out into the surrounding wilderness. Most significant for the diocese, Gillet established a school to serve as a center of Catholic education—the first in southeastern Michigan—and a religious congregation to provide its leadership.

However, the vision and zeal that marked Gillet as a pioneer in the most literal sense were suspect in the larger Redemptorist context, where contention and controversy had opened two widening rifts. The fractures existed between missionaries to America who emphasized zeal for "abandoned souls" and Redemptorists in Europe who looked dimly at adjustments in regular observance and the common life. A second rift was among factions in America, most notably the French and the Germans. Gillet sparked the Provincial's ire when, hoping to raise money for "my poor religious" (LFG to DeCH, 4 May 1891, IA; trans. by author, MA) he undertook an ambitious preaching mission in New Orleans without first seeking permission. More frequently preaching and baptizing than present in the rectory, and apparently more resourceful and willing to endure extreme economy measures than certain of his brothers, Gillet was construed by German superiors as "living and acting absolutely according to his own whims and caprices" (BH to "Consultor General," 22 Dec. 1855, AGR). In 1847, Gillet would be recalled first to New York, where he would be subjected to constrictions and scrutiny that severely strained his high-strung temperament, and then to Baltimore. After a series of miscommunications, Gillet would be accused by German superiors of insolence, of "drinking every day quantities of brandy," and of having lost his taste for religious life (BH to "Consultor General," 22 Dec. 1855, AGR). In the end, exhausted by conflict, Gillet would be maneuvered out of the congregation against his wishes (MDeD, 15 Apr. and 6 May 1849, trans. in OSPA; LFG to Rector Major, 29 May 1855, AGR).

For two years, however, in a rare match of ethnicity, temperament, spirituality, and obliviousness to the expectations of authority, Gillet and Maxis traded energy and a hope for realizing their best dreams. Characteristically, both constructed plans from existing circumstances and from visionary possibilities and immediately set out to execute them, often without full reflection on their future ramifications—and just as often without authorization.[22] Both trusted their responses to a providential

---

22. Gillet later reflected: "[I was] a young priest, full of zeal, it is true, but perhaps indiscreet zeal, without experience in the ways of God, without resources" (LFG to DeCH, 4 May 1891, IA; trans. by author, MA).

God who spoke through persons and through unfolding events. Of those beginnings, Gillet wrote: "[M]y role is limited to a mere trifle, quite simply to have taken the initiative. . . . I commenced, urged by the pressing need of offering Christian education in Monroe, without concerning myself too much about the future of that nascent work" (LFG to DeCH, 4 May 1891, IA; trans. by author, MA).

The freedom and excitement of a pioneer venture suited Maxis's vision and experience. Everything waited to be shaped—the parish, the school, the enterprise of religious life. To this task, Maxis brought her Oblate understanding of the superior's role: "It will be her duty to see that the Sisters be not overburdened with occupations, that they take sufficient repose when necessary; that in health or in sickness they never be left destitute of those little comforts which may be necessary; in a word, she will conceive for them all the tenderness of a mother" (OSPR 1829, quoted in Posey 1994, 18). Maxis would emerge quite literally as "Mother," whose sustaining spirituality, forcefulness, and care inspired the affection and loyalty of both sisters and children and whose organizational and intellectual abilities would assure the school's success.

At Gillet's prompting, Maxis sent for her Oblate companion Ann Shaaff, age 36. The two boarded with the Roderick O'Connor family—who would become Maxis's longtime friends and supporters (BW to "Rev. and dear Sisters" [WC], 24 Sept. 1936, IA)—until Gillet and Poilvache had completed the new C.SS.R.'s residence; at which time the log cabin and small frame house the priests had occupied became home for the sisters and for future boarders and "children of the house." [23] Therese Renauld (Sister M. Celestine), 23, whom Gillet had earlier invited to join the new congregation, arrived from her father's Grosse Pointe farm on 9 November to complete the founding circle. It is noteworthy that two-thirds of the (apparently white) original community were women of color. Gillet and the women apparently collaborated to sketch a provisional Rule adapted from the Redemptorist discipline; after the selection of provisions "compatible with their sex," Gillet "compiled" the whole and sent it to the bishop for his approval (MMC, 28 Dec. 1845, MA). The congregation was named "Sisters of Providence," and the former Oblates received the habit and made vows privately. Finally, there took place a ceremony intended to "instruct the Congregation [parishioners] on the religious state, of which these poor people had hitherto been completely ignorant" (MMC, 8 Dec. 1845, MA). At the first Mass, Maxis and Shaaff publicly renewed their vows. Then, at the High Mass, in a packed church, the professed Sisters led "the postulant(s) dressed in white" to a side chapel from which she reappeared "transformed, in the habit of a novice"

23. "Children of the house" were frequently orphans, but this was not always the case; for example, at least one child was *purchased* from a Protestant family (Life, 106–8, MA).

before the stunned population: "The whole assembly was as if electrified, they climbed onto the benches in order to see better" (LFG to DeCH, 4 May 1891, IA; trans. by author, MA).[24]

Immediately after the ceremony, the town's new religious proceeded to the log cabin and small house vacated by the fathers and began their life together. The Monroe Motherhouse Chronicles explain that the buildings were about 90 steps apart, and that

> [A]s it was necessary for the Community to be united during meals, and the common exercises, they were obliged to assemble, sometimes in one house, sometimes in the other; thus making this traverse ten or twelve times a day, and that in the depth of winter, amidst snow and ice, and subject at all times to storms and thunder. The roads were often so bad that they were in danger of falling at each step; this however, for them was a recreation, for they considered themselves fortunate in not breaking their legs or necks: this must be told to testify the truth, and show the power of grace. (15 Jan. 1846, MA)

The congregation grew slowly. In April 1846, Josette Godfroy-Smyth (Sister M. Alphonsine) received the habit.[25] Godfroy-Smyth, 42, was a widow who "used to visit us often" but had had to settle financial affairs before joining permanently (TMN, 14, MA). In 1849, French-speaking former students Mary Whipple (Sister Mary), 18, and Rose Soleau (Sister Mary Rose), 17, formally entered the community. Poverty and the untried nature of their undertaking engendered among the sisters a strong reliance on God's Providence, on one another, and on their Redemptorist confreres. Their common "Frenchness" strengthened their unity in a polyglot milieu ([Kelly] 1948, 68).

From the outset, sisters and fathers made plans together—from the habit design to the school prospectus, from the annual Fourth of July parish celebration (featuring a much-mentioned "German band with their instruments") to the later change of congregational title (MMC, 8 Dec. 1847, MA; GES to GM, 8 Nov. 1891, SA). In a parish situation characterized as notoriously difficult, congregational chronicles and letters evidence a shared sense of mission and a mutually energizing, day-to-day exchange of ideas, anxieties, triumphs, and disappointments (Tentler 1990, 59–60).

24. Gillet's account is problematic because he uses plural forms and places two postulants in the ceremony—Renauld and "Mrs. Whipel." Context confirms that his memory combined the reception of a later entrant, Josette Godfroy-Smyth, with that of Renauld. The Whipples were relatives of Godfroy-Smyth.

25. A woman entered the community as a postulant. After a period of formation, she received the habit and a new name, thus becoming a novice. When she had adequately incorporated the spirit and Rule of the community, the novice professed first temporary and then—sometime later—final vows. Before they were regulated by canon law, the time frame for each stage varied according to individual circumstances and needs.

The provisional nature of their frontier situation supported an operational definition of God's will: sisters and fathers routinely discerned and executed choices from the data of their internal responses to unfolding outer circumstances, particularly when those circumstances involved the needs of those persons with fewest resources. This process of situating God's will had roots both in West African and in primitive Redemptorist spiritualities[26] but was essentially divergent from the more vertical piety of the day, in which experience was suspect and the will of God was mediated through male clerics in hierarchical progression. The Motherhouse Chronicles for January 1848, shortly after the arrival of Gillet's successor, Giles Egidius Smulders, C.SS.R., illustrates the young community's discernment process, with its five characteristic elements:

1. *Interior responses to unfolding events and needs.* Maxis records that Smulders "had hardly visited the different missions ... when he felt greatly grieved upon finding so many abandoned children in every part," whom he and the sisters feared would "become Protestants ... if means were not taken to remedy their situation."

2. *Prayer with the expectation of Divine guidance.* Smulders then "received an inspiration from Heaven to make the convent an asylum for assembling these children" for sacramental instruction during the space of three summer months.

3. *Further discernment with trusted companions.* Smulders tested his "inspiration from Heaven" with those confidants most intimately involved with him: "He prayed and had prayers offered by others to know the Will of God; he communicated his thought to the good Father Poilvache, his companion, who approved of and highly encouraged it. He, at the same time, discovered this idea to the Sisters, whom he caused to make a novena with this intention."

4. *Communication with authority.* This action consistently came last, and served more to confirm what had been discerned than to request permission: "He *afterward* spoke on the subject to His Lordship the Bishop who was delighted with it" (emphasis added).

5. *Immediate execution.* Disregarding practical obstacles, the community "hesitated no longer" and swung into the course of action they had concluded was the will of God for them: "Although pecuniary means failed him, he still depended on Providence, and began at once to have preparations made in the house."[27]

This style of discernment was not the province of the clergy and

26. For a characterization of the primitive Alphonsian spirit, see Hoegerl 1976; Londoño 1995.

27. This was no simple arrangement. In May 1849, four sisters, 18-year-old postulant Mary Whipple, and one laywoman welcomed into the house thirty children, speaking three languages. The chronicles of 15 May 1849 record: "This year, we were afflicted by different diseases among the children among whom, nine were attacked, and two died of congestion and fever of the brain" (MA).

superior only. Early in 1855, the chronicles (25 Feb., MA) capture a similar unfolding, this time from the heart of a single member, Sister Mary Aloysius Walter, a one-year-professed German woman who could barely communicate in the French-speaking house. Maxis recorded that Walter

> *felt grieved* that her own country people in a foreign land should labor under these disadvantages [the German Congregation had no girls' school] and *immediately recommended the matter to God.* She soon after, *received an inspiration to take upon herself* the instruction of the young German girls . . . *After serious reflection and continued prayer, she communicated her idea to the Superiors and also to the Rev. Father who had charge of St. Michael Congregation,* both of whom highly approved of it.

Walter considered her resulting proposal to open a German school *"an indication of the Divine Will,* and therefore, [typically, this was the last, formalizing step] *with the consent of her Superiors, she readily complied.* Accordingly, on the 16th of April school was commenced under the patronage of St. Aloysius" (all emphasis added).

Walter's discernment within the community context—rather than any assignment from the diocesan ordinary—determined the first IHM outreach beyond St. Mary's proper. The notion of hierarchical authority as mediator of God's design, particularly dear to Lefevere, appears to have been foreign to the Monroe pioneers. During this period, the bishop's hand appeared little in congregational affairs; generally, he approved women for entrance, reception, and profession of vows by letter—after local deliberations had been communicated to him. Two instances, however, reveal the inherent tension between Lefevere's and the sisters' modes of perceiving and of acting on the will of God.

On 8 December 1849, Lefevere "judg[ed] it necessary to make a change" (MMC, MA) and appointed Godfroy-Smyth superior. Godfroy-Smyth was older, possessed proven practical wisdom, and was a friend of his (TMN, 42,[28] MA), and thus perhaps he expected more deference than from Maxis. Nevertheless, "she could read french [*sic*] but not write, even not her name. She could preside, she was a good housekeeper, but Mother Theresa, as assistant, had to do all the rest" (GES to FXS, 22 Nov. 1892, MA).[29] The community appears to have solved this situation by circumventing the formal appointment: "As Mother Theresa was the first, she was looked on as *the* one to whom to go, although Sister Alphonsine

28. The gloss that is handwritten on this page of Maxis's notes is in the hand of Sister Xaveria McHugh (as identified by Kelly).

29. The written records in Godfroy-Smyth's hand are two signatures, which according to Suzanne Fleming, I.H.M., appear to be stylized. Community correspondence and the Motherhouse Chronicles suggest that Godfroy-Smyth engaged in household management; she is not mentioned in connection with the schools.

was appointed superior. Mother Theresa acted at that time as Assistant and Secretary and attended to all the business of the house" (CRHC, 14, MA). At the end of Godfroy-Smyth's three-year term, the sisters endorsed Maxis as her successor (MMC, 8 Dec. 1852, MA).

The second instance occurred in autumn 1854, when Maxis, James Poirier, C.SS.R., and Ignatia Walker, a trained teacher two years in the community, thought it time to extend the congregational mission beyond Monroe; Walker was sent to Detroit to assess the possibilities. Afterwards, she wrote Lefevere: "Having visited Detroit and seeing the field there is for a good Catholic school in the center of that large and populous city, I cannot refrain from asking your Lordship to establish a branch of our House there." She envisioned it clearly and went on to present a plan for a teacher training center for outlying settlements (IW to PPL, 4 Sept. [1854], MA). Lefevere failed to act on this forward looking proposal. On the contrary, he contained the community to all but an outpost in nearby Vienna (now Erie), Michigan, until after 1860.

Further, and unfortunately both for the Redemptorist and for the IHM congregations, Lefevere gave mixed signals about his financial commitment to the burgeoning St. Mary's. When he denied a verbal agreement to meet the costs of completed parish buildings, Redemptorist superiors concluded that the chronically impoverished mission would never become self-supporting. They determined to withdraw the fathers.

## Transition to the Joos Era, 1855–59

On 1 May 1855, the Redemptorists left behind a bereft sisterhood and a smoldering bishop. Though they had given Lefevere a year's notice of their withdrawal (GR to PPL, 17 Mar. 1854, cited in Wuest 1899, 345), and Poirier had requested that a successor be named in time for the smooth transition of parish, convent, and school, Lefevere vowed to "oppose" and "prohibit" the departure (PPL to JP, 16 Apr. 1855, DAA). He challenged the decision through Rome and left the parish unattended for seven months.[30] Further, he forbade all communication between sisters and Redemptorists except for formal exchanges around entrants whom the priests had begun to send from their eastern missions (TMN, 48, MA).

The "French" era had ended; ended, too, for the meantime, were liturgy and sacraments, Friday spiritual conferences, pastor's instruction for the children, and collaborative planning for parish events. What had formed and nurtured, consoled and energized the sisters—the heart of their spiritual life together—was snatched away. Nor did things augur well for establishing the IHM congregation as "more . . . than . . . a

30. In 1858, after a nearly four-year dispute, the Propaganda Fide ruled in favor of the Redemptorists (Curley 1963, 127–29).

religious society" (TM to PPL, 9 July 1859, UNDA) with a completed
Redemptorist Rule.[31] "However great this trial may have been," Maxis
recorded in the Monroe Motherhouse Chronicles,

> we had anticipated it for a long time, and we were in a measure prepared
> for the separation as after continued prayer we knew it was in perfect
> accordance with the Will of God, who for our greater sanctification de-
> prived us of those friends, who for so many years had made so many
> sacrifices and labored so arduously for both our spiritual and temporal
> advancement, and we were thus taught to seek our consolation from no
> human source, but in all our works to look to and to live for God alone.
> (1 May 1855, MA)

Maxis responded to changed conditions with her characteristic combination of reliance on God's Providence and active solution-seeking. An
incident that occurred shortly after the C.SS.R.s' departure illustrates the
paradigm from which she both lived personally and guided the congregation. Having resolved to attend Mass in Vienna, ten miles south, for
the Feast of the Ascension, Maxis could find not a single conveyance.

> Still we did not desist from our design. I *knew by experience* that I could
> walk three miles, *Sister Magdalene was also willing;* we were in hopes of
> *finding on the way some charitable person* who could take us to our jour-
> ney's end, so it happened, after walking about 3 miles *we saw a door
> opened,* on one side of the road, and a woman sitting inside. *I went and
> asked* her if she knew any one that could take us to the Church at Erie?
> She had the kindness to search until she found a man who took us in his
> buggy. . . . In the evening *we found more than one friend* ready to take us
> home. (TMN, 47–48, MA; emphasis added)

Unprovided for, Maxis assessed what she knew by experience, then acted,
trusting that the rest would be given in a combination of opportunity
provided by God, her own assertive response, and others' willingness to
assist. She forged ahead—not alone, but with a companion. During seven
months without pastor or director, Maxis managed to admit two postulants, arranged for the profession of Sister Mary Joseph Walker, opened
a longed-for mission in Vienna, and maintained communication with

---

31. Maxis was preoccupied with finalizing the Rule in the Redemptorist tradition.
Gillet's original sketch provided a framework, but experience and reflection were needed
to assure provisions for all eventualities. Maxis had made some few additions as circumstances prompted, and her anxiety seems reasonably to have stemmed from a desire to have
the congregation protected from the shifting whims of prelates, such as she had experienced
in Baltimore and had begun to suspect from Lefevere.

Redemptorist advocates. By the time the fervent but rigid John Van Gennip was appointed pastor and director in Monroe, Maxis had confided to the sisters (one in deteriorating health) her intent to seek outside support to complete the Rule and ensure future expansion of the community.

During the next twenty-four months, even as Ignatius Walker died of tuberculosis, the earlier pattern of slow congregational growth shifted markedly. Four postulants entered—three sponsored by Smulders—and "on the increase of subjects and the numerous charges devolving on the Rev. Mother, it was judged desirable" to appoint "a distinct Mistress of Novices" (MMC, 30 Aug. 1857, MA). Maxis chose Mary Joseph Walker, twenty-one months professed.[32] Half-sister of Ignatius Walker, Mary Joseph was gentle, bright, and a trained teacher. She had converted to Catholicism nine years before (MJW to JF, 14 July 1860, MJWP, MA) and had soon entered the Grey Nuns of the Sacred Heart, where "ill health and excessive scruples" ended her postulancy within five months (Mengy. of MJW, 18 Oct. 1864, MA). In contrast, the IHM community appears to have provided a milieu that nurtured both Walker's spirituality and her leadership potential. Maxis trusted the new novices to Walker's tutelage.

Though records attest to mutual respect and affection between Maxis and pastor-director Van Gennip, an autumn 1857 letter he wrote to Lefevere signaled some apprehension. The letter appears to have followed a late summer visit by Smulders, who had delivered two entrants and celebrated another's reception. Van Gennip petitioned Lefevere to "preserve good order" by restricting the sisters' access to "too many directors" and confessors and by requiring that "no one will have the *right* to confess or instruct without your permission *in writing* or mine in word" (JVG to PPL, 24 Sept. 1857, UNDA; emphasis added). Lefevere did more. Five weeks later, the Reverend Edward Joos materialized in Monroe, bearing a blotted, sloppily scrawled letter from the bishop:[33]

> I take pleasure in informing you and all your Sisters, that after mature reflection and invocation of the Holy Ghost . . . I have nominated and constituted the Rev. Edward Joos, Superior and Director of the Sisters of the Immaculate Heart of Mary in the Diocese of Detroit. The Rev. Father Joos is truly a man of God, has great experience, and is endowed with

32. Mary Phoebe Walker arrived in Monroe from Canada on 26 July 1854; before the planned time for her departure, she entered the congregation (Life, 31–33, MA). For a discussion of Walker's life, see Suzanne Fleming's account in chap. 2 of the present volume. I am indebted to Sue for the numerous exchanges (and scholarly disagreements) that were the catalyst for my attention to Walker and to her role in the congregation.

33. The state of the letter suggests a haste and carelessness markedly different from Lefevere's typical communications, which were polished second drafts.

all the qualification [*sic*] that could be desired for the important office to which he is appointed. You will therefore receive and acknowledge him as your Superior. (PPL to TM, 5 Nov. 1857, MA)

Lefevere's description bore little resemblance to the cleric who appeared at the door. Fifteen years Maxis's junior and only one year in the country, Joos stammered through uncertain English. With no direct experience of religious life, the new superior was handed the task of directing an astonished community and its former superior general according to his own and the bishop's minds—which, it turned out, bore much similarity. Like Lefevere, Joos was possessed of a Jansenistic mistrust of human freedom and of the paternalistic view of woman's "place" typical of the era.

Appointing Joos superior when the IHM Constitutions provided for the election of a sister likely reflected Lefevere's conscious effort to curtail the IHMs' contact with the Redemptorists, who had become "anathema to him" (Kelly, SN, n.d., 30, MA). Viewed from a larger perspective, the appointment occurred as Lefevere's challenge to the "generous autonomy" in parish life, rampant in his sprawling missionary see, gained momentum (Tentler 1990, 18). With the added ascendancy of superior of the congregation, Joos transformed the director's role from a companion with whom the sisters discerned the will of God and collaborated on school and parish matters to "our dear Father," preeminent authority and guardian of regularity. Almost immediately, and apparently without consulting the members, he set out to have the congregation's purpose statement emphasize the establishment of orphan asylums rather than the mission of education Gillet and Maxis intended ([Kelly] 1948, 246). For Maxis, the intrusion presaged the likelihood that Joos and Lefevere would prescribe for the congregation according to their own biases and assumptions, with minimal comprehension of its unique life and character. Two months into Joos's tenure, Maxis's references to him as "our good Father" disappear from the chronicles, replaced by "Rev. Father Joos" or "Rev. Father Joos, Director" (2 Feb. 1858–2 Feb. 1859, MA).

By March 1859, six more entrants of varied ethnic and cultural backgrounds had joined the community. In Joos and Maxis, this generation of sisters—some as young as fourteen, neither French-speaking nor former "children of the house"—were exposed to deeply conflicting though perhaps not clearly articulated perceptions of holiness, of God's will, and of the nature of ecclesial and congregational authority. Complicating the conflict was Walker's role as novice mistress.

Unlike Maxis, Walker believed that clerics enjoyed exclusive access to God's will—even to God's opinion—concerning both spiritual and practical matters, and she appears to have afforded Joos and Lefevere a reverence approaching worship.[34] Although elements of Walker's attitude reflected the nineteenth-century Catholic ethos, the extreme deference that became her hallmark likely resulted from her ongoing struggle with scrupulosity, a radical uncertainty and anguish about even the most trivial choices in the spiritual life.[35] Until the emergence of the behavioral sciences in this century, the prescribed solution for scrupulosity consisted of allaying the anxiety associated with choice and responsibilty by submitting one's judgment to the authority of a spiritual director. In practice, this "cure" produced an arrangement in which an individual (usually a woman) laid bare her inmost struggles to an authority (usually a male cleric), who interpreted God's will for her and required, in God's name, blind obedience. Thus, at a critical juncture in her own and in the congregation's development, Walker accepted Joos as spiritual director and submitted to his guidance as she molded the spiritualities of her charges.

Maxis appears not to have grasped the underlying threat of congregational division, as she poured energy into devising a way to remove at least part of the community from Lefevere and Joos's control to a place where the sisters could flourish under a completed Rule faithful to the founding vision. An opportunity to do so came in the form of a Redemptorist-prompted request from Rev. J. V. O'Reilly in Susquehanna, Pennsylvania, that IHMs accept a mission among Irish railroad workers whom O'Reilly hoped to stabilize into farming as continental railroad construction pushed farther west (Curley 1952, 385). Maxis responded with obvious delight—and with alertness to potential resistance from Lefevere: "I cannot help expressing to you my satisfaction on hearing that it is among the poor we are called," she wrote to O'Reilly, "for it is exactly what we like. We have no desire of being established in large cities and among the great ones of this world. The location and all give me the assurance that it is the will of God we should go." She then added, "I will do all in my power to come soon. Please mention in your next, when you want us that I may meet no opposition" (TM to JVOR, 26 July 1858, SA).

34. Examples pervade the biography of Walker: "Her veneration for priests was very profound, and often in conversation she acknowledged that when in their presence, she felt such awe and reverence that she could scarcely refrain from casting herself on her knees and kissing the very ground upon which they stood . . . therefore, [she] entertained the same respect and reverence for them as she would wish to show Him whose substitutes they were" (Life, 189, MA).

35. It is my assessment that scrupulosity remained an issue for Walker throughout her life. Primary sources (personal correspondence and the Life) document her profound need for certainty from an external frame of reference, her conflicted paralysis in the face of existential choice, and her energy-draining self-recrimination for minute "failures." Although sometimes personally debilitating, such scrupulosity can also be seen in a positive light: Marcia Westkott (1986, 20–52) asserts that psychological conflicts, by their nature, constitute a critical response to the culture in which they prevail.

In July 1858, with permission from Lefevere and Joos, Maxis and Sister Aloysius Walter headed east to prepare house and school for the three sisters to be assigned to the Susquehanna mission. Maxis remained there for three months, during which time she consulted Philadelphia bishop John Neumann, C.SS.R., about completing the Rule and supplied him with a copy she had brought. Subsequent events suggest that Maxis also heard, from Neumann or others, about the availability of a second house, large enough to serve as a novitiate (PPL to JW, 2 Aug. 1859; JNN to PPL, 7 Aug. 1859, DAA).

Maxis returned to Monroe swept up by the Providence of the eastern, Redemptorist connection. When Neumann wrote inviting the sisters to a large house in Reading, Maxis carried the letter to Detroit and naïvely expected Lefevere to share her enthusiasm about further expansion in Pennsylvania (PPL to JW, 2 Aug. 1859, DAA). He did not. Maxis later recounted her annoyance: "This was such an advantageous offer for our poor institution that I was desirous of accepting it, considering the little Ecclesiastic Authority ever did in the Diocese of Detroit, for our Community. All had been done by the Redemptorist Fathers, and seeing the interest they were still manifesting for our success since they had been obliged to leave; how could we be indifferent to such blessings . . . the whole community was of the same mind" (TMN, 59–60, MA). The principals faced off not long afterwards. Summoned to resolve a potential scandal developing in Pennsylvania, Maxis expected permission to go (PPL to JW, 2 Aug. 1859, DAA). She was refused. In a blatant departure from the nineteenth-century script for a woman—particularly a "good," religious woman—Maxis stood her ground with the director in a clash of wills, perspectives, and purposes that proved disastrous. "I did not," she related later, "give up and still persisted in demanding justice" until it became clear to her that her judgment about community affairs would be held hostage to Lefevere and Joos's determinations. At that point, she continued, "I . . . asked to be discharged of the Superiorship of the Community, since I was not able to act in its interest" (TMN, 60, MA).

Joos assessed the encounter differently. His letter summoning Lefevere never referred to Maxis by name; the text and tone suggest prior negative exchanges about her between the clerics: "This morning I had a short but very important conversation with . . . *She* asked me whether Your Lordship allowed her to go or not." Joos decried Maxis's "revolt" and requested immediate action "lest she destroit [sic] the whole institution" and "involve the other houses." He concluded by weighing the revolutionary potential of the rest. Unlike Maxis, who would not submit to such oppression and tyranny he reflected, "I have known them always to be submissive and Sister Joseph (the only one I have spoken to) says they are all always disposed to submit; although they feel somewhat affected by mother's disappointment" (EJ to PPL, 31 Mar. 1859, UNDA).

Lefevere arrived the following day from Detroit, the distance and busyness that had prevented his presence at a decade of community events apparently evaporating. He deposed Maxis on the spot and ordered her, with Shaaff and Ignatia Sheeran, to Pennsylvania, from whence he demanded the return of three sisters more likely to settle down under the leadership of Walker, whom he appointed superior. Through an indignant O'Reilly, those sisters ordered to return communicated their refusal; O'Reilly railed at "how injurious it is to the well being of a school to remove those in whom the affections of pupils are concentrated, the confidence of parents, patrons, centered." He also correctly assessed that sisters who had renewed vows under Neumann "owe[d] no obedience whatever to the Rt. Rev. Bishop of Detroit save what religion in general and the gratitude of generous souls towards a former superior require" (JVOR to EJ, 19 Apr. 1859, MA). To add to this perceived assault on Lefevere's authority, the sisters in Pennsylvania sent letters to Michigan detailing the promise of the mission field in the East, the investment of Neumann and O'Reilly, and the support of parishioners.

Maxis herself responded with a lack of caution that suggests her assumption that the congregation's early unanimity of vision had survived both the increase in numbers and the accompanying diversity of ethnic backgrounds, faith assumptions, and personal needs. She also miscalculated Walker's ambivalence. Maxis encouraged three Redemptorists in a letter campaign urging the sisters in Monroe to escape east. In one, for example, Henry Gieson (12 [Apr.] 1859, DAA) wrote to Walker:

> He [Lefevere] has no right any more, neither over Mother and the two sisters that accompanied her, because he sent them out of the diocese. . . . If only you now have firmity enough to fight against Contrary Winds! Listen what you have to do. In case a rupture takes place . . . quit Monroe and join the Sisters in St. Joseph's. On the 8th of next December those Sisters that want to go . . . let them refuse to take the vows; . . . Mr. O'Connor will lend them the money, that is to be restored to him immediately afterwards. . . . Try your best! Sister! . . . May God save you out of the bondage, and speed you down to your true home because home is where the Mother foundress is.

Though the recipients were cautioned to keep the communication secret,[36] the letters found their way to Lefevere.

Lefevere feared the loss both of the sisterhood and of his jurisdic-

---

36. For example, Smulders pleaded with Xavier Eagan (then sixteen): "Now, Dear child, I wish you to burn this letter as soon as you have read it; and to speak of it to *no body* except to Mother Mary Joseph, or Mr. O'Connor, or to Sister Egidius. May God give you grace and prudence not to bring me in any trouble, as you could easily do by showing this letter (15 May 1859, DAA)."

tional supremacy. His resentment toward the C.SS.R.s, which had smoldered during the protracted dispute over their withdrawal from Monroe, was fanned into self-righteous flames by the "deep rooted rascality" of these "wolves in sheep's clothing." Lefevere assumed the Redemptorist Neumann's complicity in the scheme to remove the sisters to the East and threatened to retaliate by advertising the whole affair not only to Rome and to United States prelates but to "all Pastors of souls" (PPL to JW, 2 Aug. 1859, DAA). He also struggled with outrage that his authority had been seriously challenged by a woman of color. From that point forward, correspondence between Lefevere and James Wood (coadjutor to Neumann in Philadelphia) seethed with racist comments and plots, among them a plan to discredit Maxis by exposing her biracial background in a country poised on the brink of civil war (e.g., JW to PPL, 26 Aug. 1859, DAA, copy in MA).

As a crisis of conscience and affection exploded in Monroe, neither Joos nor Lefevere encouraged the women to clarify their own experience and convictions; instead, they pressed for formal declarations of loyalty ([Kelly] 1948, 146–47). Such pressure forced underlying ambivalences into polar opposition—"self-will" and "pride" versus "holiness" and "faithfulness to God's will"—with the clerics defining the terms. Standards that Joos and Lefevere defined as integral to faith and fidelity were, in reality, contaminated by unexamined culturally and ecclesially established gender expectations.

During that tumultuous spring, exchanges ran the gamut of individual convictions:

> Frequently was she [Walker] heard to say that were all [the sisters] to abandon her . . . she would still remain and fulfill her duty to God and her vocation, and that were she obliged to dig the earth to maintain her life she would do it cheerfully to the end, or until advised to do differently by proper ecclesiastical authority. . . . [M]any of the Sisters and Novices would listen in reverential amazement, to her fervent words of advice and counsel in their doubts as to whether they should remain in Monroe or follow their companions to Susquehanna. (Life, 56–57, MA)

At the other extreme was Mary Whipple's response to Joos's interrogation;

> I would be most willing to correspond to the views of the Bishop if I could do so in conscience, but under present circumstances I cannot do it. 2. [sic] As I know that Mother Theresa (our foundress) has still authority over me I cannot recognize two lawful Superiors. 3. I cannot consent to break off all correspondence whith [sic] those who have formed me to the religious life and to whom after God I owe everything—this is impossible. Now father this is my conscience and nothing can change it. (MW to EJ, 31 May 1859, UNDA)

Joos turned to Lefevere in near panic: "I think I am obliged to make you know every part of the sad drama *they are* playing since so long. For my part I do not know what to do or say; most all wish to go" (EJ to PPL, 7 June 1859, UNDA).

In a letter to Joos dated 10 June 1859 (UNDA), Lefevere brought the full weight of his authority to bear on the identity and on the future development of the congregation. He first expelled Whipple and Mary Rose Soleau for their "spirit of revolt," then proceeded to rend the IHM congregation in two: "With regard to those Sisters in the Diocese of Philadelphia, who by their duplicity, schism and open disobedience, have so shamefully dishonored the name of Religion they of course are forever dismissed from said Order of the Servants of the Immaculate Heart of Mary and consequently no correspondence or fellowship should be had or held with them."

By the end of July, however, most of the Monroe sisters had been persuaded of God's will in their regard.[37] Twelve had chosen to remain in Monroe, and twelve had chosen Pennsylvania. Egidius Flanagan, just professed, was the last to depart: "Sister Egidia who seemed to be the only troublesome one could not hold it any longer without loosing [*sic*] her head and disturbing the Community, and left last tuesday [*sic*] in secularibus" (EJ to PPL, 23 July 1859, UNDA). It was, in essence, a no-win situation for all concerned, and for most of the next century, IHMs struggled with the conflict between their own integrity and the powerful dictates of an inherited female script.

## Loss of Memory, 1859–91

Nineteenth-century American culture provided few models for a woman exercising initiative and responsibility for her own life. From her earliest years, the typical female child was socialized into a script that afforded her no voice for anger and no arena for exercising direct influence over her own destiny. Rather than take initiative, the acceptable woman was directed simply to make herself available, in the hope that a work suited to her, a cause to which she might dedicate herself—even a religious vocation—might discover and pursue *her*, like a conventional lover. In a culture that permitted women only the language of uncertainty and submission, the female who claimed personal and social authority

---

37. Walker (to unnamed sister in Pennsylvania, between 7 Sept. 1861 and 13 Mar. 1862, MJWP, MA) recorded that the sisters' distress had reached such an unbearable pitch that she and most others preferred enforced separation: "This . . . is the formal decree of our first Superior, and given, only after his having heard through me, the conscientious opinion of the majority of the members of our Community here, respecting the matter, viz.: that all disconnection was preferable to the unsettled and dreadfully trying state of affairs at that time." See also MMC, two paragraphs preceding entry for 21 July 1859, MA.

was seen as an anomaly—frequently a monstrous anomaly to be censured. Carolyn Heilbrun (1988, 24–25) demonstrates that although nineteenth-century women's letters and diaries reveal managerial talents and patent ambitions in the public sphere, those same women's autobiographical accounts invariably depict only their intuitive, nurturing, and passive selves. Far from a conscious artifice, women's contradictory self-presentation can be understood as an unconscious defense against culturally imposed (or sanctioned) double binds. Within this framework of female consciousness, Maxis and Walker can be seen as personifying apparently polar aspects of a dynamic congregational "self" vis-à-vis social and ecclesial gender role expectations of the time. Exploring each of their responses to Lefevere's separation decree lays the groundwork for making sense of congregational choices over the next century.

Claiming her convictions—and insisting on the authority that her treasured Rule guaranteed to IHM superiors—cost Maxis her best dream and laid on her shoulders the blame for splitting the congregation in two. Lefevere's edict surpassed her worst fears and triggered an ambivalence about her personal power that would be patent in her language and behavior until her death thirty-eight years later. Once confident and breezily straightforward, Maxis vacillated between assertions of and apologetic retreats from her own experience. For example, soon after the separation, Maxis wrote Lefevere a letter in which organizational vagaries and mechanical errors signaled her disorientation. She first begged his forgiveness: "I can only own that I did wrong and beg of your Lordship forgiveness. . . . One thing I will say and which I dont [sic] understand is that God should permit that I should be carried by my impetuous disposition whilst I did not cease to pray for His assistance." Even so, she could not keep from indicting Lefevere's constrictions on the community: "I knew the rules were not completed, that the intention of those who laid the foundation of the establishment had something more in view than to form a religious society. By the length of time we remained always the same in Monroe I thought we would do better elsewere [sic]." Then, as though suddenly wary of a blow, she retreated: "All I want is charity, union [with] the will of God, which I will never any more interpret my own way" (TM to PPL, 9 July 1859, UNDA).

Still, to the end of her life, Maxis was feistier than the script allowed. Although illegitimacy and race may have placed Maxis at a disadvantage in the mainstream culture of her time, they also situated her in a marginal context characterized more by female than by male authority. The single mother who raised her had transcended trauma and racial prohibitions to become educated and self-supporting; her mentors had fled a revolution, had established a school, and had quietly countered the weight of southern prejudice and social convention to profess religious vows. "Deprived" during her upbringing of male models of leadership, Maxis appears not to have digested prevailing gender constructs. This is evidenced by her leadership style, by her collaborative relationships with a long line of priest-peers, and by her straightforward challenges to Joos's and Lefevere's assumptions of sovereignty.[38]

In contrast, Walker personified the contradictions of female self-presentation that Heilbrun describes. Letters she wrote from her sickbed to each sister on mission offer crisp, practical advice on matters from striking a bargain for roofing material or cloth to firmly refusing inferior goods, from taking responsibility for personal health to managing scarce congregational dollars. Walker's voice resonates with affection and clarity: "Dear child," she advises Sister Gertrude Gerretsen, "[b]y all means make any contract for wood or anything else that will be for the best but take things like that into your own hands, remember you are in charge there & I am far away—Take courage" (MJW to [GG, late 1863 or early 1864] MJWP, MA). In relationships with males, however, a sweet and total submission eclipsed Walker's managerial competence. Her biography records her self-effacement and the responses of the males with whom she interacted. "She was the only one who failed to see her qualifications," the writer notes; "[S]he . . . dreaded nothing so much as exposing herself to be deceived or led into error, by acting upon her own views or judgment; and therefore she wisely distrusted herself" (Life, 173, MA). The mayor of Monroe (safe from any danger that Walker *would* appropriate any such role) proclaimed that her "capacities were such as would fit her to govern the United States with ease and order." A Chicago priest exalted her as the ideal religious woman: "She is a perfect *mass* of talents, yet simple and unassuming as a child" (Life, 185–86, MA).

This approbation notwithstanding, Walker's letters intimate the conflict beneath her surrender, a longing for some unacknowledged part of herself: "[M]y heart is not at ease," she confided to her longtime spiritual guide Bishop John Farrell, "—as long as I have so much to do that I scarcely know how to do it, I am all right, but in my leisure moments I want something that I don't know . . . though I am told to be quiet, I still feel that my heart is more divided than God wills it to be." (MJW to JF, 27 Oct. [1861], MJWP, MA).

Walker valued "above all beautiful & blind obedience" (MJW to [SJD or SMP], 11 Dec. 1862, MJWP, MA), a saving grace from God through Joos, that conferred unqualified assurance that none of her choices be "self-willed," that is, sinful. A disturbing example of Walker's harsh self-censure and scrupulous attribution of moral authority to Joos's smallest wish was preserved in her biography as a model to be emulated:

---

38. Collaborative relationships with Joubert, Gillet, Smulders, Poirier, Neumann, and Augustine Gaudet, O.M.I. (her spiritual director in Ottawa) are well documented. Maxis experienced conflict only with Lefevere, Joos, and Wood.

> One morning Rev. Father desired her to send the workman to his house
> . . . somehow it escaped her memory . . . her distress was very great as
> she could not leave her bed to call anyone, however, she prayed and
> begged pardon of God for what she called *'her wicked disobedience,'* . . .
> blow after blow she inflicted on her poor, emaciated body, which had to
> be washed almost daily with dissolved glue to prevent the bones from
> piercing the skin as her flesh was all gone. (Life, 175, MA)

That such self-recrimination was counted virtue fueled Walker's conflict;
her "obedience" drew praise from a Joos who loved her but who nonetheless maintained his position at the cost of her fragmentation.

The Monroe community's response reflected the profound conflict
evoked by loyalties to both Maxis and Walker. Following the split, Joos
and Walker professed affection for the sisters who had gone east but
simultaneously began to employ language that discounted the easterners'
values and choices. Maxis had staged a "revolt" (EJ to PPL, 31 Mar. 1859,
UNDA). Companions whose anguish they had so recently shared were
described as "dissatisfied," "troublesome," and "misled," and as "bad
spirits" that "should be removed, that the others see their wrong and
make atonement" (MMC, n.d., 1859, MA; EJ to PPL, 12 Aug. 1859, DAA).
In contrast, terms suggesting holiness would continue to be applied to
the remnant who had "chosen the sterner duty, to stay rather than to go"
(Mengy. of XE, 11 Mar. 1865, MA). In response to a suggested reunion of
the sisters, Joos declared: "I would be afraid to soil the purity of those
who have remained faithful" (EJ to PPL, 12 Aug. 1859, DAA; trans.
in Gannon, 1992, 59), while Walker thanked God that she had been
"prevented from delusion and mistaken zeal" (MJW to JF, 29 Dec. 1860,
MJWP, MA).

The language of discounting laid the groundwork for the congregation to psychologically split off Maxis and all she represented of female
authority, with both its rich possibilities and its implied threat of castiga-
tion. By attributing the painful state of affairs to the unfathomable wisdom of a good God, the sisters could both transform feelings of anger
and absolve human agents from responsibility: "[I]f Almighty God permitted such things to happen, it was undoubtedly to carry out His own
designs with regard to the Community, which are at all times so merciful,
tho' so hidden to our views" (MMC, n.d. 1859, MA).

Splitting Maxis and the eastern sisters from awareness and con-
signing them like madwomen to the collective mental attic of the congregation allowed the surviving remnant to plant its feet firmly in the place
available to it, to consolidate precious energies, and to move forward
under a clear if narrowed focus.[39] To insure and reward the forgetting of

---

39. The exile of culturally unacceptable aspects of the female self is a well-documented
subtext in nineteenth-century women's writing. See Gilbert and Gubar 1979.

earlier relationships and models for living, Joos accomplished the "development and perfection" of the Rule (Life, 69, MA) and amended the congregational purpose to highlight care of orphans. He enforced the interdict on communication with the sisters in Pennsylvania, and he reassigned their religious names to incoming novices (Mengy. of XE, 11 Mar. 1865, MA). Likewise, a newly attentive Lefevere paid out of pocket for the printing of 300 "complete little volume[s]" of the *Manual of Prayers and Rule and Constitutions* (MMC, Dec. 1861, MA) and quite suddenly bestowed a long-denied permission to reserve the Blessed Sacrament in the house (MMC, 3 Feb. 1860, MA). By 1864, the chronicles referred to Walker as "our First Superioress" (18 Oct., MA), signaling an accomplished break with the past and the virtual refounding of the congregation.[40]

### Quelling Echoes from the Attic

Few echoes drifted from the attic where old lives were locked. When they did, they were quickly and consciously quelled. The first such instance occurred in 1868, when Maxis and Renauld traveled to Monroe and Detroit to beg readmittance to the congregation. Though welcomed by Joos, Godfroy-Smyth, Gerretsen, and Frances Renauld, they were required to conceal their identities and former positions from sisters who had entered since they left. Lefevere, who would die within the year, accepted Renauld (apparently on condition of her silence) but turned Maxis away, alone.[41]

Nearly a quarter of a century later, following Maxis's death in 1892, Joos refused to accept her handwritten account of the foundation years (CFR, Aug. 1934, MA), then intervened to derail a rumored biography. In a letter to a Redemptorist superior concerning the project, Joos threatened a disturbance:

> I hope it is not true, but I have been informed that Rev. F. X. Schnüttgen intends to publish something like a life of Mother Theresa, which would necessarily revive the trouble of 1858–59. . . . My informant from the way the good Father expressed himself believes that great injustice would be done to the late R. Rev. Bishop Lefevere and to the Community of Mon-

---

40. For a thorough development of the "refounding" thesis, see chap. 2 of the present volume.

41. After Renauld's reacceptance, Maxis wandered alone in Baltimore until invited back to Ottawa. Renauld was given the name Celestine Xavier and a new place in community rank (a number assigned in order of entrance), as though she were entering for the first time. "The separation in the Community became a sealed book, and those entering the Congregation after 1860 generally knew nothing of it, so with the silence imposed on the seniors and ignorance the inheritance of the juniors, Sister Xavier was rarely asked a question about the past" (Mengy., of CXR 13 Apr. 1897, MA).

roe and for the sake of justice and truth I would in this case consider myself bound in conscience to show the other side of the question by presenting, if not to the public, at least to heigher [*sic*] authorities the different letters and documents I have kept locked up in my safe since 1858.

Joos noted he had been "Director since 1857" and signed himself "Prel. Dom. S.S. Leonis XIII," invoking his Roman appointment as vicar to suggest influence (EJ to NF, 13 Feb. 1895, MA). The provincial, Ferdinand A. Litz, assured him there would be no such biography written by a Redemptorist (FAL to EJ, 17 Feb. 1895, MA). In a stark marginal gloss, omitted in her published draft, Kelly summarized aptly: "The very name of Mother Theresa was buried in oblivion and that quite deliberately" (SN, n.d., 20, MA).

Joos and the sisters most closely aligned with him exercised immense, orchestrated control over the "secret." Nonetheless, snippets of data witness that someone managed to subvert the machinations of amnesia. The Record of the Oblate Sisters for 1934 (OSPA) recalls: "In July 1879 on the occasion of our Golden Jubilee, we received a beautiful letter of congratulation from the sisters at Monroe Michigan enclosing ten dollars in gold, and stating that they felt as if we were near to them as their Foundress had been an Oblate (OSPRe, 4, OSPA)."[42] Someone in the IHM community not only knew Maxis's racial and congregational histories but dared to own her in the midst of enforced denial.

Like pond ripples from a thrown stone, acts of owning circled slowly outward. Soon after Maxis's 1885 return from Ottawa to the West Chester IHMs, a pointed article in *St. Joseph's Advocate* again put forward the issues of Maxis's race and role—and of IHM denial of both: "And here goes to let the cat out of the bag, though he scratch! Who in these United States was the first, we repeat the *very first*, to start the holy Order of the blue-robed sisterhood cradled at Monroe, Michigan, and known, we think, as 'Sister Servants of the Immaculate Heart of Mary?' Was it not one of these four colored ladies, Sister Theresa? . . . [W]e must not wound her humility (to say nothing of her trials!) by another word. She *passed* as white, but was *passed* as colored!" ([Greene] 1885, 106–7). Distracting attention from attic voices required more and more energy, as whispers slipped under the door.

## Reinvention, 1892–1948

Factors in and outside of the IHM congregation wove the complex textures out of which emerged—less significant and far less challenging

---

42. The 1879 letter has not been located (MRC to author, 17 Feb. 1994).

than her historical self—a reinvented Maxis: the silent figure in the Founder's Day tableaux, crafted to evoke the myth of beginnings without raising potentially explosive questions of congregational self-definition.

Near the turn of the century, three events focussed the thorny question of who should be called "true founder."[43] First, in 1891, West Chester IHMs unexpectedly reconnected with Gillet, by then a Cistercian in France, and received his written account of the IHM foundation. In it, Gillet described his own role and clearly assigned Maxis first place among the three women he had brought together (LFG to DeCH, 4 May 1891, IA). Second, the 1892 deaths of both Maxis and Gillet heralded the close of the founding era and the need to formalize the record for future generations of IHMs. Maxis's published obituary asserted only that "[s]he was the oldest sister in the order, and from this fact arose the title she was known by, 'Mother,' although she never filled the position of Superioress in the order" (cited in PJW to FXS, 7 Feb. 1892, MA). This "erroneous statement" sparked intense indignation from associates with firsthand experience of the early days: Smulders, Maxis's friend of many years; F. X. Schnüttgen, C.SS.R., primary advocate for her return to West Chester; Augustine Gaudet, O.M.I., spritual director during her exile in Canada; and Genevieve Morrissey, I.H.M., student and entrant during Maxis's Susquehanna days. They exchanged twenty-one letters arguing Maxis's role as "Foundress," culminating in a resolution to collect her recorded words "quietly to prevent difficulties. Such documents must be carefully put aside until they can be used without offending anybody and at the same time telling the entire truth. *Sapienti sat.*" (FXS to GM, 4 Feb. 1892, MA). A bewildered Schnüttgen ascribed the IHMs' denial of Maxis's founding role to racial prejudice: "It is strange that color should cause Religious to have a prejudice against a very deserving person" (FXS to GM, 8 May 1893, MA).

The third catalyst around the question of founder was the death of Edward Joos on 18 May 1901. Joos's passing raised the question of whether a congregation of women who for so many years had credited their growth and accomplishments to "our dear Father" could define themselves independently of him—or of any replacement cleric. Mother Mechtildis McGrail faced the task of persuading IHMs that they were capable of moving into the new century with a woman at the helm. By what Maxis would likely have labeled Providence, Francis T. Parr, C.SS.R., arrived from New York to preach the annual retreat the following August.[44] To the astonishment of the sisters gathered in chapel, Parr

43. References to Maxis as "foundress," "Mother Foundress," and "founder" were thematic in letters by those who knew her from 1859 into the twentieth century.

44. By this time, Redemptorist spirituality had been eclipsed by the Jansenistic rigors of Joos's guidance for forty-four years.

began the exercises by presenting two small notebooks handwritten by Maxis—her recollections of the early years (TMN), which Joos had earlier refused to accept from Smulders, and her personal collection of prayers. Parr had discovered the books while housecleaning after Schnüttgen's death and "felt they belonged here in the Home of the Institute, so I am happy to have the privilege of bringing them to you" (CF, interviewed by RK, 1934, notes in MA; see also note of RK on cover of TMN, MA). The ironic contradiction between McGrail's determination to wrest congregational reins from further male domination and the community's unconscious collusion to deny Maxis's paradigmatic leadership role captures IHMs' ambivalence about their authority as women in the church and in the culture of their times.

The majority of sisters present at the retreat conference knew nothing of the notebooks or the woman whose memory and role had crystallized there; those few who held the secret, however, responded with action. In response to the decade's sharpening focus on the founder issue, a coterie of sisters who maintained powerful loyalties to Joos's memory and who had internalized his paternalistic values executed a careful strategy to promulgate a revised history.

Examination of certain original documents regarding the congregation's earliest years—accounts of the foundation by Maxis, Gillet, and Renauld, and the biography compiled just after Walker's death—reveals in each the attempt by a revisionist hand to purge evidence of Maxis's prominence, to shift the central focus to Renauld and Godfroy-Smyth, and to touch up certain of Gillet's traits that might have appeared unseemly against then-current notions of holiness. For example, in Maxis's "Notes Regarding the Foundation" (TMN, 1883, 3–4, MA), an eraser-smudged blank replaces her comment about Gillet's irritation with Germans.[45] In Renauld's "Historical Cronology [sic] of the beginning of our Community" (13–14, MA), a carefully cut-and-pasted patch obscures Renauld's report: "As Mother Theresa was the first she was looked on as *the* one to whom to go, although Sister Alphonsine was appointed Superior. Mother Theresa acted at that time as Assistant and Secretary and attended to all the business of the house." In the handwritten original and in a typed copy of this Life of Mother Mary Joseph Walker, ca. 1865–66 (both in MA), Maxis's name has been neatly left blank. Finally, the most sweeping and strategic revisions appear in a published "translation" of Gillet's account of the founding ([Shanley] 1916, 37–49).

Moreover, the coterie appears to have produced two new documents, a 1904 pamphlet (apparently no longer extant) and Loyola Shanley's 1916 *A Retrospect*, written for the congregation's diamond jubilee. A single

---

45. The reviser also pencilled comments and clarifications into Maxis's "Notes," going so far as to correct punctuation errors and French spellings.

letter attests to the existence, contents, and emphases of the pamphlet. West Chester Mother Gonzaga Rooney, who had entered under Maxis in Pennsylvania, wrote in disgust to her General Superior, Mother Camilla Maloney:

> [I]f I had read one [pamphlet] carefully, instead of merely glancing at the first pages, I should have considered the pile worthless. . . . I read for the Sisters the edifying parts, correcting, while reading, the glaring errors. . . . Chronologically, it is all wrong. It is no wonder that the Monroe Province are sensitive on the subject; for it concerns them only. Fr. Joos had no claim on us Pennsylvanians. We had no claim on him. . . . If the Redemptorists gave no advice, when appealed to, they . . . justly ignored those who were mutilating their work. . . . The miracle to me lies in the fact, that twice their number, seven hundred exist [i.e., the West Chester IHMs], have grown to even mediocrity without the aid and direction of Mons. Joos. (27 Oct. 1904, IA)

Rooney's words reflected her understanding of and distaste for the attempt to inflate Joos's contribution and to eclipse Maxis. She ended flatly: "Ther's [sic] no use trying to kill people, that don't suit us. Mother Teresa [sic] is an illustration of the inevitable resurrection. She is ever and anon appearing in type for the benefit of the public reader."[46]

The second attempt at codification of a revised history was the 1916 *A Retrospect*, which Kelly (in a gloss on the title page) attributes to Loyola Shanley. The volume reads like a collection of essays by at least two authors, with styles varying from highly ornate and convoluted to flat and unadorned. There are inaccuracies of many sorts and no documentation. A Victorian hyperbole and piousness prevail, and overemphatic attributions suggest an intent deeper than simply to convey information. Supposedly presenting to the reader a statement of the facts from original sources, the author sets out a chronology and a set of carefully crafted anecdotes that establish Renauld as the "first" IHM and as the centerpiece in Gillet's plans, with Josette Godfroy-Smyth next in priority. These are the white women from Grosse Pointe and Monroe, respectively. The volume relegates Maxis and Shaaff to third and fourth positions chronologically and renders them nearly invisible in images fashioned to evoke the founding in congregational memory. The reader cannot know that "incontrovertible statement[s] of the facts" ([Shanley] 1916, 37) have been skillfully emended: comparison with primary documents reveals strategic deletions and insertions as well as blatant revisions. Most astonishing is the use of an edited version of Gillet's original "Notice sur l'Origine" in which all references to Maxis's Oblate connection and to her primary

---

46. The "resurrection" likely refers to Reilly [1900, 1102] which names Maxis as the colored foundress of the IHMs.

role in the IHM founding—even to the IHMs' earliest title, "Sisters of Providence"—have been struck. The complicated editing process required deleting the document's original title, then painstakingly emending significant portions of the text, including Gillet's account of his inquiries into whether the Monroe congregation had survived.

These revisions served their purpose: *A Retrospect* stood as the authoritative source for further congregational writings until Kelly's time. In the commemorative volume for the community's Diamond Jubilee (SSIHM [1920]) and in the volume commemorating the dedication of the new Motherhouse-Academy complex (SSIHM 1932), the community replicated the chronological inaccuracies, sourceless citations, and even the idiosyncratic spellings of proper names that Shanley had set out. In addition, the 1927 *Souvenir Volume: Dedication of Marygrove College* (Marygrove College 1927) relied nearly verbatim on Shanley, and presumably to target an audience of "young ladies" who might be inspired to enter the college or congregation, further embellished the descriptions of Grosse Pointe Renauld's virtue and courage.

If the reinvention was meant to be an inside affair, it did not remain as such. In the first quarter of the twentieth century, an immigrant church assured of survival reflected on its own experience and on the phenomenon of religious life. At the same time, a freed slave population sought to bring forward "colored" heroes. Although individual IHMs communicated little across community lines, a succession of major superiors from Monroe and from West Chester sustained interactions that were geared to maintain tight control of IHM self-presentation.

As historians from varied quarters probed leaking stories of the congregational split and of Maxis's double connections and exile, women of spiritual depth who cared immensely for their own integrity found themselves in an untenable position. On the one hand, admitting the truth risked incurring prejudice against vulnerable IHM institutions and casting a succession of prelates—and their former advocate Joos, who had so benefited the congregation—in the worst light. On the other hand, continued denial required compromising their integrity at multiple levels, including flat denials to inquiring historians, continued manipulation of written accounts, hypervigilance over archival records, and control of congregational access to information. Faced with this double bind, IHMs intensified the machinations of denial but split off from awareness the full implications of their duplicity by relying on religious constructs. Note how Mother Ruth Hankerd, in her exchange with Sister (later Mother) Maria Alma Ryan of West Chester, placed responsibility for Maxis's demise not on human politics and choice but on God's design: "Mother Theresa was certainly a remarkable woman despite the many contradictions in her make-up. Undoubtedly she would have gone far had circumstances been more propitious in the early days. But God evidently mapped out her life on different lines for her greater glory in the only life that counts" (RH to MAR, May 1942, draft, MA).

From at least 1919 through the late 1930s, Monroe and West Chester superiors colluded to field the questions of numerous researchers, including an unnamed Baltimore Sulpician; Hugh Duffy, S.S.J., and Grace Sherwood, historians for the Oblates; Detroit Archdiocesan historian Rev. George Paré; Francis E. Tourscher, O.F.M., Edward J. Curran, and Joseph Code, S.J., all from the American Catholic Historical Society; and Leonard DiFalco, a Brooklyn parish priest who attempted to raise Maxis's cause for canonization. Together, the women resorted to maneuvers that ranged from posturing ignorance to enlisting the influence of Josephite L. B. Pastorelli, Catholic University theologian Peter Guilday, and bishops Dennis James Dougherty and Michael James Gallagher (of Philadelphia and Detroit, respectively) in negotiations for silence.[47] Mother Domitilla Donohue epitomized the IHM superiors' position in a statement to Duffy: "[W]e are convinced that silence is the fairest, wisest, and most agreeable way of committing to oblivion this subject" (DD to HD, 5 Dec. 1928, OSPA).

Superiors involved in the artifice appear to have discounted the long-term futility of denying a documented historical reality and continued to publish revisionist histories until Kelly's time. At each threat of disclosure, a chain of informed guardians acted quickly to marshal episcopal influence. In one such instance, Mother Loyola Gallagher (West Chester) informed Bishop Dougherty that "Rev. George Paré . . . is preparing for publication a history of the Diocese of Detroit. Contained in this book is a very strong letter from Archbishop Wood which . . . would be very detrimental to our community, referring, as it does to our foundresses as mulattoes. . . . I thought it wise to lay these facts before Your Eminence at once, since this publication would do untold harm to almost three thousand of our Sisters in many dioceses of the United States" (LG to DJD, 22 Feb. 1932, draft, IA). Dougherty responded to Gallagher's request for "direction and guidance in this matter" by enlisting Detroit bishop Gallagher's intervention with Paré, who in turn assured Dougherty that "my investigations were activated merely by a legitimate desire to know the truth . . . it has long since been agreed upon that there was no necessity for embarrassing the Sisterhood by blazoning intimate details of their domestic history" (GPa to DJD, 27 Feb. 1932, IA). The bishops may well have been equally reluctant to blazon the intimate details of their predecessors' attitudes and behavior. In the end, Lefevere and Wood's racism —a pivotal dynamic in Maxis's story—remained unexamined until the publication of an article in 1983 (Shea and Supan, 10–13).

Grace Sherwood, second historian for the Oblates' centennial volume,

47. Documentation can be found in letters between major superiors and to the clerics mentioned above during 1929–34, in MA and IA.

poignantly characterized the conflict between her professional integrity and her concern that no damage be done. "I have gone over it and over it, paring off things that violated my conscience as an historian in an endeavor not to give offence," she wrote to Hankerd. "Everyone has been against me in this except the Mother General of the Oblates and her assistant who, like myself, feel that the book would be spoiled for all time if anyone were hurt or injured by it. It has been a terrible thing to do without any help from your community." Sherwood encouraged Hankerd to seize the historical moment:

> Now . . . when the letters, diaries, etc. are being unearthed which establish that she [Maxis] was educated, free, competent to conduct a school, a professed religious and the daughter of a woman who gave her life for the service of humanity . . . it could be told, beautifully, and the discrepancies in the history of the IHM as told in their book [Gillespie 1921] all accounted for on the ground of this new and un-learned of data. . . . As it is, the history of the IHM . . . will not stand the test of research. . . . These are the things I wanted to talk over with you. Not how the things untold by me would affect the Oblates because their history is not affected by it but the effect that concealing them may have, some day, on the reputation of the author of the history of the IHM. (15 Dec. 1930, MA)

Hankerd did, in fact, seize the moment; with her response to Sherwood, she put an end to a near century silence. "I see nothing in the copy of Extracts from 'Oblates' Hundred and One Years' that could be deemed objectionable to us, and if that is all you have in the book that concerns the I.H.M.s I see no reason why your mind should not be at ease about your work" (17 Dec. 1930, MA). Four years later, Hankerd would go further allowing Kelly to enter the attic and face what she might find.

There is no doubt that the burial and reinvention of Theresa Maxis were prompted by the sociocultural dynamic of racism. However, historical amnesia also served the more critical purpose of distracting IHMs from having to confront the implications of Maxis's vision and voice for women in a patriarchal culture and church. Nineteenth century social and political roles were dominated by males: with rare exceptions, males governed, legislated, and sat on judges' benches and on episcopal thrones. Men controlled the forums of communication and the means of access to them; men's writing created the fictional worlds women inhabited, just as for centuries it had generated the canonized record of women's nature and role before God.

By the middle of the twentieth century, prohibitions on female self-definition and autonomy that were lifting slightly in the larger social context had not budged in the inner world of the church. Religious women have been described as enviably free for the times because they escaped the script of dependence on a man through marriage, were highly educated, and relied on the strength of a company of female friends. Along with religious women's "privilege," however, came schizophrenic messages and expectations, all the more powerful and confusing because defined as "holy." Professional religious women who forged and directed educational and charitable institutions in the church were nevertheless forbidden, under threat of censure, a voice with which to define their identity and role.

Attending to muffled voices in order to distinguish cultural dictates and to reclaim exiled parts of individual and corporate selves is the anxiety-fraught, often painful, task of maturity. Rosalita Kelly spent years attending to the echoes of attic voices.[48] In the end, she rearranged the IHM tableau figures and breathed life into them. Continued listening is a matter of historical responsibility. For the future there remain the tasks of understanding Maxis on her own terms—as a woman forced to assimilate—and of daring to embrace both Maxis and Walker, two aspects of a whole congregational "self,"[49] with both the polar tensions and the immense creative possibilities such integration implies in a culture and Church that continue to dictate female fragmentation.

48. One sister recalled: "I felt her [Kelly's] heart going out to them. . . . She talked about it a lot . . . she couldn't understand why Theresa could be left up in Canada . . . her wonderment that nobody could answer those hideous letters once a year . . . that she was so abandoned. She almost cried at that. She said if she'd been around she'd have found a way to get in touch with her" (IHM sister [entrance 1921], interviewed by author, 31 Oct. 1992).

49. Ann Chester, I.H.M., reflected: "I have been aware throughout my life of a double spirit in the Monroe IHMs: one I believe stemmed from Msgr. Joos and Mother Mary Joseph, the other from Fr. Gillet and Mother Theresa Maxis" (written interview by author, 8 Jan. 1993, copy in MA).

Mother Mary Joseph Walker, I.H.M.

# 2

# She Who Remained

## Mother Mary Joseph Walker and the "Refounding" of the IHM Congregation

### Suzanne Fleming, I.H.M.

On 27 November 1865, the Reverend Edward Joos, superior and director of the IHM congregation in Monroe, Michigan, supervised the exhuming and transferring of the bodies of nine IHM sisters, among them Mother Mary Joseph Walker (MMC, MA). In the process, Joos removed some of Walker's bones (CM, 17 Sept. 1932, MA), securing for the congregation a first-class relic[1] of the woman whom both he and her sisters regarded as the congregation's "true foundress" (Life, 223, MA).[2]

Technically, Walker was the congregation's third general superior. However, Walker and Joos, together with the sisters they governed, viewed the period of her tenure as general superior—from Mother Theresa Maxis's dismissal in 1859 until Walker's death on 18 October, 1864—as a "refounding" of the congregation. During this period, Walker fostered and modeled to her sisters a relationship with Joos that would influence the governance of the congregation long after her death.

### Theresa Maxis and the "Separation"

A Belgian Redemptorist priest, Louis Florent Gillet, had established the IHM congregation in 1845 but had departed Monroe in 1847. Over

1. A relic (in Catholic ecclesiastical usage) is a part of the body or an artifact of a deceased person who has lived an exemplary life and who is regarded as holy enough to be considered for sainthood. A first-class relic is a bone fragment as opposed to a lock of hair or a clothing fragment. A relic is reverenced to honor the memory of the deceased person.

2. The Monroe Archives contain a handwritten biography of Walker, hereafter referred to as the Life. Through comparison of the handwriting of the Life with that of a document known to have been written by Bridget Smith, I.H.M. (IMN, MA), I have identified Smith

the objections of Detroit's coadjutor bishop, Peter Paul Lefevere, all the remaining Redemptorists were withdrawn by their provincial on 1 May 1855 (MMC, MA).[3] Throughout these early years, it was Maxis—one of the women who had followed Gillet to Monroe to be founding members of the new congregation and who also was its first superior—who supplied the energy and charismatic vision which guided the young community.[4] Nevertheless, the Motherhouse Chronicles of 30 November 1855 describe the seven-month period immediately following the departure of the Redemptorists, when the congregation was without ordained male spiritual direction, as a "severe trial" of "spiritual desolation." At that time, a diocesan priest, the Reverend John Van Gennip, took over as the congregation's spiritual director; he stayed in Monroe for only two years.

Then, on 5 November 1857, the unannounced arrival of Joos, a young missionary from Belgium who had been in this country only one year, offered an unexpected challenge to Maxis's authority as the congregation's leader and superior (MMC, MA). Lefevere had given Joos complete jurisdiction over the IHM sisters, making him both director and superior (PPL to TM, 5 Nov. 1857, MA). Maxis was now to report to him. Although she outwardly submitted to her loss of authority, Maxis must have resented Joos's appointment. Her discontent crystallized in late March 1859, when Lefevere and Joos denied her permission to open a second mission in Pennsylvania (TMN, 60, MA).[5] Joos reported to the bishop that Maxis had told him she had "no Confidence any longer neither in the Bishop . . . nor you [Joos], and so you may write to the Bishop who can give me my demission" (EJ to PPL, 31 Mar. 1859, UNDA).

Accepting the challenge, Joos in the same letter put Walker, then the congregation's young novice mistress, squarely in the middle of the dispute: "As for the Sisters I have known them always submissive and

---

as the probable compiler and author of the Life. Professed just days before Walker's death, Smith, a straightforward woman of much common sense, was a close friend of Walker; see chap. 4 of the present volume for more on Smith. Page numbers used in citing from the Life are from the handwritten copy that is believed to be the original (over the years, two additional handwritten copies were made).

3. The account that follows evolved from cross-referencing numerous primary documents in the Monroe Archives and material in Kelly's centennial history (1948).

4. Maxis served as superior from the congregation's founding in 1845 until her dismissal from this office in 1859, with the exception of the three-year period from 8 Dec. 1849 to 8 Dec. 1852 when Sister Alphonsine Godfroy-Smyth held the office.

5. Maxis wrote these notes—which give an account of the early days of the IHM congregation in Monroe (1845–59)—in 1883, at the request of Father Augustine Gaudet, O.M.I., who was her spiritual director during her years with the Grey Nuns in Ottawa. They were given to the Monroe congregation by Reverend Francis T. Parr, C.SS.R., who found the document among the effects of Reverend Francis Xavier Schnüttgen, C.SS.R., in 1901.

Sister Joseph (the only one I have spoken to) says they are all always disposed to submit, although they feel somewhat affected by mother's [Maxis's] disappointment." Distance notwithstanding, Lefevere arrived the next day from Detroit. He reproached Maxis for "being head-strong and self willed" (TMN, 60, MA), dismissed her as superior, and assigned her to the Susquehanna mission in Pennsylvania. Lefevere then immediately appointed Walker as successor to Maxis.

At the same time, Lefevere must also have asked Walker what her understanding of the sisters' vows were, as these pertained to his authority. She must have answered in a manner that he held to be erroneous and for which he probably blamed Maxis ([Kelly] 1948, 143). The next day, a conflicted Walker wrote him to clarify her response:

> Pardon me, My Lord Bishop, for referring to the past—at the same time listen to one word in justification of my neighbor—The erroneous idea under which I have labored for a short time past with regard to the Vows taken by the Sisters of the Institution and of which I made acknowledgment yesterday, came to me through a very indirect and complicated channel—Mother [Maxis] is in no way implicated . . . She would have put me right had she known me to be in the wrong, as she would not, she could not with deliberate will, lead anyone astray. (MJW to PPL, 2 Apr. 1859, copy in MA)

Maxis departed for Pennsylvania on 4 April 1859 (MMC, MA). Two months of jurisdictional contention between Lefevere and Bishop John Nepomucene Neumann, C.SS.R., of Philadelphia (and their representatives) ensued. At the same time, three members of the Redemptorist congregation—perhaps prompted by Maxis—were writing the sisters in Monroe, encouraging them to follow Maxis (JMJ to CMy, 4 May 1859; HFG to MJW, 12 [Apr. 18]59; GES to XE, 15 May 1859; GES to EF, 25 May 1859; all found in PPL Letter Books, DAA).[6] Walker was again caught in the middle. She turned the correspondence from the Redemptorists over to Joos, who gave it to Lefevere. Ten weeks after Maxis's departure and after consulting with the sisters in Monroe, Lefevere ordered the complete separation of the sisters in Pennsylvania from those in Michigan. He also prohibited all contact, even written, between the two groups (PPL to EJ, 10 June 1859, MA).[7]

6. The originals of these letters were apparently destroyed. Copies are preserved in the Letter Books of Lefevere in DAA.

7. The question as to who initiated or requested the separation—Lefevere, Joos, or Walker—is of more than academic interest. The relevant chronicle entry (spring/summer 1859, MA), reads: "Things went on in this way for some time without any hopes of a change, when our Bishop found it necessary to prevent any further communication with the Sisters of the other diocese, 'until some amicable settlement could be agreed upon.' To this order of his Lordship every member willingly consented." Given her love of Maxis and

Caught in this web of suspicion and tension between Joos and Lefevere on the one hand and Maxis on the other, Walker opted for submission. Although this acquiescence may have been partly due to physical weakness associated with the early stages of pulmonary tuberculosis, it is also true that Lefevere had accused Maxis of willfulness and insubordination (TMN, 60, MA). If the sisters remaining in Monroe were to survive as a religious congregation, Walker most likely realized that she would have to create an atmosphere of cooperation with Joos and the bishop. In addition, Walker was a convert to Catholicism, which may account for the fact that she seems to have granted to both of these clergy not only respect but adulation.

## The Remaining Monroe Congregation

In this period of division and separation, the morale of the members of the congregation remaining in Monroe could hardly have been worse. For two months, the IHM sisters had witnessed the fabric of their lives rent apart by misunderstanding, hostility, intrigue, and clerical wrangling. Whatever Maxis's faults, the sisters in Monroe loved her and were now deprived of her leadership and presence.

After the formal break in June, only eight professed members,[8] four novices, and one postulant remained in Monroe; two of the professed sisters who stayed had seen blood relatives leave for Pennsylvania.[9] The three founding members of the congregation—Maxis, Ann Shaaff and Celestine Renauld—were all now in the East. One professed, Egidius Flanagan, after getting a dispensation from her vows, followed Maxis east on 21 July 1859 (MMC, MA). The four remaining novices had had to make a choice between following Maxis or staying in Monroe with Walker, a difficult decision, since all of them—Xavier Eagan, Gertrude Gerretsen, Johanna Burke, and Colette Myers—were from the East (Pr. Bk., MA). Gerretsen related in later years that she had believed firmly that she should be with Maxis ([Kelly] 1948, 774 n. 79); however, when

---

of her companions in the East, it is probable that Walker "willingly consented" only because of the contingent nature of the imposed silence—"until some amicable settlement could be agreed upon." Her own correspondence during summer 1859 does not intimate that she then regarded the separation as final. Indeed, all other primary documentation indicates that in the Monroe congregation, awareness of the finality of the breach occurred only gradually during the latter half of 1859. In addition, later congregational documents place responsibility for the separation at the feet of episcopal authority.

8. This number includes Gerard Duillette, who died on 18 Sept. 1859, and Anthony Mohr, who on 7 Aug. 1861 left the congregation, leaving vacant the position of novice mistress.

9. Frances Renauld's sister, Celestine Renauld, and Alphonsine Godfroy-Smyth's niece, Mary Whipple, were in the East.

she confided her doubts to Walker, her former novice mistress and now her superior responded: "Sister, since you desire a decided answer, I will tell you that I believe as firmly that it is your vocation to remain where you are, as I believe that Jesus is present in the Blessed Sacrament" (Life, 57, MA).[10] All four novices remained in Monroe. Eagan and Gerretsen, in that order, would later succeed Walker as superior.

By one account, the lot of the Monroe sisters was made even more difficult because of "the departure of many of the talented and efficient members of the Community, so that the responsibility of the schools, with the charge of the principal one, rested entirely . . . upon the extremely weak and delicate Superioress." The same writer goes on to say: "Ten dollars alone remained to support a community of twelve Sisters and some orphans" (Life, 57–58, MA).

Walker herself keenly felt the loss. Although she apparently held no rancor toward Maxis or the other sisters in Pennsylvania, there is nearly total silence regarding Maxis in the annals of the Monroe sisters following the separation. Walker refers in several written documents to the good intentions of those who left. In a letter to the Bishop John Farrell of Hamilton, Ontario, written four months after Maxis's departure, Walker wrote in evident pain:

> For the last some months our poor little community has labored under severe & afflicting trials, and of such a nature, that were it not for divine support & blind obedience we would have either fallen under the pressure or have strayed from the path Eternal Wisdom designed us to tread; —half of our beloved Sisterhood are now in another diocese, & owing to some misunderstanding, we know not if we shall ever again be united —however, we hope that God has not been offended, & that out of evil good will come. (MJW to JF, 1 Aug. 1859, MJWP, MA)

## Walker's Background

Walker's leadership of the remaining congregation was to be quite different from that of Maxis, in part because—despite their intelligence and strong educational backgrounds—the two women had very different personalities. The French-speaking Maxis was of San Domingan heritage, a Catholic by birth, forceful in her relationships with clergy, often impetu-

---

10. I have been critically selective in making use of material from the Life for documentary purposes, excluding obviously hagiographic passages. Although the text was compiled and handwritten by Smith, it includes (in addition to Smith's reflections) excerpts from Walker's letters and a variety of handwritten documents about Walker from other sources. The collected Walker Papers contain fragmentary documents that are obviously first drafts of material written by her contemporaries that were later used or rejected by Smith (and perhaps Joos) in preparing the Life.

ous, free of spirit, and self-confident. The English-speaking Walker was of Canadian ancestry, Anglican by birth, deferential in her dealings with clergy, and circumspect in her decision making.[11]

Hamilton Walker—a lawyer, a judge, and a member of the Anglican Church—provided for his family an affluent lifestyle. Born in 1827 and named Mary Phoebe, Walker was his daughter by his second marriage (to Jane Macdonell).[12] Hamilton died when Mary Phoebe was three years old. She became a Catholic after her mother's death in 1847, and she was received into the Church in July 1848 by a young Irish priest, Father John Farrell. In 1856, he would become the first bishop of Hamilton (KF, telephone conversation with author, 15 Feb. 1992, MA) and—following the separation of the IHM congregation—Walker's confidant and counselor.

One year after her conversion, Walker entered the convent of the Grey Nuns in Montreal.[13] She left at the end of March 1850 because of illness and the onset of excessive scrupulosity.[14] For the next five years, although she taught and even opened her own school in Cornwall, Ontario, she remained troubled by what she perceived to be her own sinfulness (Life, 25, 29, MA). Convinced of her separation by grievous sin from the God whom she wished to love and serve, she experienced doubt and fear. Joos would later say in describing this period of her life: "She suffered most dreadfully for quite a time and was, as she said, in a kind of hell because all that time she was as certain that she was to go to hell. That temptation was awful particularly at holy Communion . . . [She] thought that she was to be separated forever from Him she wished to love so much" (EJ, Remembrances of MJW, ca. 1864–65, MJWP, MA).

In desperation, she wrote to her older half-sister Ann (Hamilton's daughter by a previous marriage), who had become Sister Ignatius of the IHM congregation, telling her of the spiritual anguish and mental suffering that she was enduring (Life, 30–31, MA). Predictably, Ignatius en-

---

11. Other factors that distinguished Walker from Maxis are age and maturity in religious life. At the time of her appointment, Walker was 31 years of age and had been a Catholic for only 11 years and a religious for four. Maxis, on the other hand, was, at the time of the separation, 49 years of age and for 29 of these years had been a religious. For a fuller treatment of Maxis, see chap. 1 of the present volume.

12. Though the surname of Walker's first wife was also Macdonell, she was apparently unrelated to Jane.

13. "Grey Nuns" was the title popularly given to the Grey Nuns of the Cross of Ottawa because they wore grey habits. The formal title was changed to Sisters of Charity of Ottawa in 1968, when the congregation was incorporated.

14. A scrupulous person, in the traditional Catholic sense, sees sin where there is none and thus experiences constant dilemma in making moral choices regarding sin. In modern psychiatric theory, scrupulosity is viewed as "a form of neurosis, an obsessive-compulsive reaction characterized by unavoidable thoughts, always unpleasant, and frequently accompanied by compulsive behavior." Scruples may be "temporary or chronic, mild or severe, limited or almost boundless in extent" (NCE, vol. 12, 1967, 1254, 1253).

listed the prayers of the sisters in Monroe, and Walker went there for a visit in July 1854.

## Walker Becomes an IHM

The visit never ended. In Monroe, Walker found relief from the struggle within her.[15] Her biographer relates that "almost the moment she entered the Convent a certain calm and content seemed to again return to her heart. . . . Her sleep was undisturbed" (Life, 30–31, MA). Maxis immediately welcomed Walker as a postulant, and she was received into the novitiate on 13 November, taking the name Mary Joseph (MMC, MA).

Walker had been a novice for only about six months when, in spring 1855, the Redemptorists left Monroe permanently. The sisters were without any regular spiritual guidance. Uncertain about the future of the congregation, Walker hesitated about making her profession. With Maxis's approbation—and probably even at her urging—Walker wrote to Lefevere expressing her concern. She concluded her letter requesting profession if the bishop "think[s] there is no occasion for uneasiness" (MJW to PPL, 17 Oct. 1855, MJWP, MA). Lefevere granted permission, making no reference to her hesitation (PPL to TM, 22 Oct. 1855, MA); Walker, and perhaps Maxis, interpreted his silence to mean that Walker's fears were unfounded. She was professed on 14 November 1855 (MMC, MA). Sixteen days later, Van Gennip arrived to assume the role of spiritual director for the sisters. If Maxis had had a strategy in urging Walker to write this letter, it had paid off.

On 27 February 1856, only one and one-half years after Walker's

15. Walker's scruples appear to have been resolved during her visit to Monroe. While there, "she made a short retreat under Father [James] Poirier's (C.SS.R.) direction" ([Kelly] 1948, 95) during which she went to confession and was advised by Poirier to seek admission to the congregation (Life, 32, MA). We may better understand her situation in the light of a recent book on scrupulosity, The Doubting Disease, in which Joseph W. Ciarrocchi distinguishes between developmental scrupulosity and emotional scrupulosity. The former may be linked either to the onset of adolescence, when "some youngsters focus excessively on sin as part of their religious and social development," or to the faith development of adults "as part of a broader conversion experience: a response to a deeper exploration of life's meaning, one's faith or place in the universe. . . . Both forms of developmental scruples differ from [emotional scruples] since the person usually grows out of them. They respond either to self-reflection or advice" (1995, 15–16). The onset of Walker's scruples was at the time of her conversion and first entrance into religious life, when her knowledge of the tenets of Catholicism was limited. Given that all direct references to Walker's bout with scruples refer only to this one episode and limits it in time and that her relief from scruples came when she was deeply engaged both in obtaining spiritual direction and in self-reflection, it is likely that Walker's scruples were developmental in nature. Although it is true that she was precise, orderly, punctual, and diligent—traits highly prized in religious life—her voluminous correspondence reveals her to be a warm and compassionate woman, decisive and free of any symptoms of obsessive-compulsive disorder (see Goldman 1988, 358–60 for a description of obsessive-compulsive disorder).

entrance into the IHM congregation, Ignatius died from consumption (MMC, MA). Maxis keenly felt the first death in the little sisterhood, saying of Ignatius: "She will be the Standard bearer in our procession in Heaven" (TMN, 51, MA). Walker mourned an even greater loss—the older sister who had been instrumental in bringing her to Monroe.

Maxis placed considerable confidence in the remaining Walker sister. On 30 August 1857, she appointed Walker the congregation's first mistress of novices (MMC, MA).[16] Up to that time, Maxis had served as both superior and novice director, but as the number of novices increased, Maxis needed assistance. Years later, in relating her recollections of that fateful day in April 1859 when she was dismissed as superior, Maxis said on hearing of Walker's appointment as her successor: "I was very calm and said 'All right,' she being the very person I would like to take my place" (TMN, 61, MA).[17]

Given the relationship between the two women, Walker must have struggled with the question of whether to follow Maxis to Pennsylvania. However, constrained as she was by her own temperament and reliance on authority, she, already superioress, really had no option but to defer to Joos and Lefevere.[18] Her decision to stay, once made, enabled her to put aside her hesitations and to move forward in addressing the future of the IHM remnant in Monroe.

### Walker after the Separation

Walker faced a daunting task. The *Constitutions* by which the congregation lived and operated were inadequate and had in fact contributed

16. Undoubtedly, Van Gennip and Lefevere approved Maxis's choice of Walker. This appointment bears out the thesis that Walker's scruples were developmental in nature. It is improbable that Maxis would have entrusted Walker with the formation of young women had Walker been afflicted with emotional scruples. See also chapter 4 in which Hinsdale describes a document (purported to be in Maxis's handwriting) that advises "much consideration from the mother superior" before admitting a scrupulous candidate (144–45).

17. Again, Maxis would hardly have viewed Walker as an acceptable successor had the latter been afflicted with emotional scruples.

18. Walker's reliance on authority is well documented; a few examples will suffice. In a letter to Farrell of Jan. 1860, after describing the trials of the separation, she speaks of the peace that "is found in God alone" and attributes it to "Obedience! thou blessed plank of safety!!" In a letter to the sisters (at SJD or SMP) dated 11 Dec. 1862, she says: "[F]or everything around us reminds us of God—our vows, our rules, the bell & above all, beautiful & blind obedience." Again, to Farrell on 29 Dec. 1860, in speaking of Joos she says: "[It is] by [his] precepts we were prevented from delusion & mistaken zeal & guided in the path our loving Master designed us to tread" (MJWP, MA). The Life also describes her devotion to obedience in the person of her superior, Joos: "[S]he was convinced she could not know [God's holy will] except through him whom God had appointed Spiritual Father of the community; therefore she wisely distrusted herself, and never acted or undertook anything upon her own views or judgment" (61).

to the episcopal misunderstandings leading to the separation. Ambiguity with respect to the jurisdiction of the bishop of a diocese in which sisters staffed a mission vis-à-vis the jurisdiction of Lefevere, the bishop of the diocese in which the motherhouse was located, was a major factor in the separation.[19] In addition, the congregation was not incorporated under Michigan statutes, and the ownership of both the land and the buildings was unclear. Further, the congregation also had no clear system of education either for its members or for the formalized classroom instruction the IHMs were to do. An increase in membership was needed if the congregation were to survive and fulfill its mission of Catholic education. Many of the early vocations had originated with the Redemptorists, but the separation and the strained relationship of Lefevere with the Redemptorists diminished this source of membership.

Still, an aura of circling the wagons prevailed in Monroe during the summer months of 1859. On the eve of the sisters' annual retreat, Walker wrote to Farrell (the priest who baptized her and who was now the bishop of Hamilton): "Father! if you only knew what falls on my shoulders, you would pray for me night & day; but in all things we must thank Almighty God, for His judgments are right & his Wisdom is infinite. The Sisters are uneasy about my health, as consumption we believe is slowly doing its work" (1 Aug. 1859, MJWP, MA).[20] Joos arranged that the retreat would be conducted by his cousin, the Reverend John DeNève; undoubtedly, he hoped that these days would be a time for the sisters to put aside the past.[21] Knowing DeNève, Joos apparently trusted him to shape his message in a way that would restore peace in the little sisterhood. The

19. For a detailed explanation of the difficulties inherent in this type of situation see [Kelly] 1948, 127–30. According to Kelly, "In reality, the major consideration, the rock which sundered the congregation, was the lack of canonical legislation for just such exigencies."

20. It is in Walker's correspondence with Farrell that she first reveals the depth of her spirituality. Often expressed in the pietistic language typical of mid-nineteenth-century Catholicism and filtered through her own personality and experience, Walker's expressions of her experience of God are reminiscent of the writings of the Catholic women mystics. For example, in a letter to Farrell of 15 July 1861, she says: "I cannot understand why I feel nearer to God than at other times, and enjoy such peace of soul, that nothing disturbs me— but please don't think I do anything on my part—God has compassion on me" (MA). Again, on 27 Oct. 1861, she said: "[F]or myself I want to be good, & though I can see no violation of duty, still father, my heart is not at ease—as long as I have so much to do that I scarcely know how to do it, I am all right, but in my leisure moments I want something that I don't know—God may permit this to punish me for little infidelities, for tho' I am told to be quiet, I still feel that my heart is more divided than God wills it to be" (MA). Collectively, Walker's holographic documents reveal a woman whose mysticism—if that it be—is grounded in service and love.

21. In a letter to Lefevere of 23 July 1859, Joos assessed the situation: "Now a little hesitation seems to remain with one or two novices, but it will pass away, I hope, with the retreat. To prevent further defections he proposed "to have the election [of Walker] in form and to renew the vows of every one [sic]" during the retreat (UNDA).

Motherhouse Chronicles record that at the close of the retreat, "a settled peace seemed to reign not only through the house in general, but also in the hearts of the Sisters, all of whom, now acknowledged the Hand of God in the affairs of the past" (MMC, 7 Aug. 1859, MA).

While the sisters were in retreat, Bishop Neumann of Philadelphia clarified much of the misunderstanding between him and Lefevere. He held out the possibility of a reunion of the two IHM congregations: "Monroe as the cradle of this new Religious Community has acquired a right to be the Mother House and I think most of the Sisters [in Pennsylvania] share my sentiments" (JNN to PPL, 7 Aug. 1859, DAA). Joos, apprised of Neumann's letter remained wary of reunion (EJ to PPL, 11 Aug. 1859, DAA) and advised Lefevere: "[I]f you believe that there is a means to reunite it is necessary that the bad spirits be removed, that the others see their wrong and make atonement. . . . Otherwise I would be afraid to soil the purity of those who have remained faithful" (12 Aug. 1859, DAA; trans. in Gannon 1992, 59). Nothing came of this correspondence.[22] By 10 December 1859, two days after Walker's formal election as superioress, Joos wrote to Lefevere: "All things then are right; but now, the foundation being laid[,] there remains a great edifice to be built up" (UNDA).

## Moving Forward: Walker's Dependence on Joos

Walker and Joos worked together in building up that edifice, but Walker depended heavily on Joos. Alongside the nature of her personality and her disposition, Walker's illness with pulmonary tuberculosis confined her to bed much of the time. Sore throats, coughing, and bouts of near suffocation gradually left her emaciated. Remissions occurred, but these were short-lived.[23]

References to the state of her health frequently appeared in Walker's correspondence with sisters on assignment away from Monroe. In December 1861, she wrote Gerretsen: "Myself, up to-day for meditation, the second time in three or four weeks; but I feel strong now—how long it will last, I know not—but I do nothing except take care of myself, a fine employment for a Sister!" (MJW to [GG], [ca. 8 Dec. 1861], MJWP, MA).[24]

22. It is noteworthy that Walker's religious name was given out to an eastern novice on 24 July 1859 ([Ryan] 1967, 90). Thus, even as Neumann, Joos, and Lefevere conferred, the eastern sisters had accepted the separation as final.

23. Handwritten documents in the Monroe archives taken collectively describe the progress of Walker's disease (e.g., MMC, 18 Oct. 1864, MA; Life, 118–20, 131, MA; EJ to JF, 30 Sept. 1864, DHOA, copy in MA). For a fuller description of tuberculosis as viewed in the nineteenth century, see Mettler 1947, 468–74.

24. Many of Walker's letters are undated or partially dated and many of the addressees are not identified. In most cases, I have been able to supply the missing information by cross-referencing documents in the Monroe archives.

Ten months later, she told the sisters missioned at Saint Joseph (in Detroit) that "the Dr never saw me so bad & thought me like one not having ten hours to live—I was preparing for the last sacraments over again but got a change before morning—I may linger a time as I am but may go at any moment" ([between 8 and 29 Oct. 1862], MJWP, MA). With a touch of humor, she remarked in another autumn letter to the same group: "I am pretty smart as far as my arms, my brain, and my tongue can go, but alas! the old shanks tie me down" ([autumn 1862], MJWP, MA).

In the hope that she would be cured, Joos and the sisters in Monroe made a novena in March 1863.[25] For nine days before the feast of Saint Joseph, the sisters implored God (through the intercession of Saint Joseph) for the restoration of their mother superior's health. Walker was elated. "Will you believe it?" she wrote the sisters at Saint Joseph House. "I am so much better that I am round the house again! Yes, dear Sisters, nine days before the feast I was hardly able to turn in bed alone & dared not think of standing without being held. . . . From that moment [the beginning of the novena] I gradually gained strength until the great 19th when I was able to go to High Mass in church" ([mid-March 1863], MJWP, MA).

The remission was ephemeral, however. On 26 March, she wrote to the sisters missioned at Adrian: "I would have replied ere now, but between fits of weakness at times & many affairs to settle at other times I could not succeed til today" (MJWP, MA). Five months before her death, after telling the sisters at Adrian that "today I have [had] several bad coughing spells, but between times am quite smart," Walker concluded: "Good night, my beloved ones—I long to clasp you all in my skinny, bony arms" ([5 May 1864], MJWP, MA).

As her health failed, Walker's dependence on Joos increased. On 29 December 1860, she relayed her concern about his health to Farrell: "Please pray also for good father Director, he is killing himself before his time, with labor & fatigue—he, next to yourself, has done more for me than any one on earth" (MJWP, MA). Several weeks after the opening of Saint Joseph's mission in August 1861, she spoke to Farrell of her fear that she would lose Joos, asking: "It is not wrong, Father, is it, to ask God to leave him a few years longer?" (27 Oct. [1861], MJWP, MA). The following spring, she again begged: "Do, dear father, pray that God will leave him yet a little longer, I cannot bear to think he will ever die" (MJW to JF, 6 Apr. 1862, MJWP, MA).

Walker's biographer relates that her fear of losing Joos was in fact

25. In the Catholic tradition, a novena is a devotional practice, usually involving prayer for nine consecutive days, made in petition for a special favor. The favor is requested of God through the intercession of Mary or another saint. For a broader treatment of Catholic devotionalism, including novenas and the miraculous in nineteenth-century America, see Taves 1986.

one of her greatest trials, "for almost her whole burden and responsibility she threw upon him depending upon his advice and assistance in every event, and fearing if once deprived of that she would be left to herself" (Life, 192–93, MA). Perhaps because of her early bout with scrupulosity, the typical nineteenth-century Catholic ethos of reverence for the clergy was intensified in Walker's case. She wholeheartedly embraced Joos as Christ's representative, calling him "our second founder and reformer" (MJW to [AGS], [late Jan. or early Feb. 1863], MJWP, MA). Joos and Lefevere—whose rigid and moralistic views of religious life, of human nature, and of spirituality were tainted with the practices and piety of Jansenism—now provided the direction for the young superioress.[26]

## The New Foundation

Operating from within this framework of frailty and deference, Walker and Joos developed a model of congregational leadership that lasted for the remainder of the nineteenth century. After Lefevere decreed that there should be no contact between the IHM sisters remaining in Monroe and those who were with Maxis in Pennsylvania, the preseparation period became shrouded in silence. Whether intended or not, the actions of Joos combined with Walker's acquiescence emphasized to the sisters that the continuing congregation was really a new entity with a new mission.

Hard on the heels of Walker's formal election as superior on 8 December 1859, Joos drew up articles of incorporation. With their approval by the State of Michigan, the congregation in Monroe became a legal entity separate and distinct from the IHM congregation in Pennsylvania.[27]

26. The heresy of Jansenism originated in Louvain, Belgium, in the writings and teaching of Michael Baius, a professor of scripture at the University of Louvain. Although condemned by Rome in 1567 and again in 1579, Baius's tenets were codified by Cornelius Jansen, another professor at Louvain, and published posthumously in 1640. As a system, "Jansenism was based on a certain doctrine of justification that proposed rigorous views of human nature and the role of grace in man's salvation. . . . Jansenists were austere in their morality and they considered anyone opposed to them as corrupted enemies of God" (Neill and Schmandt 1957, 435). Although the movement was condemned again in 1643 and 1653 and formally came to an end in 1728, its rigorism and austerity lived on in the lives of many Catholics, robbing their spirituality of the richness of their faith (see Neill and Schmandt 1957, 435–43). Jansenistic piety was "inflexibly rigorist and was characterized by the tension experienced by souls weighed down by the thought of damnation. . . . Jansenists were excessively moralistic and held that humanity had to be kept in check by penitential rigor" (NCE, vol. 7, 1967, 825).

27. The wording could not be more explicit: the " 'Sisters Servants of the Immaculate Heart of Mary' residing in the State of Michigan and belonging to the Institute of Sisters Servants of the Immaculate Heart of Mary whose Motherhouse is now at Monroe aforesaid and no others shall become members of said corporation, and they may be admitted to such membership on their subscribing their names to one of the triplicate copies of these articles of agreement and association" (Art. of Incorporation, 1860, MA; emphasis added). The document is signed by the professed members of the institute.

The Constitutions (or Rule) that Gillet gave to Maxis and the other early IHM sisters in 1845 had stated that the principal work of the congregation was the education of youth by all the means available. Joos's articles of incorporation, however, spelled out a new purpose—the care of orphans, a ministry he had suggested to Lefevere about 10 months prior to the separation (EJ to PPL, 23 Aug. 1858, UNDA).[28] The chronicle entry for 6 February 1860 reads:

> The papers were legally drawn out, and the professed Sisters, being about ten in number, agreed to form an association, the end of which was the receiving of orphans and abandoned children for the purpose of providing for and educating them as far as circumstances would permit; also to establish asylums for their support, and schools for their instruction in any part of the State to which we may be called. His Lordship, the Bishop, approved highly of what had been done, and on the 7th of the following May, made over to the Trustees of the Association, a lease for thirty years of the property which we occupy; which lease was signed in presence of witnesses and duly recorded. (MMC, MA)

In spite of this official change in purpose, the Monroe sisters never abandoned their commitment to formal education.[29] Walker oversaw the opening of five teaching missions during her brief tenure as superior.

Walker and Joos turned next to the issue of the Constitutions. In a letter written to Walker at the time of the separation, Neumann had spelled out the inadequacy of the Constitutions in defining the scope of episcopal authority (JNN to MJW, 1 June 1859, copy in MA).[30] The single chronicle entry for December 1861 clarifies the reasons for the revision:

> [N]ow that missions were likely to be founded elsewhere, it [the Rule] was found to be incomplete & not sufficiently clear in many points to prevent misunderstanding: besides, as many articles had been added, and some other changes made after its approval by the Bp. in the year 1845, it could no longer be considered as an approved Rule, as these

28. Kelly states that this interest in orphans on the part of Joos may have been a source of friction between him and Maxis, who understood and upheld the original intent of Gillet in establishing the congregation (1948, 246).

29. Although Walker herself "undertook the care of as many little orphans as the house would accommodate, often even more" and felt convinced "that sheltering those little creatures was one of the works most dear ... to her Divine Spouse" (Life, 45, MA), the involvement of the Monroe IHM congregation in establishing orphanages was never extensive. The orphans who attended Saint Mary's Free School in Monroe and lived with the sisters were eventually, as a group, called Saint Mary Orphanage. Saint Anthony orphanage in Detroit was opened in May 1867, two-and-a-half years after the death of Walker; it remained under the direction of the IHM congregation for ten years ([Kelly] 1948, 247).

30. Neumann said: "As long as the rule remains unfinished, I consider it due to the Bishops, who have houses of the Community in their diocese, that no new regulation be added to the rule without their approbation."

changes had never been confirmed by his Lordship's approbation.
Therefore, at the earnest solicitation of the members of the community,
and the approval of the Bishop, Rev. Father Director, who had long seen
the necessity of what we now desired, consented to revise the original
Rule, and to provide, at the same time, for the deficiencies we had heretofore experienced. . . . [A]fter a few weeks of labor it was completed in an
entirely new form, tho' the Rule was in no ways changed, with the exception of being made clear on certain points, and provisions made for certain
cases which before had not been mentioned. (MMC, Dec. 1861, MA)

To avoid a repetition of the misunderstanding with Neumann, Joos added
the statement that the bishop of Detroit had approved the establishment of
the congregation and was its "first superior." Not unexpectedly, Joos also
regularized his own position by adding a new article providing for a director appointed by the bishop to guide the community in the latter's place.
This article gave him "further faculties and functions" to be determined by
the bishop (Const. 1861, 13–14, MA); according to Kelly, "Among the latter,
certainly, was that of superior" (1948, 245). The power denied Maxis by the
appointment of Joos as superior was denied her successors for the remainder of the nineteenth century by the codification of Joos's position.[31]

On 7 November 1861, Lefevere approved the revised Rule, personally
paying to have three hundred copies printed. He must have expected the
congregation's phenomenal growth now that all things were regularized.

Three months after Joos completed the Rule revision, Walker spoke
of Joos in a letter to Farrell: "Your visit to Monroe, My Lord, was providential, for I think you encouraged him; & he now feels more than ever
the position that God gives him to fill in our regard. He has done, and is
still doing much, in the way of making our young Community what our
loving Jesus would wish us, as religious, to be; pray that his labors may
be blessed, and that we may yet become children of God's own heart!"
(MJW to JF, 27 Oct. [1861], MJWP, MA). The reference to "our young
Community," coming as it does on the heels of Joos's Rule revision,"
indicates just how much the period from 1859 through 1861 represented
an entirely new beginning in Walker's eyes. Otherwise, her precise mind
would not have permitted her to refer to a congregation founded in 1845
as "young" in 1861.[32] Moreover, in this context, her use of the word
"position" in referring to Joos's leadership almost certainly hints at her

---

31. In reality, the only major changes to the Constitutions were: 1) the designation that
the bishop of Detroit was the first superior of the congregation and had the power "to
appoint a new Superioress provisionally" in cases when the "Superioress [was rendered]
incapable of fulfilling her charge," and 2) a new constitution that provided for a director
appointed by the bishop to guide the community in the bishop's stead.

32. In the Life, Walker's biographer also uses "the then young community" (193) in
referring to the congregation under the leadership of Joos and Walker, thus attesting that
not only Walker but also her sisters viewed the postseparation period in this light.

later view of him as "second founder and reformer" (MJW to [AGS], [late Jan. or early Feb. 1863], MJWP, MA).

The publication of a Book of Customs in summer 1863 represented a further step in codifying the lives of the sisters. In this case, there is no doubt whence the impetus came: "As in many institutions there are certain customs and observances besides the established rule . . . Rev. Father judged it advisable that such observances as were practiced among us should be compiled in one manuscript and after their approval by the chapter as lawful and useful customs, they should be subjected [*sic*] to his Lordship for his approbation" (MMC, 18 Aug. 1863, MA). The new IHM Book of Customs was approved by Lefevere on 18 September 1863. Although this book merely formalized much of what was already established practice, it assured that the lives of the sisters working in missions away from Monroe conformed in daily practices to those of the sisters at the motherhouse.

### Persistence of Preseparation Memories

And yet, despite all these efforts to create the aura of a new foundation, Mother Theresa and the preseparation history of the congregation seem not to have been entirely forgotten or suppressed. For example, at the time Lefevere had the Rule printed, he also had the sisters' prayer manual printed and bound in the same volume. A new petition, "For those who are absent," was added to the night prayers, which the sisters said together each evening. This petition is not found in any of the prayer books or manuals in the Monroe archives that predate the 1861 printed volume; it is also not found in a printed volume of the Redemptorist prayer manual, given to the sisters by Gillet and dated 1844. Perhaps Walker had found an unobtrusive way to recall publicly in prayer Theresa and her companions now in the East.[33]

Another change in practice took place in Monroe around the time of the separation. Previously, the sisters had placed the initials J.M.J.A.T. at the top of their letters, representing the names of Jesus, Mary, Joseph, Alphonsus (Liguori), and Teresa (of Avila).[34] Shortly before the separa-

33. The petition first appeared in a prayer manual for the Immaculata, Pennsylvania, sisters in 1892, the year of Maxis's death (GMS telephone conversation with author, 1 Sept. 1993); for the Scranton sisters, it first appeared in a Customs Book used by their Sister Bertrand Walton in 1895 (WR to author, 13 Oct. 1993, MA). An interpretation sometimes given the phrase is that it refers to the sisters absent on mission. I am discounting this interpretation because the petition appeared only after 1859; the Monroe congregation had had missions in Vienna, Michigan (near Monroe) and in Susquehanna, Pennsylvania, before then. No extant prayer manuals in the Monroe Archives before 1861 carry the petition.

34. The rule of St. Alphonsus guided the members of the Redemptorist congregation and was adapted for the sisters by Gillet, who was a Redemptorist. St. Teresa of Avila, a sixteenth-century Spanish mystic, was a patroness of the congregation.

tion, after Maxis had gone east, Sister Mary Rose Soleau indicated in a letter to Joos (6 June 1859, UNDA) that she "must follow our foundress Mother Theresa whom I consider to be at the head of the institution" and headed her letter J.M.J.T.A.—reversing the order of the A and the T. Walker then seems to have begun a new practice in the Monroe congregation: while usually retaining the original ordering of the initials in correspondence with clergy, she began to use the inverted form in correspondence with the sisters. The Book of Customs, approved in 1863, also specifies the inverted form for the sisters' correspondence (Custom 20, MA). Walker's successors Gertrude Gerretsen, Clotilda Hoskyns, Justina Reilly, and Mechtildis McGrail continued the practice. One explanation —perhaps the most probable—is that Walker did this to move the name Teresa to a more prominent position, thus recalling the Theresa who had played so important a part in their lives.[35]

### New Teaching Missions

If Joos took the lead in resolving the legal and technical issues of governing the IHM congregation, it was Walker who oversaw the schools. Joos, as superior, undoubtedly worked with Lefevere in determining where and when new missions would be started, but Walker appeared to see herself as mother and implementer. Bedridden, she nonetheless wrote numerous letters that reveal her grasp of educational issues, her stewardship of the scarce resources of the congregation, and her great love for her sisters.

Staffing was a problem during all of Walker's tenure. The separation left the Monroe congregation badly crippled. At Joos's urging, Walker wrote Farrell in January 1860 asking him to send new members to Monroe. Two months later, Walker reiterated her request:

35. The difference in spelling, i.e., Teresa versus Theresa, is not relevant; the early sisters consistently used variations in spelling their names. It is interesting to note that Maxis herself on at least one occasion used the inverted form. During the period of intense negotiation about her return to Pennsylvania, Maxis in a postcard to Mother Frances Henry of Scranton (dated 11 Sept. 1882) heads the postcard "J.M.J.T.A." (SA). Interestingly, there is in the Monroe Archives a holy card of Gerretsen's on the back of which is inscribed, in her handwriting, "From Mother Maxis, Oct. 1883" (Gerretsen celebrated her silver jubilee that year). This predates Maxis's return to Pennsylvania from Canada in Jan. 1885, and so it is apparent that, at least on this one occasion, they had found a way to circumvent the prohibition on communication. Thus, Maxis may have known of the practice in Monroe. My conclusion regarding the inversion is based on an examination of the extant letters of Walker, Gerretsen, Hoskyns, Reilly, and McGrail, which are held in the Monroe archives. In each case, with very few exceptions, the heading was inverted when the general superior was writing to the sisters. The practice ended sometime in the first decade of the twentieth century.

We are sadly in want of teachers—our schools are suffering and so few vocations are found in the West that for the last some months we have been obliged to have recourse to a secular teacher for one of our schools ... During our trials of last year some of our most competent Sisters (with the intention of doing greater good) left the diocese to join the other half of our beloved Community—but blessed be our Good God! things are no [sic] so far settled that no further difficulty is to be apprehended. (8 Mar. [1860], MJWP, MA)

By late 1860, the congregation numbered sixteen and Walker was able to relay to Farrell the news that "[o]ur Community is increasing, & if good St. Joseph does not send us great teachers, he sends us those animated with the true spirit of our blessed Lord, which is still better" (29 Dec. 1860, MA). On 15 July 1861, she wrote to him: "[S]ome time ago we wanted subjects, but now, we have applications from all directions" (MJWP, MA).

At Walker's death on 18 October 1864, the congregation numbered twenty-four professed, six novices, and two postulants. She had been alternately buoyed by the trickle of new members and dismayed by the illnesses of many. Within this constant flux, Walker was able to open and staff five schools. Her quick mind and ability to manage served the congregation well through the financial exigencies of the Civil War.[36] The first Detroit mission, Saint Joseph, opened in autumn 1861, followed by Saint Mary school in Painesville, Ohio, a year later. In mid-February 1863, three sisters opened Saint Mary school in Adrian, Michigan. Finally, Saint Mary (Marshall, Michigan) and Saints Peter and Paul (Detroit) opened in autumn 1864, just weeks before Walker's death (MMC, 9 and 26 Sept. 1864, MA).

In September 1862, Walker presided over the expansion of the sisters' school in Monroe, which had been founded in January 1846 by Maxis and Gillet. The sisters had "occasionally received [a small number] of children as boarders," but no distinction was made between these children and the orphans who lived with the sisters. The number of regular boarders had increased and it became "necessary to provide [for the new residents] a distinct dormitory, refectory, and recreation room" (MMC,

36. Walker, at the suggestion of Joos, used her relationship with Farrell to make sure that the patrimony of one of her sisters was safely deposited in a bank in Hamilton because the banks in the United States were "likely to fall at any moment." She wanted to have it deposited where "it could receive the interest, or after timely notice to draw it all if we required it" (MJW to JF, 24 Apr. 1864, MJWP, MA). In her next letter, thanking Farrell and sending the check to him, she adds: "I would prefer [you] to place [it] in whatever bank you may think to be the most secure, even tho' the interest would be less" (MJW to JF, 3 May 1864, MJWP, MA). In a letter dated 8 Feb. 1867 (but no longer extant), Gerretsen asked Farrell to return the money to the congregation; Farrell in his response (dated 11 Feb. 1867) indicated that the money would be sent "you by express" (MA).

MA).[37] Walker began to purchase household materials in large quantities. Though Saint Joseph was located on what was then the outskirts of Detroit, its proximity to suppliers made it a natural choice to function as the purchasing center for the new endeavor. In a series of letters written to the mission in autumn 1862, Walker appointed a reluctant Gerretsen as purchasing agent, teaching her about the finer points of making a good bargain.

Happy with a prior purchase of flannel for sheeting but concerned that "expenses [were] now so enormous that [she] fear[ed] to be imprudent," Walker advised Gerretsen to approach a "Mr [Carp]" in order to have him "keep the other piece [of flannel] for us till we find it more convenient to pay for it." However, the linen she found "perfectly useless —[I]t is *sheeting* we wanted—coarse, thick, like we got from Baltimore of which I sent you a sample—it is from 2 to 2¹/₄ yards wide and sold for 75 or 80¢ per yard. . . . [P]erhaps the Merchant will return this as it is money thrown away for us: and in hopes he will I will send it by opportunity on Monday to change it for *strong linen sheeting*" (MJW to [SJD], 20 Sept. [1862], MJWP, MA). A few days later, she sent via Joos a "draft for $150," noting for Gerretsen that "when the time for drawing it comes," the total "will be $157.50 as the interest for six months will be $7.50—this is to go [to] pay for the flannel, but if Mr. C[arp] takes back the linen in payment, the bill will be only $115, which will leave a balance of $42.50 coming to us. Be careful, dear Sister, don't slash and dash as if we were made of money—reflect first and then act with prudence" (MJW to [GG], [between 20 and 23 Sept. 1862], MJWP, MA). In a later letter, she wrote to Gerretsen:

> The bedsteads I presume are not high at 22/ but you know we cannot get *very nice* things—I suppose however, we will have to take them, but if he would dispose of them elsewhere of course I would be glad, as we can get here, without freight bedsteads that come apart for 20/ which are much more convenient than those all in one. . . . [D]on't think dear child that I blame you—no—far from it it is only inexperience & no bad will, so you need not be uneasy about holy Poverty, as you meant all for the best & God of course is pleased—don't worry one moment about anything—anyhow we should ourselves have explained matters more fully—so you see you have us to forgive too. (MJW to [GG], [shortly after 23 Sept. 1862], MJWP, MA)

37. It is possible that this "increased" number of boarders was related to the need of families during the Civil War to find accommodations for children. According to Kelly, "three little McDermotts were boarders while their mother went to be near her husband, a Union colonel stationed at Corinth" (1948, 253). See also MJW to MMcD, 19 May 1862 and 20 Mar. 1863 (MJWP, MA).

Walker concluded the series of letters by noting the efficacy of her advice: "Sr Gertrude, I must congratulate you on your improvements in making bargains—it is good to make little blunders sometimes" (MJW to SJD, [between 8 and 29 Oct. 1862], MJWP, MA).

Gerretsen would remain at Saint Joseph until Walker's death. In November 1863, she was appointed local superior of the mission house when Godfroy-Smyth returned home because of poor health. She succeeded Walker as superioress of Monroe at age 26.[38]

By early 1863, Walker could say of the congregation: "[I]n no circumstance could we recognize more clearly His divine interposition than in the increase of our members & the opening of a wider field for our labors to yield more fruit" (MMC, 19 Feb. 1863, MA). Even with the increased numbers, however, keeping missions open required sensitivity, courage, and some sleight of hand. For example, problems quickly beset the new school, Saint Mary in Adrian, Michigan. On 19 February 1863, Xavier Eagan, Johanna Burke, and Rose Groll, a novice, had journeyed by train to Adrian, and the new school had opened three days later. However, the situation deteriorated rapidly: "My heart would break if God did not support me, but by His love and grace we manage to get on happily in the midst of everything—Sister Xavier very ill—school shut up. Will return tomorrow with Sister Rose. Sister Frances & Sister Godelevia [a novice] left here today to replace them—Home, poor home! suffers a sad trial, but a mission once begun we must try & continue—Pray much for us, for everything falls on our backs" (MJW to SJD, [23 Feb. 1863], MJWP, MA).

Later that same year, she recalled Godfroy-Smyth from Saint Joseph in Detroit. With her usual attention to regular observance of both rule and custom, she wrote:

> Now that the cold weather is setting in I fear that perhaps you may suffer where you are during the winter from cold! & as Father Director told me that Sr Augustine was now strong enough to do the work alone (washing excepted) You had better return home as soon as you can conveniently settle every thing—You will be dispensed from having any one with you & come when you get ready[39]—Sr Xavier will not go to Detroit until some final settlement be made, in the mean time [*sic*] Sr Gertrude is hereby notified to act as Superioress after your departure until further orders. (MJW to AGS, 10 Nov. 1863, MJWP, MA)

Keeping schools open had far more to do with how many women were well enough for service than with the level of education each pos-

38. Xavier Eagan, as Walker's assistant, succeeded her briefly upon being formally appointed superior by Lefevere; however, she died on 11 Mar. 1865.

39. The sisters were not permitted to travel without a companion.

sessed. Walker—who, like Maxis, was well educated—was accomplished as an artist, a poet, and a musician, and she felt a pressing need for better education for her sisters. Again, she asked Farrell's assistance; after telling him of an accomplished candidate entering the following month, she added: "[W]e look on [her coming] as providential, for we have many subjects who will make such fine Sisters for school if they have a few advantages in the way of education. . . . I told [Father Director] I would ask you all about the conditions of the Normal School [in Toronto], as you, having placed one or two already there would be likely to have all necessary information concerning it" (MJW to JF, 6 Apr. 1862, MJWP, MA). Farrell's response to Walker's letter is not extant. However, nothing came of her efforts.[40] It would be several years before the congregation would have the luxury of furthering the formal education of its members. In the meantime, she herself lost no opportunity to guide the sisters in their educational endeavors.

In a letter dated 26 November 1861, Walker set Gerretsen—eager in her first classroom assignment—straight:

> [Y]ou speak about globes, but ask yourself two questions: 1st, Can I teach the globes? 2nd, Are my children sufficiently advanced for the globes? I have taught since the age of twenty and children that I presume knew a little more than those you have, but never, except to three or four, have I taught the globes. No, child, the idea of it for the present is ridiculous. Never aim at what you cannot carry through and you will succeed; but when we dabble into what we know nothing about, we expose ourselves . . . Even here [in Monroe] we have not the globes as a class in school among children whom we have had for so long a time— why then before six months have passed?" (MJW to SJD, MJWP, MA)

After Gerretsen pleaded her case, Walker relented somewhat: "As for the globe, I think I see you laugh—but I did not laugh, for I really thought what I wrote. If you think yr sister is able to give you a small one I have no objection to yr asking her" (MJW to GG, [ca.8 Dec. 1861], MJWP, MA).

Walker was unstinting in her care for the sisters on mission. Unable to visit them, she kept in such close touch through her letters and notes that her biographer would later say of her: "She was in truth the guiding

---

40. Several months later, on 25 Nov. 1862, Theresa Persyn transferred to the Monroe IHM congregation from the Sisters of Charity of Thielt, Belgium. She brought with her a copy of the Saint André method of education, which became the foundation for the future educational endeavors of the congregation ([Kelly] 1948, 320–47). It is possible that with this acquisition, Joos and Walker dropped their efforts to find outside educational opportunities for the sisters. Joos himself studied the Saint André system, translated several sections, and over the years gave pedagogical conferences based on this method for the sisters ([Kelly] 1948, 350–53).

spirit and soul of every department connected with the Institution; each claimed her time and attention" (Life, 87–88, MA).

## Walker Remembered

After the death on 18 October 1864 of the congregation's "First Superioress" (MMC, MA), Walker was enshrined in congregational memory through a handwritten 232-page biography (Life) commissioned by Joos sometime in late 1864 or early 1865. This document is a compilation of different voices, which defined for Joos and the sisters a "composite" Walker. It includes excerpts from remembrances by Joos, by the IHM sisters, and by Walker's blood sister, Hammy (MJWP, MA),[41] along with excerpts from the Motherhouse Chronicles that were either written by Walker or dictated to another sister when Walker was too ill to write herself. Joos had asked Walker while on her deathbed to dictate to Eagan the account of her conversion, and excerpts from this are also included in the biography. Joos wrote to Farrell and requested him to record his memories of Walker;[42] in replying, Farrell returned to the congregation the letters Walker had written to him (JF to EJ, 12 Nov. 1864, MA). At Joos's request, Gerretsen sent a letter to Lefevere asking that he too lend the congregation letters Walker had written to him so that copies might be made (GG to PPL, 24 July 1865, MA). The biographer—Sister Bridget Smith, who knew Walker well—wove excerpts from these collected materials, along with her own insights, into the text of the biography. In keeping with nineteenth-century practice, this document contains much that is hagiographic in nature. Often the portrait painted of Walker is that of a plaster saint—a woman of unparalleled virtue.[43]

Besides the biography, the sisters composed a litany in her honor. They prayed to her as "Mother J. who confided in Divine Providence and acknowledged its watchfulness even [in] the smallest events of life . . . Mother J. who loved the poor and saw in them the person of Jesus Christ, Mother J. who tried to give your Sisters a horror of little faults, Mother J. who received extraordinary favors from God." Each petition was followed by "Pray for us" (MJWP, MA).[44]

---

41. Hammy's remembrances were most probably written to Gerretsen in late 1864 or early 1865. The given name of Walker's sister is not known; "Hammy" is probably a diminutive for Hamilton, her father's name.

42. This letter is not extant, but Farrell's reply gives a date of 27 Oct. 1864.

43. Because this document is a compilation of many voices from many sources—some more objective than others—the text tends to slip in and out of the hagiographic style. As Kelly (1948) says of the effort to memorialize Walker, "Mother Mary Joseph was the victim of her contemporaries who did her the disservice of dehumanizing her in an unnecessary effort to make her virtue shine" (255).

44. For a discussion of litanies as a Catholic devotional practice see Taves 1986, 41–42.

Joos had a photographer take a picture of her as she lay in state. To each sister, he gave a holy card bearing this picture (ID to PPL, 23 Jan. 1866, UNDA). Either on his own or at the urging of the sisters, he saw to it that a lock of her hair was cut off and preserved.

Although the records and artifacts of most of the early IHM sisters are sparse or nonexistent, those testifying to the life of Walker are by comparison abundant. Even her eraser was kept. Over the years, two additional handwritten copies of the biography were made (MA). Walker's memory was so treasured that sometime prior to 1915 and again in 1927—the hundredth anniversary of her birth—Sister Blanche Vanderheyden (Joos's niece) painted two portraits of her.[45]

However, it was Walker's voluminous correspondence with her sisters that preserved her human side. As Kelly noted in her centennial history of the congregation, "Her letters, gathered together a month or so after her death . . . reveal, rather unexpectedly, a woman truly lovable" (255). Typical is her advice to Mary Schweiss: "I fear [you] are sick from imprudence—do, my dear child, be careful—put on yr rubbers when out in the wet & never remain with wet petticoats or stockings—You have with care, sufficient strength for yr work, but that overdone, you will fail . . . I shall sew [you] a pair of over stockings which [you] must always wear in the snow when [you go] for water or in other ways [are] exposed to cold" (MJW to SJD, 26 Nov. 1861, MJWP, MA). To Gerretsen; "I am sorry for your eyes, do something for them by all means with the advice of a doctor of course—perhaps you have tired them too much if so, you must rest from study or work or even reading for a while" (MJW to SJD, [after Apr. 6 1864, no. 1], MJWP, MA).

From her bed in the motherhouse in Monroe, Walker molded the sisters' congregational identity. It was she who first and often called the motherhouse "home" in her letters to each teaching mission,[46] letters in which she usually mentioned each sister by name. She encouraged and

45. There are in the Monroe Archives three photographs of three different paintings of Walker; the paintings themselves were most likely destroyed in the fire of 3 June 1929 in which Saint Mary Academy was burned to the ground. Of the three photographs, analysis leads to the attribution of one of them to Germain Sibbald, I.H.M., and the other two to Vanderheyden. Though Vanderheyden was not a contemporary of Walker, in 1915 eight sisters who were contemporaries of Walker were still living. Thus, it seems probable that the portraits by Vanderheyden are good likenesses of Walker, even though there is a marked difference between these and a photograph taken of Walker during her lifetime as well as one taken after her death; in these two photographs, she exhibits the extreme emaciation characteristic of a person in the last stages of tuberculosis.

46. The meaning of "home" in the Monroe IHM lexicon is distinctive. From Walker's time until the present, when a Monroe sister uses the word "home," she is invariably referring not to her current residence but to the motherhouse. The circular letters of the general superiors after Walker are consistent in this use of the term.

instructed them; she scolded them and commiserated with them. She was their mother. Having given the congregation new life, they regarded her as its "true foundress" (Life, 223, MA).

## Conclusion

On 25 November 1932—two months after the discovery of the box containing the bones from Walker's grave that Joos had saved as relics— Mary Agatha Walsh, the last sister who had known Walker personally, died. With her death, Walker's mythical presence came to an end. Memory of her faded so quickly that it was only in 1948, with the publication of Kelly's IHM centennial history, that many sisters then in the congregation became aware of Walker's place in congregational history. However, the years of Walker's leadership (1859–64) had a profound impact on the future of the Monroe IHMs.

Well into the twentieth century, the sisters continued to refer to Walker as "first Mother" (FXS to GM, 12 Sept. 1892, MA), "our dear first superioress" (MMC, 4 Mar. 1869, MA), and "the First General Superior" ([Shanley] 1915, 12). It is therefore not surprising that Walker's nine-teenth-century successors—Eagan, Gerretsen, Hoskyns, and Riley—did their best to continue in Walker's footsteps. They saw Joos, the man Walker had called "our second founder and reformer" and to whom she had deferred, through Walker's lens (MJW to [AGS] [late Jan. or early Feb. 1863], MJWP, MA). His leadership thus remained paramount until his death in 1901—long after Rome deemed the position of Director and Superior obsolete ([Kelly] 1948, 403–8, 800n. 4) So important to the life of the congregation did Joos become that Mother Mechtildis McGrail, the general superior at the time of Joos's death, had to reassure the sisters that it was possible for the congregation to continue without him ([Kelly] 1948, 132).[47]

It must be acknowledged, too, that Walker's tenure as mother "super-ioress" inaugurated an extended period of silence regarding Maxis and the preseparation history of the congregation. She did not initiate this

---

47. According to Kelly, "From the time of his appointment as superior and director in November, 1857 until the hour of his death, 'Father,' as he was always called in the community, was the center around which its life moved" (1948, 482). Over the years, Joos wrote out the conferences that he gave the sisters; these notes (in MA) exhibit much of the Jansenistic morality and spirituality characteristic of his own formation. The extent of his influence can best be understood in light of the fact that as late as the mid-1960s, his conference on charity was read aloud each Holy Thursday. In addition, it was the custom for the General Superior to read aloud one of his conferences during the sisters' annual retreat each summer.

silence and suffered greatly from its effects.[48] However, her acquiescence to authority, coupled with the love and reverence she earned from her sisters, effectively locked the congregation in an institutional "forgetting" of Maxis that endured for decades.

Still, subservience to male clerical authority was not Walker's only legacy. In a letter to her from Joos, his salutation suggests her ambiguous role: "Dear child, or Mother, what is it?" (EJ to MJW, 7 Sept. 1861, MA). She was both—like many women of her time, she faced in two directions. As she looked toward the institutional church and its representatives, she adopted the stance of a child; when she turned toward her sisters, she was their mother. Both revered her, and in both roles she helped to ensure the life and growth of the Monroe congregation. In this sense, it is easy to understand why her contemporaries called her the congregation's "true foundress."

48. The relevant passage in the Life reads: "When the separation of the Sisterhood took place, her humility traced this, as also other afflictions, to her own unworthiness; considering them as punishments for her sins and infidelities. This thought has often caused her to weep and grieve bitterly, thinking that her dear Community was suffering on her account" (186–87, MA).

The Bible as a source for prayer.

# 3

# "Not Two Exactly Alike"

## *IHM Spirituality*

### Margaret Brennan, I.H.M.

On 17 May 1883, Mother Theresa Maxis, pioneer sister and first general superior of the IHM congregation in Monroe, Michigan, wrote Sister Genevieve Morrissey of the IHM congregation in Scranton, Pennsylvania, about one of the congregation's early devotional practices:

> I had the thought of speaking to you about a practice we had in the very beginning of the institution, of each Sister procuring a kind of pocket book in which she would write all the prayers of her own selection and which suit [*sic*] her particular devotion. If the same variation exists with respect to devotions as it is with all the other works of God, that there are not two exactly alike, then I think it is convenient for every one to have their own choice for private devotions, etc. (SA)

Although Maxis had always considered the spirituality of St. Alphonsus Liguori as foundational to the new congregation, it is significant that from the very earliest days she had also been concerned that the sisters be able to pursue their own inclinations with regard to the choice of devotions through which they could relate personally to God. It is the purpose of this essay to reflect on the reality of those personal relationships and how they were expressed—and continue to be expressed today—in the lives of individual sisters who also acknowledge and consider Alphonsian spirituality as a precious IHM heritage.[1]

---

1. In response to the encouragement of Vatican II that religious come in touch with the spirit of their founders in the light of the challenges of contemporary times, some very specific efforts were undertaken to reflect anew on the Alphonsian roots of the IHM community. Studies on Alphonsian spirituality were pursued in the congregation in the summers of 1964 and 1965 through courses offered by Gabriel Ehman, C.SS.R., who also served as a tertian master for sisters making a summer of renewal. Serious pursuit of

## The IHMs' Inherited Redemptorist Spirituality

Founded in 1845, the IHM congregation in Monroe was one of a proliferation of new apostolic religious congregations of women established during the nineteenth century. For the most part, these congregations served the new immigrant Catholic population of the United States in the cities and on the frontiers or established catechetical and health centers in the "mission lands" of China and many parts of Africa and Latin America. Because apostolic congregations of religious women were still a relatively new phenomenon in the church, rules of life and spiritualities that specifically reflected their ministerial life of service as women were almost nonexistent. The general practice was to impose a structure modeled somewhat after that of cloistered religious, with an interpretation of the vows and a modified form of enclosure that allowed little interaction with "seculars" or little room for personal initiative or for expressions of individuality. At the turn of the century, these new women's groups were able to become canonical institutes with simple vows.[2]

Like the IHMs, the new apostolic religious congregations of the nineteenth century were for the most part under the control of local bishops who generally appointed diocesan priests as directors. If the religious congregation was associated with a religious order of men, the director would more than likely come from that order's ranks. In the case of the IHM congregation, Detroit's coadjutor bishop Peter Paul Lefevere appointed as directors Redemptorist priests, because the Redemptorists had helped the congregation get started in Monroe. This continued until 1855, when the Redemptorists withdrew from Monroe (MMC, 1 May 1855, MA).

The place, importance, and influence of the Redemptorists in the early years of the IHM congregation are indisputable realities that gave the sisters a stable structure of religious life. The apostolic zeal of Redemptorist Louis Florent Gillet, who drew Maxis and the other founding sisters to the Michigan frontier, instilled a vision that united the founding group and energized it for action. The continuing support of other Re-

---

Alphonsian spirituality became part of the novitiate program in the early 1960s. Bernard Häring, C.SS.R., and Francis Xavier Durwell, C.SS.R., were consultants in the major rule revision during 1960–66. Nancy Fearon, I.H.M., Margaret O'Shea, I.H.M., and Mary Jo Maher, I.H.M., have published and edited books on Alphonsian spirituality and on its connection to the IHM congregation.

2. On 8 Dec. 1900, Pope Leo XIII issued the bull *Conditiae a Christo*, which recognized the status of apostolic communities of women as religious. A religious institute, as defined by canon law, is a society in which, in accordance with their own law, the members pronounce public vows and live a fraternal life in common. The vows are either perpetual or temporary; if the latter, they are to be renewed when the time elapses (Canon 607, par. 2).

demptorists after Gillet's departure from Monroe in 1847 are important parts of IHM history. In her centennial history of the congregation, *No Greater Service*, Rosalita Kelly suggests that Maxis's request in February 1857 to the Redemptorist bishop of Philadelphia, John Nepomucene Neumann, for "a place in [his] Diocese" (JNN to PPL, 7 Aug. 1859, DAA) was centered in her desire "to bring the institute again under Redemptorist direction and to have the rule completed along the lines of that of St. Alphonsus from which the founder had adapted it" ([Kelly] 1948, 131).

There is no doubt that Maxis saw the identity and autonomy of the IHM congregation as inextricably connected to the continuing support of the Redemptorists, especially in the work of completing the congregation's Constitutions, which were an adaptation of the Redemptorist Rule. Even though the fledgling congregation was placed under the direction of diocesan priests after the withdrawal of the Redemptorists, Maxis continually sought ways and means to come once more under Redemptorist influence. This proved to be particularly difficult after November 1857, when Lefevere appointed the Reverend Edward Joos superior as well as director of the congregation (PPL to TM, 5 Nov. 1857, MA). This action led in time to Maxis's own dismissal as congregational superior on 1 April 1859 and to the eventual severing of the IHM congregation into two separate branches, one in Monroe and one in Pennsylvania.[3] In a poignant letter to Lefevere after her dismissal, Maxis once more declared her intentions:

> I will here declare, My Lord, that after the closest examination of my conscience, I cannot find that in all I did or said to get the Institution out of Michigan, right or wrong I had any other motive but the welfare of the Institution. I knew the rules were not completed, that the intention of those who laid the foundation of the establishment had something more in view than to form a religious society.—By the length of time we remained always the same in Monroe I thought we would do better elsewhere. The saying that it was for the Redemptorists is perfectly disgusting to me. I dont [*sic*] expect to be where there are Redemp. Fathers nor do I wish it, all I wish and I cannot help to wish is to have our rules attended to and it is what I have been trying to have done for years—Other motives may be given to me, but God knows all. (TM to PPL, 9 July 1859, UNDA)

Lefevere's anger at the withdrawal of the Redemptorists from Monroe had led him to forbid Maxis to have any contact with them except

---

3. In 1868, the Philadelphia diocese was divided and the new Diocese of Scranton constituted. In August 1871, the bishop of Scranton, William O'Hara, asked that the IHM sisters in his diocese separate from those in the Philadelphia diocese and form a separate and distinct order. Thus emerged three separate IHM congregations (see [Ryan] 1967, 142–43).

with regard to their forwarding of possible candidates for congregational membership ([Kelly] 1948, 125). However, the IHM Constitutions, which formed the sisters' corporate spirituality, was still clearly an adaptation of the Redemptorist Rule and spirit. Specific congregational devotions (e.g., the rosary, stations of the cross, and visit to the Blessed Sacrament) as well as formal congregational prayers (copied by Maxis into her 1850 prayer manual from the Redemptorist *Recuel de Prieres* of 1844) reflected the great redemptional themes that gave rootedness to Alphonsus's own spirituality: the Incarnation, the Passion, the Eucharist, and devotion to Mary. Community prayers until the 1960s were, with few exceptions, the same as those of the Redemptorist congregation.[4]

### Personal Devotional Practices: Poverty Books

Although an Alphonsian-Redemptorist spirituality remained the basis of the congregation's official spirituality, Maxis's recognition of the value and importance of sisters' following their own preferences and desires in cultivating their personal devotional practices indicates that she was able to distinguish between the spirituality of the congregation and that of each person. The practice of creating personal prayer books —later known as "poverty books"—that Maxis recalled in her 1883 letter to Morrissey continued in the IHM congregation for many years, becoming an integral part of the sisters' prayer lives. Strikingly, the strict common life to which the sisters adhered did not allow for the possession of any books other than the *Imitation of Christ, The Little Office of the Blessed Virgin Mary,* the congregational *Manual of Prayers,* a copy of the IHM Constitutions, (or Rule), and (beginning in 1927) a *St. Andrew's Daily Missal.* Thus, the very existence of a personal prayer book was significant.

In a poverty book, a sister could give expression to her own attractions in prayer, cultivate her own devotions, and exercise some freedom of choice. When typewriters became available, these books took on a more polished look. Many sisters had small, three-ringed, loose-leaf binders in which new prayers could be easily added, changed, and reordered.[5] Those that I have seen that belonged to deceased sisters and ones that are even now in use contain prayers, quotations from spiritual books, devotions to particular saints and to Mary, holy cards, and sometimes memorial cards of deceased loved ones.

However, not every IHM sister responded to poverty books in the same way. In an interview in 1993, a sister then in her eighties recalled

---

4. For a more detailed history of IHM prayers, see SSIHM 1987.

5. Legislation about poverty books appears as late as 1954. In the Chapter of Affairs for that year, enactment no. 17 reads: "Inexpensive ring notebooks may be used for poverty books" (MA).

with great amusement her own aversion to creating or using a poverty book as a book of prayer:

> I never had a poverty book because I never wanted one. I had an aversion to them. Early in my life, before I entered the community, I prayed the psalms. I wanted a book of psalms, nothing else. When the general superior came for visitation to the mission where I was stationed, she said to me, "I hear you have no poverty book." I answered, "No, I don't —I never have had one." And then she said, "Everyone has a poverty book and I understand that you have your own book of psalms." She said that it was not our custom: "We can have a poverty book or a missal but nothing else and so I want you to know that you have to give up your book of psalms." So I did and read the psalms when I could from the Bible. And to this day, I *still* use the psalms.[6] (interview 1)

Poverty books also became a way in which a sister could unobtrusively share and communicate affection, friendship, and support with another sister without incurring disapproval. Often a professed sister would prepare the beginnings of a poverty book for a young relative or for a woman she might be mentoring or sponsoring for congregational membership. I can recall how an IHM sister with whom I had shared my developing thoughts of a religious vocation put together a little notebook that contained some quotations of Thérèse of Lisieux, Dom Marmion, Janet Stuart, and others who had been part of our conversations. Forty-five years ago, we would not have named such sharing as spiritual direction, nor would we have been able to articulate the ways in which women have always intuitively known that they were sharing a part of themselves even as they shared their experience with God. I recognize now that the gift of that little notebook was a way of communicating friendship and encouragement and the loving presence of another in a growing relationship with God. Such overtures were never named for what they were because of long-standing dualisms that viewed human relationships as obstacles to total union with God.

The spirit of personal spiritual exploration expressed in the poverty books grew and developed in other ways as well. During the summer months, courses were provided at the Monroe motherhouse not only for academic credit and enrichment but also specifically as a means of deepening the sisters' theological knowledge. The Jesuit, Dominican, and Benedictine educators who came to Monroe inevitably influenced the sisters' personal lives as well as their professional lives as teachers.

---

6. An important assumption of feminist interpretations of history is the claim that the personal lives and experiences of women are critical to representing that history accurately. All quotations are taken from interviews taped in Aug. 1993. The interviewees were guaranteed anonymity (MA, restricted).

Poverty books as a common expression of devotion and individuality eventually disappeared as the liturgical movement and the renewal in biblical studies took hold in the congregation in the 1960s, offering new scope and breadth for personal prayer and devotion. The sisters were now allowed to choose their own sources from which to make morning meditation rather than hearing "points" read aloud by the superior. After the renewal of Vatican II, they were able to choose their own place for prayer and were not obliged to gather together in the chapel. The novices were taught to pray from the Scriptures and the texts of the daily liturgy rather than from meditation manuals or pious commentaries on biblical texts. New forms of common prayer replaced the old manuals; lauds and vespers, the official prayer of the church, replaced the former morning and evening prayers. Biblical, liturgical, and liberation theologies and spiritualities gave a new richness and depth to the more privatized devotions that had taken root in a period of the church's isolation from the modern world. More recently, the importance of individual and personal response to God and the trusting of experience as a locus of ongoing revelation of the divine has become a renewed source for theological reflection. Feminist spirituality, with its stress on relationality and interconnectedness, has highlighted and reverenced the experience of friendship and solidarity as well as a commitment to bring about an alternate vision of church and world that is both inclusive and participative.[7]

### Of Saints and Angels

Reflecting on these developments in the light of Maxis's insight about "not two [being] exactly alike" gave me the incentive to explore further the reality of personal spiritualities in the IHM congregation. I decided to conduct a series of interviews with approximately thirty IHM sisters of varying age and experience in the community. My desire was to acknowledge the personal spiritualities that have been present and continue to flow beneath that of the congregation's corporate Redemptorist/Alphonsian heritage. These interviews, which were actually more like conversations, were not undertaken with the intent of gathering statistics or tracing significant trends. My questions centered around the kind of devotions or patterns of prayer that sisters brought with them as young women entering the congregation. Did they come from family practices? Influences in the parish? Was their way of relating to God, their "spirituality" (although I did not use the term), informed by family, friends, or one's place in history? Was it influenced by their ethnic background? Was it patterned on gender? I asked further if IHM congregational practices

7. For a summary of salient characteristics of feminist spirituality, see Schneiders 1991, 87–88.

and teaching on prayer enhanced those early formative experiences. Did IHM influences encourage or discourage their development? Were there attitudes of prayer and devotion and places of meeting God that had to be relearned or were discountenanced by the congregation? What understandings of the ways of God and images of God were learned? Have those images changed? Did the IHM Rule and its devotional practices provide an ambiance for prayer? What or where were the sources of strength in times of darkness and discouragement? Where was the presence of God found and experienced most tangibly?

The women I interviewed often spoke of the "spirit of the congregation" as something almost tangible to them, though none felt it necessary (or perhaps even possible) to describe it in terms that were particular or specific. What was clear to all of them was the realization of belonging to a community of women who were committed to the congregation's spirit, to its mission, to the world, and to deeply caring for one another. Within this common congregational spirit, however, a large measure of freedom and room for individual expression in terms of personal devotion also existed—without ever having been officially encouraged or even endorsed.

Two instances, among many others, illustrate this reality very well. Both were about the power and place of saints and angels in the formation of personal spiritualities. In the first instance, I spoke with two women—separated in age and in entrance into the community by fifteen or twenty years—whose spiritual lives grew and deepened through their internalization of the "little way" of Thérèse of Lisieux and through devotion to the archangel Raphael. One of the women expressed it this way:

> It seemed to me that the "nitty-gritty" of our lives as novices was so narrow and circumscribed—especially since we could not read the papers nor hear the nightly news. Even after profession this seemed true when we returned to the convent after a day of school. When I discovered that Little Thérèse—a cloistered Carmelite—had been named patroness of the missions, I received a new incentive. Belief that her "little way"—doing small and insignificant things with great love—could be a source of grace, courage and perseverance for a tired and discouraged missionary because of our interconnectedness in the Body of Christ gave broader parameters to what seemed at times to be such a narrow world. I suppose that I would be less "romantic" about it today, yet I still believe that we can be sources of spiritual energy and new life for one another. (interview 5)

In the second case, I saw how devotion to the power and presence of the archangel Raphael had taken on a public dimension for Sister Mary Jerome Sanford. Aside from her teaching at Marygrove College, Sanford found time to spread knowledge of this angel of happy meetings. With

ecclesiastical permission, she published pamphlets, and a large correspondence poured into the college recounting favors received through
the intercession of this messenger of God.[8] Sanford died in 1952, but the
account (recorded in her menology) of the quasi-mystical experience that
was to shape her own spirituality is perhaps relevant to IHMs of all eras:

> Almost by chance it would seem, God directed her during this period of
> study at Notre Dame to the Heavenly Friend who was to hold her soul
> in his hands throughout the long later years of grinding and molding.
> She went into the library one day in 1920 or 1921 to look for a
> Latin book. Her eyes lighted upon a book in French by Ernest Hello,
> which, because she did not know the author, she opened to page through
> it. In it she found an essay on the "Holy Angels," and she read, with
> one of those flashes of light and joy that the Holy Spirit sometimes
> grants a soul, the now familiar passage on the Angel Raphael, Angel of
> Happy Meetings. Her soul was stirred to the depths. This, she knew,
> would be a companion prayer for the rest of her life—at this time she
> did not realize that rather than the prayer, it was Raphael himself who
> would be her companion for the rest of her life. (Mengy. of MJS, 27 Dec.
> 1952, MA)

### The Influence of Home and Catholic School

Almost without exception, every woman with whom I spoke had
come to the congregation with some spiritual formation from her home
and from her education in Catholic schools. For the most part, these
early formative experiences provided the ground upon which their own
personal spiritualities developed. Those who had entered the community
from Redemptorist parishes often spoke of a special devotion to Mary
rooted in Mother of Perpetual Help Devotions. One sister recounted:

> All my life I have had a strong devotion to Mary and have loved the
> rosary even though I no longer say it every day. I also love to pray in
> the presence of the Blessed Sacrament. While our IHM community life
> emphasized both these forms of prayer, I would have to say that I had
> already been shown the depth and beauty of such devotions by living
> in Holy Redeemer Parish, attending Mother of Perpetual Help Devo-
> tions, the yearly mission, and the Stations of the Cross in Lent. These
> were family events, deeply formative, I believe, for all of us. I know that
> even today my brothers and sisters, though not what I would call deeply
> religious, will still search out these places and kinds of prayer—espe-
> cially in times of need. (interview 7)

8. For a recounting of this devotion, see McGrath 1952 (copy in MA).

Almost all those who entered religious life from IHM high schools in the 1930s, 1940s, and 1950s had learned the fundamental principles of uniting prayer and action through the influence of the sodality, retreats, Catholic Action, and young Christian student movements that exerted such influence in the pre-Vatican years under powerful figures such as Daniel Lord, S.J. Devotion to Mary, which took a number of forms, said something to these young women that carried over into active service such as visiting the sick, working in soup kitchens, and playing with children in low-rent housing units. One woman with whom I spoke was very clear on how her years at Immaculata High School had laid the foundations of a spirituality that was built on the Gospel and was committed to action:

> What I felt during my high-school years was an excitement and a firm sense of commitment to the poor. I realize now that what we understood as Catholic Action was really a kind of formation. In our small-group meetings we were actually doing a kind of social analysis though we did not use those words—and we were expected to be about real service rather than simply giving out of our abundance at stated times of the year. I believe that the seeds of my vocation were sown in those years and in a particular way through the example I saw in the sisters. It made IHM life appear to be very attractive and worth the gift of my own. (interview 4)

On the other hand, another woman who had had similar experiences in her high school days felt that after entering the community her spirituality seemed to regress:

> After so much involvement in high school and learning to appreciate the value of discussions about how the Gospel challenges us in our daily life, I felt very "let down" after I entered the community. I did not really feel that I was taught to pray even though we were given time. Life seemed to be so "turned in on ourselves." I often felt suffocated and so much of formation did not make sense to me. We made so much of things which struck me as having very little consequence and looking back I marvel that I took it so seriously. But then, maybe it did more good than I think! (interview 8)

### The "Unwritten Rule" Against Contemplative Prayer

In the years prior to Vatican II, a sharp division existed between ascetical and mystical theology, and these differing theologies each had a strong influence on different expressions of spirituality and forms of prayer. The ascetical life was thought to be the common and ordinary way in which most persons were led to God. It consisted of the struggle to acquire habits of virtue, fidelity to vocal and mental prayer that followed a set formula, and a strict observance of the rule that was the measure of sanctity and perfection. Spiritual reading books for the most part were about the acquiring and practice of virtue or recounting the lives of saints and of other holy persons who exemplified such an ideal. The mystical life, on the other hand, was not something to which an ordinary person should aspire. Union with God that was deeply affective, together with calls to silent contemplative prayer that was not only wordless but also without any kind of discursive thought, was believed generally to be a special gift and invitation given to very few persons. Moreover, those who sought guidance in more simplified and quiet prayer were generally counseled to doubt such inspirations and to walk the safer, surer paths of discursive mental prayer.

Two or three persons whom I interviewed shared their struggle with trying to articulate calls to prayer that moved from rational considerations to a centering and wordless presence of God.

> I remember going to my superior one Sunday morning during retreat and wanting to talk about my prayer. I had found that the way in which I had been meditating no longer nourished or inspired me. When I went to morning meditation, I had no desire to do any conscious reflection or considerations on a text nor to use my mind. I told her that I felt drawn instead to just "be there," to enter into my heart and to rest somehow in the presence of God who seemed to be within me. I must say that the superior was very kind and tried to be understanding. But her advice was not too helpful. She said that perhaps on Sunday mornings when we had more time for prayer I might try praying as I described, but that I would probably grow more in union with God if I was faithful to the Rule which described our morning prayer as *meditation*, and that meant using our mind to consider the points, make resolutions, and relate my prayer to my duties. After all, we *were* apostolic religious! (interview 6)

Another woman confided her fear of revealing a strong call to contemplative prayer within the framework of the congregation. For many years, she struggled with doubts as to the authenticity of her call, and only in the last decades of her life did she find the encouragement to trust in and to follow what she always sensed to be of God:

> I do think that I had some mystic experiences in prayer, and I was very attracted to the writings of women such as Elizabeth of the Trinity and Margaret Mary Alocoque. Devotion to the Sacred Heart and prayer before the Blessed Sacrament were very nourishing. But I didn't know

what to do about these experiences and I couldn't find anyone who seemed able to help me. Spiritual direction, at that time, was considered generally to be quite extraordinary. For a time I was part of a group of other sisters who used to meet on Saturday afternoons to prepare the Sunday liturgy together. That kind of sharing helped—but it was not encouraged. (interview 10)

There were also exceptions, however, to this "unwritten rule" of not encouraging the cultivation of more contemplative modes of prayer. One of the women interviewed recounted how, even as a novice, she was gently goaded and challenged to take up the ways of more simplified prayer and was given books to read that nourished the desires she had been able to share with the novice director:

For a time my charge was dusting the novice directress' office. She had a bookcase full of volumes that enticed me—like the works of Teresa of Avila, Catherine of Siena, books on prayer by Caussade, Lallement and other classics. She must have noticed me dawdling over them and very carefully removing them to be sure that I dusted them well. After I had done all the required reading—*three* volumes on *Christian Perfection* by Rodriguez (which I raced through)—she carefully and skillfully put me in touch with a whole new world of prayer which provided me a foundation that I shall always be grateful for. (interview 2)

### Vatican II and After

For those women who entered the congregation on the eve of and after Vatican II, the framework for prayer changed dramatically. The women whom I interviewed who came in the mid-1950s, 1960s, and 1970s had no need nor any inclination to have or to make poverty books. The concept itself would have been quite foreign and meaningless to them. Each of these women came to the community with her own copy of the Bible, from which she learned to pray, and was given intentional instruction on prayer and the opportunity to read the great teachers of prayer such as Saint Teresa and St. Alphonsus. Moreover, these young women were nourishing their own spirituality in the study of biblical, liturgical, and systematic theology, which by this time had become an integral part of their formation. As a result, many of these young women had a low tolerance for certain devotional practices that did not stimulate, nurture, and foster a spirituality that was rooted in the liturgy and in the Scriptures and that was related in some way to the mission of the church toward the transformation of society. Such a formation proved to be highly rewarding and fulfilling for many who entered the community in those years. One sister summed it up very succinctly and positively: "I came to the community with 100 percent desire and I got 110 percent answer to that desire" (interview 3).

Other women who came at this same time remember the emphasis placed on mission and recall being encouraged to live on the edge of the new frontiers where the church was engaging the world's joys and sorrows, hopes and longings. One sister reflected very cogently on the creative tension that this could engender:

> I recall a lot of discussion and instruction around the spirit of the congregation and learning that holiness had something to do with living out the challenge presented in Luke's Gospel, Chapter 4. Study of St. Alphonsus and wanting to be with the poor appeared as a congregational ideal. As I reflect on those formation days after nearly thirty years of ministry, I do see in us as IHMs a group of women with a sharpened corporate, critical consciousness of the signs of our times and of how we as religious in the church should be there. I think, too, that this can be problematic for us at times. You know, "wanting to be everywhere when we see so many needs" and so risking being nowhere! (interview 11)

Women who had been in the congregation for fifty years or longer also reflected on the new insights and on the great sense of freedom that came from the opening of the Scriptures in a new way. It is not that these sisters had not read the Scriptures or heard them read many times; what was different was learning how to pray out of the Scriptures in a more personally intentional way. The opportunity and the experience of making individually directed retreats became for many a kind of school of prayer. One sister who had lived on several missions with younger sisters expressed with genuine joy how she watched the young sisters praying the Scriptures and was not beyond asking them how they went about such reflection: "When I saw those younger sisters so able to talk about the Scriptures and relate it to our lives today, I felt so thrilled—and whenever we had a prayer service for some occasion, they made it so beautiful and they were able to find just the right texts. And when I would ask them how they go about it, they made it sound so easy!" (interview 12). Another woman, who has had a long career as superior on the missions and as a school principal as well, spoke simply, gratefully, and not without humor about a young temporary professed sister who was obligated to come to her for what was called "catechism of the vows" in preparation for final profession. That young sister became a source of new spiritual awakening for this woman, who herself became a grateful learner: "One of the greatest gifts of my life was to have [her] as a young student teacher. She was a threat to many in those early post–Vatican II years, with her inquisitive and searching mind which was critical in the best sense of the word. I looked forward so much to my Sunday morning conversations with her about the vows because I learned so much from her, and I'll always remember what she said: 'I don't care how much they box me in as long as they don't put a top on it' " (interview 9).

## A Congregational Spirituality in the Midst of Pluralism

Not many of the women I interviewed would be ready to say that their changing and nuanced experiences of God were motivated by an intentionally formulated feminist consciousness. However, reclaiming their experience and learning to trust it, to share it, and above all to act on it is evidence of a new spirit in our midst that moves toward new horizons and new depths. Although I did not raise specific questions regarding changing images of God, I did sense that we *do* have various images for God—and that they *do* change. For some, there is pain and loneliness in coming to realize that the images of God, of the church, and of the world that they desire so deeply to live out of have yet no homeland in the deep places of the heart.

There is no doubt that the women I interviewed were also deeply rooted in the congregation and in the sense of a congregational spirituality. Living side by side, both in community life and in the ministry of education, they forged strong bonds in a gravitational field of attraction that linked religious faith and human friendships in ways that enhanced both, even if this was not openly articulated and sometimes not officially approved. Fidelity to a Rule of life that remained unchanged for well over a hundred years instilled a spirit among IHM sisters that remained intact even through the changes of Vatican II. Today, on the edge of a new millennium in an emerging postmodern world, fidelity to that same spirit has committed the members of the congregation to sustained interaction around the weighty question of what it means to belong to one another as we struggle with a plurality of beliefs and values (Assembly '93 Outcomes, MA).

Commitment to the struggle of belonging to one another has been part of IHM history from the very beginning of the congregation. It reflects in large part the passion of Theresa Maxis to form the congregation as a religious order in the spirit of the Redemptorists, who had given it birth with a commitment to mission on the frontiers of faith. Grounding the IHM congregation in this heritage has given it a sense of stability, but now that the diversity of personal spiritualities and devotional practices that have always been present has been consciously and intentionally articulated, there is a renewed desire among the members to name and to own what belonging to the IHM congregation means today.

## Feminist Spirituality and a Sense of Belonging

Although the formation of feminist spiritualities and their impact on the corporate spirituality of the congregation were not specifically a part of my interviews, I do believe that feminist perspectives are operative in the IHM theologies that inform relationships to God, to one another, and to the world. Spirituality, of course, includes more than an interior life or a life of prayer; theologian Anne Carr describes it in its widest meaning "as the whole of one's spiritual or religious experience, one's beliefs, convictions, and patterns of thought, one's emotions and behavior in respect to what is ultimate, or to God" (1988, 201). Such a definition has further connotations for women. The emergence of a critical feminist consciousness that grew out of the women's movement in the late 1960s had—and continues to have—important ramifications both for theology and for spirituality, as Christian feminists seek to inform and to transform their lived experience of faith. Shared reflection has raised critical questions about inherited patterns, expectations, and assumptions regarding gender and about how such conjecturing has not only stereotyped but also falsified ways of thinking and acting ascribed to men as well as to women. In Carr's thought, a Christian feminist spirituality is a way of relating to God that is mindful of the cultural restrictions placed upon women, is critical of women's dependency upon men and of women's nonsupportiveness to one another, and is invitational in calling all persons "to wider visions of human mutuality, reciprocity, and interdependence" (1988, 208).

Feminist spirituality, like feminist theology, consults women's experience and reverences the relational and embodied way that women both come to and "check out" truth. Feminist thought is grounded in an ecological ethic that sees the relationship of all reality in an interconnected web of diversity, subjectivity, interdependence, and community. At the same time, however, it prizes autonomy, self-actualization, and the individual and unique way in which each person approaches the transcendent God who is also immanently present in all created reality. Elizabeth Johnson pictures this cosmic reality as a circle of mutuality grounded and sustained by the Spirit who, as the great creative Matrix, attracts it toward the future: "The Spirit of God dwelling in the world with quickening power deconstructs dualism and draws in its place a circle of mutuality and inclusiveness. . . . The Spirit creates matter. Matter bears the mark of the sacred and has itself a spiritual radiance. Hence the world is holy, nature is holy, bodies are holy, women's bodies are holy" (1993, 60).

I suspect that most qualities of feminist spirituality, in one way or another, have found a home in the lives of a great number of IHM sisters. At the same time, the varying degrees in which feminist perspectives have been internalized—as well as the further realization that there are those who have neither endorsed nor accepted its premises or its practices—are realities that are very much at the heart of the differing values and beliefs that challenge the sense of belonging. As women religious more consciously claim a feminist spirituality, the initial movement is to deconstruct the learned patterns of imaging and relating to a God who was presented in patriarchal and androcentric images, concepts, and models of behavior. More often than not this leaving behind is a dark and lonely journey of unknowing. However, as we begin to share our stories and memories individually and collectively, the small snippets of experience where we have trusted insights and perceptions that flow in our lives like silent underground rivers come together to reveal ways in which the Creator Spirit was present and active in surprising ways. Practically speaking, this means searching in oral and written history for the hidden and unarticulated traces of intuition and of freedom of spirit that mark the subtle and artful presence of Wisdom and the courage to trust it.

It is my growing conviction that the diversity of spiritualities operative in a congregation where "not two [are] exactly alike" does not take away from the spirit that bonds us so deeply to one another in the common history and heritage we share. The breadth and depth of those differences among us are rooted in an emerging postmodern consciousness that is influencing our ways of thinking, feeling, and responding to the realities of our time. The challenge that faces us is the seriousness of our commitment to sustained interaction around the foundational issues of faith and of life that form the basis for our belonging to one another and for our common dedication to the mission of Jesus in a contemporary church and world that is dramatically different from that which gave us birth and growth, though it is rooted in its heritage and tradition.

PART TWO

# The IHM Life Cycle

# The Context

## Margaret Susan Thompson

Just a few years ago, the concept of a religious life cycle would have seemed odd or anomalous, even to many members of vowed congregations: the term "cycle" connotes ongoing process and development, but religious life typically was defined in static terms, usually as a "state of perfection." Additionally, "cycle" suggests curved lines and fluidity. In the past, if any linear images came to mind, they almost surely were rigid, straight, and hierarchical, pointing upward to sources of authority within the community and church and, ultimately, to a God in a celestial heaven.

The very existence of this section in a book about sisters, then, is indicative of how much change there has been in the past few decades in understandings of religious life. What these essays also reveal is that religious life was never as rigid and as static as prescriptive literature or formal constitutions might suggest. Despite prohibitions against particular friendships, for instance, camaraderie and companionship were the rule rather than the exception. A standardized habit merely inspired greater creativity in sisters' efforts to assert individuality in their appearance than otherwise might have been the case. Meanwhile, the personalism and concern reflected in the tenures of novice mistresses like Bridget Smith were echoed at the end of individual sisters' life cycles by the compassionate care offered to elderly and disabled sisters by women like Flora Collins, Francina Ryan, and Gertrude Sweeney. Thus, although only Mary Ann Hinsdale among the authors of this section employs the term "small subversions" to characterize the contrast between what happened and what (legalistically speaking) was supposed to happen, it applies equally well to the subject matter of the other chapters.

Of course, Carol Quigley's essay is an important caution not to overstate the degree to which individual differences and frailties were accommodated. Historically, the IHMs were representative of nearly all religious congregations in exhibiting little understanding of or capacity

113

to respond to members affected by mental illness. Rather, this was a condition too often left undiagnosed and untreated or, worse, blamed upon the lack of docility or lack of religious spirit of the sufferer. In contrast to the generosity toward aged members that Jane Shea demonstrates was displayed consistently throughout IHM history, and the centrality that the elderly have been understood to have in the life of the community, the mentally ill tended to be ignored, shut out, or put away— sometimes with tragic results. Here again, the IHMs were hardly unique; similar patterns are evident in the annals of most congregations. Few sisters, however, have been so forthright as those from Monroe in undertaking such a self-critique.

Moreover, there is another dimension of life cycle evident in this section and, indeed, in many other essays in this volume. The IHM community itself seems to have evolved over the course of its history, passing through at least three distinct and discernible phases: the pioneer, the institutionalized, and the post–Vatican II phases. The first era was characterized by a great deal of flexibility, trial and error, and humaneness in the introduction and implementation of regulations. At such a time, the founder(s)' charism is not only evident but still incarnate in the founder her- or himself, and so there is a vitality—almost an urgency—that precludes rigidity. In the case of the Monroe IHMs, that first period was relatively short, generally coincident with Mother Theresa Maxis's presence in the community and, beyond that, in the memory of those who knew her well.

After the pioneer phase, in this as in other congregations, a time of institutionalizing ensued. Rules became more clearly specified and enforced; uniformity was normative and individualization required risks. The regulations that Joan Glisky describes in her essay on the prohibitions against friendships and the novitiate practices that Hinsdale discusses are reflective of a time and a mindset that historian Mary Ewens has insightfully designated "the Great Repression" (1978, 23). For the IHMs, this period lasted for about a century, from the arrival of Father Edward Joos as ecclesiastical superior until the beginning of renewal in the 1960s. The religious life that emerged during this timespan is what most people —including many sisters—believe to be the normal or typical form that it has taken throughout history, an understanding that is both erroneous and unfortunate, because anything else is thereby classed as odd or aberrant.[1] In the United States, moreover, this was the period when the private side of religious life was lived in greatest isolation from the general pub-

---

1. One need only read about previous historical periods in which new forms of religious dedication emerged to appreciate how little can be considered typical or normal about any form of religious life. For a useful survey that covers the nearly 2000 years of women's religious life, see McNamara 1996.

Si vous avez besoin d'un hébergement pour la rencontre du 10 février, me faire parvenir, le plus tôt possible les informations suivantes: votre nom, la date de votre arrivée et de votre départ. Vous pouvez me les faire parvenir par télécopieur (613-236-0825) ou par courriel (crcres@web.net) Merci de votre collaboration.

If you need accommodations for the February 10th meeting, please forward the following information, as soon as possible: your name, your arrival and departure dates. This can be done by fax (613-236-0825) or by email (crcres@web.net)  Thank you very much!

lic; women "left the world" when they entered the convent. For this reason, the detailed (and substantiated) information on the novitiate and on interpersonal relationships provided by these essays is particularly necessary and welcome. Here, for example, is the inside story on topics (such as nuns' hair, habits and underwear, recreation, and daily schedule) that, even today, seem to evoke limitless curiosity in people—including sisters who entered after these practices were largely ended and the veil was lifted, literally and figuratively.[2] It is for this era of rigid conformity that verification of the humanizing "small subversions" is especially important, as a corrective to the impressions left by rulebooks, by popular media, and by traditional prescriptive religious writing.

After Vatican II (1962–65), of course, much of what typified at least the official version of life during the institutionalized period underwent fundamental change. A woman joining the IHMs today finds little resembling the regimentation that Hinsdale describes, and she learns that friendships are not only tolerated but strongly encouraged. However, the strong and well-defined personalities who are evident throughout this book and throughout all eras of IHM history, as well as the widespread and long-lived memories of close relationships that Nancy Sylvester discovered in her interviews with older members, suggest that there is perhaps more continuity in the IHM life cycle than may previously have been appreciated.

Thus, in understanding the IHMs—both as individuals and as a community—we may again turn to anthropologist Mary Catherine Bateson, who suggests that there is a circular dimension to the time line of our daily lives:

> Because we are engaged in a day-by-day process of self-invention—not discovery, for what we search for does not exist until we find it—both the past and the future are raw material, shaped and reshaped by each individual. . . . These are lives in flux, lives still indeterminate and subject to further discontinuities. This very quality protects me from the temptation to interpret them as pilgrimages to some fixed goal, for there is no way to know which fragments of the past will prove to be relevant in the future. Composing a life involves a continual reimagining of the future and reinterpretation of the past to give meaning to the present. (1990, 28–30)

In many ways, this section of *Building Sisterhood* is the most innovative in its concept and, one might hope, the most likely to inspire comparable work by members of other orders—work that can add to the

---

2. For example, on the "Sister-L" Internet discussion list (the majority of whose participants are sisters), discussions of topics like habit design, choice of religious names, hair provoke some of the liveliest and most extended discussion.

fleshing out of what women's religious life was truly and generally like in the American past. For now, it provides the provocative suggestion that "sisterhood" in congregations such as the IHMs was, after all, a reality in something more than name only.

Exiting as novices.

# 4

# "The Roughest Kind of Prose"

*IHM Socialization, 1860–1960*

Mary Ann Hinsdale, I.H.M.

Although the IHM's pre–Vatican II formation experiences may not be unique compared to other apostolic congregations of women in the United States, recovering specifically IHM stories of convent socialization, is, as feminist historians and folklorists have recently shown, essential to "claiming our roots." According to the feminist folklorists, "acts of coding—covert expressions of disturbing or subversive ideas—are a common phenomenon in the lives of women, who have so often been dominated, silenced, and marginalized by men" (Radner 1993, vii).[1] Such coding may be deliberate, or it may be unconscious. It is this essential ambiguity that protects women from those who might find their messages disturbing. In discussing these covert expressions, folklorists "attend to the aesthetic choices people make, their ways of bringing beauty and entertainment into their daily occupations and of ritualizing their identities. They focus on the art *in* the everyday: the saving games that make the repetitious drudgery of house or factory work bearable; the clever stories that buffer with laughter pent-up anger at the boss or husband; the expertise of stitchery or stepdance or carpentry that evoke sustaining admiration and empathy from those in the know (Radner 1993, viii). No matter how seemingly mundane or homegrown the coded expressions of IHM socialization may seem "the silencing of [women's] stories in history," says Carolyn Woodward, "works to silence us in the present" (1990, 49).[2]

1. Many examples of such coding are found in the volume edited by Joan Newland Radner. The material cited from interviews in this essay on IHM socialization is taken from audiotapes that remain in the author's possession.

2. So many first-person accounts of convent life abound that they practically constitute a genre of "nun exposés." These range from intelligent considerations such as Bernstein 1976 and the collection edited by Ann Patrick Ware (1985) to the naïve but nevertheless charming [Danforth] 1956. The late 1970s and early 1980s saw a spate of "tell all" publica-

Important in illuminating the IHM socialization process are the personalities and written instructions of the IHM ecclesiastical director, the Reverend (later Monsignor) Edward Joos, and those of the IHM novice mistresses (the chief mentors who were responsible for formation), outlining the specified requirements for entrance into the congregation and the rhythm of daily convent life. However, the recollections of the sister-initiates themselves are important also. Their anecdotal history reveals how, despite the pervasive emphasis on uniformity and on abnegation of self-will, they managed to retain a certain sense of autonomy and self-directedness by turning "everyday acts" into "small subversions."[3] My research in this area also uncovered a lost IHM memory: the story of Bridget Smith, a nineteenth-century novice mistress whose philosophy and mentoring style stand in stark contrast to the socialization experience of most IHMs formed in the pre–Vatican II years. This discovery alone makes revisiting the topic of preconciliar religious formation a worthwhile exercise.

## The Road to Perfection

Before Vatican II, like other women who joined religious congregations or "institutes," the women who wanted to join the Monroe IHMs expected that they would leave "the world" (in this case, the dominant culture of the United States) and enter an esoteric domain of prescribed duties and customs. This "religious life" offered the opportunity to "advance on the road to perfection."

All who aspired to this life were required to undergo a period of initiation known as novitiate, which the Novitiate Directory (a manual that sets out the rules of novitiate life) describes as having a twofold goal: "a trial by [both] the Congregation and the subject and a preparation for the religious life" (ND, 1957, 11, MA).[4] The entering sister's life, an earlier

---

tions, whose book jacket blurbs claimed they "read as novels": Kelly 1978; Armstrong 1981, 1983; Upton 1985; Wong 1983. Examples from the late 1980s and 1990s are more "hard edged" and political in tone: Violet 1988; Ferraro and Hussey 1990; Lieblich 1992. The formation accounts in many of the books mentioned here are similar to the experiences of Monroe IHMs; in particular, see the essays in Ware 1985 and Curran 1989. Curran's account is a serious anthropological study which utilizes recent feminist scholarship on the body.

3. For the concept of "everyday acts" becoming "small subversions," I am indebted to Hochman 1994.

4. Strictly speaking, the formation of religious sisters takes place in two stages: the postulancy and the novitiate. The postulancy (*postulare*, "to ask") is so named because the candidate is asking for admission into the community. The novice member lives the full life of the community while being educated about the demands of the three traditional vows of poverty, chastity, and obedience, which she professes at the end of her novitiate. For IHMs, as for most U.S. religious, the postulancy lasted from six to nine months and the novitiate for one or two years, one year of which became known as the "canonical" year after the

version of the manual stressed, was to be "diametrically opposed to that mode of living which regulates itself by the simple impulses of nature. It considers as nothing, and tramples under foot, the things that are loved and esteemed by the world, seeking and choosing for itself whatsoever the world dreads and holds in abhorrence" (1902, 26, MA).[5] Over the years, some of the wording of this manual would be ameliorated, but one thing remained constant: the novitiate was to be "a preparatory school of virtue, where novices are initiated into the religious life" (1902, chapter 2, MA).

That life certainly appeared mysterious to outsiders. Although the IHMs professed "simple vows," their rules and customs were considered especially strict.[6] The sisters took new names, wore habits (a uniform period-piece dress) and veils (each stage of convent initiation being marked by a different color), and kept a defined daily schedule, or *horarium*, that included a rhythm of prayer and ascetical practices. Rules also regulated contact with outsiders (called "seculars"), including the sisters' own families (Const. 1920, art. 197). Candidates themselves would frequently arrive at the convent door with little information about the culture of the life they were about to embrace. Such was the experience of a young woman from Flint, Michigan, who entered the IHM congregation in the early 1940s:

---

1917 promulgation of the Code of Canon Law. In the early days of the community, the length of these induction periods varied considerably. Alphonsine Godfroy-Smyth, for example, entered as a postulant in Apr. 1846; she received the habit the following month and was professed in Aug. 1847. By contrast, Mary Soleau, who became a postulant in Sept. 1849, entered the novitiate fifteen months later in Dec. 1850. By 1855, the IHM Motherhouse Chronicles use the phrase "the year's novitiate being completed" when writing about professions, indicating that this had become a regular practice. The novitiate was extended a second year beginning in 1877 (MMC, 16 Oct., 1877, MA). At the end of the novitiate, after receiving the approval of the general superior and her council, the novice made final vows. This practice was maintained until 1913, when sisters made temporary vows for three years at the conclusion of the novitiate. Beginning with the 1956 reception class, the temporary vow period was extended to five years, after which a sister made final vows. After Vatican II, the nomenclature for temporary vows was changed to "promises," which were taken for three years and renewed for a period not to exceed nine years before final vows.

5. In the 1957 version, an opposite tack is taken. The words "diametrically opposed" are omitted, though the dualism between "religious life" and "the world" still remains: "The spiritual life developed in the novitiate is far superior to that mode of living which regulates itself by the simple impulses of nature. It is a full flowering of the Christian life which, by virtue of the merits of Jesus Christ, is a participation in the life of God" (1957, 12, MA).

6. Women who live an enclosed, monastic style of life (most often contemplatives) and take solemn vows are referred to as "nuns." "Sisters" are women who take "simple" vows and belong to active, apostolic congregations. The distinction between simple and solemn vows has mostly to do with the disposition of inheritance and the complexity of the process for being dispensed from the vows.

I needed a letter from my pastor, but [he] said he didn't know me and couldn't write a letter unless he was my director. So, he proceeded to give me spiritual direction for three months. I had to go to mass and communion every day, go to confession weekly (to him), and come to see him for a weekly conference. At these conferences he would read to me about "the sublimity of religious life" and how it was a superior state to the lay state. Most of this went right over my head. (IHM sister [entrance 1942], interviewed by author, 29 July 1993)

## The Influence of Joos

The IHMs who guided the novices through the formative stages of religious life were entrusted with a great responsibility—the future of the community, literally, lay in their hands. However, in the early days of the congregation—particularly following the controversial departure from Monroe of the first IHM superior, Mother Theresa Maxis—the influence of the IHMs' ecclesiastical director, Joos, on the socialization of new candidates was inestimable.

Belgian Redemptorists, notably Louis Florent Gillet, initially assumed direction for the fledgling IHM community in 1845, but they came into conflict with Detroit's bishop, Peter Paul Lefevere, and left Monroe in 1855.[7] After the departure of the Redemptorists, the sisters were placed under the direction of the Reverend John Van Gennip.[8] In 1857, Van Gennip wrote to Lefevere to complain that the IHM institute had too many directors (no doubt referring to the sisters' many Redemptorist contacts, which were kept up despite their withdrawal from the diocese) and to suggest that the bishop should either replace him or give him the sole right of being the congregation's director (JVG to PPL, 24 Sept. 1857, UNDA, trans. in MA). In response, the bishop sent the Belgian-educated Joos, then a thirty-two-year-old curate who had been serving St. Anne's parish in Detroit, to be "superior and director" of the Monroe IHMs (PPL to TM, 5 Nov. 1857, MA).

Joos literally "ruled" the community for the next forty-four years. In addition to directing retreats and holding frequent conferences for the sisters, he was the key architect of both the first revision of the IHM Rule (also called the Constitutions), which received approbation from Lefevere

7. Gillet issued the invitation to Theresa Maxis to travel westward to work in Michigan. Redemptorist Fathers Egidius Smulders and James Poirier assumed responsibility for the sisters' spiritual needs after Gillet withdrew.

8. There is some confusion as to whether Rev. Henry Rievers also served as director, or whether he simply filled in for Van Gennip when the latter was away. The chronicles for 5 Nov. 1857 record that "Rev. Van Gennip had been appointed director of the Community on his arrival in the parish; but after some time the appointment was transferred to Rev. Wm. Riebers [sic] who filled the office until the fall of this year" (MA). See also [Kelly] 1948, which refers to Rievers as "the Monroe director of earlier days" (455).

in 1861, and the version of the Rule that was submitted to Rome in 1885, which received a "decree of commendation" in 1889.[9] As "Father Director" of the congregation for more than four decades, Joos has been remembered mostly with love—but at times with mild irritation. Some sisters referred to him as "our father," but others recall having to ask his permission for the least little thing, such as taking a bath or purchasing a corset.[10]

In addition to his own considerable influence on the socialization process of new members (his conferences appear alongside Gillet's in the appendix to the 1902 edition of the Novitiate Directory,[11] Joos saw to it that the IHM Constitutions spelled out the qualifications, characteristics, and duties of the office of the mistress of novices. The sister holding the position had to be an exemplary religious, professed at least ten years and thirty years of age. She was also to exercise her office with "zeal, discretion, charity and holy strictness." Exhorted to "have a motherly love for all," she was to be "vigilant in regard to their perfect observance of rule and correct every fault firmly but kindly." She herself was to be an example and was reminded that "she will never succeed in fulfilling her charge if she does not make the novices die to their own will and opinion and become generous souls" (Const. 1920, arts. 143–46).

Such admonitions were not Joos's invention, nor were they unique to IHM novice mistresses. A perusal of the standard books in use in novitiates during this time period corroborate that "dying to one's own will"

9. According to Kelly (1948, 403), Bishop Caspar Borgess (Lefevere's successor) probably ended the practice whereby Joos gave the sisters' annual retreat. Xaveria McHugh, I.H.M., mentions that Joos's weekly conferences were "taken down when delivered" and as late as twenty-seven years after his death "are read to us during our annual reteat every summer vacation" (1928, 167–68). Borgess had attempted a revision of the Rule in 1876. He and Joos were at odds about the role of director, and it is clear that Borgess did not approve of the degree of authority that Joos held in the congregation. Nevertheless, it was Joos's version of the Constitutions (substantially the same as the 1861 version) that was submitted to Rome in 1885. For a history of the writing and revisions of the Rule, see [Kelly] 1948, 59, 403–8, 485–89, 560–63.

10. Mary Joseph Walker often referred to Joos as "our father." Jane Shea, I.H.M., recalls that in the early 1960s, when she was ill in the infirmary, an older sister would come to her door and say: "Take out your Sacred Heart badge; we're going to pray to our father to make you better. It's his anniversary" (conversation with author, 5 Aug. 1993). It is not possible to document the practices about the need to request permissions, but the "oral tradition" about the corset was mentioned by a number of sisters whom I interviewed, all of whom conveyed the attitude that such demands were felt to be an "imposition" and exceeded the bounds of authority held by an ecclesiastical director.

11. The 1902 directory for novices appears to be essentially the same as that written by Mother Mary Joseph Walker in the 1860s, with the addition of quotes and examples from St. Alphonsus. An appendix contains "Compendium of the Rules of Politeness" and "Extracts from the Conferences of Fr. Gillet and Msgr. Joos." It was approved by Bishop Samuel Foley in 1902.

was a hallmark of religious virtue and that mistresses were to instruct their charges accordingly.[12]

Under Joos and the novice mistresses he supervised, it might be expected that strict observance would be the theme of the IHM novitiate. In actuality, however, life as an IHM novice during Joos's directorship seems to have been rather homey and human. Only after Joos's death did the atmosphere become one charged with legalism and with concern for minutiae.

### Early IHM Novice Mistresses

In the earliest days of the congregation, the role of novice mistress and general superior had been combined, because the numbers were so small. In 1857, however, Maxis appointed Walker as the congregation's first separate novice mistress. Walker only had one novice and two postulants to mentor, and so she also took charge of the "boys school" (a classroom in the basement of the building attached to St. Mary's church). She was novice mistress for two years before she was appointed general superior by Lefevere as a consequence of Maxis's removal and exile.

In addition to Maxis (1845–57) and Walker (1857–59), nine other women served as mistress of novices during Joos's nineteenth-century directorship: Anthony Mohr (1859–61), Alphonsine Godfroy-Smyth (1861), Frances Renauld (1862), Xavier Eagan (1863), Theresa Persyn (1863–68, 1869–70), Clotilda Hoskyns (1868–69, 1879–85), Bridget Smith (1870–73), Genevieve Kelly (1873–74), and Justina Reilly (1874–79, 1885–94).[13]

Mohr (the former Margaret Mohr of Baltimore), who had received the habit in May 1858 and had pronounced her vows the following February, succeeded Walker as novice mistress a mere two months after her own profession. She was "dismiss[ed] from [her] office" because of "trying circumstances" after serving as novice mistress for only two years (MMC, [15] June 1861, MA). Two months later, on 7 August 1861, "discouraged and unhappy in her vocation . . . she left the community" (MMC, MA).[14]

---

12. See, for example, the three volumes of Rodriguez 1929.

13. Technically, Sister Leocadia Delanty was also novice mistress during the nineteenth century, given that she began her term in 1894. However, since the majority of her tenure was in the twentieth century, I have not included her here.

14. No information is available as to the "trying" circumstances surrounding Mohr's dismissal from office; not until the late 1960s would anyone entrusted with the formation of new members ever again leave the congregation. The mystery surrounding Mohr's departure from the congregation is exacerbated by a pencilled-in note made by archivist Rosalita Kelly on a listing she made of the congregational novice mistresses. After Anthony Mohr's name, Kelly indicated that she "left the congregation, advised to do so, more later *viva voce.*" (See "List of Mistresses of Novices from the Beginning to the Assignment of Sister Leocadia" (MA). Kelly died in 1964 and I could not find anyone who recalled her mentioning this story.

After Mohr's departure, Alphonsine Godfroy-Smyth, Frances Renauld, and Xavier Eagan each took a turn at exercising this office. Their brief terms of service were probably due both to the small number of Monroe novices at this time and to the pressing needs of the community's teaching missions.[15]

Theresa Persyn served as novice mistress for a total of six years. Aside from Maxis, Persyn was the oldest and the most experienced religious to have served in this capacity; she had transferred to the Monroe IHMs from Belgium, after spending almost twenty-four years as a Sister of Charity.[16] She served as novice mistress twice, under four general superiors, during an enormous growth period for the congregation.[17]

Clotilda Hoskyns was first appointed novice mistress in 1868. She had only been in this position a year when she was appointed to serve as general superior, following Mother Gertrude Gerretsen's resignation. After Justina Reilly was elected superior, Hoskyns returned to the novitiate for six years (1879–85). According to her biographer, Xaveria McHugh, Hoskyns lived up well to Joos's expectation that novice mistresses should be firm but kind. "[W]hen a young girl breaks home ties and tears herself away from all that is dearest in life and enters the novitiate," McHugh pointed out, "she is more in need of kind and loving sympathy, and tender guidance, than at any subsequent period of her religious career" (1928, 84). To illustrate Hoskyns' sensitivity to her

15. After fourteen months as novice mistress, Godfroy-Smyth (Mohr's successor) was appointed superior of St. Joseph's, the first mission in Detroit. Renauld replaced her but served only five months before being sent to Adrian to open a new mission. Eagan then filled the office, but only for four months, until she became assistant general superior. Kelly describes the novitiate of this period as "often with one postulant or novice and sometimes none"; by contrast, after only six months following the separation, the novitiate in Pennsylvania totalled 22 (1948, 241, 151).

16. Having always wanted to be a missionary, Persyn wrote to Lefevere in 1861 that she wanted to "work with the Indians." Lefevere forwarded her letter to Father Joos, who wrote her back a discouraging letter, telling her that because the country was at war, it was not a propitious time for her to come (not mentioning that "the Indians" no longer populated the banks of the River Raisin) and that he really had no use for her unless she could contribute to the teaching mission of the order. Undaunted, Persyn made contact with Joos's cousin in Louvain, Father John DeNève, who suggested that she take a teaching course at the St. André Normal School in Bruges while she awaited her dispensation papers. Persyn arrived in Michigan at the end of 1862, bringing with her the famous "St. André system," which would characterize the IHM approach to education well into the 1940s ([Kelly] 1948, 249–51). (For a history and description of this method, see [Kelly] 1948, 317–47.)

17. Persyn served under Walker, Eagan, Gertrude Gerretsen, and Hoskyns. During Gerretsen's administration, twelve postulants were admitted in 1865, fifteen in 1866, fourteen in 1867, and twelve in 1868. This is a great many, when one considers that in the four-year period from 1860 to 1864, thirteen postulants were admitted, all of whom left. In fact, Rev. John DeNève, Joos's cousin, actually chided Gerretsen for admitting too many postulants (JDeN to GG, 10 June 1866, MA).

charges' vulnerabilities, McHugh recorded an incident in which Hoskyns discovered a postulant having tea in the kitchen before setting out to deliver an important message as her mistress had bidden. Rather than chastising the girl for not obeying promptly, Hoskyns humorously turned the incident into a teaching moment for the whole novitiate, by teasing the sister about it at recreation that evening (1928, 88–89).

### Bridget Smith

Bridget Smith was mistress of novices from 1870 until 1873.[18] Born Mary Agatha Smith, she entered the IHMs in August 1862 at the age of fifteen, having graduated from the Mercy Sisters' St. Xavier's Academy in Chicago. After only two years in the congregation, she had to withdraw for a time because of poor health, but she returned to Monroe in 1864 and was again received as a novice.[19] Her profession took place in a private ceremony on October 13, 1864, five days before the congregation's general superior, Mary Joseph Walker, died. One of Walker's last acts was to name Smith mistress of the boarding school ([McHugh] 1928, 192).[20]

Smith seems to have had a mesmerizing effect on everyone she met —students, their relatives, priests, sisters, even complete strangers. There seems to be no doubt that Smith was captivatingly beautiful: "She was tall, slender, and exceedingly graceful. Her perfect poise and many graces of person, joined to a winning sweetness and gentleness of manner, would have made her an exceptionally beautiful woman; but when you add to all this the charm that intense holiness of life throws around and over nature's gifts, you have a beauty that is beyond the writer's power of description" ([McHugh] 1928, 199).[21] The following that Smith attracted

18. My information about Smith's life is drawn primarily from [Kelly] 1948 and [McHugh] 1928. Although McHugh knew Smith personally and spells her name "Brigid," I use Kelly's spelling, "Bridget," except when quoting from McHugh's book.

19. According to McHugh, "The novitiate in which Sister Brigid was trained was not a large one. There were not more than five members at any given time" (1928, 189).

20. According to Suzanne Fleming, I.H.M., the original handwritten biography of Walker located in the Monroe IHM archives almost certainly was written by Smith; see chap. 2 of the present volume.

21. How, or why, McHugh became Smith's biographer is intriguing. Enough references exist in [McHugh] 1928 to suggest that she herself was a pupil at the Academy when Smith was headmistress there. For example, she includes herself in an anecdote about senior Academy girls skeptically debating the merits of religious life: the "iciness in Sister's tone . . . told *us* that she had heard all" (1928, 206, emphasis added). Another story tells of Smith's powers of persuasion, which involved "bribing" a student to do something by promising to leave the student her crucifix when she died. It is clear that McHugh's knowledge is firsthand, because she was the girl in question: " 'O promise me, dear ———, and I'll will you this (her crucifix) when I die . . .' The girl mentioned above wears the 'blue habit' today; and the crucifix . . . a frequent reminder of one to whom she owes more than these pages can tell" (1928, 205–6).

among the students and even some of their relatives—some of whom insisted "[s]he . . . looks like the Blessed Virgin"—was almost cult-like ([McHugh] 1928, 200). However charismatic, though, her interactions with girls at the crossroads of adolescence were apparently marked by kindness and humor. According to McHugh, "Sister Brigid's way of dealing, even when serious faults were committed, left no bitterness rankling in the heart of the one corrected; but on the contrary, drew souls to God" (1928, 207).

Smith's own notes, however, made during the three years in which she served as novice mistress, provide the most solid testimony about her character. One of the most detailed but least known accounts of the IHM novitiate that survives, these notes also provide valuable evidence about the way new members were socialized into the community during its first twenty-five years of existence.

Indeed, compared to the strict rules that characterized the novitiate handbooks of the twentieth century, Bridget Smith's instructions for novice mistresses seem warm and practical. For example, she wrote that "mistresses may allow novices to go to town when necessary to make small purchases for the Novitiate or themselves with their own pocket money, to make presents to one another, or to others" (though she cautioned against the latter, adding, "discretion is to be used as it is rather to be avoided")(BS, IMN MS, MA). Novices could also

> take fruits from the garden or house, to eat on some very particular occasion . . . go to the Doctor's to consult him in regard to health . . . have his recipe filled and used provided they pay for it with their own money . . . write to their parents (and others when proper!) . . . see them in the parlor; the mistress may see them herself when necessary and permit the Novices to show them the house and have their meals prepared and served when it would look ill to do otherwise. (BS, IMN MS, MA)

The novice mistress may have been central to preserving the community ethos, but in Smith's estimation the heart of her task was the inculcation of a religious spirit of "generous heart and reasonable mind." With respect to the congregation's Rule or the laws of the church, Smith believed the novice mistress' main goal should be to prevent legalism. In handwritten instructions, she advised:

> Another thing to which she [the mistress] should pay persevering and earnest attention is the correction of the false and stiff notions many come with regarding the teachings of the Church and the practice of virtue. Narrow views and stiff notions in a religious who should properly have generous heart and reasonable mind, is a constant source of trouble to her superiors and more or less so to her companions. Their views of the H. Rule and observances are just as small as in regard to

other matters and even more so and they never seem to know at least in practice, that the Church has a *spirit* which can at all times be followed, even if her commands cannot, and that it is the same with each religious institution in the Church. It would be almost useless to tell such persons that the spirit of the rule must often guide them and even in some particular cases, actually take the place of the rule, but when a Mistress finds some one so inclined, she may be pretty sure that novice has more than an ordinary share of *self will and self love.*

She may be inclined to excuse the novice and say she is over exact and scrupulous, but in doing so she will only increase the burden of her superiors who will have to contend with it after that Srs profession and it is not common to correct things after profession that were neglected during the novitiate. (BS, IMN MS, MA)

Concerning the formation of new members, Smith made it clear that her counsel was not her own invention but was rooted in the "tradition" of the community:

It has always been the aim and advice of Superiors of this Community to avoid the two extremes in receiving candidates, whether for the veil or for profession; not to be too exacting and strict, and not to be too easy, and a Mistress would do well to consider from time to time what an important point this is for her. If she is too strict she may have to answer to God for many lost vocations, and much good that might be done, if these vocations were saved and developed by her. On the other hand, if she is too easy and is willing to have almost any one received she may have a terrible account to give of the relaxation or damage done the Community by such a course. It is therefore essential that a Mistress understands her Superiors' views on this subject and conforms herself to it in order to do the good that is to be done and to work with them for this end.[22] (BS, IMN MS, MA)

## Justina Reilly

Despite Smith's charismatic personality, it was Justina Reilly, appointed novice mistress in 1874, who was to have the more enduring impact on the congregation's formation practices.[23] Reilly directed the novices in two stints, for a total of fourteen years. Her spirituality emphasized religious life as a "battleground" and, correspondingly, religious formation as a kind of "basic training." Her instructions to novices epitomize this viewpoint: "The religious life is fundamentally a life thoroughly

22. In Joos's handwriting, the annotation to this document appears: "Sister Bridgitt's writing at my request." Kelly has crossed out the second "t" and added "Smith" to this notation.

23. Genevieve Kelly, who had been assistant to Hoskyns, replaced Bridget Smith shortly before the latter's death in 1873. She served as novice mistress for 21 months, until Reilly's appointment.

warlike. There is open war between grace and nature, the spirit and the flesh. In this warfare there is no truce nor rest and the soldier lays aside the sword only to receive the crown" (JRi, IN, MA). To emphasize her message, she wrote: "Do not think I am sitting here to pass the time away telling you that religious life is poetry. It is the roughest kind of prose" (as cited in [Kelly] 1948, 415).

Likewise, the view of religious obedience that Reilly taught her novices was thoroughly uncompromising and hierarchical: "Our superior holds the place of God in our regard. The will of our superior is the will of God. On receiving a command never reason about it no matter how imprudent the command may seem to you—Obey blindly you will not be held responsible for the consequences. Your place is to obey, not to decide whether a command be prudent or not, entertain a great respect for the person of your superior. When you meet her or are in her company, think she is an oracle of God for you." However, the book bearing Reilly's name also contains the following—perhaps a reminder to herself? —spelled out in capital letters: "BE MORE READY TO ENCOURAGE THAN TO REPROVE. BE MORE KIND THAN JUST" (JRi, IN, MA).[24]

## The Twentieth Century

### Leocadia Delanty

Reilly's views on the religious life were kept alive well into the twentieth century by Mother Leocadia Delanty, who based her instructions to novices heavily on those that Reilly had developed. Delanty held the position of novice mistress for forty-four years (1894–1938), longer than any other woman in the congregation; her assistant and successor, Sister Mary Hubert Manion, served in the office for eighteen years (1938–56). Together, for more than half a century, these two women placed a definite spiritual imprint upon the IHM community, one that departed considerably from the emphasis on the "spirit of the Rule" that the congregation had known under Smith and her predecessors. Literally hundreds of IHM sisters received their novitiate training under the direction of Delanty and Manion.[25]

24. Several books exist labeled "Mother Justina's Instructions." Many of the quotations found in these books appear to be passages quoted from books or retreat conferences which the novice mistress thought worthwhile matters for novitiate conferences. These instruction books were passed along from novice mistress to novice mistress without emendation. Thus Reilly's instructions may also have been used by Hoskyns and Delanty as well. We are grateful to former novice mistress, Margaret Brennan, for this insight.

25. In 1993 more than 600 of 833 IHMs had been novices under either Delanty or Manion. Likewise, Kelly observed at the time of the congregation's centennial in 1945 that "three fourths of the present congregation . . . were formed by her [Delanty] to the Immaculate Heart way of life" (1948, 744).

During Delanty's tenure as novice mistress, much of the novices' and postulants' instruction concerns manners and deportment:

> Do not act familiar with priests.
> Do not make faces.
> The chest, being the 'Zone of Honor' should be expanded and kept up, and regarded as the leading part of the body both in standing and sitting and walking.
> Acquire the beautiful habit of cleanliness at table, avoid having crumbs around your plate, also leave your plate as free from refuse as possible; pick bones clean. (LD, IN, MA).

She also instructed her turn-of-the-century postulants[26] and novices in "womanly" behavior:

> #11  Where is the power of a woman? In her quiet dignity and proper reserve.
> #12  What is said of quiet dignity? There is nothing finer[,] it seems to be the best quality of a woman, it teaches how to bow, how to smile, how to receive and dismiss friends.
> #13  Who is the most perfect mirror of womanly perfection? Our BLESSED MOTHER.
> #14  Na[m]e two things of which a true woman should not speak? Of her health nor how occupied her time is.
> #16  How is a foolish woman known? By her lightness of manner and the disposition she has of wishing to attract attention.
> #29  Give an example of showing difference of opinion without contradicting. Say "I was impressed otherwise." (LD, IN, MA)

During Delanty's time, it became customary for religious to prepare for profession of vows by memorizing portions of *Catechism of the Vows*, a compendium of questions and answers that had been translated from the French (Cotel 1893, 1925). Mary Daniel Turner, S.N.D.de.N., and Lora Ann Quiñonez, O.P., have observed that its pedagogy is based upon a view of knowledge as derived from assertions of fact, with little or no emphasis placed on experience:

> The catechism proceeded, topic by topic, to pose questions like "What is a vow?" "How do the vows of religion enable us to surmount the most serious obstacles to the love of God?" "What is perfection?" "What are the obligations of a Superior towards his [sic] inferiors in regard to

---

26. Postulants and novices were both officially under the care of the novice mistress until 1926, when Sister Vigilia Burns was named the first official mistress of postulants. Before this time, Sister Genovefa Guerin (assistant to Leocadia Delanty) and Sister Jane Frances Cleary had charge of the postulants.

poverty?" "Is a permission given by a Superior valid under his successor?" . . . Very succinct answers consisted of definitions, norms, lists of
obligations, and distinctions among degrees of culpability—all asserted
as *fact*. The questions had been formulated by others (chiefly ordained
males) and were designed to instruct the neophytes on topics the authors
considered important. The answers were standard and indisputable,
basically distillations of the church's law governing religious life.
(Quiñonez and Turner 1992, 33)

During the first half of the twentieth century, experience as a source of
knowledge about religious life and how it should be lived generally
received short shrift. The prevailing dualistic worldview, which diametrically opposed the sacred and the secular, placed emphasis on "received"
knowledge contained in formulas and prescriptions: "Existing theory was
there before new members arrived and would remain when they
moved on. It was applied deductively to concrete and everyday problems" (Quiñonez and Turner 1992, 33).

Still, in Delanty's novitiate, there are hints of a warm humanity.[27] She
wrote frequent, encouraging letters to her novices working in schools
away from Monroe. To a sister in 1903, she wrote: "My dear Sister Celesta,
How sorry I am to hear that you had your teeth extracted. Was there no
way of saving them? I have been slow in answering your letter but you
know how time is stolen away in the novitiate. Try not to have any more
out and if he is a *good* dentist then have whatever is necessary done,
but done well, for [there are] no teeth like your own" (LD to CD, 4 Apr.
1903, MA).

During her term of office, Delanty also allowed the novices to publish
an occasional newsletter, the novitiate *Echoes*, which was sent to the
sisters on mission away from Monroe. This gossipy rag told who was
sick and reported on various novitiate doings such as picnic suppers,
games of croquet (which Mother Leocadia often won), and "Simon
Says." Considering that the Novitiate Directory forbade sisters to "relate
the news of the day" and warned that "no extern when relating gossip,
town talk or worldly news of any kind should ever be able to say 'I heard
it at the Convent of the Sisters of the Immaculate Heart of Mary' " (ND,
1903, 79), the November 1928 issue could be considered quite daring.
It tells of a Halloween party at which costumed postulants told the novices that "a man had been murdered and they had to verify it." Blind-
folded novices were taken one by one to "the morgue," where, the *Echoes*
reports, they had arranged "skinned grapes for eyes, spagetti [sic] for
veins, soaked marshmallows for brains, a glove stuffed with ice and

27. See chap. 6 of the present volume, which also illustrates Delanty's concern for
personal relationships.

porridge for a hand, and a basin of thickened water for his blood" (Nov. 1928, 2, MA).

Another example of Delanty's empathy for her young charges is seen in the story one of her novices tells about being sent to teach in one of the Monroe parochial schools. One day, she was asked by the principal to move a statue of the Sacred Heart; while she was taking it through a doorway, she lopped off the little finger of one of its hands. When the principal saw this, she berated the sister for her lack of judgment and said that she certainly must not have a vocation. Instructed to bring the statue to Delanty and to inform her of her grave lack of judgment, the sister boarded the "little green gosling" (the novitiate bus) in tears, toting the statue and enduring the curious stares of her classmates (who, all being in silence, could not ask her what was wrong). When Delanty came to her office after dinner, she found the Sacred Heart and the novice waiting outside her door. "Come in, dear little sister, and put that statue on the desk. Now tell me what happened," coaxed Delanty. Weepily, the novice related all the details, including the principal's conclusion that she did not have a vocation. When she asked Delanty for a penance (as was required), the novice mistress said to her: "Just leave the statue by the door. You've had quite enough penance for today" (IHM sister [entrance 1932], interviewed by author, 27 July 1993).

### Mary Hubert Manion

By contrast, the record of the novitiate under Delanty's assistant, Mary Hubert Manion, is sparse. The archives contain no record of her instructions, but she is vividly remembered by those who spent time under her tutelage from 1938 until 1956. Two pictures emerge. One is of a staunch protector of the Rule, who took seriously her charge to test the vocation of the young sisters; the other is that of the first novice mistress with formal theological training, who was torn and anguished by the pressures put on her to supply qualified teachers for the many schools which the IHMs were opening.[28]

Images of Manion as a warm, caring person during her tenure as novice mistress are rare.[29] Understanding comes mostly from her cowork-

28. The first view was expressed to me by many sisters who had Manion as their novice mistress; the other is held by those who were her associates among the formation personnel. For the record, although Manion is remembered as having an advanced degree in theology, her transcript indicates that she took courses in philosophy for four summer sessions (1924–27) at the University of Notre Dame and earned a master of arts in the department of philosophy on 3 Aug. 1927 (MRO, MA).

29. Only one of the sisters that I interviewed from Manion's novitiate (entrance 1940) spoke enthusiastically about her: "The one thing I remember her teaching us is that love covers everything. That helped me in some tight spots. I loved Mary Hubert. I cried when I left the novitiate." Typical of most other novices was the sister (entrance 1947) who said:

ers. "I remember the advice she gave me when I was appointed mistress of postulants," said one. " 'Don't be afraid to put your arms around them,' she said. 'They come so darn young and in such crowds and go out too soon.' And those days we were told we couldn't touch each other, you know. Hubert was human" (RMcD, interviewed by author, 7 Feb. 1994).[30] Another said:

> I became her [Manion's] assistant in 1952. It was during those years that I came to know the person who anguished so deeply. . . . She served for many long years as the assistant to Mother Leocadia—and it was especially during the years when Mother Leocadia was very elderly that the burden of being the assistant weighed so heavily upon her. Her own intellectual acumen and the prevailing of "death to one's own will and desires" were the ambient of the tension under which she labored. Often during those years she confided to me the anguish of her conscience. Her own sense of "what should have been" against the prevailing understanding burdened her more than anyone could know. (MB to MK, 17 Dec. 1977, MA)

Manion's inability to integrate her own intellectual and emotional understanding with the ideals of spiritual formation at the time (a tension that some would say applies to Delanty in her later years as well)[31] captures the mindset that characterized religious life in the first half of the twentieth century. The prevailing thinking was that religious life was

> an enduring "essence," untouched by the passage of time . . . impervious to alterations in human arrangements. Canonical definitions . . . gave "religious life" its existence, its legitimacy, and its value. . . . One might chafe at restrictions, find them incomprehensible, even rebel against them. Ordinarily, however, such attitudes would have been judged a

---

"The novitiate [under Mary Hubert] was not particularly memorable for me. You were always asking permission for things. I suppose that was to teach you something. But sometimes, it was like a threat. Denying permissions was used as a punishment, but mainly the atmosphere was threatening, like 'what makes you think you're going to be professed?' You lived in fear of being sent home."

30. The injunction against the sisters touching one another stated: "The Sisters should refrain from all effeminacy such as holding hands, locking arms, in fact touching or fondling one another in any way, as those things are not in keeping with a true religious spirit" (GLS, 25 Oct. 1922, 13, MA).

31. According to a sister who was a novice under Delanty, the atmosphere of the novitiate then was definitely "anti-intellectual": "Reading books were locked up. You were never supposed to express your opinion. It was particularly difficult for older novices. I remember Stella Law, she was a music teacher; how hard she found it. On the wall was painted 'Obedience is better than sacrifice.' It wasn't until I got out and read Tanquery that I learned that charity, not obedience, was the highest virtue" (IHM sister [entrance 1932], interviewed by author, 30 June 1993).

problem of the rebel (who was said to "lack a vocation"), or of the
community (which had grown lax), or of temptations against one's vocation (the work of the evil spirit). (Quiñonez and Turner 1992, 36)

However, the 1950s already harbored the winds of transformation
that would bring sweeping changes to religious life—and thus to novitiate socialization. Pope Pius XII's instructions to apostolic congregations
of sisters and the beginnings of the ferment that would blossom into
Vatican II planted seeds that would question the conceptualization of
religious life promoted in the Delanty and Manion eras.[32] Already in the
1940s, IHM novices under Manion's direction used Latin/English missals
at Mass; for one novice, who said she didn't realize it at the time, the
missals were a saving grace.[33]

### Beyond Mentors: Formation Through Clothing

Pre–Vatican II spirituality stressed that religious were to be considered "spouses of Christ." For a time, IHM reception ceremonies symbol-
ized this by having those receiving the habit enter the chapel wearing
bridal gowns and white shoes.[34] During the ceremony, the postulants so
garbed would disappear to a room below the chapel, where they were
helped to dress in the habit by a professed sister who had some tie to
the new novice. Sometimes, this was the moment when they would also
have their hair cut; in later years, especially with the larger reception
classes, hair would be cut a few days afterwards. Although many sisters
report that having their hair cut was just "something one did" or that "it
went with the territory," some sisters have traumatic memories of this
event:

32. The 15 Sept. 1951 allocution of Pius XII to teaching sisters, stressing the need of
adaptation of customs and forms that hindered their service, and the epochal national and
international congresses of major superiors held in the U.S. and in Rome during 1950–52
are discussed in detail in Meyers 1965, 45–84. See also the discussion of the role of Pius XII
in chap. 11 of the present volume. The liturgical movement (which had actually begun in
the 1920s) and the Sister Formation Movement also did much to catalyze this change. A
brief but good overview of the liturgical movement can be found in Chinnici 1989, 177–85;
on the Sister Formation Movement, see Beane 1993 and chap. 11 of the present volume.
33. This sister, now in her 60s, confided: "To my idea, the novitiate was a boot camp.
The main goal was to keep out of trouble. Spiritual books were limited to [Rodriguez's]
*Christian Perfection.* You had to have permission to read anything else. We didn't even have
a Bible. Luckily, we had the missal. I used to read it for the scripture. I think it was my
saving grace" (IHM sister [entrance 1947], interviewed by author, 7 May 1994). IHMs had
introduced the *Missa recitata* at Marygrove in 1927. Although the sister I interviewed could
not remember the name of the missal she used, it was probably the 1954 edition of the *Saint
Andrew Daily Missal,* compiled by Dom Gasper Lefebvre. For a review of other innovative
liturgical practices adopted by IHMs during this period, see [Kelly] 1960.
34. This practice was discontinued in 1956 when reception classes began wearing their
postulant garb to the ceremony.

A day or so later, we were informed that there were haircuts being given at a certain time in one of the cells on the novitiate floor. The senior novices were giving haircuts. You thought, haircut—short, maybe like a boy's. That's what I thought, anyway. The door opened and I saw Doreen Lynch, who had beautiful reddish blonde hair and gorgeous skin and a beautiful face, and the razor was going up her head, taking her hair off! It was like I was sort of in shock. I did not want to touch my head. I didn't want to wash my head or touch my head. It got to the point where I knew my head was scaly, but I could not bring myself to touch it. I could see the outline of my head's shadow reflected on the tubroom wall. I thought I looked like someone right out of Auschwitz. There was no preparation for it. No theology for it. It was just cold turkey.[35] (former IHM [entrance 1954], interviewed by author, 3 July 1993)

To the prospective IHM, the most tangible indication that she was entering another world was the list of clothing and other necessities that she was required to provide for the period of postulancy and novitiate. Rooted in practical need, clothing requirements ensured sartorial uniformity.[36] However, like the haircuts, they also were designed to extend the formative power of the religious community to one's body and to make it more likely that one would take on ways of thinking and acting that were consonant with one's new status.[37] One of the earliest lists, dating back to the 1860s[38] and in general superior Walker's handwriting, requested the following:

35. Haircuts were also symbolic of the status of one's vocational discernment and of one's piety. According to this former novice, "You didn't go on your own to get your haircut. People who might be going home were told not to get their haircut." In the 1960s, one had to have permission for a haircut; still, it was considered "virtuous" to ask for a short haircut, which could be taken as an indicator of one's intention to persevere.

36. This practice can be traced back to the late 1860s, when the IHM congregation was a mere twenty-five years old. The Civil War and the 1859 separation of the IHM congregation in Michigan from that in Pennsylvania had left the Monroe IHMs quite impoverished. This situation, together with an influx of 80 new postulants between 1860 and 1870 (not all of whom stayed), probably motivated the sisters to compose a list of "required items" for candidates who desired to enter the congregation as a means of holding down costs. Kelly attributes the increase of candidates to the great wave of Catholic immigrants to the U.S. between 1830 and 1850 (1948, 247–48).

37. Michel Foucault regards religious orders as the "masters of discipline" and as "the great technicians of rhythm and regular activities," and sees them as responsible for developing the major discourse on the body in Western culture (1977, 150, 135–69). Using Foucault's analysis, Curran (1989, 125–28) argues that the ascetical practices of pre–Vatican II religious women (particularly those associated with postures and with food) aimed at the production of docile bodies; this is a strategy, she notes, also used by the military. I find Foucault's and Curran's insights relevant to my discussion here in that they recognize that seemingly trivial bodily actions (including dress) serve to subordinate the individual to the values of the institution in the name of self-mastery.

38. The dating of this list to the 1860s is based upon a handwritten notation made by Kelly, who observed that "black quilted skirts and shawls date back to that period."

Dower ($100.00)
Expenses of reception to the Holy Habit ($50.00, besides pocket money)

*List of Clothes*
4 dresses, two of which are to be of black material
1 bolt of unbleached cotton
10 yards of *white* cotton flannel
12 towels
24 handkerchiefs
2 black quilted skirts
6 pairs of shoes
1 pair of rubbers
6 pairs of woolen stockings
6 pairs of cotton stockings
1 toilet and work box, furnished
1 shawl for winter use
Besides these articles, please bring all your clothes that you now have
    on hand.

*Bedding*
1 feather pillow
2 comforters
2 quilts
1 blanket
6 sheets
6 pillow cases
8 yards of ticking (unmade). (Cloth. L, MA)

In the formation records of the IHM archive, one finds comparable lists from the Sisters of the Good Shepherd (St. Louis, Missouri), the Sisters of St. Joseph (Nazareth, Michigan), and the Sisters of Charity (Cincinnati, Ohio), which bear the notation "borrowed from," indicating that the IHM list was probably based in part on these lists.[39] The IHM list, however, showed a greater simplicity, if not starkness, with both a smaller dowry and smaller quantities of certain items being required.[40]

    39. The IHM habit was designed in a similar manner of consultation ([Kelly] 1948, 59–62). This practice of informal (and later, formal) networking among women religious continues in the present in matters of formation, governance, and strategies for dealing with church authorities (see Quiñonez and Turner 1992).
    40. For example, the IHM list asks for six pillow cases while the Good Shepherd list asks for a dozen (in addition to twenty yards of pillow case linen); the IHM list does not mention "nightgowns," but only "one bolt of unbleached cotton," while the Good Shepherd list asks for a dozen long nightgowns and the St. Joseph Sisters require "four light calico night dresses." Most noticeable, however, is the difference in the dowry figure: the Good Shepherd Sisters ask for "a dowry of $500 to $5,000 at profession" (in addition to $200 for "expenses of Novitiate"). Apart from the mention of the $100 dower listed by Mother Mary

The IHM list makes no mention of "linen," "silver forks and spoons," "white stone china," or "ten yards of red flannel," all of which appear on the other lists. Perhaps the IHMs' aim was more in keeping with the notation that appears on the St. Joseph sisters' list: "Let it be understood that when there is a question of a vocation, inability to procure articles required, is not a sufficient raison [sic] to neglect corresponding to God's grace. In such a case, write plainly to the Superioress, and in no instance will a worthy subject be rejected on account of poverty" (LP, SSJ, n.d., MA).

Fifty years later, in 1948, when the congregation could be regarded as definitely established, the entrance list had been shortened considerably. Ready-made clothing had become more acceptable, cutting down on the need for so many raw goods. The IHM Customs of the Congregation from this period required that postulants come with the following articles:

> Two regulation uniforms—$30.00, three black ties, three black silk or rayon slips, four sets of underclothing, three nightgowns—long sleeves, three aprons, four towels and four washcloths (large size), necessary toilet articles, one dozen large handkerchiefs, two pair oxfords (military or cuban heel), one pair rubbers, three girdles, four brassieres, four pair black lisle stockings, one bathrobe, one pair bedroom slippers, one laundry bag, one black umbrella, one black suitcase of medium size, furnishings for sewing box, and one woolen blanket. They shall also bring a *Daily Missal, Webster's Collegiate Dictionary,* Baptismal Certificate, Confirmation Certificate, and a letter of recommendation from the pastor. (CC 1948, appendix, 5–6, MA)

By the 1960s, convent clothing had become somewhat standardized, with companies such as Jameson's of Chicago specializing in manufacturing the specific items required by many orders. The IHM postulant outfit of skirt, blouse, and cape was ordered from the Daisy Lee uniform company in Detroit, which also supplied parochial school clothing. Certain unique items (i.e., veils of blue faille, black crepe bows, and blue-checked aprons with extra large hems that could be let down when the postulant received the habit) were made in the convent clothes room or by sisters assigned to the schools from which the candidates entered. In addition, a postulant had to make various items of religious dress that she would wear as a novice (i.e., pockets, black slips).

Changes were made in the early 1960s that allowed novices and postulants to wear "worldly" underwear, as the sisters gave up "waists" for brassieres and "chemises" were replaced by white tee shirts.[41] They

---

Joseph, and $50 for novitiate expenses, the IHMs do not seem to have required a dowry after the 1860s.

41. A waist was a tight-fitting vest made out of muslin (flour sack material), which buttoned down the front; it was worn over a chemise, which was made out of the same

could also wear panty girdles and garter belts to hold up their black cotton stockings.[42] However, maxims such as Thomas à Kempis's "the religious habit does not make the religious" were still invoked, and the young sisters were cautioned against vain practices.[43] Ironically, one could argue that despite such admonitions, a great deal of time was spent in caring for one's appearance. The sewing, mending, cleaning, and pinning together of one's wearing apparel—though it could be gotten down to a system and was done at regular intervals—actually consumed a great deal of time. At the same time, interviews with sisters who were in formation during the 1940s and 1950s suggest that these occupations afforded the young women with outlets for relieving the monotony and homogeneity imposed by uniformity of dress.

### Redefining Beauty

A former IHM who was a novice in the 1950s recalled:

In the novitiate we redefined what counted as beauty, or looking good and feeling good about yourself as a woman. The standard became a

---

material. According to the sisters that I interviewed, there was some difference of opinion concerning whether one wore bras under or over the chemise. Novices were allowed (in view of poverty) to wear the brassieres they brought as postulants until they wore out (in some cases, they were practically in shreds when they were discarded). The nightwear of IHM novices was often the source of some amusement for the new postulants. The sisters wore no bathrobes, but over their flour sack nightgowns, they wore the black petticoat and a shawl. A special white cotton night cap replaced the day cap that was worn under the veiled bonnet. A new postulant who ran into a novice so attired on her way to hang up stockings to dry in the attic was often overcome by laughter—and thus, incurred guilt for breaking solemn silence.

42. As mentioned earlier the 1948 Customs of the Congregation (art. 9) had prescribed a clothing allowance that applied to all sisters: "one cloak with winter cape; two habits and scapulars, a third one of each may be retained if it is fit to wear, two pair of sleeves may be given with each habit; two veils; one girdle (belt); two capes; six bonnets, including those well worn; four neck bands; twelve linen handkerchiefs and a number of cotton ones; four chemises; four pair of drawers and two sets of winter undergarments; three waists, three aprons, including an old one; four day-caps and four night-caps; two night-dresses; five skirts; viz., two flannel if needed, and two wash skirts; three pair of hose; one good corset and an old one; two pair of shoes and one pair of rubbers; one pair of elastic garters. Also the needed number of toilet napkins and washcloths."

43. Thomas à Kempis's classic The Imitation of Christ (1585) was often read during the sisters' silent breakfasts. One of the innovations that novice mistress Alphonsine (Helene) Barry brought to the novitiate in 1956 was that she gave every novice a mirror. Up to that point, sisters were forbidden to look at themselves in mirrors; my interviews uncovered great ingenuity on the part of the earlier sisters, who grew quite adept at checking their appearance while dusting glass-encased bookshelves or by surreptitiously using the glass panes in the chapel doors or even the light switches! (IHM sisters [entrance 1943, 1947, 1950], interviewed by author, 18 Apr. and 7 May 1994).

clean-shaven head and a clean band.[44] We washed out our band every night and plastered it to the wall to dry. So every morning, we peeled it off, like velcro. Since the habit was not washed, except in the Christmas vacation and one other time, you cleaned it by taking the hem out, also taking off the fringe which guarded it from scraping on the ground and fraying. We undid the hems of our sleeves also. The schedule of our lives never provided a time to wash the habit and dry it (it was wool, it took time), so you took it apart, pressed the entire thing, and sewed it up again. Looking beautiful for Easter or Christmas was having a habit in which the hems had been completely pressed out and turned up and sewed neatly, but it wasn't pressed down. To have sleeves which were puffy at the bottom became a sign of beauty. (former IHM [entrance 1954], interviewed by author, 3 July 1993)

Other sisters recall that having puffy hems was simply a way to practice poverty and that they were encouraged not to iron creases in hems or cuffs in order to prevent the garments from wearing out.[45]

The practice of altering the habit in small ways seems not to have been confined to the novitiate, judging by the mention of certain practices in the written instructions for the superiors of the professed sisters. The Guides for Local Superiors (1922–45), for example, listed restrictions concerning sisters' dress, admonishing "no linings with V-necks" (7, MA),[46] Nor should bonnet boards "be rounded, nor should the veil be joined in the back without permission. Neither veil or cloak bonnet may have extra pins on the outside, nor the band, for the purpose of being smoother be pinned at the side" (11, MA).

Novices wore white veils, and having a clean veil was prized:

[In the fifties] you had an elastic which attached in two places, to hold your veil off the shoulders, so to have a clean veil that flowed gracefully over your shoulders was preferred. And the bonnet—not a brand new one—because the cardboard made it stick out from your face and you couldn't pin it tight enough. But when it got molded to your head, when it was really tight, that was looking really good! It should come out a little beyond your glasses if you wore them. To have it back was not beautiful; to have it forward so it framed your face, that was great. You also tried to preserve your veil from getting creased. You flipped the veil back over the chair so you wouldn't sit against it. If your band went up

44. A "band" was a strip of white linen with draw strings around the top. It was folded, wrapped around the head, drawn together with the strings, and pinned in the back. The linen-covered cardboard bonnet (with veil attached) was then anchored to the band with pins.

45. This response, which I received from two sisters who had entered in the 1930s and 1940s, indicates that such a practice had obviously become charged with new meaning in the 1950s.

46. A lining was worn between the habit and the underclothing.

high so a widow's peak would show, or if you went for a while without getting a hair cut and a hair would straggle out, this was bad. (former IHM [entrance 1954], interviewed by author, 3 July 1993)

To have their scapulars pressed, to have their crucifixes and miraculous medals shined, was the height of fashion, for which all self-respecting IHMs aimed.[47] A sister who was a novice in the 1940s remembers another novice running toward her on a recreation day, gleefully waving two pieces of cardboard: "Look what I found—perfect for a veil board!" (IHM sister [entrance 1945], interviewed by author, 5 Aug. 1993). Folding one's veil, then placing it between two pieces of cardboard and tucking it under one's mattress, was another "beauty trick."

Once a sister's postulant bras wore out she had to make a vest, or "waist." According to the testimony of sisters who wore them, one was most comfortable wearing the chemise first, then the vest, with buttons all the way down. Apparently, some newly professed sisters decided to experiment with a new trend with regard to the waist and began making (and wearing) them so they would button down the back. "It became the subject of one of Mother Ruth [Hankerd]'s readings at the Hall," recalled one sister ([entrance 1940], personal communication to author).

By means of constant performance, certain gestures (i.e., the flipping-out of the scapular before prostration, the flipping of the veil over the back of a chair) became ritualized—and a recognized art form. The custom of "pinning up" before doing the dishes or one's household charge was one such gesture. The goal was to accomplish the operation in one move: first, the sister rolled up her outside sleeves (the inner sleeves, or "blues," could be pushed up but not removed, except for the most messy jobs), then she would take the hat pin that each sister kept pinned under the flexaline cape and put it between her teeth, while raising her knee in order to put the hem of the habit within reach; next she would take the hem and scapular together and fold it, drawing it tightly around her waist. The pin was used to fasten the two sides of the thick hem together. Pinning-up quickly and gracefully was the mark of an accomplished IHM.

## Scheduling Uniformity

A novice's life was also rigorously scheduled. Both a rationale for and a description of this regimen appeared in the 1902 Novitiate Directory:

47. IHM sisters wore the miraculous medal instead of a cross at the end of a fifteen-decade rosary that hung from their belt. The miraculous medal devotion stems from the 1830 apparition of the Virgin Mary to St. Catherine Labouré. According to Ann Taves, "On one side, the medal depicted the Virgin standing on a globe, crushing a serpent beneath her foot. Rays of light emanated from her outstretched hands. The words, 'O Mary, conceived

As good order is the life of a well regulated Institute, the Sisters shall make it their duty to observe most strictly the following regulations: They shall rise in the morning at the first sound of the bell, without in the least giving way to sloth, thinking that it is God Himself who calls them; Entertaining themselves with holy thoughts, they shall dress with the greatest modesty;
Afterwards, make the sign of the cross, and recite the usual morning prayers, offering to God all the actions of the day;
Then, prostrate they shall say three Aves and ask her blessing while in spirit kissing her hand;
And having kissed the floor, before and after the three Aves, they shall kneel and with arms extended, say one Pater and Ave in honor of their yearly Patron.
Assemble in chapel for meditation
Assist at Holy Mass with great devotion and recollection
Breakfast
Manual work/study until 11:45
Particular examen (the subject of which the Sister should recall before leaving her cell)
12:00 (in silence) go to dinner
Te Deum in Chapel after dinner
After chapel, repair to refectory, kitchen, or other departments for charges.
After these charges, recreation.
Study/manual labor from 1:30–3:00
3:00 Spiritual reading (from a book selected by the Mistress)
3:30 1/3 of the rosary (On Sundays and Thursdays it may be said privately during free time)
4:00 Free time
4:30 Visit to the Blessed Sacrament and the BVM
5:00 Study or Instructions
6:00 Supper, followed by recreation
8:00 Silence, except on Sundays and Thursdays (may be spent before the Blessed Sacrament, in writing instructions received, or in studying the prayers or the Catechism of the Vows)
8:30 Night prayers
9:30 Last signal shall be given, when all unnecessary lights shall be extinguished and each Sister is strictly commanded to be in bed. (ND, 1902, chapter 4, MA)

As with the code of dress, the young sisters often came up with ingenious ways to mitigate the strictly scheduled program. For example,

---

without sin, pray for us who have recourse to thee' were inscribed around the figure. The other side depicted the hearts of Jesus and Mary, the one crowned with thorns, the other pierced with a sword. The first medals were struck in 1832 . . . and approved by the pope in 1942" (Taves 1986, 37). See also Powers-Waters 1962. Catherine (1806–1876) was a Daughter of Charity, the female congregation founded by St. Vincent de Paul in France.

in some novitiate classes during the 1950s, a subtle vying went on for being the first person to arrive in the chapel in the morning. The first novices to arrive before morning meditation would go up to the front before the statue of Mary and lay prostrate to pray. As one woman remembered,

> When you would get there, you would kneel down and flip your scapular out in front of you—that was a very important gesture, flipping out that scapular in front of you—and prostrate yourself. In order to be there first, you had to have your dressing down to a system, lay out the clothes and so forth. This was not so much a matter of competing in virtue, as it was a way of giving yourself time which wasn't prescheduled. You could get fifteen free minutes this way. (former IHM [entrance 1954], interviewed by author, 3 July 1993)

### Celebrating Individuality Through Chores

Novitiate chores (called by IHMs "charges") were another sphere through which individuality could be celebrated. Although the Novitiate Directory, like the IHM Constitutions, consistently exhorted the novice to the practice of humility and self-denial, there were certain assigned duties in the novitiate that carried more status than others. Anything to do with the chapel, for example, was considered more important and a privilege. "Mother's bundle" also accorded a certain prestige, though it was understood that it went to those more proficient in sewing: a novice who had this charge attended to the novice mistress' minor mending or reironed items that came back from the convent laundry crudely pressed or starched.

The worst charges were washing the dishes in the infirmary or in the "fourth section," where the youngest boarders at the academy ate. "They could really do a job on the mustard containers," recalls one sister (IHM sister [entrance 1943], interviewed by author, 7 May 1994). Some of the more prosaic novitiate duties—such as folding towels, making beds at the Hall, or serving meals to the sisters and the academy boarders—befell everyone at one time or another. Although the chapel and "Mother's bundle" might be the lot of a privileged few, no one was exempt from having a turn at what was perhaps considered the most distasteful job: collecting the bag of used sanitary towels from the lavatories.[48] Though such a chore was a rather obvious necessity where so many women of child-bearing age were congregated, this responsibility was carried out

---

48. Although by today's standards the sisters' sanitary choices would be considered both medically sound and ecologically correct, it was the spirit of poverty that prescribed the continued use of sanitary towels when these were no longer in vogue among post–World War II women in the U.S. Paper sanitary products were not adopted at the mother-house until 1967.

with such utter discretion that it could only be done at a certain time (during noon dishes) and a prescribed route was to be followed.

Despite the hard work that was part of novitiate life, many sisters still remember postulant and novitiate charges positively. A former IHM sister who entered in 1954 recalled: "You received a sense of accomplishment if you could learn the drill. It was like learning a trade—learning how to buff the floors, the scrubbing bees. You never ate between meals, but on scrub days you could" (interviewed by author, 3 July 1993). A sister who entered in 1943 said: "My favorite charge was painting. I don't know how I got to do it, but I used to like the fact that when I came into chapel for visit [to the Blessed Sacrament] the whole pew would know what I had been doing from getting a whiff of the fumes" (interviewed by author, 7 May 1993).

### Choosing the Right Candidates for the IHM Life

From its very beginnings, the IHM congregation required candidates who desired to enter the community to fill out an application form. Initially these forms, like the clothing lists, were patterned on those used by other religious congregations. The questions they contained shed light on the kind of woman for which the IHMs were looking.[49] Among the "vital statistics" requested were whether the candidate was free from debt and hereditary disease and whether she was "necessary to one's parents." Compared to those on the borrowed application forms, the IHM entrant questionnaire put more emphasis on psychological health and intellectual ability. For example, the candidate was asked: "Are you of a lively or a quiet disposition? Are you subject to any innate fault; such as, violent anger, melancholy, or strong attachments? Is there any special disease hereditary in your family or relationship, such as, insanity, epilepsy, hysteria, cancer, consumption? What was the last grade you completed at school?" These questions are not surprising for a congregation whose apostolic work was the Christian education of youth; furthermore, they are indicative of the high priority that the congregation gave to education, something not mentioned on any of the questionnaires that were used as models.[50]

49. Application forms from the Sisters of the Good Shepherd (St. Louis), the Sisters of the Holy Cross (Notre Dame, Ind.), the Sisters of Charity (Cincinnati), and the Sisters of St. Joseph (Nazareth, Mich.) were used in developing the IHM form (AF, MA).

50. It is interesting that the following questions are omitted from the IHM questionnaire:

Can you bring an outfit of clothes sufficient for the period of your Novitiate?
What are your means?
Should you at any time leave or be dismissed will you be satisfied to receive such of your effects [that] are not lost and money that remain[s] over and above your expenses while in the House?

An 1865 directory for novices, used by the IHM congregation in Scranton, Pennsylvania, and purported to have been written by general superior Maxis, has a similar list of questions:

> When a subject desires to be admitted to the Order, inquiry is usually made on the following subjects:
> 1. What is her motive for seeking to enter religion? Why does she suppose her vocation is for this Order?
> 2. Whether she is liable to any suit-at-law, on account of promise of marriage—as executrise—trustee—or some other title?
> 3. Whether she is guardian to a minor?
> 4. Whether any reports have been current to the disgrace of herself, or any member of her immediate family?
> 5. Whether she at any time conformed to a heretical worship?
> 6. Whether she was born in lawful wedlock?
> 7. Whether she has any property?
> 8. What is the nature of the property? How is it secured?
> 9. Whether there is any disease hereditary in her family?
> 10. Whether she or any of her family was ever afflicted with insanity?
> 11. Whether she is subject to any infectious or severe chronic distemper?
> 12. Whether there is any member of her family to whom she owes such duty, as to be left without means of support, by her embracing a religious life?
> 13. Whether she has been in religious life before?
> 14. Whether she has been scrupulous?
> 15. Whether she makes meditation?
> 16. What are her practices of piety?
> 17. Whether she constantly restricts herself to one Confessor?"[51]
> (SA)

---

> Do you find yourself never to claim any salary or remuneration whatever, for labor or services while in the Community? (AF of/CSC, CSCA, copy in MA)

Throughout its history, the IHMs never required repayment of educational, medical, or other expenses incurred during formation, although in the twentieth century it is clear that such remuneration was welcomed. From at least the 1920s, however, candidates signed statements assuring they were debt free and that they would exact no payment for services rendered should they leave the congregation.

51. This document, in Maxis's handwriting, bears Sister Genevieve Morrissey's name on the flyleaf. Morrissey had been received into the Pennsylvania congregation in 1860 at old St. Joseph's, Susquehanna, where she came to know Mother Theresa very well (Gannon 1992, 99–160). She became Sister Assistant to Sister Mary Frances Henry, the second superior at Scranton, in Aug. 1877. Because Maxis did not leave for Ottawa until 1867, the document was probably written by her while she still was in Pennsylvania. It is not known whether these rules were observed in Monroe. Certain conventions, such as instituting a novitiate in any branch house where there were at least five novices and various kinds of "capitular assemblies," were practices that the Monroe community did not follow. Monroe

In this document, considerably more latitude is given to the general superior to interpret the answers to these questions than the Monroe document allowed. Maxis's notes say that "affirmation in the case of No. 10 or No. 2 would be a necessary cause of exclusion, as it would be in No. 12 if the person or dependent were a parent. In No. 3 the office of guardian would be an obstacle, but it is one from which the subject may free herself. Nos. 5, 13, or 14, if answered in the affirmative would demand much consideration from the mother superior, as would No. 6 in the case of a negative" (SA).

An examination of the injunctions concerning admission of candidates to the novitiate given in the 1948 Monroe book of customs indicates that in ninety years not much had changed concerning the candidate questionnaire:

> The applicant for admission to the Novitiate must have led an exemplary life and be of a reputable family.
> As one of the principal objects of the Institute is the education of youth, it is necessary that the young lady, if she has not the ability to teach, should at least have the capacity to learn or to fulfill well other duties of the Congregation.
> Inquiries are usually made as follows: What is her motive in seeking to enter religion, and why has she chosen this Congregation? What is her name, age, place of birth, and the name of her parents? Whether her parents are living? What is her occupation and education? What are her financial circumstances? What is the state of her health? Whether the family is free from insanity or other hereditary disease? Whether she has been in religious life before? Whether she is free from indebtedness or other obligation?
> A testimonial to her character and morals is to be obtained from her pastor or some other priest. (CC, 1948, appendix, 5–6)

The admission standards found in the IHM Constitutions reflect the canonical stipulations of the 1917 Code of Canon Law. Novices had to be at least sixteen years of age, and "only in an exceptional case, sanctioned by the Council, may one who has completed her twenty-eighth year be received." She had to have sufficient education or aptitude to "make herself useful" and be of legitimate birth, of sound body and mind, and free from hereditary disease or "remarkable natural deformity" (Const. 1920, art. 15). She had to present baptism and confirmation certificates, and "accurate inquiries [must] have been made beforehand about her

---

had one central novitiate, and the tasks of the capitular assemblies (such as consultations concerning candidates, admitting postulants to reception, novices to vows, and reviewing the household accounts) were handled by the General Council. The "chapter of faults," however, was observed in Monroe.

disposition and the correctness of her morals" (1920, art. 16). Candidates who had been vowed members of other religious orders needed a certificate from the superior of that institute with the knowledge of the bishop in whose diocese she was located. Those who had been in novitiates or postulancies of other communities also needed to be recommended by "one of the major Superiors of that Institute" (1920, art. 16).

Distinctions between "invalid" and "illicit" admissions also reflected the legal concerns of canon law.[52] Those considered to have been received invalidly were converts to non-Catholic sects; those under the age of sixteen; those compelled to enter by force, by deception, or through grave fear (or, if the superior was induced to receive them in this manner); those who were legally married; those under vows in other congregations; those who were guilty or may in the future be accused of a grave crime (Const. 1920, art. 19). In contrast, illicit admission was incurred in the following cases: those burdened with debts that they were unable to discharge; those engaged in secular affairs for which they had to render an account, and from which the congregation may have had reason to fear trouble or embarrassment; daughters who had to support their parents or grandparents, and mothers whose presence was necessary to their children (Const. 1920, art. 20).

One of the greatest membership increases in IHM history occurred during the 1950s and 1960s.[53] Although none of the canonical entrance requirements were abrogated, congregational leaders at this time placed greater emphasis on personality traits. In a 1955 letter sent to sisters writing recommendations for candidates about to enter the postulancy, the following unsigned paragraph appears: "Is she socially acceptable? If she is a 'queer' no matter how she measures up in other ways do not hesitate to say so. Many times anti-social girls look forward to convent life as the answer to their problem, and find it only intensified by constant association with the same group. Often these girls are the last to leave" (MA).[54] In the confidential report that referees were to submit, respondents were asked to rate the candidate in terms of thirty-eight descriptive characteristics. There were no written instructions given as how to use

---

52. The distinction between invalid and illicit is a technical canonical distinction; invalid admission meant a person could never be considered a sister, but an illicit admission could be corrected.

53. This was true of nearly all religious communities in the U.S. following World War II (Ewens 1989, 39).

54. It is difficult to determine what the writer might have had in mind by the use of the word "queer." Though the word is often used as a slang word for "homosexual," Ruth McDonell, I.H.M., who served as mistress of postulants during that time, insists that "homosexuality was not the issue here. The word 'lesbian,' for instance, was never uttered. I think the word here refers more to a 'social misfit.'" (RMcD, interviewed by author, 9 Feb. 1994).

these labels, but apparently those that applied to the candidate under consideration were meant to be circled: "worrisome, diligent, childish, sincere, vain, scrupulous, love of ease, cooperative, persevering, perfectionist, stubborn, eccentric, selfish, tactful, resentful, moody, 'good mixer,' daydreamer, industrious, respectful, impetuous, boastful, 'breezy,' 'griper,' generous, show-off, dependable, suspicious, 'hotheaded,' critical, cheerful, sensitive, fearful, self-opinionated, quarrelsome, emotional, anti-social, prone to alibi" (Con. Rep., MA).

Given the expectations of religious life during this period, it seems fair to conclude that the most fitting candidates were those who would be able to keep the IHM Rule with its emphasis on self-abnegation, poverty, humility, and zeal.[55] Still, as one sister commented in an interview, "I had no idea that the spirit of the congregation was 'self-abnegation and love of the cross' before entering. My first inkling of it was when Sister Mary David [Moore] told me at breakfast, 'Little sister, *IHMs* do not put butter and jelly on their crackers!' " (IHM sister [entrance 1943], interviewed by author, 8 May 1993).

## Conclusion

When juxtaposed to the long novitiate reigns of Leocadia Delanty and Mary Hubert Manion, the nineteenth-century IHM novitiate under Bridget Smith appears to have been much freer. Perhaps the smaller numbers and the poorer religious preparation of candidates encouraged a more "maternal" atmosphere in the novitiate. Even though other nineteenth-century novitiate mentors, such as Mary Joseph Walker and Justina Reilly, seem to have pushed for "strict observance" in their official instructions, their writings evidence a more compassionate understanding of the young candidates. Walker's letters reflect a great concern for the religious education and for the developing spirituality of the young sisters on mission;[56] Reilly's instructions indicate that she, too, spent a great deal of her time teaching the novices basic catechism. Practically

55. A sampling from the 1955 Postulants Guide describes the ideal candidate as "Marylike" and the postulate as the time "to learn the spirit of the Community to which Christ has called us, and to prove, through docility" the acquiring of "apostolic virtures" such as "quietness of voice and action, a cheerful countenance." The postulant also must "avoid unrefined laughter or tones of voice or an uncontrolled manner, all of which are incompatible with religious dignity." The "examination of conscience" is also instructive: "Am I careless or indifferent to work assigned me? Have I an undue curiosity or concern of matters in the world—my family, former acquaintances, world conditions? Am I jealous, envious? Do I avoid others through resentment or other motives? Have I manifested worldliness by calling others nicknames? Have I particular friendships?" (5, MA).

56. See "Letters of Mary Joseph Walker," transcribed and edited by Suzanne Fleming, I.H.M. (MJWP, MA).

speaking, the candidates who entered the IHM congregation in the nineteenth century were neophytes in their faith, and this may be why novice mistresses of that era advised their successors to be gentle and to "go easy" on their young apprentices. However, one can observe a similar maternal care in the letters Leocadia Delanty wrote to young sisters during the crowded novitiates of the twentieth century. Thus, attributing Smith's freedom to the cozier atmosphere of the nineteenth century is not sufficient.

A possible explanation for the difference in tone might lie in the ferment in the U.S. Catholic church at the time of the First Vatican Council (1870–71), but it is doubtful that this council had any great effect upon nineteenth-century IHM mentors. The influence of the so-called Americanist controversy is another possible avenue of investigation, though here, too, it is unlikely that the IHMs—who were under such strong Belgian influence during the nineteenth century—would have been affected by the republican ideas associated with Americanism.[57] Looking elsewhere, we may note that young Bridget Smith was educated by the Mercy sisters in Chicago before joining the IHMs. Investigating whether any of her ideas are based upon observations of these sisters, who were greatly involved in post–Civil War social issues and who championed women's freedom to serve outside convent walls, would be an interesting pursuit.[58]

My own interpretation of the differences between the two centuries has to do with the fact that apostolic religious life during the period in which Smith served as novice mistress had not yet been codified. Even while governed by an essentially dualistic spirituality, greater freedom was found in American religious life during the nineteenth century (particularly in new communities located on the frontier) compared to the strictures that would be introduced in the 1917 Code of Canon Law. Nineteenth-century religious congregations were allowed considerable latitude in matters that would later become strictly and uniformly regulated (e.g., disposition of property, dress, contact with outsiders). This explanation, however, though plausible, does not seem completely adequate. I believe one can still detect something of a kindred spirit connecting the twentieth-century mentors tied down by codification and by the

57. Chinnici contrasts the spirituality of "Americanism" (derived from the main features of the so-called Americanist heresy, which championed such values as self-reliance, interdependence, conscience, and democratic government, and associated with Isaac Hecker) with the spirituality of the "immigrant church," which stressed obedience to authority, the weakness of the natural virtues, and a vertical relationship between the hierarchy and laity (1989, 87–133).

58. Healy 1992—a particularly vivid description of conditions affecting the Sisters of Mercy during the late nineteenth century—sheds some light on the difficulties of leading a structured, semicloistered religious life in the Midwest.

internalized expectations of higher authorities and the less canonically encumbered sisters of the preceding century. In general, IHM socialization between 1860 and 1960 had more in common with Reilly's "roughest kind of prose" than with Smith's preference of "spirit" over letter. However, perhaps the recovery of the latter bit of history can still stir some dreams for the future that lies ahead.

Why, one must ask, do most IHMs not know about Smith, when the Monroe archives contain nearly as much of her writing as they do of Reilly's? Some light can be shed on this, I believe, if one examines the accounts of IHM socialization practices for instances of what feminist folklorists call "coding": the covert attempts that women undertake, either deliberately or unconsciously, to disguise what might be deemed subversive or disturbing to those who have the power to dominate, silence, or marginalize them. If coding was not taking place during the adoption of new aesthetic standards within an imposed uniformity of dress, then why did my IHM informants thoroughly relish recalling these stories? As they reminisced, many of the sisters I interviewed expressed a sense of self-satisfaction in recalling the risks they had taken or the hurdles overcome that they had not previously recognized as such.[59]

In their discussion of strategies of coding, feminist folklorists Joan N. Radner and Susan S. Lanser distinguish between "implicit," "complicit," and "explicit" coding. An explicit code is usually apparent to those who cannot decipher it. Complicit coding is collectively determined ahead of time and is later adopted by an entire community; passwords and code names are examples of complicit coding. I would argue that in the socialization process, much of what IHM novices defined as "beautiful" or as "status" housework involved implicit coding. This kind of coding is characterized by three features: it is undertaken in situations of risk; it is ambiguous in that neither the fact of coding nor the key to the code have been made explicit; and there is an indeterminate intentionality (meaning that it is uncertain whether coding has actually occurred or what the nature of that which is encoded is). The risk element in implicit coding refers to "those occasions when the code has been adopted to provide safety or freedom, rather than simply pleasure or play" (Radner and Lanser 1993, 4). Again, I would argue that the novice coding was not merely play or diversion; rather, it entailed risk in the sense that it arose out of the context in which a young woman's selfhood was put at risk. In other words, the dress and work status codes functioned as a means of

---

59. For example, this definitely seemed to be the experience of the former IHM who suffered the traumatic haircut and enjoyed the puffy sleeves; in the interview, she was relishing what she now knew to be her authentic conviction about these matters. So too was the sister who realized that she had creatively found a way to meditate on scripture without asking permission by using her daily missal.

"self" preservation in a situation geared to annihilate the self (whether for a noble purpose is not the issue here).

Thus, even in pre–Vatican II religious life, young sisters succeeded in developing coping strategies that allowed them a certain measure of self-expression, outside authorities and monitors notwithstanding. Despite what on paper (i.e., in the official church and congregational documents) resembled an otherworldly "boot camp," designed to obliterate all sense of individuality and of creative expression, some sister-initiates and at least one of their mentors managed to survive as particular individuals within the subculture of religious life. Today, some of their devices may strike us more as quaint than as "subversive"; nevertheless, these everyday acts helped preserve a sense of self, despite the best efforts of both external and internal authorities to stifle individual personality and to obliterate singularity.

"Seldom one, never two, always three or more."

# 5

# The Official IHM Stance on Friendship, 1845–1960

## Joan Glisky, I.H.M.

Recently, a dear friend and I, both of us members of the Michigan IHM congregation, celebrated a friendship now in its fourth decade. In writing this essay, I thought often of this friendship and of the many others energized or generated because of it in my life.

I recalled how this friendship started—the spontaneous, affectionate interest shown in me that reached through all the barriers and restrictions that I thought my "religious" commitment demanded. I remembered the mutual discovery and sharing, the encouragement and support through the ups and downs of the years, the occasions enhanced by our presence to one another, the extension of our ties to each other's friends and family, the shared ministries, retreats, trips, and vacations. I remembered the ways we fashioned to maintain contact: there were the little written accounts of our thoughts and activities surreptitiously exchanged at community meetings, workshops, or at other opportunities for seeing each other; there were the permissions—so daringly sought and so gladly received—to send occasional letters or cards.

I thought, too, of the rough moments—the mistrust from some local superiors, the questioning by the mother general, the watchdogging by a self-appointed sister, our being transferred to different and distant missions. I felt again the anguish of hours of conscientious self-scrutiny, testing this friendship against the claims of Rule, custom, and community expectations of "being general" in my relationships.

With the changes prompted by Vatican II, increased visits and communication became possible. I remembered how, during those post–atican II years, my novitiate-damaged confidence in the goodness of having friends—close friends, longtime friends, occasionally-seen friends, friends in community and outside—was slowly restored.

While researching the subculture in which my religious-life friendships first emerged, I sometimes had to turn away from the documents. Even as my research renewed a zealous excitement about religious life, I felt again the moral burdens, the heavy, limiting claims of the Rule smothering me. Still, I believe I have been through some very fulfilling years. The tensions of this sometimes rigorous journey have balanced out in sustained energy for life and mission in this Godward congregation that has become for me a community of friends.

## Friendships and the Pre–Vatican II IHM Rule

As with every religious congregation, the intended spirit and practice of IHM life—including the congregation's official posture toward relationships between members—is spelled out in the congregation's Rule, also referred to as its Constitutions.[1] From the congregation's founding in 1845 until 1960—when, moved by the winds of change sweeping a path to Vatican II, the IHMs began a radical transformation of their way of life —the IHM Constitutions remained substantially unaltered.[2] Surprisingly, they do not discuss "friendship" as such. The word is used only once, and then it is in the negative light of "particular friendship." To under-

1. Mary Jo Maher, I.H.M., in "A History of the Constitutions" ([H of C. 1960s], 3n. 1, MA), states: "The terms *rule* and *constitutions* are used interchangeably in this study, as this has been done traditionally in the Congregation. In its strict sense and in ecclesiastical law, rule means the fundamental precepts of religious life as proposed by the ancient founders (e.g., Rule of St. Benedict). 'In contrast with the rule thus understood, the constitutions contain the laws which are characteristic of the different institutes and which regulate their principal obligations' [Creusen 1953, 194]. In those institutes which do not follow an ancient rule, the constitutions take the place of the rule."

2. The Monroe Motherhouse Chronicles of 28 Nov. 1845 describe the drawing up and approval of the earliest Rule. Redemptorist Louis Florent Gillet's original Constitutions received only slight modifications from the IHM congregation's first general superior, Theresa Maxis; see the 1845 Constitutions written in Maxis's hand (art. 56, 62, 75, 82, MA). There were some changes in 1861 (MMC, Dec. 1861) when the spread of missions beyond the diocese and continued growth evoked a call for clarity in governance; the new edition of the Constitutions, approved by Bishop Peter Paul Lefevere, was explicit in naming the bishop as the first superior of the Institute and authorizing a director who was to act in his absence (Const. 1861, art. 19–23, MA). Twice again, major revisions were considered but not adopted (RK, n.d., DLHR, 5–10, MA). In 1900, Mother Mechtildis McGrail initiated revisions to obtain Rome's approval, which was finally achieved in 1920 (Pope Benedict XV, "Decree of Final Approbation," 26 July 1920, Const. 1920, I–II). Not until 1954 was another revision initiated (Chapters 1954 and 1960, MA); this revision, however, was not realized. Thus, most citations from the Constitutions are taken from the 1920 edition. There does exist a document titled "Modifications to be Introduced into the Text of the Constitutions of the Sisters, Servants of the Immaculate Heart of Mary of the Archdiocese of Detroit" (MA); the text of this document notes that these modifications are in conformity with the enactments of "the General Chapter, 1960" and that their implementation will be in 1961 and 1962. A small eight-page Rule insert of these changes, given to each sister, is dated 1961 (MA).

stand how the congregation viewed friendship, therefore, it is necessary to look more broadly at the way in which the Constitutions addressed personal relationships among the members.

The prescriptions of the pre–Vatican II Rule were direct and unambiguous; however, obedience to their demands frequently generated some tension, especially in regard to friendship. This is perhaps ironic, given that the most foundational norm of the Rule was for the members to love one another: "Charity being the spiritual cement of the Congregation all the members ought to have but one heart and one soul, loving one another with an affection founded rather upon supernatural than natural motives" (Const. 1920, art. 10, MA). This is the wording in the Rule as approved in 1920, but it scarcely differs from its earlier expression by founding Redemptorist Louis Gillet in 1845: "The members of our Institute if they wish to form but one heart and one soul must above all and necessarily be invested with the bowels of charity and love one another reciprocally with a love founded more on spiritual motives than natural ones" (Const. 1845, trans. by MAW, 4, MA). The IHM Constitutions directed the congregation's mother general (also variously called superior, general superior, mother superior, or major superior) to uphold this practice of love: "The Superior has a special obligation to see that all the requirements of charity, as prescribed in the Constitutions, are fulfilled by each sister; and she must correct at once those who fail in its practice" (Const. 1920, art. 119). Clearly spelled out in other articles were the harms flowing from dissension, competitiveness, labelling or ridiculing one another, criticism, and interference in each other's work (Const. 1920, art. 11–13).

These straightforward prescriptions were deemed essential to the end and spirit of the congregation. Love was what the congregation was about because love was the law of the Gospel, as Paul affirmed in Romans 13:10: "Love is the one thing that cannot hurt your neighbor; that is why it is the answer to every one of the commandments." Certainly, love is at the heart of genuine friendship; thus, in so situating the life of the sisters in the context of love, the Rule indirectly supported the development of friendships.

In addition to designating mutual charity as the norm of religious life, the Constitutions supported friendship by basing the community's structure on permanent commitment. IHM community life was not intended to be a "come-and-go" sort of arrangement. It was an entry into long-term patterns of relationships, a call to realize the promise of three vows made "for the rest of my life" (Const. 1920, art. 26). "It is absolutely understood that no one is admitted to profession unless she is fully determined to persevere in her vocation, as a member of the Congregation until death," the constitutions stated. "By profession the subjects and the Congregation become so intimately united that no one may leave or be excluded except in accordance with the Sacred Canons" (Const. 1920, art. 28).

One might expect that to enter solemnly into lifelong relationship with a group of women committed to loving one another would be to set oneself directly on a path toward long-lasting and proven friendships. Additionally, the IHM constitutions supported reciprocity of affection through the prescription of a "common life." The ideal of the common life arises from the earliest communitarian or cenobitic practices in the fourth century. It derives from the New Testament description of the early Christian community in the second chapter of Acts: "The faithful all lived together and owned everything in common; they sold their goods and possessions and shared out the proceeds among themselves according to what each one needed."

The Constitutions hint of the role of the common life in the IHM congregation in naming the congregation's primary goal: "To advance the sanctification of its members by seclusion from the world and the practice of religious observances" (Const. 1920, art. 4). Common life enabled this seclusion from the world; it placed the members in physical proximity in an intensive faith atmosphere, where they could sustain one another in attaining the congregation's goals and realizing their vowed commitment. Members were to realize the common life in ways that were detailed in numerous articles of the Constitutions. They were to practice shared ownership of goods—food, clothing, living spaces, work materials, and gifts—whose use and disposition were under congregational control (Const. 1920, arts. 31, 36–39, 55–57, 193). They were to move together through the day from one common exercise to another: prayer, meals, work, recreation (Const. 1920, arts. 159–72). They were not to leave the house unaccompanied or without permission (Const. 1920, art. 195); while serving as teachers in schools away from Monroe, they were to live in local communities that very rarely numbered less than three.[3]

In all its parts, the IHM Constitutions assumed this common-life structure as a basic tenet. Indeed, entrants were scrutinized and tested carefully for their ability to live amicably and closely with others. If accepted, the community would accompany them through formation and profession to departure in death. It was a life pattern reminiscent of that described in the scripture story of Ruth and Naomi: "Entreat me not to leave thee, nor to return from following after thee. For whither thou goest, I will go, And where thou lodgest, I will lodge. Thy people shall be my people, and thy God my God. And where thou diest, I will die; and where thou liest, I will lie; and nought but death shall part thee from

---

3. "In establishing a new Mission it is necessary to observe strictly the following conditions. First there will never be less than three Sisters for one house, two of whom, at least, ought to be professed" (EJ, IFS 1863, MA).

me" (paraphrase of Ruth 1:16–17, Jackson 1994, 68). At the basis of this sort of common life was friendship.

## Rule Provisions that Discouraged Friendships

Mutual love, permanent membership, and common life, then, were foundational mandates in the pre–Vatican II Constitutions, prescriptions inviting the forming of friendships among the members. However, the Constitutions also contained at least six interrelated provisions that discouraged friendships between IHM sisters. Each provision stemmed from some concern or insight gleaned from centuries of experiencing the spiritual quest and the interplay of human passions in religious groups.

The first restrictive provision emphasized the individual member's solitary pursuit of sanctification. In naming the congregation's goal as the sanctification of each of its members, the Constitutions correctly placed ultimate responsibility for making choices with the individual, protecting the basic moral principle that the final choice for good or ill lies with the individual person. What the Constitutions did not fully honor were the benefits of solidarity and bondedness in the pursuit of the good and the transcendent. For example, the Rule stated that the formula for holiness was the practice of twelve foundational virtues: "faith, hope, charity or the love of God, charity towards our neighbor, poverty, purity of heart, obedience, meekness and humility of heart, mortification, recollection and silence, prayer, self-abnegation and love of the cross. These virtues are the foundation upon which the Sisters should endeavor to raise the edifice of their perfection, assisted each month by the patronage and the protection of one of the Apostles" (Const. 1920, art. 4). Here, reliance on the saints, a practice common in most religious communities, deemphasized the need for the support of community members. Where human assistance might be beneficial, the Rule seemed to assume that seeking out the superior was sufficient. In matters of spiritual struggle or in the daily discernments of life and work, members were to see this congregational authority as the immediate principal conduit of God's call: "The vow of obedience implies the obligation of obeying the commands of lawful Superiors in all that concerns, either directly or indirectly, the life of the Congregation, namely the observance of the vows and Constitutions. The Sisters obey the General Superior as they would God Himself. . . . The Local Superiors, in the houses they govern, are entitled to the same obedience and respect" (Const. 1920, arts. 45–47).

Supporting this individualistic pursuit of perfection and further limiting the building of relationships was the Constitution's emphasis on solitariness and silence. The IHM sister was enjoined to "love and cherish solitude, live in the presence of God by frequent and fervent ejaculatory prayers, and keep strict silence in the prescribed times and places"

(Const. 1920, art. 64). Although solitude and silence are traditionally recognized as essential in the pursuit of a reflective and prayerful life, the IHM Constitutions interpreted silence to be an all-encompassing feature of community life, an ironic requirement for women whose profession was teaching. Over two-thirds of the sisters' days were marked as "silence days," where conversation with one another was allowed only at recreation times (the permissible noontime recreation was usually not possible on school days). The afternoon was marked as a time of stricter silence to honor Jesus' agony on the cross (Const. 1920, art. 67). After-school chatting was unknown. From 8:30 P.M. until after meditation in the morning, a "solemn silence" was to be observed—a time that did not permit even a whisper (or a glance), except in emergency (Const. 1920, art. 68). Even during recreation times, conversation was confined to certain places and not allowed in "the chapel, sacristy, dormitory, Sisters' cells, adjoining corridors, and the refectory" (Const. 1920, art. 66). By custom, there was to be no conversing while traveling on the street.

This strictly commanded, all-pervading silence—mandated to support an individual pursuit of sanctification, while also protecting the individual's well-deserved right to privacy in large groups—was scarcely conducive to the establishment of friendships. Friends need time to talk with one another; they need idle time as well as work time to explore and enjoy their mutualities and differences.

A second provision in the IHM Constitutions hindering the formation of friendships was the attempt to homogenize the membership by stripping away personal freedom and possessions, personal tastes and characteristics. "The members of the Congregation shall lead a perfectly uniform community life," the Constitutions stated (Const. 1920, art. 36). "Perfectly uniform" tended to gain ascendancy over the ideal of common life. Instead of a plurality of personalities realizing community from the rich resources of their diversity, the ideal became sameness in everything. The Rule looked askance at distinctions in garb, in room furnishings, in additional materials for work or enjoyment. Sisters were not to express personal tastes or preferences and they were to have nothing for their personal disposition, not even a picture to lend or freely give away (Const. 1920, art. 39).

The vow of obedience ensured compliance: "Since the spirit of the Congregation consists principally in self-abnegation and the renouncement of self-will, the Sisters shall endeavor to excel in this virtue, obeying blindly and cheerfully the wishes and the commands of their Superiors, unless it is certain that the action commanded is sinful; because in doubt it is always better to obey" (Const. 1920, art. 49). In this regard, the novice mistress was reminded that "she will never succeed in fulfilling her charge if she does not make the novices die to their own will and opinion" (Const. 1920, art. 146). Submerging one's tastes and preferences in this way made the self more difficult for others to know and to befriend —and as time passed, one risked not even knowing oneself.

A third discouragement to the making and keeping of friends imposed by the pre-1960s Rule was the view of the members that it promoted. The sisters were seen as "subjects," dependents or children who should leave personal choices to others deemed more able and mature. Thus, the superiors, the local bishop, and (for over half a century) the congregation's appointed male director held the reins controlling friendly exchange among the members.[4]

Evidence of this attitude (at least in regard to the younger sisters) can be found as late as 1920, when Mother Domitilla Donohue, requesting Rule modifications, wrote Archbishop Bonaventure Cerretti, assistant secretary of state to Pope Benedict XV and longtime supporter of the congregation's Rule approval process. Among the desired changes was a petition that professed sisters not be allowed to take part in congregational elections until they had completed seven years of perpetual vows, "in order to foster a spirit of dependence in the young; here in America experience proves at present, the great need of keeping them in a state of humble subjection" (Kelly n.d., OHC, 5, MA). The comment accompanying Rome's negative reply was equally revealing: "By other means the Superior General should endeavor to maintain the younger Sisters in due subjection" (Kelly n.d., OHC, 6, MA). Although the Rule never specifically referred to the members as children, the cultural and religious climate of the nineteenth and the early twentieth century invited their being viewed and responding as such. Little evidence has been found that the IHM congregation was influenced to any degree by some of their contemporaries' calls for women's full equality and for repudiation of their treatment as children and as dependents.[5] In 1952, however, against a background of more than a century of directives to be childlike, Mother Teresa McGivney (1942–54) highlighted the ambiguity in the expectations placed on the members when she remarked in a Rule reading: "We act

4. In referring to the IHM women, the Rule most frequently used the terms "Sisters," "members," and, several times, "Spouse" (of Christ) (Const. 1920, arts. 4, 42, 43, 54), terms that could evoke womanly interdependence and mature reciprocity. The term "subjects" is used twice, in articles 28 and 58; twice, in a rule members came to know by heart, is enough to foster an attitude.

5. The first woman's rights convention took place in 1848 in Seneca Falls, New York, three years after the IHMs' foundation. The convention was publicized in the *Seneca County Courier* on 14 July 1848 as "a Convention to discuss the social, civil and religious rights of women." The women who shaped these events were active during the latter half of the nineteenth century; their actions were publicized broadly. Such names as Angelina and Charlotte Grimke, Elizabeth Cady Stanton, and Lucretia Mott rose to the fore. Of course, the negative press that such conventions and these women aroused allowed for only the most independent and courageous of women to participate; religious sisters, constrained in near-cloistered or cloistered conditions, were hardly in a position of independence.

like children sometimes, instead of developed women" (TMcG, Com. Con., 7 Aug. 1952, MA).

Formation practices fostered a sense of dependency from the moment a candidate entered the community. Generally, young prospective IHMs moved from the security of their own homes into the convent home, where a mother superior and a structured daily schedule called them to a transfer of dependencies.[6] It was not uncommon for girls to enter even before finishing high school, thus not completing adolescence before assuming the vocations of their adult lives. Perhaps it was lingering adolescent behavior on the part of some sisters that evoked this remark from Mother Ruth Hankerd in a 1941 Rule reading: "It would be sad, indeed, to know that our Sisters were now losing this dignity through loud talking, calling to one another, even going so far as slapping each other on the back in a common schoolgirl fashion" (RHN, 4, MA). Hankerd also scolded:

> Some Sisters receiving letters from girls would be ashamed to have the letters seen. The light frivolous spirit in which they are written is such that it shows how familiar these girls have become with those to whom they are writing. To see a line like this—"I am sorry I did not write to you every week as I promised" is very childish, indeed, on the part of the Sister who asked her to "write every week" or even, I might say, to write at all. . . . Try, Sisters to keep your religious dignity at all times and in all places. Don't be little girls with the children. (RHN, 9, MA).

The potential for developing friendships between mature, self-possessed persons was threatened when the sisters viewed themselves as dependents, as children, and as subjects and when their Rule of life promoted such a view. By internalizing this attitude, members chanced the loss of confidence in their ability to make personal choices and, particularly, to form relationships of deep mutuality characterizing friendships.

### Particular Friendships

Perhaps one of the greatest deterrents to friendship in the pre-1960s IHM Constitutions were provisions indicating that personal friendships

---

6. Numerous examples of this practice can be found. The chronicles of Most Holy Trinity Convent are typical. They record the graduation of young women who immediately thereafter enter the community by accompanying the sisters returning to the motherhouse for summer vacation. For example, the 18 June 1917 entry reads: "Graduating exercise held. Diplomas and gold medals conferred on the Misses Pearl Hogan, Sadie Weiss, Rosalind Shanahan, Helen Donahue and Eva Cragg. The Misses Shanahan and Cragg accompanied the Sisters home to enter the Novitiate." And for 23 June 1925: "Sisters returned to the Mother House for vacation taking with them five postulants from the High School" (HTC, MA).

threatened two valued congregational aspirations: the desire to respond to the Gospel call to universal love and the desire to be faithful to the vow of chastity.

As previously observed, the Rule called for "an affection founded rather upon supernatural than natural motives" (Const. 1920, art. 10). The supernatural motive was understood to stem from Jesus' command in the Gospel to "love one another; just as I have loved you" (John 13:34). Every Thursday, IHMs reiterated this gospel call to love by a public reading before dinner of John's account of Jesus' washing the feet of his disciples (Const. 1920, art. 180); on Holy Thursday, the Rule mandated that the superior read to the community particularly on the practice of charity (Const. 1920, art. 181). Anything "natural" was understood to be militating against the realization of these supernatural aspirations to mutual charity—witness the effort to have the novices die to their own will and opinion, or the call to an ideal, uniform life devoid of any distinctive personalities or achievements.

Coupled with the gospel ideal of love of all was the vowed commitment to the chastity of a celibate. The Rule of St. Alphonsus, from which the IHM Rule was derived, mentioned the danger of particular friendship in the context of charity; the 1911 IHM Constitutions mentioned it in relation to chastity: "One who seeks only self-gratification, or who is given to particular friendships, is far from the perfection required by the vow of chastity" (Const. 1911, art. 33).

This prohibition against "particular friendships" does not appear in the IHM Constitutions until 1911. At that time, Mother Mechtildis McGrail had the Rule of St. Alphonsus printed along with the text of the IHM Rule. It is not clear why or how this reference to particular friendship found its way into the Constitutions and into the section on chastity at this time, although it is clear that the term was used in other religious congregations of women as well. Clearly, it had some relationship to the Alphonsian Rule, where the text reads: "The members should, for the love of Jesus Christ, love one another with an all embracing love and indeed more than their friends and relations. Hence, there shall never exist among them particular friendships from which the total destruction of charity and the ruin of the entire community usually result, but they shall be attached to one another, collectively and singly, regardless of talent, nationality or rank" (PRAL 1961, 11–12, MA).[7] In this context, it

---

7. Compare this 1906 translation by W. G. Licking, C.SS.R., of the *Primitive Rules and Constitutions of Saint Alphonsus Liguori* (reprinted with permission in Monroe in 1961) with the IHM Constitutions of 1911, article 33, and the almost identical text in 1920, article 43. In their treatment of chastity, the earlier Constitutions speak more of restricting relationships with men (particularly ecclesiastics) and of prohibiting them from entry into the living quarters of the sisters, especially their rooms.

appears to be a restriction on too close or too familiar friendships between Redemptorist priests and brothers.

In interviewing IHM sisters, I found that they too understood particular friendship as a threat to charity and, with older sisters, less frequently in relation to chastity:

> [Entered 1923] Mother Leocadia explained it very carefully to anyone that wanted to listen. Particular friendship meant you and I exclusively—these people who were always together. There was no such thing that I can't have friends. The word Mother Leocadia used most was "exclusive." You were supposed to be general. (ITM, interviewed by author, 25 Apr. 1994, MA)
>
> [Entered 1926] We weren't told why it was there. We were just told not to be going regularly with the same person. I thought it was just so we would be general with one another and try to treat everybody the same. I didn't connect it with chastity at all. (INe, interviewed by author, 25 Apr. 1994, MA)
>
> [Entered 1938] We were the first class that had Mother Mary Hubert all the way through. She was always giving the speech, "Seldom one, never two, always three or more." She always had her eye on some of us—some who got along real well. She kept an eye on us. (IHM sister quoted anonymously, interviewed by author, 25 Apr. 1994, MA)
>
> [Entered 1945] I had no idea of what they were driving at, to be honest with you. I was told to take James Ellen cookies and milk [she was ill] and I went back to get the plate. That was wrong. I saw her twice in one day. You couldn't work together with the same people. We went to clean in G wing and someone got in trouble because she was cleaning with us the day before. What it did was make us feel you really couldn't have a close friend. And I've heard other people say that. (PA, interviewed by author, 26 Apr. 1994, MA)

Still, some older sisters did have intimations of the prohibition being related to chastity:

> [Entered 1923] You knew particular friendships were morally wrong. They were always spoken of by the novice mistress and superiors in a lowered tone of voice. Yet you never really knew what they were —only that they must be avoided at all costs. (EC, interviewed by author, 8 Apr. 1994, MA)
>
> [Entered 1926] When I was in the novitiate, I did wonder if it had something to do with chastity. (DH, interviewed by author, 25 Apr. 1994, MA)

The term was unfortunate, as was the tone of its presentation. It set up conditions for a too-quick suspicion of innocent attractions of members for one another. It deterred the healthy exploration of promising relationships by setting up an immediate suspicion of danger.

To protect chastity, the Rule called for limiting spontaneity by "a firm and constant custody of the senses, especially the eyes . . . [a] grave and religious manner . . . a recollected exterior" (Const. 1920, art. 42). Undoubtedly, mindfulness, inwardness, and self-control are essential to realizing the vow of chastity, but what the pre–Vatican II constitutions failed to authorize and to describe was a healthy spontaneity in relationships and ways to balance such normalcy with a habit of celibacy for the sake of the reign of God. This prevailing fear of particularity in friendships, of their threat to chastity and to charity as well, hindered—and sometimes eclipsed—the formation of strong friendships among the sisters.[8]

### Monitoring Behavior

Another hindrance to the forming of friendships in the IHM Constitutions was the legislation for monitoring the behavior of the sisters. Apart from the watchful eye of God, sisters were under the daily scrutiny of their superiors—both general and local—and the monitress. Until the Constitutions were revised for pontifical approval in the early twentieth century, they also allowed for the oversight of both the bishop and the appointed director (Const. 1861, pt. 2, const. 1 and 2, MA). After the death of the congregation's director, Monsignor Edward Joos, in 1901, the strong control of a male director was greatly diminished, and in 1913, the bishop's authority to make adjustments in the Constitutions and to direct the internal activities of the community was finally eliminated ([Kelly] 1948, 483–88).

According to the constitutions, this monitoring role of the superiors and monitress was to be discharged in a caring but firm manner. In regard to the mother general, they stated: "It is her duty to watch over the exact and strict observance of the Constitutions, never dispensing for an indefinite time or without reason" (Const. 1920, art. 117). The local superiors were to exercise the same role on their missions (Const. 1920, art. 139). The monitress was to assist the mother general in her surveillance: "The Monitress is, as it were, the Guardian Angel of the Congregation. She must charitably warn every member who evidently neglects any of her religious duties, unless, in order that a suitable remedy may be applied, she judges it more to the purpose to acquaint the Mother General of the fault; the Monitress, however, shall not reprove or admonish in public"(Const. 1920, art. 128).[9] In addition, in the earliest years, the Rule

---

8. See chap. 6 of the present volume for more discussion of particular friendships.

9. Earlier, the monitress role included correction of the superior as well. Roman authorities indicated to Joos in his submission of 1885 that "[t]he article on the obligation on the part of the monitress to warn the superior when the latter failed in her duty was either to be 'tempered in its severity or omitted altogether,' since if such a condition existed its correction would have to come from higher authority" (RK, n.d., DLHR, 10, MA).

prescibed a regular manifestation of conscience to the superior, a practice expunged from the Rule by a papal decree in 1890.[10]

Such unremitting supervision of the members reinforced their sense of dependency. It sustained a conviction of inadequacy to meet the responsibilities of one's commitment, and it supported a feeling of being moved by outside rather than by internal motivation. Such scrutiny, while safeguarding religious practice, also put severe limits on the sharing and sustaining of relationships. For example, sisters were corrected for sitting next to a particular sister too many successive nights at recreation. If the relationship persisted, they were reported to the mother general, who not infrequently took measures to separate the sisters in question (see chapter 6 in this volume).

Superiors monitored sisters' behavior, their dress, the appearance of their cells or sleeping quarters, even the arrangement of their closets and drawers of personal belongings. Individuality submerged itself in community practice. As Janice Raymond has observed with respect to women's religious friendship,

> Where the tension between individuality and community is kept, privacy is preserved in the midst of an intense and deep community spirit. Within communities of religious women, privacy helped individuality flourish. Where the tension was not kept, especially after the imposition of the rule of enclosure, the lives of nuns were in essence made the public property of the community by petty rules, concerns, and purposes. The private time and space needed for friendship was also limited, and a kind of communal surveillance mechanism against particular friendships was encouraged. The community became "big sister," comparable to an internal CBI (Convent Bureau of Investigation) for the monitoring of particular friendships. (1986, 110–11)

Finally, the Constitutions curbed the forming of friendships by curtailing the sisters' social contacts. The cloister-like regulations imposed by the pre-1960s Constitutions restricted communication with the other sisters, with students, and with "necessary" others, such as family, parents of students, or medical or other professionals. Visits in the parlor, visits to persons outside the convent (including family members), and letter writing were not done without specific permission (Const. 1920, arts. 194, 197, 201). Food, which is often the occasion of social contact, was not to be taken outside the refectory, where the sisters usually ate in silence, sitting in rank according to their date of entry (Const. 1920, art. 193).

Besides limiting the possibilities of widening a circle of friends, such

---

10. Pope Leo XIII, Decree "*Quemadmodum*," promulgated in Dec. 1890.

narrowing of contacts hindered the development of a mature context for social interaction. Raymond's observation is apropos: "The rule of enclosure cloistered more than the physical space and mobility of religious women. It also circumscribed their minds" (1986, 101). Usually entering in their late teens, members often lacked wide experience of models of human interaction; if they had not had an outlet into the world of work through the field of education, such socialization would have been even more limited. In any event, the boundaries experienced proved sometimes to be hurdles never overcome sufficiently to permit development of mature friendships. More than once, sisters have confided that having kept the Rule prohibiting particular friends, they found themselves after two or three decades with no close friends.[11]

### Upholding the Rule's Stance on Friendship: The Role of the Superiors

Traditionally, the IHM congregation's superiors played an important role in upholding the community's Rule of life as it pertained to the formation and maintenance of friendships. They maintained a remarkable similarity of practice, reasons for which are not hard to find: the unchanging character of major articles of the Constitutions; a strong desire, long pursued, to gain from Rome recognition as "real" religious; and the generally long tenure of women in leadership roles.[12] Certainly

11. One sister remarked: "I felt I wasn't supposed to relate to people. I became a workaholic" (IHM sister [entrance 1945], interviewed by author, 25 Apr. 1994). Another said: "The way I handled it was by playing ping pong with anyone who wanted to recreate with me. If you played ping pong, you didn't have to engage in conversation and get personal" (conversation with an IHM, 30 Apr. 1994). And another: "I had a Sister in high school who was partly responsible for my vocation. I felt I should not have had a particular friendship for her and I kept her at a distance. I know I hurt her by putting up a barrier. Also, Sister —— with whom I had been in school since the ninth grade. I set up a distance from her, too. We had been very close. To this day we are still somewhat estranged" (IHM sister [entrance 1926], interviewed by author, 25 Apr. 1994).

12. Theresa Maxis's own desire to be a member of a real religious community kindled her desire for the congregation to have a recognized rule of life and comcomitant status within the church (TM to PPL, 9 July 1859, UNDA). Ultimately, this desire within the congregation was realized in 1920 with its recognition as a pontifical institute, i.e., one receiving a relationship of identity and protection from the Pope.

Although ill health and strain led to short terms of office for Mary Joseph Walker, Xavier Eagan, and Gertrude Gerretsen, the rest of this period under study saw seven general superiors whose years in office numbered nineteen, eighteen, or twelve years. In addition, Joos was the director for forty-four years, and three novice mistresses had long-term roles and broad influence in that role: Justina Riley (fourteen years, followed by a twelve-year role as general superior), Leocadia Delanty (forty-four years), and Mary Hubert Manion (eighteen years). Finally, council members held leadership roles for similarly long periods.

significant in this regard was the constant communication that each superior maintained with the membership, in which she reiterated and interpreted the letter and spirit of the Rule. Undoubtedly each superior's
personality contributed to the flavor of the interpretation, but each
woman was seen nonetheless as a sign of constancy in upholding the
Constitutions.

Until the first establishment of a mission house in Vienna, Michigan,
in 1855, all members lived at the IHM motherhouse in Monroe. Accordingly, communication in the first ten years was immediate. For this reason, these years yield few letters or written directives interpreting the
details of the Rule. Mother Theresa Maxis (general superior during 1845–
48 and 1852–59) wrote abundantly, but her extant letters mainly concern
the early division of the community (see Gannon 1992). Nonetheless, she
exercised a formative impact on the nascent community and was vigorous in her desire that they should prove themselves good religious,
formed in their Rule of life. In 1857, Sister Mary Whipple testified to
Maxis's efforts to develop religious who lived their Rule: "I see notwithstanding our strict observance of the Rule and the great vigilance and
good example of Mother Superior the state in which the community is in
at present and which seems to be growing worse instead of better, from
the great and pressing want of suitable members, and a residing director
who would take an interest in our spiritual and temporal welfare." (MW
to PPL, 25 May 1857, Gannon 1992, 24–25).

Mother Mary Joseph Walker (1859–1864) had more reason for written
communication to the sisters, as mission locations began to increase. In
addition, letter writing was a major channel for her leadership because
tuberculosis frequently kept her confined to bed. With Walker, the call of
the sisters to strict submission took on a sweetness. She gave firm correc-
tions with skillful charm. To one sister at St. Joseph's mission in Detroit,
she wrote: "Thank you, Sister Gertrude, for taking my reproof so well—
if I were a little severe in my manner, forgive me" (MJW to SJD, [23 Feb.
1863], MJWP, MA). She shared the everyday happenings of the community with the sisters on the local missions, and like Maxis, her spirituality
was so integrated with every aspect of life that it flowed easily throughout her messages. In another letter written to Sister Gertrude Gerretsen
at St. Joseph's, Walker manifests her upholding of religious practice: "I
grant it is a little sacrifice not to be at home on the day of so many
ceremonies; but even if I could conscientiously say 'come,' I would not—
for then I would deprive you of the means of making such a cheerful
sacrifice—You may say I am very hard, but you know me of old, I believe" (MJW to [GG], [ca. 8 Dec. 1861], MJWP, MA). Walker saw herself
clearly as a mother to her children, beginning her letters with such
phrases as "My dear, very dear children" (MJW to [SJD], [Sept. 1861],
MJWP, MA), or "Beloved Children in our Lord" (MJW to [SMP], 15 Sept.

1862; MJW to [SMA], 28 Sept., 1863, MJWP, MA), and signing them "Your devoted Mother in Jesus Christ" (MJW to [GG], 23 Feb. 1864, MJWP, MA), "Adieu! Your Mother" (MJW to [CB], [ca. 28 Sept. 1863], MJWP, MA), or "Love to all, Old Mother" (MJW to [GG], 1 Sept. 1864, MJWP, MA). (This "Old Mother" died just before her thirty-seventh birthday.)[13]

## Handbooks, Guides, and Rule Readings

As the community grew and spread geographically, successive general superiors contributed their insights on the relationships desirable among the sisters through handbooks of instruction or guides for local superiors—and, during the summer, through "Rule readings." These channels reinforced the contradictory understandings surrounding friendships already present in the Constitutions. As the years passed, the intrusions of the surrounding culture also elicited rules specific to the times.

The congregation's collection of Rule readings and of local superiors' guides is incomplete. Sometimes the Rule readings seem to be notes made by some sister in attendance; sometimes the commentary was recorded more formally and typed and distributed, perhaps to local superiors or to sisters not able to be present. The superiors' guides often lack dates of publication and a number of them are handwritten, some by several different hands with directives inscribed over the years. Guides span various time periods. They were revised from time to time, the last extant one covering September 1966–August 1967 and titled "The Sisters' Guide." Included in these guides are admonitions first given at Rule readings, announcements made by the general superior in meetings with local superiors, and guidelines sent from the motherhouse to be included in the guide. The guide is named variously "Superiors Guide" or "Handbook of Instructions"; one is titled "Practices the Spirit of the Institute require and Superiors wish to have occasionally recalled" (SFM, MA). Sometimes the texts have no title. Guides brought to the Monroe archives from various closed missions are written by different hands but have many identical passages—clearly directives sent from the Monroe motherhouse. Some guides, however, have insertions found nowhere else. Sometimes the same directives have variations in wordings in the texts of different missions. However, despite these peculiarities, this body of material evidences an underlying consistency of teaching that affected the formation and the maintenance of friendships.

In both the superiors' guides and the Rule readings, as in the Constitutions, the call to charity between sisters assumes priority of place and is revealing of the congregational leadership's attitudes toward friendship.

---

13. For a fuller treatment of Walker see chap. 2 of the present volume.

Monsignor Edward Joos, the longtime director of the congregation, described the prevailing tone in an 1889 conference inserted in the 15 August 1952 edition of a guide for local superiors:

> First of all you are sisters. This should remind you of the strong and tender union that ought to exist among you. You must be Sisters in deed as well as in name having one for another such love as is found among sisters in a good and happy home in the world. . . . [Y]our love for those whom you call your sisters should be greater than that which you had for your natural sisters. I do not say that you should feel a greater affection for them, or even as great an affection, but "feeling," as I have so often told you, is nothing. (Joos Conf., 25 July 1889, 5–6, MA)

Various superiors' guides reiterated the necessity of charity, manifested in courtesy, in reverence, and in mutual assistance. As their roles in school and in parish expanded, the members received further guidelines about kindness and respect relative to children and to priests as well as respect for the work of sisters preceding them at a school. Local superiors, too, were to be kind and loving: "Be a real Mother to all at all times," says one entry (GLS, 15 Oct. 1922, 9, MA).

The call to uniformity, as a safeguard of the common life, is almost as strong as the call to charity. Mother Domitilla Donohue (1918–30), in a prefatory letter to local house superiors receiving new editions of the guides, wrote: "The 'Guide for Local Superiors,' which we are sending you, has been compiled to help you in the fulfillment of your many duties and to bring each of our Houses to greater uniformity of practice" (GLS, 25 Oct. 1922, MA). The succinct injunction of one telling entry is "Work against innovations" (GLS, 15 Oct. 1922, MA).

Local superiors often repeated the practices from the earliest Rule that proved restrictive of friendships, including limits on visits and traveling, rules of silence at specific times and places, and limits on letters, notes, and gifts. One superiors' guide admonishes: "Knowing the letter of the Rule the Sisters should observe its spirit and not write notes to another sister nor receive them without the permission of the Local Superior, if they reside in different houses. This refers also to postals. . . . Better not to ask dispensation of the Rule lightly, as extra sleep, recreation, etc. If given, be thankful, and enjoy it, but love to keep the Rule" (MCM, 9, MA). In 1941, Mother Ruth Hankerd (1930–42) reminded the sisters: "When you leave a Mission, write to that Mission, but not back and forth to individuals. You know yourselves what this could lead to" (RHN, 2, MA). Later, she emphasized that "the more we can get away from sending notes to one another, the happier our Community will be. Sending notes to individuals makes others unhappy, brings about hurt feelings, etc." (RHN, 10–11, MA). This is the same Hankerd whose papers in the congregational archives include letters of tender correspondence with a dear sister friend of many years. In 1945, Mother Teresa McGivney (1942–54) reminded the local superiors: "Sisters, don't give permission for sisters to go to each other's cells. You say it is an act of Charity. Most everything then is going to be an act of charity . . . Just say, 'That is the Rule, Sister, and we have to keep it' " (Superiors Mtng., 11 July 1945, 2, MA). Likewise, a 1952 admonition from McGivney reads: "The things we learned in Novitiate should be practiced until we die" (SFM, 57, MA).

As the years passed, IHM cloister-like practices shaped new directives. Admonitions to resist the distractions afforded by technology specified not listening to the victrola and the radio except occasionally, not reading the newspaper, avoiding overuse of the telephone, limiting nighttime entertainments such as parish musicals, not reading light literature and novels, and, in the late 1940s, limiting the viewing of movies. Over the years, the emphasis on controlling spontaneity recurred in the guidelines on body control—no swinging arms, use a moderate tone of voice, no unnecessary noise, no loud laughter, no unnecessary movements of the head, no swinging of beads (i.e., the fifteen-decade rosary IHM sisters wore attached to a belt at their waist). "It is considered more religious not to swing the beads," said one superiors' guide, noting that it was very desirable to have "a uniform disciplined exterior" (MCM, 17, 27, MA).

Most notable in regard to personal relationships were the limits to signs of affection noted in some of the superiors' guides. "Avoid holding the hands of young girls while conversing with them, or anything that savors of familiarity," advises one guide, which goes on to add that "[s]isters should not be too demonstrative in kissing and not do it in public" (MCM, 14, 18, MA). Likewise, another guide warns: "Avoid touching one another" and "avoid counting money at recreation; having gold-fish in the school rooms" (SGG, 24, item 3, MA). And yet another guide cautions: Avoid "taking notice of a Sister's birthday in any way; kissing seculars, or when doing so, only once" (GLS, 25 Oct. 1922, 5, MA). Later, the same guide states: "The Sisters should refrain from all effeminacy such as holding hands, locking arms, in fact touching or fondling one another in any way, as those things are not in keeping with a true religious spirit" (GLS, 25 Oct. 1922, 13, MA).

In addition to the cautions against physical contact were the ones warning against informal self-revealing conversations: "Shun the private conversations of those who can injure your spirituality and always avoid undue confidences particularly with seculars." In addition, sisters "should avoid such expressions as 'dearie,' 'darling,' etc. in addressing one another; or speaking of another Sister as her 'lady ship.' Through delicacy of feeling the subject of nationality should be avoided as much as possible" (MCM, 2–4, MA). In 1899, Mother Justina Riley (1879–85, 1894–1900) warned:

Where two sisters sleep together [in the same room] if silence was not a rule they could go to their cell and visit all day and no one would know anything about it so you see where the harm might be done. . . .

Above all things do not give your confidence to anyone outside of your superior and I would say shun a sister who does it. Yes, shun her positively. . . . There is nothing which so surely undermines a vocation than giving and receiving confidence. Besides it is a sign of a very weak mind, to say the least it is not noble mindedness. (JRi Inst., 10 Aug. 1899, MA)

A 1907 guide entry admonished: "Do not give ten cents to Sisters to buy presents for one another. Watch communications—too much writing of letters. Do not ask Sisters who have left your mission to visit during the holidays. Do not give undue confidence to a sister on the mission or talk to her about another" (GLS, 9, 7, MA).

On the other hand, Donohue remarked in the 1920s that "[t]he Summer vacation at Home has always meant for the Community, bodily rest, mental improvement, and *a strengthening of social ties*" (DD, Com. Con., 1, MA, emphasis added). McGivney later supports this need for "strengthening of social ties" when she says: "Let us look upon recreation as a very important exercise of the day. The makers of our Holy Rule did; that is why they gave us very definite time for relaxation. In most of our houses, we do not have the noon recreation, so we should make an effort to recreate at night. We need it in order to be socially healthy" (TMcG, Com. Con., MA).

Some of the superiors' directives aimed to develop the sisters into refined women, whose conversations were free from boorishness and insensitivity. Others were guardians at the gates of their vow of chastity, mindful of the admonition from *The Imitation of Christ* that was read every morning in the refectory, "Resist beginnings" (Thomas à Kempis 1940, chap. 13, 18). Still others reflected Victorian restrictiveness or efforts at group control. In any event, collectively, for the 115-year span from 1845 to 1960, the communications to the members from their elected superiors expressed faithfully the tenor and the letter of the law set out in the IHM Constitutions, maintaining the tension between the limitations placed on establishing lifelong friends and the community's orientation toward establishing such friends.

## Conclusion

With Vatican II, a new spirit—with its own benefits and shortcomings —emerged in religious communities. The IHM congregation became a forerunner among religious congregations in affirming the emerging life-giving, growth-promising movements that supported the shaping of a community of friends. With this energy, the old Constitutions and superiors' directives were transformed or set aside to integrate fresh understandings. Another chapter of struggle for mutual solidarity and affection began to unfold in the lives of sisters. In a future era, the success and the shortcomings of this changed view in building enduring bonds within the community and beyond will call for another assessment.

On the way to berry-picking.

# 6

## PFs

*Persistent Friendships*

Nancy Sylvester, I.H.M.

[A close friend is] a person who accepts you as you are and truly loves you. One with whom you can share intimate thoughts and feelings and know they will be treated with reverence and respect. One with whom you are comfortable, at home, and at ease in a feeling of mutuality. (quest. 7)

I believe a close friendship involves trust, loyalty, love and the ability to keep confidences, to be able to face the truth when a disagreement arises. (quest. 5)

It's mutual—a peer relationship (at least, if ages are different, it must be an equal relationship). It grows with time and the willingness to work through conflicts. Friends support, listen to each other, encourage, draw out talents and gifts . . . no jealousy or holding back of honest feelings. (quest. 18)

These eloquent testimonies to friendship are offered by women who have lived from forty-five to sixty years as vowed religious in the congregation of the Sisters, Servants of the Immaculate Heart of Mary, based in Monroe, Michigan.[1] They entered religious life in the first half

1. Interviews conducted by the author (MA, restricted) in 1992 and questionnaires compiled by the author in 1993 (MA, restricted) are a major source of information for this essay. There were fifteen two-hour interviews conducted with sisters; the age breakdown of these sisters is as follows: nineties (3); eighties (6); seventies (1); sixties (4); and forties (1). There were thirty-five questionnaires completed by sisters; the age breakdown of the sisters returning questionnaires is: eighties (1); seventies (11); sixties (10); fifties (8); and forties (5). Sixteen sisters, ranging in age from forty-five to ninety-two, also participated in a one-hour discussion session. The sisters interviewed were women whose names surfaced repeatedly when other sisters were asked who should be interviewed about friendships. The questionnaires were made available during a congregational assembly in the summer of 1993;

of the twentieth century, when the rules and regulations that governed IHM life restricted their ability to make and foster friendships. "Never one, seldom two, always three or more" is a saying many of these women remember being taught as novices. The jingle was a device for remembering to avoid "particular friendships," or PFs. What constituted a PF, however, was not always clear.

"No one ever said! You just guessed what was meant," said one seventy-year-old sister (quest. 6). Sisters were accused of having a particular friend if "you sat next to a person two nights in a row" (interview 11, 15 Aug. 1992), took a walk with the same person, or even sat next to the person in choir where seats were assigned (interview 13, 5 Sept. 1992).[2] A sister who entered the IHM congregation in 1923 stated:

> It didn't take me long to discover that you were not supposed to be with one person for any length of time but I found that it was just a part of me to recognize certain people and I seemed to have a feel for them—a mutual kind of feel. . . . I knew that whatever these "particular" friends were they were really something—and yet you thought you were guilty if you had a friend. You did not know what a PF was. I didn't know anything about lesbian[ism]. Somehow or other it was labeled wrong, yet we did have friends. (interview 5, 22 July 1992)

For women who entered the IHM congregation between the 1920s and the 1950s, friendships were a suspect but significant fact of congregational life. The official negativity toward friendships that prevailed during this period created a powerful tension between positive personal experiences of friendships and the Rule's admonition that particular friendships were morally wrong. Significantly, perhaps, such a tension had not been so pronounced in the earlier history of the congregation.

### Friendships in the Early IHM Institute

The very beginnings of the IHM congregation were rooted in friendship. In autumn 1845, two Oblate Sisters of Providence—Sister Marie Therese (who would become Mother Theresa Maxis, the first general superior of the IHMs) and her friend and companion of seven years, Sister Ann Constance Shaaff—left the Oblate community in Baltimore, Maryland, and traveled to Monroe, Michigan, to work with Father Louis Gillet, C.SS.R., to establish a Catholic school and a new noncloistered religious institute, which became the IHM congregation. Within the next six months, these two women had been joined by two others, twenty-

---

the one-hour discussion took place during that same assembly. Participation in both was voluntary.

2. All material cited from interviews is taken from edited transcripts of the audiotapes (MA, restricted).

four-year-old Therese Renauld, later known as Sister Celestine (MMC, 9 Nov. 1845, MA) and Josette Godfroy-Smyth, a forty-two-year-old widow who later became known as Sister Alphonsine (MMC, 14 Apr. 1846, MA).

These four women worked and lived together for three years before any others joined them. Gillet formulated a provisional Rule for them, adapted from that of his own Redemptorist order. (This was a common practice among such groups of religious women in this period because there was no comprehensive body of church law governing the formation of such institutes until 1917.) Gillet's Rule prescribed a daily schedule of religious exercises that included meditation, Mass, a visit to the Blessed Sacrament, and spiritual reading. It also incorporated other aspects of male Redemptorist life, including the observation of long periods of silence, limitations on correspondence, and the practice of never traveling alone. Love of God and of others was key. Although the Redemptorist's founder, Alphonsus Liguori, stressed that particular friendships violated charity and threatened community, the new IHM Rule incorporated prohibitions regarding particular friendships in terms of a violation of chastity.[3]

However, these first years were not conducive to living the ordered and uniform life that would become the hallmark of twentieth-century religious life. The accounts of those early years—both from Maxis's "Notes" and from Renauld's "Historical Cronology [*sic*]"—indicate that they freely adapted the Rule to respond to the circumstances that they faced. The result seemed to strengthen their commitment, both to their vocation and to one another. According to Maxis, "From the time we met and commenced to live in community, the rising hour was at 1/2 past four. Sr. Mary Ann and Sister M. Celestine slept in the old Presbetery [*sic*] and I, with a girl in the other house, here we would meet for prayers and meditation. . . . [S]ometimes they [the priests] would be absent. . . . [I]n this case we would make the Stations of the Cross: to this we gave the name of 'White Mass' " (TMN, 11–12, MA). In 1916, Loyola Shanley, I.H.M., recorded Renauld as saying that "[o]ur furniture was in keeping with our surroundings, a small table, two chairs, a three-legged stool, and a bench. But the sacred memory of those early days has never faded away. That home was filled with life and light and love which no darkness overshadowed, no desolation made drear" ([Shanley] 1916, 34).[4]

By early 1859, the congregation numbered twenty-four women. How-

3. Through the centuries, prohibitions against particular friendships have been classified in these two categories: as an offense against charity, and therefore harmful to life in community, and as an offense against chastity, which referred to undue intimacies with the opposite or same sex. See Raymond 1986, 91–93, and chap. 5 of the present volume.

4. Though this quotation is not found in Renauld's "Historical Cronology," it is probable that Shanley was paraphrasing an oral tradition of the congregation. The two women lived in community together from 1888, when Shanley entered the congregation, until 1897, when Renauld died.

ever, owing to a series of disagreements and misunderstandings between and among Maxis, Detroit's coadjutor bishop, Peter Paul Lefevere, and Redemptorist bishop John Neumann of Philadelphia (who had invited Maxis to open an IHM mission in his diocese), Lefevere on 1 April 1859 discharged Maxis as IHM superior general and banished her from Michigan to Pennsylvania. A few Redemptorist priests, probably in collaboration with Maxis, tried to persuade all the sisters to leave Michigan and come to Pennsylvania; when Lefevere became aware of this, he permanently split the two groups (PPL to EJ, 10 June 1859, MA). He forbade all communication among the sisters, perhaps sensing that ongoing letter writing might lead to his losing the sisters still under his jurisdiction. At this time, eleven sisters were with Maxis in Pennsylvania and thirteen remained in Michigan.[5]

After the separation, Mary Joseph Walker succeeded Maxis as superior of the Monroe sisters. In an effort to keep the congregation alive, she and the Reverend Edward Joos (whom Lefevere had appointed director and superior of the congregation in 1857) tightened congregational discipline. They focused on revising the original Rule and by 1863 completed a Book of Customs, which specified the Rule in practical behaviors and included a section entitled "Instructions for Superiors." They also completed a Book of Instructions for Superiors; both were to be tools in establishing "uniformity of action" as "the bed-rock of the common life" ([Kelly] 1948, 254).

Although friendship itself was rarely mentioned in the new Book of Customs, behaviors that might foster friendships were restricted. For example, the twenty-fourth instruction for superiors reads: "Although the Sisters be not forbidden to see occasionally their relations and friends still it should always be remembered that long visits as well as frequent ones, are not without danger and therefore should not be allowed. For good reasons, though, females who are relations to one of the Sisters within the second degree, can be allowed to stay in the convent for a longer time, but not over two nights: men never." However, the text went on to say that "[t]hese regulations see no objections that friends of the house, or former boarders or such like should be allowed to spend a few days at the Convent" (BC 1863, sec. 24, MA). Thus, despite efforts to make the Monroe sisters more disciplined, it seems that a spirit of leniency still infused community life, a leniency that facilitated the sisters' ability to make and to sustain friends despite official prohibitions against special bonds of affection. This was true even for those charged with enforcing

---

5. Though traditionally the IHM congregation is described as having been "divided in half" at the time of the formal break on 10 June 1859, technically this statement does not apply until 21 July 1859, when Egidius Flanagan, I.H.M., joined Maxis in the East, giving equal numbers in each location.

these prohibitions. For example, despite the Rule's prohibition against favoritism, there is evidence that as general superior, Walker developed a deep affection for Susan Quinlisk, who lived with the sisters from the age of six and then entered the community. When Quinlisk died on 28 April 1871, the Motherhouse Chronicle entry stated: "Her lively, very happy disposition endeared her to everyone, and our dear Mother Mary Joseph who regarded her as her own child admitted her as a Candidate just before her departure [death], at the same time giving her as a last gift her own beautiful name to be assumed at her reception. Mother's ring was at the same time given her, and reserved, as Mother Joseph desired, until our favored little Sisters's profession" (MMC, 28 Apr. 1871, MA).

Likewise, the incidents and stories that Sister Xaveria McHugh related about Mother Clotilda Hoskyns (IHM superior during 1869–79 and 1885–94) in her 1928 book *Mother Mary Clotilda and Early Companions* resemble the type of daily and personal experiences usually recorded in a diary or journal, indicating that the sisters shared information about family background, feelings toward each other, and other topics of conversation—even though they were cautioned against sharing such intimacies. For example, McHugh included the family tree of Hoskyns's father, Edwin Bennet Hoskyns, emphasizing his noble English lineage and acknowledging that he was not Catholic. (Hoskyns herself, however, in an instruction about charity in conversation with one another, points out "never mention nationality, for we are all one" [CH IN, 145, MA].) McHugh also wrote of Hoskyns's affection for the chief infirmarian, Flora Collins: "[F]or if our saintly Mother had any favorite among her blue-robed daughters, that favorite was Sister Mary Flora—and deservedly so." Well aware of this apparent contradiction of the Rule, however, McHugh carefully qualified her statement: "The word 'favorite' is not to be here understood in any unworthy sense of the term. Our dear Mother's big heart had room for us all" ([McHugh] 1928, 61).

In effect, Hoskyns seems to have balanced a willingness to dispense with some of the order's most cherished customs—she reportedly readily dispensed with silence at meals if there was a good reason, which included the sisters being unusually tired—with upholding the tone she thought appropriate for religious life ([McHugh] 1928, 50). One novice recorded that Hoskyns asked the sisters "to make a resolution . . . to keep out of our recreations all worldly talk, such as dress, marriages, weddings and all such not suited to our vocation" (CH IN, 148–49, MA); under miscellaneous points, the novice recorded an injunction to "avoid kissing strangers. It is unbecoming" (CH IN, 150, MA). The very need to address such behavior probably indicates it was occurring, and the gentle reprimands stand in contrast to the more rigid interpretation of the Rule in the coming years.

McHugh herself also seems to have had close friends. Her personal file contains three letters, two from the Reverend Joe McManus (dated 1873 and 1878) and another from Stella Trainor, the daughter of a woman she had taught at St. Mary's Academy (dated 1930). These letters demonstrate that these were long-standing friends. For example, in his 2 October 1878 letter to McHugh, McManus reflected: "When I look back and think of the time we first met and now. I, a young priest, and you, a gay girl, what a change. You now a Spouse of Christ. . . . [A]nd I a priest still surrounded by all the dangers of the world and more especially those of seeking to please others & to satisfy others. I sometimes envy you your happy state" (MRO, MA). Likewise, Trainor's letter of 24 March 1930 indicates that she and McHugh corresponded regularly. Trainor's mother had just passed away and she was sending McHugh some of her mother's things: "The enclosed photographs of Monsignor [Joos] came to light. Nowhere would their possession be so appropriate as in Monroe. Therefore they go to you. The picture of Mama I also send." She continued: "The enclosed magazine you may be familiar with? It has been coming to me for some time. With no permanent address I have renewed my subscription in your name and hope you will receive and enjoy its contents." She ended by stating that she "[w]ill mail itinerary and full information later," as she was setting sail for the Eucharistic Congress (MRO, MA). The very fact that McHugh saved these letters indicates that the custom not to save correspondence in order to be free of possessions either went unenforced or was something McHugh felt free to ignore.

Similarly, it was well known in the congregation that Mother Mechtildis McGrail, general superior during 1900–1918, and Mother Leocadia Delanty, novice mistress for over forty-three years beginning in 1894, were close friends. "[Mother Leocadia's] novitiate companion and spiritual friend for long years was Elizabeth McGrail, who is revered in the community as Mother Mechtildis," wrote Sister Ann Loretta Murphy in a 1945 reflection (Mengy. of LD, 24 Apr. 1945, MA). More publicly, Kelly's centennial history of the congregation notes: "The two newcomers met in the novitiate and from that day spent their lives together in the furthering of the interests of the congregation" ([Kelly] 1948, 481). Thus, Delanty was well aware of the positive benefits of close personal relationships. A 1902–3 novice notebook on Delanty's instructions indicates that Delanty recognized the natural inclination to find "a sister who is particularly pleasing to us. We show this feeling towards her by kissing her again and again, dancing around her for joy, and taking special pains to inform her of all the news we can and taking [her] around the house" (NC, no. 5, 21 Nov. 1902, 2, MA). However, she also points out the tension between such particular affections and the requirements of religious life. In the same instruction, she discusses the "faults of the body," including "immoderate demonstrations of friendship and loud laughter" (NC, no. 5,

21 Nov. 1902, 2, MA); likewise, a section on chastity says: "Avoid all familiarity and touching each other, and above all being familiar with children or others" (NC, no. 5, 28 Mar. 1903, 60, MA).

However, although earlier generations of IHMs had accepted this tension between the Rule's call to discipline and the sisters' need and desire for close friendships, in the years following McGrail's tenure as general superior any congregational sense of permission to interpret the Rule with a bias in favor of allowing and cultivating friendships seems to have disappeared.

### "Keep the Rule and the Rule Will Keep You"

This changed atmosphere was the result of a number of shifts taking place within the IHM congregation, the Catholic Church, and society in general. Most immediately, the shift had to do with McGrail and her desire to keep control of the congregation in the wake of Joos's death in 1901.

For forty-four years, Joos had filled the influential role of appointed director and superior of the IHM congregation. Some sisters were convinced that "his death would mean, if not the collapse, at least serious deterioration in the religious life and spirit of the community" ([Kelly] 1948, 483). McGrail was very aware of the sisters' fears that first summer after Joos's death:

> Calling the members of the community together before their departure for the missions, she told the assembled body that she was aware of the anxiety that had been expressed. Then she reminded the Sisters that the congregation was the work of God, not man, and that He would, therefore, see it through. . . . For its part, the congregation had but one fundamental requirement to meet if it were to remain fervent and strong, and that, she pointed out, was the faithful observance of the rule. ([Kelly] 1948, 483)

Paradoxically, McGrail—the congregation's first general superior to be free of male supervision—chose to prove her ability to govern by requiring strict uniformity of life and by limiting the sisters' interactions ([Kelly] 1948, 485–90). When disagreement over the need for a male director developed and threatened to fracture the community, she prohibited sisters from communicating between missions, a seemingly temporary measure that was never rescinded.[6] Her advice, "keep the Rule and the Rule will keep you," shaped congregational life for the next several decades.

6. Based on a conversation with a former IHM general superior (summer 1992).

## Official Church Recognition and Social Fears

McGrail's turn-of-the-century call for a stricter observance of the IHM Rule also coincided with a shift in the church's attitude toward noncloistered women religious. In 1900, Pope Leo XIII issued *Conditae a Christo*, which marked the first full recognition of noncloistered institutes of women like the IHMs. Together with the 1917 Code of Canon Law, it set forth the procedures for official recognition as a pontifical institute and the elements that constituted an authentic religious congregation of this type. Although Rome's actions in many ways benefited religious congregations—official acceptance of these congregations into the Roman Church offered them heightened status and a greater freedom of movement in fulfilling their mission across diocesan boundaries—they also signified increased control of the everyday life of women religious, for which there were centuries of precedent (Raymond 1986, 73–78).

Rome moved to officially sanction (and thereby to control) the new institutes of noncloistered religious women at a time when the larger society was growing fearful of the emerging independent woman. At the turn of the century, social attitudes toward female friendships shifted significantly.[7] Nineteenth-century white upper-class society was one in which women and men lived and operated in separate spheres. Often, marriage was seen as a practical economic necessity and the way to raise a family; it was not always assumed that one's marriage partner was to be the source of affection or emotional support. Women often sought that kind of companionship and support from other women. In many cases, nineteenth-century women had very intense—even passionate—commitments to other women. From diaries, correspondence, and novels of the time, it is clear that many women opened up their hearts and souls to their female friends. They uttered expressions of overwhelming love and promises of faithfulness. They lived to be together. When separated because of marriage, they awaited visits from each other. Often, the husband vacated the bedroom, leaving the two friends to spend the night together, embracing each other and showering affection upon each other. Women kissed each other and walked hand in hand. Such friendships were even sometimes called "romantic friendships."

In today's culture, the immediate reaction to such intimate relationships is to wonder if they were sexual, but feminist historian Lillian Faderman has concluded that most nineteenth-century romantic friendships did not involve genital sexuality. For centuries, women had internalized the social views that romantic love and sexual impulse were

7. Two key sources that I used in developing this section of the essay are Smith-Rosenberg 1985 and Faderman 1981.

unrelated and that women had no sexual passion. Genital sex was deemed the prerogative of the man and was performed primarily for procreation or for the pleasure of the husband (Faderman 1981, 15–20).

By the second decade of the twentieth century, however, romantic friendships had become suspect. Faderman discerns a number of forces behind this shift. First, as a result of the opening of opportunities for higher education to women in the later nineteenth century, women of the early twentieth century were better educated and more economically independent than ever before. Many had become involved in organizing for social causes. This new breed of educated, independent, and progressive women often rejected traditional marriages but had long-term relationships with women.[8] They pooled their resources—financial, emotional, and physical—so that both partners succeeded in careers and had their personal needs fulfilled. As the Irish writer Edith Somerville wrote in 1917, "The outstanding fact, as it seems to me, among women who live by their brains, is friendship. A profound friendship that extends through every phase and aspect of life, intellectual, social, pecuniary. Anyone who has experience of the life of independent and artistic women knows this" (cited in Faderman, 205–6).

Second, the national feminist movement, launched by the Seneca Falls Woman's Rights Convention of 1848, had grown in strength. "[F]eminist gains had the potential of shaking the traditional family structure," Faderman states. "If women could hope for an education and jobs and political equality, they had no need to marry unless they truly desired to" (Faderman 1981, 237). This possibility threatened the prevailing world view that women existed only in relation to men and that women needed men to survive.

Third, beginning in 1869 with the writings of Carl von Westphal and continuing with the work of Richard von Krafft-Ebing in 1882 and that of Havelock Ellis in 1897, a new psychological theory emerged that depicted love between women in a morbid light and associated it with insanity and disease. These men developed a category of "true invert." Ellis argued that the main way to distinguish "normal" women from true inverts was that normal women would naturally pursue relationships with men if given the opportunity (Ellis and Symonds 1897, vol. 1, 132). Ellis further argued that the independence encouraged by the women's movement "often led to homosexual behavior, especially if women took jobs, since at work they would come into frequent contact with like-minded women and they might find love where they find work" (Ellis and Symonds 1897, vol. 1, 147–48). Faderman has shown that most of the so-called lesbian cases that Ellis (and later Freud) cited were cases of

---

8. Of the women who received Ph.D.s in the U.S. from 1877 to 1924, three-fourths did not marry (Faderman 1981, 186).

Victorian and post-Victorian women whose love relationships were non-genital (Faderman 1981, 17). Thus, the attack on homosexual behavior was aimed at the kind of behavior exhibited by the previously accepted romantic friendships. In a climate in which women were becoming more educated and more economically independent and in which society was becoming more open about sexual matters, women's expressions of affection and love for one another had become suspect among those who feared a breakdown of the traditional moral order.[9]

The women who entered the IHM congregation during this period were influenced by these cultural shifts. At the turn of the century, one IHM novice wrote:

> Among the questions which press for solution in this opening year of the 20th century, none are more prominent or interesting than those which concern the place of woman in the social life of today. The sex problem, as it is called, meets one at every turn. Current life, current literature are full of it. All ages, all classes seem confident to discuss it. It enters into the frivolous small talk as well as the most sublime utterances of the statesman and the devious. Contemporary journalism, as well as contemporary philosophy deals with the theme; the fiction, the drama of the day, all bear witness to its popularity; more than one noted novelist has risen to fame by weaving into creation of his fancy, some particular theory with regard to this question of the hour.[10] (NC, MA)

By the 1920s, society's message of the danger and immorality of close female friendships among educated and independent women was permeating all aspects of life. This shift converged with McGrail's renewed emphasis on the strict observance of the IHM Rule (and its many prohibitions against particular friendships) and with the order's becoming a pontifical institute. Little remained of the nineteenth-century congregation's sense of permission to interpret the Rule or congregational customs with a bias in favor of allowing and cultivating friendships. It is no wonder that some sisters developed a malformed, guilt-ridden understanding of what it meant to have friends. The specific sanctions against particular friendships (a term that did not appear in the IHM Constitutions until 1911) only reinforced this situation.

### Sanctions Against Particular Friendships

Perhaps the most serious sanction imposed on a sister who was suspected or accused of having a particular friendship was that of denying

---

9. For an understanding of how this affected the U.S. see Cook 1992, 288–302.

10. Taken from the "Infant Jesus Circle" notebook of Sister Mary John Cavanaugh, born 1877 and received on 12 June 1900.

or delaying her vows. One sister who entered the congregation in the 1940s was accused of having a particular friendship while she was away from Monroe on mission and under temporary vows. The accused sister denied the charge, but the local superior refused to recommend her for final vows, an action that led the general superior to deny the sister's participation in the final vow ceremony with the rest of her entering "class." She reflected on that painful episode in an interview, remarking on "the whole trauma of the time. We were so identified with our class. You could not discuss it with anyone. Nobody knew" (interview 11, 15 Aug. 1992).

Other sanctions included embarrassing the sisters involved: "Sisters would be yanked out of choir practice or at another time when we were all assembled someone would be called out" (interview 13, 5 Sept. 1992). Sometimes a sister's mission assignment was changed: "People paid the price for friendships. The next year both people were changed or at least one was and the other was left at the mission" (interview 5, 22 July 1992). Levying general suspicion and judgment on the accused was another tactic. "The reputation that we would have PFs would go with us on mission," recalled one sister (interview 10, 20 July 1992). "People would talk," remembered another. " 'Those two are always together' " (interview 9, 22 July 1992).

For many IHM sisters, congregational confusion regarding particular friendships resulted in much pain and suffering. Some sisters interviewed said that they took the teachings on particular friendships very literally and that they did not have friends for years, in some instances for as long as twenty-four years (DG, 1 July 1993).[11] Others said that they knew sisters who had died never having had friends. Significantly, however, some of these sisters' contemporaries—women similar in age and in formation—responded differently to these same teachings and sanctions.

### "I Knew I Was Not Supposed to Have Friends But . . ."

The sisters' tightly scheduled and closely monitored daily routine, substantively unchanged from 1918 until the mid-1960s, removed many of the usual ways in which one makes and sustains friendships. Silence was observed most of the day, and there were many prohibitions regarding personal contact with others. Within this circumscribed lifestyle, however, a remarkable story emerged.

In reflecting on how they responded to the congregation's official teachings on friendship, some sisters interviewed indicated an inner sense of freedom to make up their own minds. "I never believed it," said

---

11. References from the discussion group are taken both from handwritten notes and from an audiotape (MA, restricted).

one. "Every friendship by its nature is particular" (DG, 1 July 1993). Said another: "Well I told her [the superior] my mother told me to be very particular about the friends I chose. I got put into retreat for a week on the head of that" (interview 12, 19 July 1992).

Many more sisters attributed their positive attitude toward making close friends to other (often older) sisters who had close friends and to superiors who bent the rules and who understood the beauty of friendship. One sister reflected: "I knew I was not supposed to have friends but I had seen Sister Anthonita [Bryden] who loved people and had friends. . . . Anthonita was not afraid to tell me that I was special to her, even as a child in school" (interview 11, 15 Aug. 1992). Another sister shared this memory: "I always noticed that superiors I lived with had very close friends. Their friends were the ones they would like to invite over. You would hear them talking about their friends. Their actions told you that this was okay, that along the line you would have friends yourself" (interview 7, 22 July 1992).

A third sister remembered specific instances:

> One sister, Sister Mary Vincent [Corice], was in trouble all her life for particular friendships. Once a neighboring mission came to visit. A close friend of mine was on that mission. Sister Mary Vincent pushed us into a room together and said, "Talk." She knew we wanted to talk together. Also my first superior at Mt. Clemens was wonderful. I talked to her about my experience in the novitiate. She was very good. She told us not to tell any of the neighboring missions what she would do for us to make life a little more pleasant. After school she would tell someone to order ice cream sundaes or pack a picnic and we would go out. It gave me a sense of freedom to know that everything was not frowned upon. (interview 10, 20 July 1992)

Sisters in the IHM congregation met their future friends in the same way most women do. Some women entered with their childhood or school friends. One of the sisters in her nineties (who entered while McGrail was still general superior) recounted a story about her entrance day:

> There were five of us who came that day. We all graduated from St. Vincent's, Detroit. We made up our minds that we would have our goodbyes at home and that our families were not coming with us. So we said goodbye at our homes and met at the interurban [streetcar] station. Our whole class was there to say goodbye. We got on the interurban and came down. Now we didn't stop at the convent right away. We went to Hagan's to get a cantaloupe sundae because we thought we would never see ice cream again. (interview 1, 21 July 1992)

Those sisters that arrived in Monroe that day continue to be friends.

Most IHM sisters made friends with the women who entered with them at the same time—those in their "class"—or with those near them in years. Their "next-in-rank" often became a friend: "rank" was usually chronologically determined by the date and time of arrival of each candidate at the motherhouse,[12] and sisters did many things according to rank such as eating, sleeping, and praying. Other IHM sisters met their friends while teaching school, while attending college and graduate classes together, or while working together on household chores.

### "Summer at Home!"

When asked how they maintained the friendships that they made during formation, the sisters' universal response was "Summer at Home!" When the school year ended, all the sisters left their missions and came back to the Monroe motherhouse to study. They filled the dormitories of the girl's academy and the school for boys on the Monroe campus. The sisters were assigned sleeping quarters according to rank, and so those closest in age—those who had shared formation—slept and ate in the same buildings. There was still a schedule, but it was not as strict as during the school year. There was more time for recreation, for cherry-picking in the fifteen-acre orchard and berry-picking in the gardens at the motherhouse—both sites part of the eight hundred-acre farm that the IHMs owned and managed ([Kelly] 1948, 706).

Great commotion and laughter marked "homecoming" day, as sisters who had not seen each other for nine months reconnected. One sister who entered the congregation in 1925 related her memory of those days and the "date books" they used:

> When we came home we had little books, the size of our examen book. It had all the dates in there of July and August. You asked people if they would go out with you this night [during free time] and that way you never went out twice with the same person. But you had so many friends that you wanted to go out with them and find out how they got along this past year. We used to get our dates fixed up within the first two days. We were not supposed to be talking. Of course, the little date book we kept in the summer went in the waste basket or the fire when we went back on mission. (interview 8, 23 July 1992)

Favorite places to meet these "dates" were on the green benches that dotted the lawn outside the Hall of the Divine Child (the boy's military

---

12. At the time of final profession, each sister was assigned a number, which then permanently maintained the same chronological rank.

academy) and in the berry patches where sisters picked berries side-by-side and talked with their companions. Some of the English teachers who were in their eighties at the time of the interviews remembered being part of a group known as "Beowulf's Den," whose members met at the academy every summer to share their love of English literature. Others remembered the "Mystics," a small group of sisters who met to share prayer together in a special spot by the infirmary every summer in the 1930s.

To a greater or lesser degree, such gatherings were not encouraged. Another sister in her eighties recalled that Sister Clare Willetts, who was in charge of the sisters at the Hall of the Divine Child, gave homilies on friendship. She told the sisters "that when they left chapel and went down the stairs whomever they met at the door would be God's choice for them that night at recreation." This sister remembered how some of the sisters would ask each other earlier in the day, "Would you be God's choice for me tonight at recreation?" and would make a date. They then would figure out how the two of them could end up going out the door together. "It was clear that there were friends," she remarked—and clear that there were ways of getting around the expected behavior (interview 5, 22 July 1992).

One sister in her seventies remembered how she used to skip events with her friend while at the motherhouse. One priest in particular "drove us nuts" so they would go in one door of the room and out the other (interview 10, 20 July 1992). Other sisters spoke about going up to the motherhouse attic and meeting friends there.

### Backrooms and Communication Undergrounds

Although "summer at home" offered a prime opportunity for bolstering old friendships and for making new ones, it was not the only occasion for this to occur. A sister in her sixties recalled how Fuchs, the religious goods store in downtown Detroit, was a great meeting place for friends on mission in that city:

> We would find out that one of the schools was preparing for Holy Communion and that some of the sisters would be going to Fuchs to buy what was needed. Well, if my friend was at that mission, I would suggest that we should also go downtown that day. And so, we would meet and stop at Sanders, the candy store, and buy a sundae and go to Fuchs which had a back room where we could sit and eat as we were not allowed to eat in public. (interview 12, 19 July 1992)

Because the sisters were not allowed to phone each other or to write letters without the permission of the superior, some of them created an underground system of communication that employed the lay people who would deliver stationery, laundry, eggs, etc., to the various convents in and around Detroit. One person that some of the sisters remembered was the stationery man. He would carry the news from one convent to the other: sisters told him what was happening and it was his responsibility to pass the news on when he arrived at the next convent. Some sisters even subverted the mail system. Every sister was to leave any letter she wrote opened in the superior's office. The superior in turn would have the right to read it and then place it for the postal person to pick up. However, some sisters knew when the postal person arrived and waited until the mail appeared and then slipped their letter into the pile (interview 12, 19 July 1992).

## The 1950s and 1960s:
## A Gradual Relaxing of Negative Congregational Attitudes

Although many sisters subverted the external rules and regulations that shaped their lives, the mixed messages regarding particular friendship affected the general patterns of how sisters in the IHM congregation related to each other and how they dealt with the accompanying emotions. According to a sister in her late sixties,

> Nobody was served by this strange attitude toward friendship because it created a community [of women] which was afraid to be human, to be expressive of their own feelings. What kind of a mindset did it lay on what could have been life-giving relationships if you turn it into "this is sick" or "this is a taboo"? Part of the strength of the human person is to share who you are, what you dream. The crazy things you were asked to do in the name of virtue, to deny yourself as a human being! (interview 11, 15 Aug. 1992)

Still, the freedom to openly acknowledge special friendships in the IHM community seems to have increased in the late 1950s and into the 1960s. One sister interviewed shared a very important moment from her years as a temporary professed in the late 1950s. At this time, those sisters who had taken vows for three years continued to live and study at the motherhouse. The sister recalled how she told the sister in charge of them that she

> was preoccupied and struggling with an attraction I was feeling for another sister in our group. She received my words with compassion. She then told me that what was very important for me was that I not close down or become distant from that sister. She encouraged me to simply keep my circle of companions inclusive of many. In that way, she

said, the other will come into perspective. I always have felt grateful to her for such wise and understanding words. (DG, 1 July 1993)

Likewise, a sister in her early seventies recalled her first mission experience and the friendship that developed between herself and the superior. The young sister really did not know how to teach, and so the superior took every opportunity to slip into her classroom and observe, so that she could assist the young sister in improving her teaching. Through the years they were together, they shared a variety of experiences. When the superior was changed to a different mission, the young sister wanted to say goodbye. She approached the superior and "the superior kissed me, not in the customary fashion on both cheeks, but rather a kiss and embrace" that conveyed the emotion she was feeling. The young sister was "so glad to know that sisters could feel that way" (discussion with IHM sister, July 1993).

Was there any sexual expression of sisters' affection for one another among the IHMs? Although there are intimations that some sisters shared sexual intimacy, the preponderance of what the interviewees talked about was just plain close relationships—without sexual connotation.[13]

This gradual relaxing of congregational attitudes toward friendships coincided with other shifts in the larger church and in society—the church renewal of the mid-and late-1960s and the second wave of feminism. In this period, fewer women entered the congregation, and rank was abolished. Local schools began to close, as did their adjacent convents. Sisters attended a variety of universities in pursuit of new professions, and they no longer came home in the summer. Many sisters participated in the women's movement and in the emerging national organizations of sisters who worked for justice in society and in the church. The prohibitions regarding particular friendships became obsolete in the face of new understandings of psychology and of human development. There was no longer any need to subvert or to circumvent the Rule, for there was freedom to make personal choices about one's day, work, housing, and friends.

13. There is evidence that in 1929, a sister fled the mission she was on with another woman (interview 7, 22 July, 1992). Another story well-known in the congregation concerns two sisters who left their habits in the field behind the motherhouse and ran away. Whether those relationships involved genital sexuality is unknown. In one interview, a sister in her 40s recalled an older sister approaching her while she was in formation and making a sexual overture to her. The older sister eventually left the congregation (discussion with IHM, 3 July 1992).

## The Last Twenty-Five Years

Over these past twenty-five years, the congregational understanding of close friendships has changed dramatically.[14] Sisters speak of "a new openness to manifesting one's love" (quest. 10), of being "less fearful regarding friendships" (quest. 29), of a "realization of the beauty of true friends" (quest. 19), and of the importance of close friends in one's life (quest. 13). Many sisters associate their increased freedom to make and to sustain friendships over these past several decades with personal growth in spirituality, with risk-taking in ministry, and with new ways of thinking. Close friends have enabled them, they say, "to remain sane" (quest. 1), to "be myself" (quest. 2), and to "stay in the convent" (quest. 7); friendships, one sister said, "were essential to my well being and development" (quest. 10).

Because the majority of IHMs are in retirement, many are caring for friends who are sick and dying. One sister interviewed at age eighty-one told of how she cared for her friend ten years her senior, who was dying of cancer. They had lived together since the mid-1960s, until they returned to the motherhouse to retire and her friend was taken to the infirmary: "I am with her all day. I go up after breakfast, eat lunch, go back at 3 P.M., stay until supper, go back after supper till she goes to bed. Sometimes she wants me to stay there at night; lately she says, 'I am going to sleep so you go.' We pray together at night" (interview 9, 22 July 1992). Other sisters told of friends getting ill and how they stayed in the hospital or at their bedside during the dying process.

Death comes often in a community of aging women, and so funerals become an occasion for friendships to be acknowledged and celebrated. During the wake service, individuals remember the life of the person and her impact on theirs. Friends often help prepare the liturgy, do one of the readings, or even give the homily.

After death, the memory lives on. The sisters who have died are not forgotten. They are remembered and invoked to be with those who are still alive. At particular times—a year after their death, or at the end of a calendar year—there might be a special remembering. One of the oldest members of the congregation interviewed told of such an occasion. She came to the community with her high-school friends and they had remained friends ever since. One of them had died during a particular year, and she was asked by the superior of the house to participate in the special liturgy remembering all the sisters who had died that year. "I said

---

14. In response to the question "Has your understanding of, or attitude toward, close friendships changed over the years?" only eight out of the 35 respondents answered in the negative.

I would love it," she recalled. "I took my walker as I don't trust myself without it. I took the special carnation up. Many people said what a good job I did. Did I ever appreciate taking that flower up!" (interview 1, 21 July 1992).

## Conclusion

IHM sisters were persistent in forging friendships even under adverse circumstances. There existed a tension between the externally defined norms regarding *particular friendships* among celibate women in community and the life-giving experience of close *persistent friendships* among these same women. At different stages in congregational history, the bias of interpretation shifted between these two poles. Although scars remain from those times when personal experience was sacrificed to externally defined norms, for the most part the sisters in the congregation chose to make and to sustain friendships.

With rare exception, the IHM sisters answering the questionnaires knew that there were IHMs with close friends and that sisters who were close friends played an important part in the history and mission of the IHM congregation. Almost everyone can name who the close friends were—among them Theresa and Ann, Clotilda and Xaveria, Mechtildis and Leocadia, Ruth and Miriam, Marie Isabel and Mary George. Today, such persistent friendships are considered life-giving and essential to the congregation.

Serving trays to sisters in the infirmary.

# 7

# Emotional and Mental Illness in the IHM Congregation, 1845–1980

## Carol Quigley, I.H.M.

Emotional and mental illness within the Michigan IHM congregation is a topic about which little has been written—records are scant in the earlier years of the congregation's history and, later, when more abundant, are restricted by confidentiality. However, it is clear that in every period of its history, the congregation has counted among its members some who were afflicted with emotional and mental disturbances.

To attempt to define or even to describe mental or emotional illness is less easy than to describe its opposite, mental health. The *Dictionary of Behavioral Science* offers as criteria for mental health the following five characteristics: "Realistic perception, emotional balance, social adjustment, achievements commensurate with potentialities, and self-esteem" (Wolman 1989, 214). In this essay, I will explore the phenomenon of the lack of mental health in some IHM community members and will discuss how the congregation has responded. I will also suggest that aspects of congregational life and attitudes may have negatively affected the mental health of its members.[1]

### Mental Illness in the Nineteenth-Century Congregation

The IHM congregation was established in autumn 1845 when Sisters Theresa Maxis, Ann Constance Shaaff, and Theresa Renauld accepted Father Louis Florent Gillet's invitation to begin a new religious community of women in Monroe, Michigan. Concerns about persons evidencing

---

1. For purposes of confidentiality, names are not used unless already public knowledge; all cases used are of deceased IHMs, all of whom died before 1980. Case materials for each person were drawn together by the author, to be used only as research material for this essay (MA, restricted).

emotional difficulties arose as early as 1853, when Maxis, the community's first general superior, wrote to the Archdiocese of Detroit's coadjutor
bishop, Peter Paul Lefevere, that Sister Mary Whipple, who had joined
the small Monroe congregation in 1849, was suffering some maladjustment to religious life. "You know that she is in poor health," Maxis stated,
"and she always needs something new, some distraction to excite her or
else she lets herself go into a fit of melancholy. And I have observed that
every time that an occasion presented itself for going out or for distracting her, she seems much better. All her weakness leaves her in this
case, and she acts like a vigorous person, which gives me to think that
her mind is more sick than her body" (TM to PPL, 1 July 1853 UNDA;
translation, MA). This restless spirit, however, did not appear to impede
Whipple's overall functioning within religious life.[2] In June 1859, Whipple joined Maxis and other members of the Monroe IHM congregation at
a mission in Susquehanna, Pennsylvania.[3] A misunderstanding led to her
becoming discontented there, and on 17 August 1866, Whipple became a
novice (Sister Mary of Providence) in the Congregation of the Grey Nuns
of Ottawa; it was with this same congregation that Maxis spent her years
of exile and lived again with Whipple, who did not die until 1891 ([Kelly]
1948, 152–54).[4] What distressed Whipple in Monroe may have been simply cabin fever; the best cure, it appears, was brief, periodic returns to
the world Whipple had left when she took her religious vows. Maxis's
insights into this matter were both helpful and healthy.

If, in the congregation's opinion, Whipple's melancholia and restlessness did not mark her as unsuited for religious life or render her unable
to function within it, signs of more acute disturbances in other sisters did
have that effect. The congregation's leaders tended to turn away such
candidates as soon as their condition became apparent. In 1864, for example, Paulina Franklin left the community after six months as a novice.
Nine days before her departure, a passage in the Motherhouse Chronicles
(a day-by-day record of important events) stated:

> [Paulina] complained in the evening of being tired and was sent to lie
> down, but on awaking some hours afterwards was found to be quite
> childish. Medical treatment was resorted to but no good effects resulted;
> she continued for some days to grow yet more wild and it was finally
> decided that it was best she should return home as soon as sufficiently

2. Whipple served as superior of a local convent three times: Vienna, Michigan; St.
Joseph, Susquehanna, Pennsylvania; and Saint John the Baptist, Manayunk, Pennsylvania
([Kelly] 1948, 146; [Ryan] 1967, [460], 112).

3. For an account of the separation in the IHM congregation, see [Kelly] 1948, 124–50,
and chaps. 1 and 2 of the present volume.

4. For an account of the years of Maxis's exile with the Grey Nuns of Ottawa, see
[Kelly] 1948, 214–35.

restored, as the Doctor said she would always be subject to these fits of insanity. Accordingly on the 4th of June, we were obliged to our great regret, to part with our dear little Sister, for by her exemplary piety and sweetness of disposition, she had endeared herself, not only to her Sister Novices, but also to the Superioress and the whole Community. (MMC, 4 June 1864, MA)

Most reports of sisters' departures in the nineteenth-century chronicles are far briefer than this account. More typical is the notation made about another novice who was sent home at the same time as Franklin. She left, the chronicler reported curtly, "because the superiors found her as 'wanting in vocation' " (MMC, 12 May 1864, MA). The phrase "wanting in vocation" may or may not imply the existence of a mental disorder in this candidate, but the attitude of superiors in dealing with her situation is evidence that not all dismissals were handled in the same way. The account of Franklin's dismissal is detailed and compassionate, capturing both the surprise of the community at the "insanity" that could exist parallel to her "exemplary piety and sweetness of disposition" and their genuine regret at having to dismiss her in order to preserve her own equilibrium and that of the community. The account also captures an early instance of the congregation's efforts to treat mental illness medically. Even as they accepted the advice of a physician, however, there is a sense of regret and sadness about her suffering and about the congregation's loss of a promising young member, whom they had previously regarded as fitting in well.

The experience of a Paulina Franklin, however, may have led the community to become more precise in naming the qualities that it sought in candidates. The congregation's nineteenth-century leaders included a woman of special compassion and balance in the person of Bridget Smith, who served as novice director during 1870–73.[5] In an undated commentary written for the congregation's director, the Reverend Edward Joos, apparently at his request, she describes various facets of formation. After stating the need for a certain degree of intellectual acumen in potential sisters, she comments on the necessary qualities of mind for religious life in such a way as to suggest she is, in fact, speaking of the need for emotional health:

It is not necessary to be of so quick a mind as will understand a thing before it is half-said but it is necessary to be able to understand without receiving an hours [sic] explanation of what needs no explanation at all, and also that the mind whether, quick or not, be *strong* and capable of understanding the rule and spirit of the Institution, and that it can bear

5. For a fuller description of Bridget Smith, see chap. 4 of the present volume.

the restraints of rule without danger to health of mind or body, *particularly the mind*. If weak minds are received they can hardly be corrected for their faults through fear of upsetting them and causing uneasiness which might prove fatal, and so they may live for years giving disedification which they perhaps will never see or correct. (BS, IMN, MA)

The nineteenth-century story of the IHMs is also not without its example of institutionalization. Sister Louisa Walsh, born in Ireland, entered the congregation and was formally received in 1867, making vows the following year. From approximately 1870 on, however, she resided at St. Joseph's Retreat in Dearborn, Michigan, an institution for the mentally ill operated by the Sisters of Charity. She recovered her reason a few weeks before her death in 1885, but the cause of her death was listed as insanity (Mengy., 9 Sept. 1885, MA).

### Twentieth-Century Cases

Twentieth-century evidence of emotional and mental disturbances among members of the IHM community is more plentiful than for the nineteenth century, with a wider range of expressions. Like their nineteenth-century counterparts, twentieth-century IHM leadership personnel continued to exercise caution with candidates for membership who showed a family history of or disposition to emotional instability. Leaders also continued to rely on medical doctors for advice. The first item on the agenda for one meeting of the governing council in 1934, for example, was "[t]he advisability of receiving a postulant [candidate] whose mother is in an insane asylum. . . . It was decided to report her case to [the doctor] and abide by his decision" (CM, MA).[6] A 1935 entry in the council minutes concerned a novice with a possible psychosomatic illness: "She has been ill all during her novitiate and although every effort has been made, the Doctors have failed to find the cause of her disease. Outside of her health condition she is a very desirable subject. The question was left open" (CM, MA).

Because decisions about new members would last a lifetime and would vitally influence the whole congregation, any expressions of doubt about a candidate's suitability were treated very seriously, and sometimes a decision could take months. One member under temporary vows evoked this response from the council: "[A]ll feared that in her present state of mind she will not be able to assume the responsibility of the vows" (CM, MA). After this initial evaluation, however, the council took

---

6. In this essay, dates for minutes of council meetings and for menologies are not cited for reasons of confidentiality.

five months for the decision to be finalized: "She has not improved, although she shows no bad spirit, she evidently has no vocation. It seems kinder to dismiss her than to keep her until her vows expire in January. All felt this procedure would be best" (CM, MA).

Some who found IHM life incompatible after their final vows were able to recognize their own emotional unhappiness and to act in their own best interests, as evident in the minutes of one 1929 general council meeting: "At this meeting our Rev. Mother General informed us of Sister ————'s determination to leave the Community—because she could not endure the strain and is unhappy. Her conduct for the past three years has been disedifying in her disregard for the Holy Rule, and sad as it is, all the Council Members favored her getting a dispensation" (CM, MA).

One member who eventually left the community in 1948 sent signals of emotional distress that in hindsight seem quite clear (case I, 1, MA). Through the symptoms of physical health problems, her own deep unhappiness emerged. She had been assigned to kitchen work, but after a dozen years, she reported that the work affected her health. When her place of work (but not the work itself) was changed, she began to request and to receive many highly unusual exceptions from the Rule, such as several months at a sanitarium living and dressing as a lay woman. After returning to regular convent routine, she found the habit material intolerable and its weight detrimental to her health; she felt heavily burdened and probably unheard, both in her spoken and her somatic language. She subsequently lived with her family for six months—again an extraordinary permission. One of the physicians consulted in her case noted: "She has been to innumerable doctors, specialists, and cultists; to many hospitals and sanitariums. She has had most every kind of clinical and laboratory test and examination. She has traveled near and far. . . . Many and most of her complaints are bizarre and unworthy of credence" (case I, 2, MA). He later suggested that she was a danger to younger members and a "menace" to religious life because of her demoralizing effect on the group. The only relief, in his view, was for her to leave religious life, although he questioned if even that would bring her happiness.

For years following her departure, that former member corresponded with Mother Theresa McGivney, then general superior of the community. These lengthy epistles were cast in pious language and expressed great gratitude to the community. Still, her problems did not cease—her marriage to a man many years her senior put her squarely back into domestic work (case I, 2, MA).

While some of those who sought vows in the IHM congregation were turned away because those in authority judged them unable to keep the

Rule[7] or because they eventually signaled their own emotional distress at trying to do so, others remained in spite of their deep unhappiness. Often enough, such persons, by virtue of their unacceptable or hypercritical behavior, made life miserable for those who shared community with them or for those who were their students.

The menology of a member who died in 1970 draws such a picture. An avid reader of literature and a student of classical languages, she gradually became preoccupied with worries—especially about the future of the country—and eventually returned to the Monroe motherhouse "suffering from many emotional problems" (case G, 1, MA). She was diagnosed by a psychiatrist as a passive-aggressive personality.[8] Her behavior, "including yelling anathemas at her sisters and complaining of too much noise," sometimes required hospitalization. Although she lived as a virtual recluse in the community, participating little in its daily life, she remained a member for over thirty years. One friend said that she shared a meal with her sisters only at the time of her twenty-five-year jubilee. The community cared for her for decades because she was a member of the congregation who had committed herself to it for the rest of her life. Ironically, though, some of the congregation's own ambivalence is evident in the very fact of allowing this rather aberrant form of IHM life to go on within the motherhouse itself.

At times, however, there shines through the accounts of the emotionally ill stories of a different type of frustration. One member's record describes her as "unusually gifted as an artist [who] studied art with masters, but felt her limitations, one being her inability to take over the Art Department at the opening of Marygrove College." A friend wrote that she "possessed a high social intelligence prompted by a sensitive nature," adding that she was also "a perfectionist in high degree" (case F, 1, MA). It is striking to note that the latter years of the sister's life (after her retirement) were marked by "not only a break in physical health but a mental break from time to time." For three subsequent autumns, she spent time at Mercywood Hospital, a psychiatric facility in Ann Arbor, Michigan. Each time, after a month of treatment, she was discharged with new medications. Apparently, her condition was severe enough to lead the professionals in charge of her care to consider shock therapy, but she was considered "a poor risk" because she had earlier been diagnosed with a heart problem (case F, 3, MA). It may be that with time in her

---

7. Council minutes, for example, note as a cause for dismissal of one sister: "Although her novitiate is nearly completed, she has not been able to adjust herself to the religious life."

8. This diagnosis in contemporary terms might well be considered phobic avoidance of contact, judging from the behavior described. The symptoms do not coincide with the term passive-aggressive as defined in American Psychiatric Association 1987, 356–58.

retirement to reflect on her life and her work, the great heartache of not being at Marygrove surfaced each fall, just as the new school year began. Her perfectionism may have dictated a goal to which she could respond only with an annual acute reenactment of her own sense of failure. The writer of her menology sacralized the suffering of this sister, comparing it to the agony of Jesus (Mengy., MA).

As in the nineteenth century, there were times in the twentieth century when a sister's mental difficulties required that she be institutionalized for extended periods, even for a lifetime. One member's menology records such a situation with considerable understatement: "While on the missions, it was noted that her mind was deranged." This sister spent the last thirty-three years of her life, until 1930, at St. Joseph's Retreat. The menology concludes: "When she was brought home, her poor body was as crippled as her mind. . . . A few days before her death, her limbs and arms began to relax and her face took on a very calm, peaceful expression" (case E, 1, MA).

Another member entered in 1924 with a glowing epistle from her pastor: "Seldom have I recommended an applicant seeking admission in the religious life, with the confidence and satisfaction inspired by the character, virtues and spirit of Miss ———— . . . . She has inherited the twin virtues of piety and faith of an apostle, the constancy of a martyr." The very qualities that elicited such high praise, however, might in hindsight suggest a defensive rigidity hinting at future problems. Although one mourner at her funeral remembered that the sister was "prostrate with grief that she was not allowed to go home for the funeral" of her father during her postulancy, there were few signs to the untrained eye that beginning in 1937 she would spend nearly a quarter century suffering from chronic psychosis (case H, 1, MA). To the trained eye, however, the combination of initial symptoms and subsequent loss of touch with reality might suggest the profile of a victim of childhood trauma (MCSu, interviewed by author, 9 Apr. 1994, MA).

Sometimes a sister would begin to manifest symptoms of concern to herself and others only a few years after her final profession of vows. One such member began a forty-year history of illness in 1932. "Patient has symptoms to almost every organ or system of organs . . . in the past few years," recorded the first doctor consulted. "As soon as one complaint clears up, another complaint appears elsewhere. . . . Patient has a functional nervous disease with hypochondrias. . . . However, it has been impossible to delve into her life very intimately to determine the source of this conflict in her mind." After giving results of the physical exam, the report indicates "psychoneurosis and hysteria," with this added note: "There seems to be a terrific functional element present with a revolt to her tasks" (case J, 5, MA). Fifteen years later, another physician wrote of the same sister: "I am of the opinion that her condition of discomfort and state of ill health is only psychological, rather than on a physical basis" (case J, 6, MA). The numerous doctors called in to treat this sister usually began their treatment with great compassion, ordering batteries of tests and retests, and then signing off the case with a recommendation of psychiatric treatment. Apparently, the doctors seldom conferred among themselves. About the time of the sister's twenty-five-year celebration of religious life, the psychiatrist recommended hospitalization at St. Joseph's Retreat. He was upset that he had not been informed that "she'd been in St. Joseph's Retreat several years ago and on several occasions had treatments from other psychiatrists." Given that he had himself noted one month earlier that "Sister is a pathological liar" (case J, 8, MA), his frustration was clearly directed at his professional peers, not at the sister herself.

One IHM member born at the beginning of the twentieth century manifested problems shortly after her first profession of temporary vows. As the IHM general superior wrote in a letter some thirty years later, "Though by nature timid, shy, retiring, it was not until Sister was living on mission that she began to manifest deep moods of depression, crying day and night and unable to do her work. Her despondency exaggerated the natural shyness, timidity, and sensitiveness. She appeared very inhibited and awkward and irregular menstrual periods aggravated her mental condition. A guilt complex developed and make it very clear that Sister was in need of psychiatric care" (case K, 2, MA). These statements were written in appealing to Rome for approval to accept this member for final vows, fifty years after she entered the community; permission was granted, this sister having demonstrated, in the opinion of leaders, fidelity to her religious commitment to a heroic degree. Her return to the motherhouse from St. Joseph's Retreat—after a quarter century there— enabled her to experience a freedom of mind and body. The convenience of the regular services of a psychiatrist provided at the motherhouse safeguarded her progress toward relative independence. Based on her psychiatrist's recommendation, she enjoyed a short trip to California and gradually was able to move more freely throughout the motherhouse and, eventually, even to take on some responsibilities.

Another member who was brilliant suffered paranoia. The daughter and granddaughter of college professors, she prayed continually for the conversion of her father to Catholicism. Her request was answered on his deathbed; some in the congregation interpreted her suffering as a "payment" on her part to God for this favor. Her autobiography (something each retired member has been required to write since the 1970s) mentions only her work, providing little else to reveal her personality. The last decade of her life included no teaching, owing to the symptoms of paranoia. Her psychiatrist stated she was "antagonistic toward her superiors and her environment and manifested this antagonism by an attempt to undermine the policies and principles and the Holy Rule of the religious" and recommended her removal from teaching and from "contact with the laity" (case L, 4, MA).

There is, perhaps, no more poignant expression of emotional conflict than the act of ending one's own life. For one to choose one's own death witnesses to intense struggle at the core of one's existence. In 1970, one member made that choice, and her family and community were left without answers. With the new openness of communication in the congregation, then general superior Margaret Brennan wrote in a letter to all IHMs: "On Monday morning, September 28th, Sister —————— was found dead in the lake in the back of the motherhouse just before 8:00 A.M. Subsequently, we discovered a brief note Sister had left, indicating that she could be found there. Because of the circumstances surrounding the death a police report was necessarily filed which listed the cause of death on the coroner's report as 'suicidal death by drowning' " (case M, 2, MA).

This sister had lived with the struggle of mental illness for many years and had been hospitalized several times. One year before her untimely death, she was diagnosed as manic depressive, since renamed bipolar disorder. An unsigned note in her file indicates that she had been despondent for a few weeks before her death; with the advice of a medical doctor to see her "own doctor," the writer of the note recalls, "she thought this meant she would have to re-enter a mental hospital for treatment and this she did not want to do" (case M, 1, MA). The sister's own description of her work for the community is a list of miracles that she thought were visited upon her or her pupils while she was their teacher. She peppered her account with "the miraculous cure by St. Francis Xavier of a form of lockjaw I had from having a wisdom tooth extracted" and "eight miraculous full-blown roses" sent by "[t]he Little Flower" in response to the "prayers of the second and third graders." She continued: "The day after Father Van Antwerp blessed me with the relic of St. Anne—[my] goiter had vanished, which was considered miraculous because I had it for nineteen years" (case M, 3, MA). No church authority has yet authenticated any miracle.

## Treatment of the Mentally Ill

In providing treatment for the mentally ill, the congregation reflected the times and the treatments current during those times. Not all of the treatments would stand the test of holistic approaches today. One can shrink in horror, for example, at the number of sisters who underwent electric shock therapy. That there were any lobotomies—and there were —may seem incomprehensible to later generations (case P, 6, MA). History also bears the marks and wounds of the fact that some sisters were forced to live apart from the congregation for years, even decades. Ordering a change of scenery, i.e. a different teaching or work assignment, in an effort to see if a situation in the local convent was responsible for the problem was one common response to symptoms of emotional distur- bance. Unfortunately, when the problem persisted (as it often did), con- gregational leaders usually ordered another change of assignment instead of seeking the causes of the problem. The case of the domestic cited earlier is one example.

The IHM sisters' fear of the emotionally troubled was not unlike the fear of most families who faced the same phenomena. Recognizing the limits of their authority in professions other than their own, IHM superi- ors generally complied with and deferred to the professional advice of doctors from outside and to the nurses and other caregivers within the community.

The IHM healthcare professionals working at the motherhouse in- firmary tried to balance compassion for a friend and sister with the care dictated by professional standards. Interviews with several of the women who have served in this capacity since the 1940s make clear that their love of the members took precedence and that they attempted to integrate kindness with the best known methods at the time. They changed treat- ment, safeguards, and their own attitudes just as soon as they believed a better course was indicated for the patient. The caregivers interviewed also told tales of desperate patients who would attempt an escape, either from the motherhouse infirmary through a window or from life itself through an overdose of drugs. Once, a knife-wielding patient nearly car- ried out prior threats on one of the sisters. Often the patients in that state would be medicated and sent to the hospital for more intensive care. On their return, the patients were given increased sedatives and were iso- lated; too often they were not kept busy or involved. The care they re- ceived reflected the fact that the community had too few sisters trained to treat the mentally ill and managed only to maintain relative peace.

By the mid–twentieth century, however, advances in treatment dic- tated closer collaboration among those in authority and those providing care. Group meetings with superiors from the congregation, the member involved, and professionals began to be held in order to guarantee the best possible treatment (case J, 2; CM, MA).

During the early 1970s, great changes took place in the care of sisters who suffered more severe forms of emotional or mental disturbance. The closing of St. Joseph's Retreat forced the community to seek alternatives to institutionalization. Benefiting from advances in the behavioral sci- ences, the congregation designed new and more humane living situations for all sisters, but especially for those who returned "home" to the moth- erhouse. Although one leader of the infirmary can recall the flaws of the transitional period, the main goal of "getting the sisters home" was a clear and conscious choice. That choice required updated education for those who would work most closely with the returning members as well as general education for the other sisters (Info., Oct. 1973, B. 14, item 3, MA). Even by the time of my research, however, many of those interviewed felt that training in the mental health areas has not kept pace with the needs of the community.

Some of the choices involved renovation of space to accommodate the needs of those leaving St. Joseph's Retreat. These changes had, as a primary purpose, to safeguard the patient more than to placate the unfounded fears of others living in the motherhouse. Staff persons entered into greater dialogue with psychiatrists, learning in advance the side effects of psychotropic medication rather than discovering them as they affected the sister who took them. The onsite services of at least a part-time professional began at that time (and has since become a permanent part of congregational life). Therapy expanded to include crafts, music, and much more contact with the other sisters; colorful furnishings replaced the neutral or uniform shades of earlier years. Clothing expressed the taste and comfort of the wearer.

As the congregation expanded its works, many more members entered the counseling professions—some as therapists, some as psychologists, and still others as spiritual directors. The stigma of mental illness began to diminish as ongoing education enabled all to see the wide range of mental illnesses and the possibility of prevention of some of the routine pitfalls of human life and development. Fearful attitudes died more slowly.

## Contributing Factors

In assessing the incidence of mental illness in the IHM congregation from the period of its founding in the 1840s until the modern era, it is impossible not to question whether the conditions and constraints of religious life—a life intentionally separate and different from the "normal" way of life "in" the world, among family, one's own possessions, and other social conventions—have had a significant part to play in causing or exacerbating some sisters' problems. Most of the IHM caregivers interviewed for this essay (some of whom have cared for sisters whose histories span the last fifty years of IHM life) agreed that although a contributing factor to mental illness was frequently low self-esteem (often developed in childhood), this condition was worsened by congregational pressure to perform or to conform. The pressure to be a "good" sister exerted a particular stress in an atmosphere that demanded perfection and often fanned the flames of unfounded guilt. Those interviewed cited in particular the problems posed by the extreme uniformity instilled by a Rule of life that was intended to facilitate the pursuit of "holiness."

Emphasis on the strict observance of the congregation's Rule (or Constitutions)—with its equation of the "good religious" with the law-abiding IHM citizen—increased from 1917 on, when religious congregations such as the IHMs were brought under the jurisdiction of official church law (Benedict XV, *Codex Iuris Canonici*, 1949, Canons 487–681). The IHMs brought to the new code of church law a dedication to seek perfection in all its facets. They committed themselves with a passion to be loyal daughters of the church. The IHM Constitutions, approved by Rome at the time of the formal ratification of the congregation in 1920, gave a faithful reflection of the church's expectations. What was IHM and what was of church law were often indistinguishable.

The observance of each and every slightest rule received the superiors' utmost attention, and the "community woman" was one who perfectly mirrored the ideal described in the written word. Even for the healthy, the strain of being perfect increased pressure. Beginning in this period, virtually every hour of every day was regulated. The rising hour was 5:00 A.M., followed by meditation, morning prayers, and Mass; prayer also occurred at 11:45, 4:30, and 8:30. Meals were eaten after Mass, at noon and at 6:00 P.M. following the study hour. The community assembled at 7:30 P.M. for recreation. At 8:30, strict silence began and by 9:30, all were "strictly commanded" to be in bed (Const. 1920, arts. 160–63, 168–71, 198).

Not only time but also the way the sisters interacted with each other was highly regulated. "To preserve the spirit of charity, they shall carefully avoid all disputes and whatever could give the least cause of dissension; they must not sustain their own opinion with obstinacy, endeavoring to take advantage of their learning or endowments; but let each readily yield to the others in a spirit of humility and charity," read article 11 of the Constitutions. "Even in jest, the Sisters, either professed or novices, are not permitted to address a companion except by her religious name," instructed article 12.

The importance of discipline is clear in the articles of the Constitutions that address speaking and reading. "Silence is observed the entire day, except during the hours of recreation; The Sisters speak only through necessity and give careful attention to silence of action," stated article 66. In the case of reading, stated article 43, "The members of the Congregation are strictly forbidden, without special permission, to read novels, either in book or serial form, the daily papers, or other periodicals not commonly used for school purposes. Laxity in this matter might easily cause the loss of vocation and lead to the destruction of the Congregation." In general, according to article 58, the members were to "render an entire and faithful obedience to the Constitutions. Though these do not bind under penalty of sin, yet their willful transgression is rarely without fault. Love of regular observance is necessary in every circumstance, that the Sisters may preserve the true religious spirit." Such regulations gave rise to great uniformity, and the slightest exception was immediately apparent to all, which only increased the pressure to conform.

With the financial hardships of the Great Depression in the 1930s came additional demands for a disciplined community life. The hard times were exacerbated by the need to rebuild the congregation's St. Mary Academy (destroyed by fire in 1929) and to initiate construction of a new motherhouse, as well as to pay off the mortgage incurred to build Marygrove College only a few years earlier. The council minutes report numerous cases during this period in which obedience to the Rule seemed to be the sole criterion of a sister's goodness, both as a person and as an IHM. The least discrepancy of observance could cause a sister to be judged as unfaithful to her vows or as unworthy of IHM membership. Because no one article of the Rule was said to be more important than another, there was little distinction between small infractions and major omissions—both were of equal wrong because both disregarded "the Holy Rule." Although no article of the IHM Constitutions specifically called for such scrupulous attention to every jot and tittle of the law, community practice dictated such strict observance. Each Friday, the superior had the responsibility of reminding the local community of the Rule and any lack of respect to it that she had observed.

The prevailing assumption—"if you don't have a vocation when you enter, you will receive one"—left little tolerance for those who were tempted to leave. The fear of infraction led to scrupulosity and perfectionism. If breaking silence and lack of charity were of comparable importance, it is little wonder that daily life could seem overwhelming. If the bell was the voice of God, what else mattered? And if one failed to respond to that bell, had one disobeyed God? At times, the pressure left a sister with little peace. One recourse was simply to leave reality, even if that choice was unconscious.

### Feminist Connections

Still, despite the qualities of IHM religious life that may have had a negative impact on the mental health of some of the members, much of the IHM experience with mental illness closely resembled that of the secular world. Recent scholars of women's history and culture, for example, have argued that narrow, confining definitions of "woman's place" (especially in the nineteenth century) may have led some women to retreat into illness as a means of escape from prescribed social roles. The cultural understandings of "true womanhood" that operated well into the nineteenth century—understandings that defined women as "pious, pure, submissive, and domestic"—themselves prompted some women to "act out" noncompliance through depression or "hysteria" (Welter 1976, 57). For IHMs—whose spirituality, ethos, and Holy Rule sacralized precisely the conventional definitions of true womanhood—the pressures to conform were doubly intense, as were, probably, the temptations to escape those definitions through some form of self-punishment. It is certainly possible that the moodiness, restlessness, agitation, and melancholia reported of some sisters during the nineteenth century may have stemmed from the same factors as those that plagued their lay sisters.

Even for those women—lay or religious—who could put on the "outer garment" of compliance or who could appear to embrace conventional behaviors, the inner self might still be resistant. Historian Barbara Welter recounts, for example, the work of the Boston physician Harriot Hunt, who often found herself treating women patients who "exhibited the outward signs of those societal conventions which denied them knowledge of their interior life." Hunt noted in one case: "Mind had been uncultivated—intelligence smothered—aspirations quenched." Welter continues: "Very often she [Hunt] treated not the disease . . . but the soul of the women who consulted her." One woman, challenged by Hunt's words " '[Y]ou have hugged your chains,' responded, 'I know no language in which to utter myself.' " Welter calls this comment "possibly the most succinct summary of woman's emotional problems that the nineteenth century has provided us" (Welter 1976, 60–61). The same comment might be made about IHMs, schooled in silence and self-abnegation and often rendered speechless about their own individual gifts and self-identity.

If women who struggled to comply with traditional notions of womanhood or of religious life were sometimes conflicted enough to suffer emotional instability, so too were women who did not meet the socially expected behaviors. Women who resisted marriage and motherhood or who chose careers or other means of self-fulfillment could pay the price in emotional uncertainty. Patricia Vertinsky, in *The Eternally Wounded Woman*, illustrates the lot of such women in the nineteenth century:

> For many female intellectuals in the late nineteenth century, the attempted transition from domestic to professional life was characterized by nervous disorders and periodic depression. "New women" and nervous illness seemed to go together, and neurologists readily fashioned treatments which were designed to ease the anxieties of female patients by defusing their ambitions and resocializing them to their traditional sphere and its familiar obligations. (1990, 212)

As professional educators who might be considered "female intellectuals" and as women who asserted that there was a different way to live life than in marriage (even if they did so for reasons that were not overtly feminist, nor even self-consciously countercultural), religious sisters went against the mores of what "properly" constituted women's role. No matter how life choices were couched in religious language, for some IHMs, the internal conflicts over competing definitions of womanhood—wife and mother vs. competent professional vs. humble religious vs. ambitious intellectual—might well have been expressed in forms of nervous disorder or periodic depression. Injunctions to such "new women" to keep the Rule, to examine one's conscience, or to pray may not have been effective treatments because they were the religious equivalents of "defusing their ambitions and resocializing them to their traditional sphere and its familiar obligations."

Treatments might also have been ineffective—or too effective—because they were designed by men to keep women "in their place." IHM leadership did defer to professional, largely male, advice regarding mental illness and its treatment. In many instances, the deference given to the authority of the doctor resembled closely that given to the parish priest, who exerted nearly absolute authority over the parish schools in which the vast majority of IHMs taught. Not surprisingly, doctors who considered women patients cured when they returned to their "familiar obligations" and not cured when they continued to act in inappropriate ways would have found their advice respected in a religious community that valued uniformity and conformity.

Commentators on women's experience of mental illness in the twentieth century often seriously question the accuracy of the male professionals' diagnoses, particularly their reluctance to consider cultural reasons for emotional instability. In *Women and Mental Illness*, for example, Agnes Miles writes:

> The feminist argument is that women become depressed because they have reasons to be so; that their position in society is one of disadvantage *vis-à-vis* that of men. Indeed sociologists have documented that women's education, employment, power, prestige, and opportunities compare unfavourably with corresponding aspects of the male situation. . . . Research, not primarily into the causes of depression but intent on portraying the nature of women's lives within the social structure of contemporary Western societies, has identified . . . many unsatisfactory and, indeed, stressful features of the situation of women. (1988, 10–11)

However, these "stressful features of the situation of women" have often been twisted into a double standard or a double bind when women seek treatment. Reacting—in many ways logically—to the conditions of their lives, women are then castigated for doing so, as doctors "reinforce their guilt feelings and encourage their notions that something must be wrong within themselves" (Miles 1988, 64). In *Women and Madness*, Phyllis Chesler argues that "the real oppression of women" does lead to "real distress and unhappiness"; that "the conditioned female role of help-seeking and distress-reporting" does naturally lead to "patient 'careers' as well as overt or subtle punishment for such devalued behavior"; that "the double or masculine standard of mental health used by most clinicians" does lead to "perceiving the distressed . . . female as 'sick,' whether she accepts or rejects crucial aspects of the female role"; and that "comparatively limited social tolerance for 'unacceptable' behavior among women" does lead to "comparatively great social and psychological pressure to adjust—or be judged as neurotic or psychotic" (1972, 118).

This latter factor of social intolerance determines both how patients perceive their own condition and status and how others react to them. Reporting on a survey of women psychiatric patients, Miles writes:

> Most respondents were worried that the fact of their having psychiatric treatment would produce negative reactions among their social circle. . . . Expectation of negative attitudes were most forcefully expressed when discussing the vexed question of whether or not to tell relatives and friends that one is seeing a psychiatrist. Many respondents said that as a general rule they kept quiet about it, telling only those within their immediate social circle. (Miles 1988, 70–71)

These reactions are not surprising in view of social attitudes toward the mentally ill. She further reports: "Numerous studies have demonstrated that stigma is attached to mental illness, that people reject and discriminate against the mentally ill and that these negative attitudes change very slowly, if at all" (Miles 1988, 68).

Such attitudes existed within the IHM community for many years. Accepting the judgment and the mores of a double standard of mental health and acting like their counterparts in society, IHM sisters sometimes characterized the mentally ill naïvely and uncritically. Moreover, once the stereotype or stigma attached itself, it usually lasted a lifetime. Members caught innuendoes and body language from their peers and superiors alike that suggested that a mentally ill sister, whether she was currently in treatment or not, could not be relied upon as others could.

The feminist connections, although not always clear throughout IHM history, nonetheless can be substantiated by the foregoing authors. Looking back at nearly 150 years, there are times of foresight, others of regression. IHMs tended, albeit unconsciously, to follow similar paths of critique, flight from reality, and the unhealthy submission of the women of their time.

## Conclusion

As a congregation, the IHMs have had their share of mentally ill members. They have, for the most part, treated them with the best known methods of the time, but they have suffered the same pitfalls as others who followed their best instincts.

The Rule set up a kind of tension between the call to the holy and the call to the work of the day, which for the vast majority of IHMs from 1845 to 1970 was teaching. For those who could hold the tension in balance, life could be challenging; but for some, the tension itself did not aid the pursuit of health or happiness, much less holiness. To assert that IHM life or its rules caused maladjustment or mental illness would be simplistic; to propose that they exacerbated some individuals' problems would be fairer.

As for the future, the movement toward a critical feminist perspective may constitute the best preventive measure for some potentially ill members. As women, including IHMs, assume not a role but their rightful place in church and in society, they will create an improved quality of life among themselves.

The "Glass House," the windowed extension to the infirmary, was built on stilts for sisters with tuberculosis.

# 8

## In Health and Sickness

### *IHM Health-Care Delivery, 1845–1993*

### Jane Shea, I.H.M.

In the early 1960s, because of a serious illness, I spent a year at St. Mary Infirmary, the IHM health-care center attached to the congregation's motherhouse in Monroe, Michigan. Fifteen years later, I became a caregiver in that same institution, serving as administrator. Each time, I became aware of both the sister nurses' and the congregational leadership's deep dedication to ensuring that patient care was not separate and distant from but rather attached and connected to the life and mission of the congregation. Unlike many religious congregations—who house their retired and infirm members in separate buildings or in congregational hospitals on a distant campus—the IHM congregation strives to keep all members at "home" in the IHM motherhouse, where they may enjoy the companionship of their sisters. The IHM infirmary has always been intentionally an extension of the main motherhouse building. I believe that this culture of integrated health care, which I have observed during my own lifetime, had its roots in the early history of the congregation, when a "family" spirit prevailed.

### Frontier Conditions

From the beginning, the very survival of the congregation was threatened by the harsh conditions of pioneer life. In 1845, the original three IHM sisters, under the direction of Redemptorist priests, braved frontier living in Monroe: "They occupied two small houses, situated about ninety steps from each other. . . . They were obliged to assemble sometimes in one house and sometimes in the other" (MMC, 15 Jan. 1846, MA). Mother Theresa Maxis recorded that "it required the assistance of the brothers to break the ice in the river in order to draw water; for drinking purposes we had to send for it near the Church where there was

211

a well. We had a little shed for [a] kitchen in which there was besides the cooking-stove an old cupboard in which the dishes were kept, on rainy days we had to go with an umbrella to take them out, likewise in the little refectory we would often be sprinkled" (TMN, 13, MA).

Father Louis Gillet, the Redemptorist founder of the congregation, was the first to mention the unhealthy condition of Monroe; in a letter to the coadjutor bishop of the Detroit diocese, Peter Paul Lefevere, on 3 March 1846, he stated: "Your Grace knows, without doubt, of the ravages that an unknown and very special kind of sore throat is working here. It is very much more yet in Toledo [Ohio] and the Baie" (UNDA; Eng. trans. in MA). In her account of the founding of the congregation, Mother Theresa Maxis recorded that in January 1848 an epidemic of spotted fever ravaged Monroe. The sisters and pupils were spared, but one of the Redemptorists, Father Francis Poilvache, died. When viewing his remains, Maxis and the pupils spontaneously kissed his hand (TMN, 19–23, MA). No board of health existed to regulate such naïve indiscretions in dealing with communicable diseases.

Probably the greatest medical threat to the future of the newly formed congregation was the prevalence of tuberculosis. A simple cold often ended in pneumonia or in tuberculosis. Sister Ignatius Walker, the first of the congregation's sisters to die, was a victim of tuberculosis in February 1856; love of teaching and zeal for her students had apparently prompted her to conceal her illness (MMC, 27 Feb. 1856, MA). Such behavior would also prevent early detection and treatment, but in the 1850s the sisters would have been unaware of the disease's contagious properties, which were not proved until 1868 (Major 1954, 892).

Maxis admonished her little community to avoid colds and sickness by wearing their flannel petticoats and rubbers when going to and from their teaching duties. Despite such warnings, she too complained that Monroe was a place of sickness, as in a letter of 11 March 1859 to Lefevere: "Allow me, My Lord, to say that all I said about the constant sickness existing in our Community is not an imagination it is too true F. [Edward] Joos [appointed by Lefevere in 1857 to be the congregation's director and superior] knows knows [sic] it the cause. I dont [sic] know, we live here as other people do, but every one who comes fall [sic] sick, I always took it as a trial of God, and did not speak of it as long as we had no better place" (UNDA).

Maxis herself was also often sick. Writing in 1883, she recalled: "I had a spell of sickness [in 1857] caused by overexertion, was really in danger; not being able to procure ice, which the Dr. prescribed to be applied to my head, Sister Ann kept cold water. Being that I was not good enough for God, I did not die then" (TMN, 54, MA).

In 1859, there was a controversial split in the congregation: Maxis and eleven of the congregation's twenty-four sisters settled in the diocese of Philadelphia, where Redemptorist John Nepomucene Neumann was bishop. Mother Mary Joseph Walker was appointed mother superior of the remaining Monroe congregation, with Joos serving as the community's director and superior. At the time of the separation, Walker was herself a victim of tuberculosis.

## The Call to Live "Poorly"

Walker spent much of the five years that she led the congregation in the small infirmary room of the motherhouse. Because of her own suffering, she had great empathy for the sick, but this empathy was often in conflict with her desire for the sisters to live "poorly"—in accord with their vow of poverty and with the early traditions of the community.

This ambiguity comes through in a letter to Sister Gertrude Gerretsen. Walker first notes the carelessness of a sister on the mission in looking after her health: "Sister Josephine [White] . . . behaves so badly, after all the charges I gave her to beware of the cold & to wear her flannels & her drawers—Let her not by any means, come home in that way, for we are not allowed to be instrumental in our own sickness—This is not the poverty that God calls us to practice, for our Dr's bill will come to much more than a flannel jacket or an extra bed covering." She then urges Gerretsen to "[t]ry to keep well yourself & be not scruplous [sic] about keeping warm & comfortable—if you want anything, let me know (MJW to [GG, ca. 8 Dec. 1861], MJWP, MA).

However, when arriving at the new St. Joseph Mission (the first of the congregation's missions in Detroit) in 1861, Walker was delighted to find the convent very "poor." Indeed, the house had been a barn. She did not want this poverty to be embraced to the detriment of the sisters' health, however: "To the [local] infirmarian she gave very wise and beautiful instructions telling her that her responsibility was very great, and that it was her duty to see that the sick did not suffer for anything, but to use all proper means of affording them relief in their sufferings" (Life, 117–18, MA).

When Mother Clotilda Hoskyns was elected general superior in 1869, she appointed an infirmarian, Sister Flora Collins, whose special charge was the care of the sick. Collins was not a nurse and was still a novice, but she had distinguished herself for her devotedness to her invalid mother before entering the congregation and was for this reason deemed qualified for the position. Collins served in the capacity of infirmarian for thirty years. She displayed much practical common sense and empathy for the ill ([McHugh] 1928, 61–62). Mary Xavier Turner notes in her history of health care in the congregation that "Sister Flora's unusually large endowment of common sense and good judgment enabled her to identify an illness and treat her patients skillfully. The doctor, when called, agreed with her diagnosis" (1984, 3, MA).

Like Maxis and Walker, Hoskyns was committed to the care of the sisters. She was more than kind to the sick; she was devoted to them, frequently serving them with her own hands: "[S]he would insist on climbing those stairs many times a day just to inquire how [a] Sister was feeling . . . sometimes she brought a nice drink; again it was some little dainty to tempt the appetite" ([McHugh] 1928, 68). However, Hoskyns too expected the sick to behave in all things as true religious. The following points taken from a book of instructions given when she was mistress of novices illustrate that she was still very much a woman of her times, seeing religious conduct from a monastic and Jansenistic perspective that stressed the justice and order of God rather than compassion and mercy:

> 1. Try as much as you can to hide your pains and sufferings from all except those to whom you should make them known.
> 2. Never mind it, when not noticed by any one.
> 3. Try as much as possible to spare the Infirmarian, and let her have her night's rest.
> 4. Never find fault with the doctor.
> 5. Never complain of the food no matter how much you may dislike it. . . .
> 6. Never complain to any one of anything whatever.
> 7. Show gratitude for every favor or act of kindness. ([McHugh] 1928, 69)

### Farmers' Breakfasts and Other Remedies

Untimely deaths were frequent during the early history of the IHM community. In 1863, Sister Liguori Lafontaine died at the age of twenty-nine; in October 1864, Walker, aged thirty-six, succumbed to tuberculosis. A number of young sisters died as novices. Early IHM chronicles vary in reporting the illness and cause of death among the sisters. Some just mention "a lingering illness, a cold not thought to be serious, ill a few days," and others offer no cause whatever. In the decades between 1860 and 1890, eight novices pronounced their vows on their death beds. Records also show that between 1870 and 1890, death claimed some two dozen young professed sisters who had been in the community less than 10 years (Turner 1984, 2, MA).

In response to this threat, a "farmer's breakfast" of meat or eggs and potatoes began each IHM day in an effort to build up stronger constitutions to resist tuberculosis, the "white plague" that was causing the deaths of so many young sisters (Turner 1984, 2, MA). The practice of eating two pieces of bread or toast each morning remained a novitiate "must" into the 1950s. It was essential that sisters remain strong and vibrant for their mission duties.

The battle against disease was no more sophisticated outside the convent. Prior to the Civil War, "the American doctor was quite simply ignorant, and even his post–Civil War successor did not receive the training expected of a doctor today. Few medical schools before 1860 required more than two years of attendance, almost none provided clinical experience for their fledgling physicians" (Wood 1974, 5). Nurses learned their trade on the job, assisting doctors in hospital wards, but with little book knowledge of correct practice. (Ellis and Hartley 1988, 22). Florence Nightingale opened the first school of nursing in 1860, and by 1890, nursing had established itself as a respectable and suitable career for women (Ellis and Hartley 1988, 24). However, home remedies still governed much medical care: "Practically every cookbook or family health manual had several headache remedies. . . . 'Take a tea-spoonful of powdered charcoal in molasses every morning, and wash it down with a little tea; or drink half a glass of raw rum or gin, and drink freely of maywood tea' " (NFM 1852, as cited in Welter 1976, 66).

## Healthy Femininity

According to historian Ann Douglas Wood,

> Self-sacrifice and altruism on a spiritual level, and child-bearing and housework on a more practical one, constituted healthy femininity in the eyes of most nineteenth-century Americans. Dr. Clarke of Harvard, who believed that girls of the 1870s were ill because they were quite literally destroying their wombs and their childbearing potential by presuming to pursue a course of higher education intended by nature only for the male sex, was very much a spokesman for the doctors of his generation. (1974, 7–8)

Women like the IHMs—who not only vowed celibacy and set about acquiring knowledge themselves but also conducted schools for young women as their mission and ministry—were, of course, a special case. However, despite the fact that congregational attitudes toward health and disease were shaped by their own leaders, those attitudes were strongly influenced by contemporary male perspectives.

Joos, whose influence lasted for the forty-four years that he was director and superior of the community, illustrated these attitudes in his spiritual conference on the "Care of the Sick" given to the sisters during a summer vacation in the 1880s:

> Your Holy Rule says that those who require extras may have them and therefore Superiors having at heart the preservation of the health of the Sisters ought to act wisely and kindly in this respect, but they must not be over-solicitous. Strong sensible Mothers in the world do all they can

to keep their children in good health and the wise performance of their little duties, while foolish and indulgent Mothers spoil them by excessive attention and keep them home from school for every little headache . . . A passing weakness scarcely requires a remedy, but each Sister must act so that if illness should come she may be able to say that it was from no imprudence on her part. How often have I not seen a Sister between two windows in a direct draught—and known too, that having contracted a cold she tried to hide it. I would like to know what idea such a one has of the Fifth Commandment! (EJC, "Care of the Sick," 1, MA)

Such stern admonitions created an attitude of fear and suspicion of getting sick and being forced to be absent from teaching or other assigned duties. Nothing was to inhibit the work and mission of the congregation. A tension between personal well-being and devotion to duty became a problem for some sisters, who felt that it was wrong to get sick even though they were aware of the care and support that the sick received each day in the infirmary.

## IHM Nurses

By the turn of the century, health care in the United States had become more sophisticated and more professional. This shift also occurred in the IHM community, for in 1897, a registered nurse, Ellen Ryan, joined the congregation. Ryan was a mature, thirty-year-old woman who had trained at Grace Hospital in Detroit; before entering, she had established a school for nurses at old St. Mary Hospital, also in Detroit. Receiving the name Sister Francina, she was accepted into a congregation whose ministry was, strictly speaking, teaching, but her thirty-five years of religious life were spent in ministry in the infirmary. She attended every dying sister, was present at every surgery, and had complete charge of the daily operations of the infirmary (Mengy., 30 June 1931, MA).

During Ryan's administration, the isolation unit—called the "glass house"—was added to St. Joseph infirmary wing, east of the IHM convent chapel. The unit was so named because of the many windows on three sides of its riverfront location. In accord with the current medical theory of rest, sunshine, and nutritious food, the several tuberculosis patients could benefit from ample pure air and sunlight to hasten their recovery. This arrangement continued under Ryan's direction from 1903 until a new infirmary was completed in 1932 (Turner 1984, 6, MA).

Ryan spent the summer months each year in Detroit to care for sisters recovering from surgery. She set up a convalescent center at the IHM mission of Holy Trinity Convent in old Corktown, Detroit. A note about these surgeries is found in the Superiors Guide of 1907: "The sisters should be very reserved in speaking about operations of a private nature as they are indelicate subjects for conversation" (SGG, 33, MA).

Ryan's skill did not go unnoticed in wider circles. For example, Bishop John Foley requested that she care for him in his failing years. Foley had been a frequent visitor to Monroe during his episcopacy in Detroit and was aware of the excellent care that Ryan provided. He was in ill health for the last fifteen years of his life and a virtual invalid from 1914 until his death in 1918 (Tentler 1990, 119). Ryan cared for him at the episcopal residence, receiving some relief on the weekends from other IHM sisters; she rendered this service while still in charge of the infirmary in Monroe (Mengy., 30 June 1931, MA).

Several other nurses joined the congregation in the second decade of the twentieth century: Sister Marie Camillus Ryan in 1913, Sister Mary Mark Dwyer in 1916, and Sisters Marie Adelina O'Donnell and Gertrude Sweeney in 1918. Like Ryan, "these Sisters gave full care to our sick Sisters and students in the old Motherhouse, including food preparation and room care" (Turner 1984, 7, MA). There were no eight-hour shifts—these women were on call twenty-four hours a day. Their sleeping rooms were located next to the infirmary corridor so that they could easily be reached at night. In times of emergency, they worked around the clock. Later, in the mid-1920s, three more trained nurses, all with considerable experience, were accepted into the congregation. One, Sister Raefella Keenan from New Orleans, was on active duty in France in a front-line hospital during World War I. On returning to the United States, she was assigned to a temporary hospital during the 1918 influenza epidemic (Turner 1984, 8, MA).

During the early 1900s, the congregation established a lasting relationship with the Grey Nuns, who operated St. Vincent Hospital in Toledo, Ohio. Many doctors on the staff of this hospital served the IHM sisters *gratis*, a great boon in a time when health insurance and Medicare did not exist. Dr. Fred Douglass deserves special mention. Mother Domitilla Donohue, general superior, wrote a letter of gratitude to him on 7 August 1923: "Though our words cannot adequately express the deep gratitude we feel for your continued acts of benevolence, it is some satisfaction to offer our sincere 'Thank you.' You have certainly manifested the noblest attributes of a great physician—knowledge, skill and exceeding charity—and merited our lasting gratitude" (DDP, MA). When Sister Jamesetta Rhoads was appointed to assist in the infirmary in Monroe, she received her practical training at St. Vincent's, working on night duty with one of the Grey Nuns' sister nurses. On 3 June 1929, when a fire threatened the IHM Monroe motherhouse and destroyed the academy that the IHMs had operated since 1846, the Grey Nuns offered to transfer the infirmary residents from Monroe to the hospital in Toledo (JR, interviewed by author, Jan. 1993). Although it was not necessary to accept this generous offer, it conveyed the close ties that the women in the IHM congregation had developed with the women in Toledo.

IHM membership grew dramatically during the decade of the 1920s.

Membership numbered 456 in 1920, the year of the diamond jubilee celebration of the founding of the IHM congregation: by 1930, the membership was 677 (OCD, 1920, 1930). Although most of this growth was due
to new vocations, increased longevity and improvements in general
health care were also factors. In addition to the increasing professionalism
of the IHM health-care staff, there was an emphasis on health education.
For example, during the 1920s, James Walsh—a physician, philosopher,
and author of *Eating and Health*—lectured the sisters every summer at the
motherhouse. Walsh stressed that the means of prolonging life was to
"eat something raw every day and drink at least seven glasses of water
every day" (MMC, 1–2 Aug. 1927, MA). However, the "die with your
boots on" attitude toward work and retirement still prevailed. In a letter
to Donohue in 1924, a sister wrote: "I read recently that there are three
'Ds' which we ought to avoid—the Doctor, the Devil and the Dumps"
(DDP, MA). In the Superiors Guide of 1919, the local superior was cautioned that she must obtain permission from Monroe for a sister to have
an X-ray; permission for extra rest had to be obtained on a weekly basis,
and no young sister was expected to ask this permission unless she were
sick (GLS, MA). Much of this attitude was considered virtuous rather
than a neglect of one's personal well-being.

### The 1932 Infirmary

The new infirmary, completed in 1932, brought about a significant
change in IHM congregational health care. After the 1929 fire destroyed
the academy building—and realizing the need for a new motherhouse—
plans were put forth to build new buildings further west on Elm Avenue.
To preserve the connectedness and unity of all the members, the infirmary was made part of that new "home." It was to be a separate area,
but it would be attached to the motherhouse. Sisters would continue to
visit the sick without leaving the building, and likewise the sick could be
brought to activities held in the motherhouse proper and join in community prayer in the chapel. Thus, sick sisters would always be active members of the congregation. It was also hoped that this structure would
provide for all needs in regard to the sick and the retired for many years
to come.

The dedication volume of 1932 describes the new building:

> The infirmary consists of five floors. The first is equipped with work-
> rooms, the clinic, and the large diet-kitchen from which the smaller
> diet-kitchens on each floor are supplied. The main floor provides bright,
> airy rooms for the sisters who are no longer able for active duty. In the
> west corridor of this floor is an exquisite little Chapel, where day and
> night dwells the Divine Physician of souls. . . . The third floor, though at
> present unfinished, is intended to be the operating section of the Infir-

mary. The fourth floor is devoted to contagious diseases. There, by means of sunny rooms, abundance of fresh air, and an exclusive sunporch, the best of care and treatment may be given those afflicted. Besides an office, each floor possesses a large solarium, cheerily furnished and overlooking St. Joseph lake, the Grotto and a broad stretch of woodland. (SSIHM 1932, 75–76)

The new building was erected during the leadership of Mother Ruth Hankerd and Sister Miriam Raymo. Hankerd's main objective was to retain the family spirit of the congregation—the "home spirit," as she so often reminded the sisters. The spreading complex of large buildings was not to change the spirit of poverty and of simplicity of the original struggling community on the River Raisin. Hankerd was very active in the final preparation of the building for occupancy, and on 28 April 1932, she accompanied the first seven tuberculosis patients from the "glass house" to the fourth floor of the new infirmary (Turner 1984, 12, MA). During her years in office, she made a visit to the infirmary a part of her daily schedule when she was in Monroe (JR, interviewed by author, Jan. 1993).

Sister Gertrude Sweeney succeeded Ryan as head nurse in the new building in 1932. Sweeney had received her training at St. Mary Hospital in Detroit and was a great friend of Ryan's. She followed many of the practices of her mentor, guiding the infirmary during the growth periods of the 1930s and 1940s. Sweeney was not only a good nurse but an able administrator. A more professional atmosphere prevailed in the new infirmary than in the old facility; for example, the sister nurses all wore white habits and veils distinguishing them as nurses (formerly, only the nurse in the "glass house" wore white). Throughout the 1930s and 1940s, sister nurses provided complete care, both day and night. The nurses slept near the nurses' station, which was equipped with a signal light to alert them of any patient in need. It was not until 1950 that a regular night nurse took the night shift (Turner 1984, 14, MA); this relieved the other nurses from twenty-four-hour duty, but days off and rotating schedules were still unknown. The need for more outpatient clinic time prompted two senior nurses, Sister Joella Poupore and Sister Gracelma Beavis, to provide care for the sisters in residence at the motherhouse (Turner 1984, 13–14, MA).

## The 1950s: The Need for Professional Staff

In the early 1950s, during Mother Teresa McGivney's second term as general superior, the council saw the need for an increased number of sisters to care for the sick. The congregation had never trained a sister as a registered nurse, for it had always relied on those who entered the community already possessing this training. Therefore, educating nurses was a new venture. Between 1952 and 1954, three sisters trained for nursing degrees at Borgess Hospital in Kalamazoo, Michigan, and earned their state certificates. These sisters—Laurella Jarboe, Louise Jarboe, and Eileen Semonin—served the infirmary for many years. The community also sent Sister Trudy Baltes to the University of Michigan in 1951 to obtain a degree in pharmacy. Baltes set up a professional pharmacy that not only served the infirmary but also filled requests from many of the IHM missions. This service was economical and also provided another link in sister-to-sister care (Turner 1984, 18, MA).

Beginning in 1928, the Marygrove College infirmary served the post-surgical and recovery needs of sisters missioned in twenty-five Detroit parishes. A well-equipped infirmary was set up in the south wing of Madame Cadillac Residence Hall, the resident building for Marygrove students and faculty. Sisters Ann Raphael Brady and Mary Mark Dwyer served the students and sisters there from 1928 until 1948. Nursing care for sisters was transferred to Marygrove's new convent building in 1949. The "visiting" nurses who served the Marygrove convent infirmary during the four decades of its operation not only provided patient care but also visited the Detroit hospitals, checked with doctors on patients' progress, and accompanied sisters to appointments with doctors (Turner 1984, 64–65, MA).

Back in Monroe, the increasing number of sister patients required that the academy patients—until then housed on the infirmary's third floor—be transferred to space in the academy building. This floor in the infirmary now became home to chronically ill sisters. Lay staff were hired to take over the housekeeping tasks, and the diet kitchen on each floor was discontinued. The central diet kitchen supplied trays, which novices assisted in serving. Retired sisters who were not patients assisted in feeding patients, writing letters, reading, and visiting. A program entitled "Adopt a Sister" involved the whole community and proved very helpful for the nursing staff. Each IHM local mission adopted a sister patient; she became a real part of that mission, praying for their needs, and in turn receiving personal attention (as well as sundry items and notions) from the mission sisters.

Despite such measures, however, infirmary staffing remained inadequate. During Mother Anna Marie Grix's administration (1954–66), five registered nurses, four licensed practical nurses, two aides, and five lay assistants cared for fifty permanent patients and the many patients who spent limited time in the infirmary. The need for more space for retired sisters was also evident. Housing in the motherhouse was not adequate for the number of sisters who had belonged to the large entrance classes of the early twentieth century and were now retiring. The 1932 building designed for the long-range health care of the sisters had reached its capacity in just thirty years. In 1960, the membership numbered 1,407—almost double the number of IHMs in 1930 (OCD 1960, 83).

## The Need for a Retirement Center

A 1959 study on "The Health and Longevity of Today's Sisters" revealed that since the turn of the century, the control of tuberculosis and
other communicable diseases—to which members of a close community
like the IHM congregation were especially prone—had added fourteen
years to a twenty-year-old nun's life expectancy (Fecher 1959, 67). Therefore, the number of religious sisters living beyond the age of sixty could
be expected to increase greatly.

Concerned about these statistics, the leadership of the IHM congregation decided to build a retirement center for those women who were
ambulatory and able to take care of themselves but who welcomed retirement after a lifetime in the classroom. A large rose garden at the west
end of the campus seemed an ideal location for this building. Again,
however, there was a concern that the retired sisters not be housed in
a separate building from the motherhouse. Accordingly, the architects
provided a plan for a new five-story wing attached to both the infirmary
building and the motherhouse. A landscaped courtyard known as Lilac
Court had to be sacrificed, but everyone was pleased that the new Liguori
Hall would be part of the motherhouse, reassuring the "at home" continuity (AMG, interviewed by author, Jan. 1993; CM, 28 Mar. 1961, MA).

Another improvement in the health-care system of the 1960s was the
hiring of a house doctor. In September 1962, Dr. Edward Laboe, a physician who had been on call to the IHMs some time before retiring, decided
to come out of retirement to administer the clinic several days a week.
An office was arranged for him on the first floor. This was a real boon for
many sisters, who now no longer had to travel for appointments. Laboe
came regularly to the clinic until 1971, when he retired a second time. Dr.
Thomas Snider then became the regular doctor and has remained in this
position through the 1990s. He comes to the infirmary five days a week
and is on call whenever necessary (Turner 1984, 23, MA).

## Post–Vatican II Health Care

In the wake of Vatican II and of the changes in religious life away
from the old monastic model to a more active ministerial model, a congregational committee was formed to make an in-depth study of the personal well-being of IHM sisters. A 1966 community-wide "opinionaire"
revealed that the stress and tensions of modern living and the demands
of the teaching apostolate did not fit the age-old traditions of monastic
discipline. The data presented a picture of very enduring but very weary
women. Recommendations for an improved health-care plan for all of
the members of the community—not just the sick—were made to the

1966 Chapter in the "Report of the Committee on Personal Aspects of IHM Religious Life" (MA). These recommendations could be summarized as:

1. A one-year moratorium on accepting any new teaching obligations.
2. Establishment of a community board of health.
3. Twenty percent of future graduating classes of junior sisters be trained in health-care fields.
4. Yearly physical examinations for all sisters.
5. Vacations with no fixed horarium.
6. An eight-hour shift for all nursing personnel.
7. Personal health education.
8. Care of sisters with emotional problems.

These recommendations resulted in a new awareness that it was time to deal with the conflict between being a virtuous religious and meeting the health-care needs that resulted from the stress of modern day apostolic commitments. IHM sisters began developing a holistic attitude toward their personal well-being. Vacation time became the norm rather than the exception, a more relaxed daily schedule relieved stress, and sisters developed educational programs to encourage phased retirement. An initial screening of physical examinations began in August 1966. Superiors encouraged a lighter work load in teaching after age sixty-five. The community purchased a vacation spot on Lake Erie in Canada (known as Crawfton Inn) where sisters could relax and enjoy each others' company.

Several young sisters began studies for nursing degrees; even a few sisters who had been teaching for many years decided to enter a new phase of ministry and studied for licensed practical nurse certification. The number of lay staff in the infirmary increased each year. In 1973, a new staff person was appointed to carry out administrative responsibilities, thus freeing the nurses for professional nursing care (Turner 1984, 18, MA).

Integration of IHM health care with all dimensions of IHM life demanded new approaches to health-care service. A two-pronged reorganization focused on changes in staffing policies and on patient care. One of the sister nurses was appointed director of nursing, whose duties were to coordinate patient care on all floors. Staff sister nurses were encouraged to give several years of service to the IHM community and then to have the freedom to opt for work at an outside health-care institution. They attended workshops, joined professional organizations, updated techniques, and collaborated with health personnel in Detroit. Their schedule now included weekly days off, and sister nurses were also encouraged to live away from the infirmary in a community situation. Lay nurses and staff increased each year, so that it was possible to have either a registered nurse or a licensed practical nurse on each floor, assisted by several nurses' aides.

In 1962, the closing of St. Joseph's in Dearborn, Michigan—a mental hospital where three IHM sisters were patients—added another major dimension to IHM patient care. They and ten other patients who were suffering from nervous breakdowns or Alzheimer's disease were now housed on the infirmary's third floor. Dr. James Dawson, a psychiatrist who visited this floor twice a month, urged that these patients be kept active and stressed the importance of their engaging in group work. Thus began the Reality Orientation program, conducted by Sister Elza Laszlo. Laszlo loved working with these women and provided daily hours of enjoyment in education, music, art, and just plain fun to occupy their days. Dawson also had appointments with outpatients during his visits to Monroe, adding to the preventive aspect of provision for good mental health (Turner 1984, 26–28, MA).

### St. Mary Health Care Center

In 1982, the infirmary was named St. Mary Health Care Center. By this time, the facility had again expanded, for now the retirement center, Liguori Hall, had full-time nursing care. Two nursing stations were arranged to care for the needs of sisters residing in Liguori. A physical therapy department was also added on the ground floor to assist in the rehabilitation of stroke patients and those suffering from arthritis or from broken bones. Laboratory and X-ray services provided by a technician from the local hospital were also housed on the first floor. A pastoral care department began to coordinate the care of the spiritual needs of the patients. The forerunner of this ministry was Sister Ann Joseph Fix, who during the 1960s and 1970s had made a daily visit to every patient, had corresponded with relatives of the aged and infirm, and had been at the death bed of every IHM sister.

At century's end, St. Mary Health Care Center operates on a modern professional basis providing assisted, intermediate, and total patient care. The goals of the present administrator, Sister Elaine Aldridge, promote collaborative team leadership and the participation of the residents in their own care. The staff of 143, of whom nine are IHM sisters, view their service as a partnership in congregational ministry. They have shown that although professionalism is critical, its achievement need not result in institutionalization nor blur the "home" concept.

The Center's mission statement, developed in 1993, states:

> In accord with the mission of the Sisters, Servants of the Immaculate Heart of Mary, St. Mary Health Care Center provides an opportunity for specialized health care services focusing on holistic care in an environment that enhances the quality of living for its members. The daily operations are reflective of shared ministry for all who give and receive care at St. Mary Health Care Center. Each patient is made aware of her

rights, which include provision for her care and information relative to
this care. She is entitled to continue to exercise her rights as a member
of the congregation by participating in religious, community, and social
activities. (SMHCCB, 1993, MA)

This mission statement reflects and preserves the unifying spirit and
traditions of the congregation while also acknowledging a more holistic
attitude toward health care. The buildings in Monroe will forever give
evidence of the aim of past superiors who wished to keep the health-care
center a vital part of community living. Women who model the pattern of
Flora Collins, Francina Ryan, and Gertrude Sweeney continue to provide
loving care for all the members of the congregation. With the support of
congregational leadership and of every sister, this special IHM health
care continues to be a visible and dynamic reality today.

# PART THREE

# Authority, Leadership, and Governance

# The Context

## Margaret Susan Thompson

For the better part of a millennium, obedience was the most important component of governance in vowed communities. The political dynamic of religious communities has undergone more change in the decades after Vatican II than in the seven centuries since St. Clare set down the rules for her Poor Clares. Regarding the role of the abbess (or superior) in the religious order that she founded in the thirteenth century, Clare wrote:

> I also beg that sister who will have the office to strive to exceed others more by her virtues and holy life than by her office so that, encouraged by her example, the Sisters may obey her not so much out of duty but rather out of love.... But the sisters who are subjects should keep in mind that for the Lord's sake they have given up their own wills. Therefore I ask that they obey their mother as they have promised the Lord of their own free will. (Armstrong and Brady 1982, 231)

The Monroe IHM Constitutions of 1861 reflect the same adherence to obedience and to absolute authority, but with more institutionalization: "The Sisters will also obey, as they would God Himself, the person whom the Bishop will have appointed Superioress, or whose election he will have sanctioned, even though she were only a novice, provided she be invested with legitimate authority. Every one will bear towards her all the esteem and respect possible, considering in her the person of Jesus Christ Himself, of whom she holds the place" (Const. 1861, MS, 31).

By the 1980s, however, the revolutionary impact of the Second Vatican Council had transformed the very structure of the order:

> [Many sisters] have moved steadily away from hierarchical organization. They have adopted participative procedures for the conduct of government.... At the basis of these developments in practice are pro-

227

found theological convictions about the dignity and equality of persons, the inalienability of personal freedom and responsibility, the right of every individual to justice, and the irreplaceable value for community life of full participation by the members. (Schneiders 1986, 93)

By the middle of the twentieth century, religious communities had become microcosms of the large secular corporate institutions that collectively prescribed the day-to-day structure of life in the developed world. Congregations of sisters are communities, but they also are formally structured organizations, with clear juridical status in both civil and Catholic canon law. It is fortunate for everyone affected by vowed communities that transformations such as these have occurred, for these communities are complex corporations, which may own vast amounts of property and operate numerous institutions. Although the Monroe IHMs have never administered hospitals, they have run a college, several private schools (boarding and day), children's homes, and a massive headquarters (or motherhouse) containing offices, residential quarters, chapels, archives and exhibit areas, dining facilities, and a state-of-the-art health care center.

Thus, the governance of religious congregations is a tremendous practical undertaking, one of significance not only to members but also to employees and to the people served by the congregation. Were skillful management all that leadership had to provide, it would be enough to engage the talents of bright and diligent individuals. However, those charged with heading groups such as the IHMs also bear substantial responsibility for the spiritual, emotional, social, and professional well-being of their sisters. In short, the form and quality of governance is crucial. In the two essays of this section, Amata Miller, Maryfran Barber, and Mary McCann—all with firsthand experience—provide two helpful but very distinct perspectives on leadership roles and styles in twentieth-century IHM history. At the same time, the contrasts between these two essays offer potent testimony to the extensive changes that religious communities have experienced in recent decades.

At first glance, Miller's essay might appear to do little more than to describe the consequences of a single, if defining, event: a massive fire in 1929 that destroyed the IHM motherhouse. That it was not only rebuilt but constructed on a scale that still leaves new visitors to Monroe gasping —and that this was done during the Great Depression by a group of women vowed to poverty—certainly makes for a good story. Moreover, the fact that the two women most responsible for this undertaking, Ruth Hankerd and Miriam Raymo, were IHM sisters and close friends who relied on and supported each other personally and professionally does more than lend a human dimension to this account; it confirms and reinforces the insights concerning the centrality of friendship that Glisky and Sylvester offer in earlier chapters of this volume.

Within these pages, however, Miller has done more than provide a compelling narrative. She has subtly and carefully offered a view of how leadership could and did function in the world of the "total institution" that was religious life in the period before Vatican II.[1] Stated simply, Hankerd and Raymo succeeded in what they undertook not only because of their not inconsiderable personal abilities but also because they could and did exercise enormous power over their organization and over their hundreds of "subjects," vowed firmly to obedience. They could and did compel their sisters to endure austerities and financial sacrifices far beyond even those demanded by an already rigorous vow of poverty. They could, without fear of much overt dissension from the ranks, take risks that might have jeopardized the very security of the congregation, had they failed. In the process, they could even enjoy privileges, however small (hot dogs and hamburgers), that they never considered extending to the others, especially in a time of crisis.

Hankerd and Raymo were able to behave as they did not because they were exceptional individuals (although Miller gives ample evidence to suggest that they were) but because of the complex nature of the authority they exercised. In the context of religious life, such authority derives not simply from the consent of the governed (although IHM superiors were and are elected) but also from what both they and their followers were convinced was a form of divine will. "The voice of the superior is the voice of God" is one of the hoariest clichés of religious life as it traditionally has been lived, but it was accepted as legitimate and even as attractive. As one American sister, a representative contemporary of Hankerd and Raymo, once put it: "Through my obeying another—I know this for a certainty: I can never make a mistake. . . . I can still never fumble, if I follow His directions coming to me through my superiors" (Joseph 1958, 38).

Religious orders are voluntary associations. Early-twentieth-century women entered and remained in groups like the IHMs because they embraced the values and assumptions underlying this state of life. The enculturation process that Mary Anne Hinsdale describes in her essay in this volume reinforced the convictions and attitudes that candidates brought with them to places like Monroe. Thus, leadership of the sort that Hankerd and Raymo exhibited received willing and even enthusiastic support. Sisters responded generously to the demands placed upon them when the motherhouse had to be rebuilt not because they were coerced

---

1. For the "total institution" concept, which frequently has been applied to religious life, see Goffman 1961.

but because their commitment to what their community represented was all-embracing. In short, one must appreciate the mutuality that was inherent in pre–Vatican II religious governance, however dictatorial it might appear. When it succeeded—as it clearly did in the case recounted here—it did so more by virtue of faith than of force. Morever, that success was considered a corporate one, not just an accomplishment of the superiors.

Still, the system was autocratic and hierarchical, grounded in a worldview in which both superiors and subjects (or "inferiors," as they were designated in many constitutions and commentaries) believed that God spoke in a special and determinative way through those placed in positions of authority. However, one of the most significant outcomes of Vatican II was an alternative vision of the church as a radically egalitarian body of believers who together comprised the People of God (see Dulles 1974). Within such an understanding, authority no longer was entrusted to just a few but instead was to be exercised collectively. Within a very short time, women who had been trained to see themselves as obedient daughters—whose principal obligation was to implement, with humility and eager alacrity, God's will as expressed by their superiors—were called upon to govern themselves in collegial, co-responsible, and participatory ways. The essay by Barber and McCann describes the sweeping nature of the changed expectations that electrified religious life after Vatican II, as well as the tensions, difficulties, and short-term failures that (perhaps inevitably) ensued.

The important thing to keep in mind when reading about the IHM's representative assembly is how rapidly these new understandings came into play and how radically they transformed sisters' expectations about themselves and about their religious congregations. Although the IHMs were among the first to implement such an experiment, they were by no means the only community to do so—or to experience the sort of "dark night" that Barber and McCann depict.[2] Thus, if the Miller essay is representative of leadership in the earlier era, the Barber/McCann piece is illustrative of events in more recent times.

Unlike the story of Hankerd and Raymo, that of the RA does not conclude with a happy—or even a definitive—ending. Although the IHMs and their peers today are unquestionably more comfortable with participatory and broadly based notions of authority than were sisters a generation ago, contemporary religious life is still a "work in process." Through the 1990s, books on community life have been published with such titles as *Religious Life: The Challenge for Tomorrow* (Yuhaus 1994) and

---

2. Perhaps the most self-examined congregation is the Sisters of Loretto; see Sanders 1982 and Ware 1995. For other examples of self-analysis, see Chittister et al. 1977 and Ware 1985.

*Living in the Meantime: Concerning the Transformation of Religious Life* (Philibert 1994).[3] Clearly, vowed women (and men) on the cusp of the twenty-first century have not concluded their evolution into what they still hope to become.

3. Monroe IHM Margaret Brennan has essays in both volumes; Sandra M. Schneiders, the Monroe IHM whose work is cited at the beginning of this essay, has one in the Yuhaus volume.

Good friends—Mother Ruth Hankerd, I.H.M.,
and Sister Miriam Raymo, I.H.M.

# 9

# An Enterprise of Sisterhood

*Building the IHM Motherhouse in the 1930s*

Amata Miller, I.H.M.

On 3 June 1929, a disastrous fire gutted St. Mary College and Academy in the southeastern Michigan city of Monroe. Though no one was injured, the destruction of the newly renovated building—housing their premier educational institution—was a crushing blow to the IHM congregation ([Kelly] 1948, 518–22). Keeping all-night vigil at the site of the tragedy, and providing sandwiches and coffee to those who had come to help fight the blaze, were the two women who together would lead the IHM congregation through the rebuilding process: Sister Ruth Hankerd, who would become the general superior in 1930, and Sister Miriam Raymo, who would be her partner as congregational treasurer (MR and RH, S of F, audiotape, 1962, MA).

Although the congregation was already heavily in debt from the building of Marygrove College in Detroit, there was apparently never a question about whether to rebuild the school. The morning after the fire, the officers of the congregation (a group which included Ruth and Miriam) met to plan for what to do "until a new Academy is erected."[1] Detailed arrangements were made about where to house and to teach the students of the various grades so that school could open on time in September 1929 ([Kelly] 1948, 523).

The fire also raised another need that these women determined to address. Without the academy, there would not be enough space in Monroe to house the more than eight hundred IHM sisters, and so the summer of 1929 would be the first time in its history that the whole IHM congregation would not be able to return to Monroe for the summer (CM, 4 June

---

1. The Minutes of the Council Meeting on 4 June 1929 (the day after the fire) record favoring the housing of the high school students at Marygrove "next year or until a new Academy is erected" (CM, MA).

1929, MA). The inclusion of this fact in the customarily terse, factual record of the official proceedings testifies to its importance for the IHM community. The chronicles of Holy Trinity convent in Detroit noted that not being able to return to the motherhouse made it the saddest summer in the sisters' memory (HTC, MA).[2]

Left standing across the street from the destroyed academy, on the banks of the River Raisin, was the IHM motherhouse. In 1929, this was a jerry-built complex, the result of successive expansions of the "First St. Mary Academy" and of the original frame convent from 1860 to 1895. Under the risk-averse financial philosophy of Monsignor Edward Joos (director of the congregation from 1857 to 1901), nothing was ever built until the money was in hand, however great the need or ultimately wasteful the process. (The community's chronicles reveal that the sisters were aware of the additional expense entailed in this practice [(Kelly) 1948, 277–78]). As a result, by 1929 the aging complex was badly in need of replacement.[3] As Miriam observed in a taped conversation with a group of the congregation's youngest members in the early 1960s, even though the fire was "a terrible, terrible tragedy," it was also a "blessing," because without it they would probably still have been down on "that corner" (MR, R from A, audiotape, 1963, MA).

In 1930, Ruth—by then IHM general superior—requested of Pope Pius XI the canonically required permission to borrow $2 million to build a massive new complex that would include both a new academy and a new motherhouse. She stated the reasons succinctly: "Our Academy with its entire equipment was totaly [sic] destroyed by fire June 3, 1929. The present Motherhouse built about sixty years ago to accommodate a small community, is rapidly falling into decay, but at its best would be wholly inadequate for the needs of the present Community numbering about eight-hundred-twenty-five" (RH to Pius XI, 8 Sept. 1930, MA).

### The Underlying Motive for the Project

However, a deeper purpose motivated this community of women to undertake a $2.6 million building project in the midst of the Great Depression,[4] when simply rebuilding the academy would have been

2. Holy Trinity Convent (Detroit) Chronicles, vol. 2, 1912–35, 79–80.

3. Notes to the author (6 Aug. 1993, MA) from Sister Rita Archambeau describe the "terrible memory" of the long galvanized trough used for washing one's face and for brushing one's teeth and of scaring rats and water bugs out of ground-floor toilet facilities by slamming the door as one entered the poorly lit compartments. She also observed that despite the discomforts, "we were one big happy family."

4. Prospectus for $3,100,000 first mortgage serial and sinking fund bonds, 23 Oct. 1936, MA.

enough for the moment. In Ruth's 29 September 1931 letter to the congregation, she concluded with a prayer: "That God may bless all your efforts in the good work you are doing for souls, while we labor to build for you a temporal home with strong walls and solid foundations, and that the spiritual union founded on love and sacrifice will ever grow more firm is our constant prayer for you all" (MA). To this day, the IHM community commonly refers to the Monroe motherhouse as "home." "Home is where each one lives for the other, and all live for God," says the plaque that Ruth placed in the new motherhouse foyer.

According to IHM community historian Sister Rosalita Kelly, this emphasis on "home" stemmed, in part, from Ruth's own mother's sense of the importance of making a home for the family ([Kelly] 1948, 678). However, the motivation that inspired and that justified mortgaging everything to build such massive and enduring buildings—and that evoked from the women of the community such a concerted and cooperative effort to see the project through—was stronger than that, being grounded in the particular experience of the IHM congregation, a congregation that had been "orphaned" in its earliest years. Redemptorist Louis Florent Gillet had left Monroe in 1847, two years after bringing the three founding members together; the rest of the Redemptorists left Monroe in 1855. In 1859, the bishop of Detroit banished the community's first superior, Theresa Maxis, along with two companions. These three joined three other IHMs who were running a school in Susquehanna, Pennsylvania. The bishop of Detroit enforced a strict separation between the two communities.

This experience of being orphaned seems to have undergirded the Monroe community's custom—not common among women religious of the time—that all members would come together at the motherhouse each summer, instead of remaining in the local convents attached to the schools where they taught (CM, 4 June 1929). Because of this "homecoming" tradition, it was especially important to the IHM community that it have a complex of buildings large enough to accommodate all of the members during the summer months. The scope and solid structure of the new complex of motherhouse buildings, in addition to providing this accommodation, underscored the value the community placed on security and on permanence.

A second reason for committing themselves to such a large project would have been the experience of the Joos era of building—a thirty-five-year period (1860–95) of almost continual construction of a wing here and a room there, only as much as the money at hand permitted. The end result (as well as the experience of constant building over all those years) seems to have left in the community a desire for something that could accommodate new needs without continual additions.

## The Project

On 10 May 1932, the *Monroe Evening News* carried a long article describing the newly completed IHM Motherhouse and Academy. Under the title "Impression of Stately Beauty Surrounds St. Mary Buildings," the author praised "the remarkable achievement of the Sisters in financing, planning and constructing this collection of architectural masterpieces." To convey the size and scope of the buildings, the writer continued: "The ensemble is too big for immediate comprehension. One must walk around it first. Then walk through it. Walking through it is not an easy thing, you need a guide and lots of fortitude. There are many miles to walk . . . The effect is one of mingled magnificence and peace." The building project was reportedly one of the largest going on in the country at the time, and skilled tradesmen came from long distances to work on it —743 men were working on the construction site in December 1931.[5] There are 3 million bricks in the buildings, three hundred thousand square feet of tiling, five carloads of copper water pipe in the hot and cold water system, and twenty carloads of Vermont slate for the roofs (MR, R from A, audiotape, 1963, MA).

In his essay "The Builder's Art" in the publication commemorating the dedication of the buildings, Henry E. Brennan, the builder, wrote: "The successful combination of the aesthetic and the practical, together with economy of the original cost and the cost of maintenance—the hope of the owner and the objective of the architect and builder—is strikingly exemplified in these buildings." The safety and health of the students, Brennan continued, was "the first and all important consideration in the planning and construction of these buildings—the point about which the Sisters were most solicitous" (SSIHM 1932, 83). Beauty and sentiment also received careful attention. The curved marble staircase in the academy entranceway was cut from a single block of Tennessee marble; this reduced the amount of marble used but increased the hours of labor. The grotto from the grounds of the old motherhouse was disassembled stone by stone (with the help of the boys from the boarding school) and rebuilt behind the new building. A thousand trees were transported by sleigh during the winter from the community-owned island in the River Raisin just in front of the new site. The trees were transplanted in the back of the property for landscaping after the construction was finished (MR, R from A, audiotape, 1963, MA).

Materials and furnishings from the old buildings were incorporated

---

5. In Sister Miriam's menology, it is noted that "[t]he new Motherhouse and Academy were the largest private building projects of the year, 1932." See also CL of RH, 21 Dec. 1931, MA.

into the new. Most of the bricks from the burned academy were reclaimed and formed the inside layers of bricks in the new motherhouse's twelve-inch-thick walls (MR and RH, S of F, audiotape, 1962, MA). An altar from the old motherhouse chapel was taken apart, each stone marked with a number from the blueprint, and reassembled seven years later by crafts-men from the firm that had originally built it. Likewise, furnishings of all kinds were brought from the old motherhouse. Only gradually were new furnishings purchased (MR, R from A, audiotape, 1963, MA).

The plans also called for some things that the congregation could not afford to complete at the time of the original construction. The mother-house chapel was not built until 1939. The fourth floor of the mother-house had to be left unfinished until the 1940s (CM, 3 Feb. 1932, MA). Also, the drawings called for a tower in the center of the two buildings, atop which would stand an eleven-ton marble statue of Mary, carved from a solid block of Italian Carrara marble. However, the congregation did not have the $175,000 to build the tower, so the statue was placed (and still stands) in a ground-level grotto at the spot where the tower would have been (MR, R from A, audiotape, 1963, MA; [Kelly] 1948, 699).

## Financing and Refinancing

Fortunately, thanks to the financial foresight of its prior leadership, the congregation in 1929 already owned the land for the new buildings. During the administration of Mother Mechtildis McGrail (1900–18), 176 acres were purchased at a site about half a mile west of the motherhouse; by the mid-1920s, the site totalled 300 acres.[6] The congregation's original intention had been to build a college on this piece of land, but in the early 1920s, the bishop of Detroit requested that the college be built in Detroit ([Kelly] 1948, 576). Thus, in 1930, the land was available for a new acad-emy and motherhouse.

During the administrations of Mechtildis and of her successor, Mother Domitilla Donohue (1918–30), the congregation acquired St. Mary Farms, another group of properties that played a key role in the financial story of the 1930s. A 1929 appraisal of community assets valued the Farms at $250,000 (RH to Pius XI, 8 Sept. 1930, MA). The congregation purchased additional farmland even during the financial duress of the early 1930s (CM, 5 May 1931 and 5 May 1934, MA). By 1936, the commu-nity had nine hundred acres of farms, raising beef and dairy cattle, pigs, and poultry, along with the feed for all of these animals and vegetables

6. Motherhouse Chronicles for 24 Sept. 1904 record the purchase of the 106-acre Park Place for $10,000; on 9 Oct. 1912 is recorded the purchase of the adjacent 75-acre Ilgenfritz farm. Additional adjacent pieces were purchased for a total of 300 acres ([Kelly] 1948, 493, 576).

of many varieties and fruits in orchards and groves (Prosp., 23 Oct. 1936, MA).[7] According to the congregation's centennial history, the purpose of these farms was to "reduce the cost of living and make it possible to initiate and carry through a necessary and extensive building program." Moreover, if the farms were of large enough scale, food could be supplied to the boarding schools and to the college. This would enable the community to offer education at tuition rates affordable to the "average American," thus widening the opportunities for education, particularly for women ([Kelly] 1948, 703–6).[8]

Another of the congregation's assets was Marygrove College in Detroit, whose buildings and sixty-two acres of land were valued at $4 million in 1929. On the perimeter of the campus were twenty-five acres of land that the congregation had platted into lots for sale for housing. As of 1929, the remaining lots were valued at $250,000 (RH to Pius XI, 8 Sept. 1930, MA).[9]

However, in order to buy the land and build Marygrove, the congregation had incurred a mortgage debt of $1.5 million at 5.5 percent. All of the congregation's land and buildings had been pledged as collateral (CM, 13 Nov. 1926; CBM, 13 Nov. 1926 and 14 Oct. 1927, MA). Keeping up with the semiannual payments of $200,000 on this debt was a heavy responsibility as the congregation faced the need to rebuild in Monroe.

The financial challenges facing the IHM community in 1929 would have been daunting even in a time of national prosperity, but this was the period of the deepest and longest depression in the nation's history. Though unemployment statistics were not kept regularly, it is estimated that as many as 4.5 million persons were unemployed in 1930. Michigan was one of the states in which the banking crisis was most severe, and Detroit's auto industry was severely hit (Mitchell, 1947, 92, 129–30).

In their 1930 request to Rome to be allowed to borrow $2 million, the congregation's leaders revealed their plan for paying the interest and for repaying the principal: "The present income derived from Marygrove College, St. Mary Academy, and sixty parochial schools, if carefully managed, should enable us to set aside yearly about one-hundred-twenty-five to one-hundred-fifty-thousand dollars for interest and principal. Due to present financial conditions in the United States and what we like to consider a special blessing of Divine Providence, we are hoping to secure a long time loan at the very low rate of 3.5 percent" (RH to Pius XI, 8

7. For a full description of the scope of the farms, see [Kelly] 1948, 703–7.

8. See also Council Minutes of 23 Jan. and 1 Sept. 1928, 31 May 1934 (MA).

9. It is interesting to note the financial sagacity apparent in the fact that in order both to develop the neighborhood around the college and to generate some income, the community used some of the college land to create a series of lots around the perimeter on two sides and hired a real estate agent to market the lots. The community built Tudor-style homes on some of the lots to set the style for the neighborhood.

Sept. 1930, MA). Rome granted the permission with the requirement that the debt be reduced as soon as possible, at a yearly rate determined by the bishop of Detroit, and that he be notified annually about the progress of the debt reduction (Vatican to MJG, 13 Oct. 1930, MA).

Specifically, the plan was to refinance the 5.5 percent, $1.5 million Marygrove mortgage debt at a lower rate of interest and at the same time borrow the $2 million for the new buildings, pledging as security the Marygrove land and buildings and the land in Monroe. The day after the communication came from Rome, the IHM corporation board authorized the general superior, Mother Ruth Hankerd, "to proceed with the necessary business of securing funds to the amount of $3,500,000 for the purpose of refinancing present indebtedness of the Corporation and for the erection of the new buildings." She was also authorized to engage an architect to draw up the plans (CBM, 14 Oct. 1930, MA).

The hoped-for 3.5 percent interest rate did not materialize in 1930; instead, the $3.5 million could be secured only by paying 5 percent, a reduction of only 0.5 percent from the rate on the earlier mortgage (CBM, 22 Jan. 1931, MA). Though acquiring the loan was in itself a major accomplishment, given the circumstances of the time, the terms proved extremely onerous during the next few years for the cash-strapped congregation. Meeting each of the new semiannual payments of $100,000 required community-wide sacrifice. Still, the congregation never missed an interest payment and managed to reduce the principal by approximately one-half-million dollars by 1936 (MJG to BCZ, 15 Sept. 1936, MA).

The IHM leadership continued efforts to find a way to refinance the loan at lower rates and for a longer time period. The IHM archives contain extensive correspondence in 1935 and 1936 about contacts from and with many firms seeking to assist in this effort. A 1935 letter from the congregation's attorney, Oliver Golden (who thought it unwise to try to refinance the loan), observes: "They [the IHM leadership] are constantly contacted . . . by folks desirous of playing Santa Claus" (OG to RN, 14 June 1935, MA).

In August 1935, Miriam, as the community's treasurer, wrote to B. C. Ziegler, a Wisconsin company that had worked with other Catholic institutions, that the IHM congregation wanted to refinance its outstanding $3.27 million debt at a rate of 4 percent and extend its maturity (MR to DJK, 12 Aug. 1935, MA). It should be noted that such refinancing was a task of some magnitude and delicacy. It required "calling" the original bonds, i.e., notifying the present bond holders that the 5 percent investment would no longer be available to them and that their principal would be returned to them. Then, investors for new bonds at the lower rate of interest had to be found. Not until October 1936 were the terms of refinancing finalized. Once accomplished, however, this greatly reduced the semiannual payment burden on the congregation. The debt, now $3.1

million, would be extended at rates ranging from 3 to 4 percent, with semiannual payments of $37,500 for the first six years, dropping to $25,000 for the rest of the period, with a balloon payment of $2.225 million due on 1 January 1952 (CBM, 10 Oct. 1936; Prosp., 23 Oct. 1936, MA).

One can imagine the collective sigh of relief when the general superior's letter of 27 November 1936 arrived: "I know you are all rejoicing with us over our successful refinancing, and that you are anxious to know some of the details." She described the "very intensive study" and consultation that preceded the choice of Ziegler as the underwriter, and reported the terms and the fact that most of the bonds had been readily sold within a week of the offering. She concluded with expressions of gratitude: "So you see God has wonderfully blessed us by enabling us to keep intact our credit and this has been accomplished only by the cooperation of every Sister in the community" (CL of RH, 27 Nov. 1936, MA).

The minutes of the IHM council and corporation and the general superior's letters to the community for the rest of the decade evidence that the debt had now become manageable. The congregation could now afford to attend to other needs, such as a new barn and tractor for the farms, replacement of mattresses at the boys' boarding school, and a house for the engineer responsible for maintenance of the complex (CM, 3 Feb. 1937, 5 Feb. 1938, and 2 Aug. 1938, MA). Moreover, on 23 September 1938, the council approved the building of the new chapel. Though no more could be borrowed, the money was in hand: since 1931, Miriam had been keeping in a separate fund for this purpose all the gifts that had come to individual sisters either from legacies or from their relatives.[10] However, economies were still needed. The purchase of new furnishings was postponed until there were sufficient funds; the sanctuary was downsized by twenty feet, reducing the chapel's seating capacity to nine hundred from the one thousand originally planned. Purchasing unpaneled pews saved $500 (CM, 16 Nov. 1938, 27 Dec. 1938, and 7 Jan. 1939, MA).

On 24 December 1939, when the first Mass was offered in the new motherhouse chapel, the building project was completed. The IHM congregation had managed to weather the financial crisis by a series of complex negotiations coupled with countless individual economizings and initiatives. Moreover, this was achieved by a community of women in an era when women's roles in the economic arena were limited almost exclusively to low-skilled and clerical positions and when women were hardly expected to have a high level of financial acumen.[11]

10. Sister Miriam tells this story herself in handwritten notes found in her personal file (MA); it is also noted in [Kelly] 1948, 699.

11. See the extensive treatment of women's economic status during 1920–40 in Chafe 1972, chapters 2 and 4.

## The Women Who Led the Project

Two women carried the burden of leadership during this project. In accord with the custom of the time, Mother Ruth Hankerd, general superior of the congregation from 1930 to 1942, was most visible; Sister Miriam Raymo, IHM treasurer from 1924 to 1948, was less so. However, it is an accepted fact among the members of the IHM community that it was Miriam's financial and practical genius that made the rebuilding project possible.[12]

### Ruth Hankerd (1886–1963)

Margaret Hankerd, who would become "Mother Ruth," was born into a prosperous Michigan farm family, attended high school as a boarder at St. Mary Academy, and entered the IHM community three days before her seventeenth birthday in 1903. At the age of thirty, she was chosen to be a local superior (principal and leader of the IHM community in a parish school). Ten years later, she was elected by her sisters to be first assistant, the second highest office in the congregation. In 1930, she became general superior, first as temporary successor to Mother Domitilla Donohue (who died suddenly of a heart attack) and then through election to her first six-year term. She was reelected to her second term in 1936 and in 1942 became first assistant to her successor, Mother Teresa McGivney, who had been a member of Ruth's council throughout the twelve years of her general superiorship.

Thus, Ruth had the task of leading the community with a firm hand through the financially challenging period beginning in the 1930s. Her experience as part of the governing group during the building of Marygrove College and the academy fire gave her knowledge of congregational financial realities and of the manner in which past crises had been handled. She also had the credibility that this experience gave her within and outside the IHM community. Beyond this, according to the congregation's centennial history, "[t]he making of the home a place to be lived in and loved was inbred in Mother Ruth, and, while the achievements of her administration were many and great, she will be longest remembered as the renewer of the family spirit in the congregation" ([Kelly] 1948, 678).

12. On the permanent record folder in the personal file for Margaret Raymo (Sister Miriam) under "Special Services" are typed the words: "During Sister's term of office she supervised—built—Marygrove College, the new Motherhouse and Academy, the Chapel, directed the financial affairs during the depression, bank moratorium,—inaugurated a system of financial concurrence of the missions with the Motherhouse" (MA). The sister-scribe neglected to mention the building of Immaculata High School.

One means of building "family spirit" during these years was the writing of regular one-page "Circular Letters" to the members of the congregation (found in MA). These monthly missives usually began with the salutation "Very dear Sisters," ended with "Lovingly yours," and expressed a confidence that those to whom she wrote shared her own love for the congregation and would respond to all of her requests for help. "We know how anxious you are to hear of home and the opening of school," she wrote the members on 14 September 1932; on 27 February 1933, her letter read: "I know you have all been making strenuous efforts to save in every way." A few months later, on 12 April, she told the sisters: "We are very anxious that the college enrollment be greatly increased and are trusting you to urge attendance at Marygrove upon those of your graduates who expect to attend college."

Moreover, Sister Prudentia Brand told of Ruth's daily visits to the kitchen, to each infirmary room, and to the print shop to inquire personally about each sister's family and personal concerns. When summer assignments were made, Ruth remembered those who liked night air and those who did not and made the room assignments accordingly. Prudentia remembered Ruth as "really a Mother" but as one who was also stern and expected you to do what she asked as she asked it (PB, interviewed by author, 4 Aug. 1993).

Ruth openly shared her sense of the heavy financial burden with the members of the congregation. "While steel framework proclaims that our New Convent Home is really taking form . . . we gaze almost bewildered and wonder how we shall ever be able to equip the buildings since every available cent must go for brick and mortar," she wrote them on 23 September 1931 (MA). The following February, her words were: "Though the burden of building is great, and will be for a long time, the thought of the loving, loyal Sisters devoted to the interests of our dear Community sustains us in the work" (CL of RH, 4 Feb. 1932, MA). On 27 February 1933, she wrote: "You have, no doubt, heard of the Right Reverend Bishop's order to close the parochial schools on May the twenty-sixth. This entails a great hardship—a deficit of about $30,000 which we were depending on for our July interest. . . . [L]et us implore Him [God] to help us in our dire need" (MA).

Ruth lived in a spirit of gratitude and reliance on God, on St. Joseph (patron of household affairs), and on her sisters. "Although no large donations are materializing, still dear St. Joseph is doing his work quietly," she observed before reporting the gift of an auto and truck from Henry Ford in September 1931 (CL of RH, 29 Sept. 1931, MA). The following October, she wrote: "It is amazing what He [God] has done for us within the last few months through the united efforts of the Sisters" (CL of RH, 26 Oct. 1932, MA). She more directly acknowledged her reliance on the sisters: in December 1933: "Our grateful thanks to each dear Sister for her loving cooperation, for through your striving and united efforts, we feel very hopeful about the interest burden in January [1934]. Thank you again for helping to lift this great burden" (CL of RH, 6 Dec. 1933, MA).

In addition to her commitment to the rebuilding, she was constantly concerned both about increasing membership and about improving the sisters' educational preparation. In almost every letter to the community, she reminded the sisters to pray for an increase in members: "Looking ahead to June, 1932, the completion of our building. . . . How shall we respond to the increased demands of our schools?" (CL of RH, 2 Apr. 1931, MA). Again, on 27 February 1933, she wrote the congregation: "You will be interested in hearing that we have nineteen postulants. Seven came this month. We are trusting that you will have a goodly number ready for June" (MA). Likewise, in February 1934, there was much deliberation and prayer over "who to send for higher studies at the Catholic University next year" (CM, 22 Feb. 1934, MA). Later that year, the council decided to send three for graduate degrees in chemistry, biology, and education, so as to enable Marygrove to meet the latest standards of the accrediting institution (CM, 16 June 1934, MA). Two years later, four were sent to Notre Dame and another to Catholic University (CM, 22 Feb. 1936, MA). In 1937, the council investigated purchasing a house of studies in Washington D.C., adjacent to Catholic University (CM, 3 Feb. 1937, MA). The following year, "the dire necessity of sending more sisters away to study was discussed at some length," and the suggestion was made that "some of the very young members" be sent to Marygrove for their undergraduate training (CM, 29 Jan. 1938, MA). This latter was a radical departure from the past practice of getting one's education over many years through summer courses offered at the motherhouse.

In sum, the IHM congregation had at its helm during these years a woman who had natural qualities of leadership, the necessary decisiveness, and the foresight to plan for the future that she envisioned for the community and for its educational works. Some remember her as a woman of stern demeanor and piercing eyes (MCS, M of MR, audiotape, 11 Mar. 1974, MA). As revealed by her own writings and those who knew her well, however, she was a woman who had great love for the community and a maternal commitment to building family-like relationships among its members. Her gifts matched her challenge of providing a "home" for the family.

### Miriam Raymo (1875–1965)

Margaret Jane ("Jen") Raymo was one of the five children of Mary and Joseph Raymo, owner of a Detroit hardware business. Margaret was educated in the Detroit public schools and at Detroit Business College before entering the IHM congregation at the age of 21.[13] In 1919, while serving as principal and local superior (a position she held for eight years), she received her baccalaureate degree, earned over many summers, with emphasis both in music and in business administration (Mengy. of MR, 2 Mar. 1965, MA).

Her talent in music was evident in her early ministry; in one of her first assignments, she organized a band whose fame earned her the nickname "the Band Sister." However, it was her talent for business that had the greatest impact on the congregation. In 1924, she was elected treasurer, a position she held until 1948. "Her business acumen was recognized by influential lawyers and industrial leaders as well as by the casual 'knight of the road,' " wrote her menologist, Sister Marie Chantal. "They all learned it was no use to try to put anything over on Sister Miriam" (Mengy. of MR, 2 Mar. 1965, MA). In a letter after her death, the regional manager of the company that held the mortgage wrote:

> She was certainly the most remarkable, capable businesswoman I have ever had the pleasure of meeting. . . . She knew every brick in each one of your numerous buildings. I might add that she also was familiar with every entry in the voluminous abstracts, that were three or four feet high when piled one on top of the other. Her knowledge of every detail in connection with the operation of your farm was also quite amazing . . . she would be able to tell us within the fraction of a penny the cost of plowing an acre of ground with a diesel engine tractor as compared with a gasoline engine tractor. (SCT to LS, 12 Jan. 1966, MA)

In the IHM community, Miriam's commitment to St. Mary Farms is legendary. She was always seeking ways to improve the yields. A generation of IHM sisters can remember being enlisted in her plan to put colored glasses on the turkeys to prevent them from harming one another. Fewer are aware that she instituted experimental breeding of the beef stock to increase its meat yield. Marie Chantal reports carrying the news from the exultant farm manager to Miriam's sickbed that "Agnes has a calf." To this, Miriam responded: "Agnes who???" Then, after a moment, she chuckled, "Not Agnes; you must mean, the Angus" (MCS, M of MR, audiotape, 11 Mar. 1974, MA).

Miriam was also a determined and creative fundraiser. In the earliest years of her twenty-four-year tenure as treasurer, she was confronted with the necessity of raising as much money as possible for the building of Marygrove College. The major fundraiser, netting $100,000, was the Marygrove Festival, a week-long Detroit-area effort in which every parish

---

13. Her personal file simply indicates that she attended Detroit Business College, but there is no evidence of an earned degree or certificate there or of any transfer of credits (MA).

and school, all the Catholic men's organizations, and all IHM graduates were involved ([Kelly] 1948, 582–83). To advertise the event, Miriam arranged with her friends at Selfridge Air Force Base to drop festival brochures from their planes (Mengy. of MR, 2 Mar. 1965, MA). To get prizes for the various booths, Miriam personally visited the presidents of major Detroit businesses. Marie Chantal, who accompanied her, describes how they always had a prearranged appointment with the "top man" and how Miriam always asked directly for what she expected to receive: "How she would manage to get to the top was a secret of her own and of her particular warmness, her way of writing letters, her way of calling up and making appointments. She always called the president direct." Miriam's view of fundraising was what one hears from specialists today: "Go to the top people. You do them an honor" (MCS, M of MR, audiotape, 11 Mar. 1974, MA).

When the community needed some new vehicles, Miriam presented the case in a personal letter to Henry Ford himself. In the same letter, she added the personal touch of inviting the Fords to a quadrille at the Academy, informing him that the young women there were learning his favorite pastime, old-fashioned dancing, and were anxious to dance with him at the upcoming ball. (It seems that Ford's secretary had several daughters in the school, and he had been instrumental in the hiring of a famous dancing teacher there). A personal response from Ford came back, saying that the vehicles would be on their way and that he and Mrs. Ford would be happy to attend the ball (MCS, M of MR, audiotape, 11 Mar. 1974, MA; CL of RH, 29 Sept. 1931, MA).

That Miriam was respected as a businesswomen in the Monroe community was evidenced at the time of the national banking crisis. Two of the banks in Monroe had failed and there was fear for the third, the First National. Late one evening at the motherhouse, the top civic leaders and executives of the major paper companies then headquartered in Monroe met with Miriam to develop a strategy to prevent a run on that bank before the Federal Reserve in New York could forward additional cash. The plan was simple and ingenious. Marie Chantal was sent with quarters and half-dollars and the community bank book to stand in the deposit line. Miriam herself and several other sisters joined her there. They were commissioned to deposit a quarter at a time and then go back to the end of the line and to talk to as many people as possible, trying to build confidence that the bank would not fail (MCS, M of MR, audiotape, 11 Mar. 1974, MA). The strategy worked; the First National Bank withstood the storm (personal communication of a longtime bank employee to JSh, 14 Mar. 1994).

During the building process at the motherhouse, Miriam made daily rounds to check on the progress being made. She oversaw every detail; nothing escaped her. One morning, she looked up at the lights and noted one misfit out of eight. On the morning the bricklaying was to begin, she arrived at the scene after a few courses were up, only to find that the mortar being used was not the prescribed yellow color. She went to the persons supervising the bricklayers, who said: "It is not specified." She retorted, "Stop laying those bricks." She recounted later, "I knew those specifications from A to Z." The work was redone. (MCS, M of MR, audiotape, 11 Mar. 1974, MA).

In addition to the tales of Miriam's business skill and acumen, memories of Miriam are replete with engaging anecdotes that reveal her as a warm and loving human being of many diverse talents and interests. Spiro Micallef, who worked as IHM master carpenter for fifty years, summed her up this way: "She was a brilliant woman. She could do anything. She was like my mother to me" (SM, interviewed by FM, audiotape, 26 June 1986, MA). In a tender letter for Miriam's Golden Jubilee, her dear friend Sister Mary Judith Connelly wrote: "I never could tell you how I have marveled, not at your business ability, but at your all-round ability. You are as motherly as my grandmother wa[s] and can cook as well . . . and you can build a college or swing a loan as neatly as you can fry an egg. You are at ease with Jerome [one of the congregation's longtime employees] or the Cardinal and you can make both of them feel at ease" (MJC to MR, 29 Aug. 1948, MA).

Her skill at needlework was well-known, and she used it as a means of service. Her menologist records an instance when one of the sisters needed a new habit to start school at the University of Notre Dame. Miriam had just finished making one for her niece to wear at her vow ceremony, and said, "It wouldn't take anything to whip up another . . . besides I wouldn't own a niece who wouldn't give up her habit to help a Sister" (Mengy. of MR, 2 Mar. 1965, MA). In her "retirement" years, she made meticulously handcrafted vestments, an enterprise to which she brought the same high standard of quality and beauty that she demanded in the construction of the buildings she oversaw.[14]

Miriam was a woman who spoke her mind plainly and forcefully; she described herself as a "straight shooter." The story is told that one day, she approached a sister during the dishwashing process and asked her what she was doing. When the response was "I'm saying aspirations [short prayers]," Miriam retorted, "Quit saying aspirations and wash the dishes!" (Mengy. of MR, 2 Mar. 1965, MA). When she assigned to an

---

14. A text displayed on the desk used by Sister Miriam, now in the Monroe Archives, reads: "Miriam loved beauty, whether in its natural wonder . . . or prepared by some gifted person. She was a wonderful seamstress and delighted in making vestments . . . She loved art in all its forms—provided not too abstract! The design, the planning, the simple beauty and foresight of the Motherhouse/Academy complex is still a matter of astonishment to professional architects and builders."

astonished Marie Chantal the task of purchasing the year's apple supply
and the young sister protested that she didn't "know an apple from an
onion," Miriam shot back disgustedly, "Well, that doesn't mean you have
to remain an ignoramus, you know." She then proceeded to provide her
secretary with books and market field trips to educate her for the task
(MCS, M of MR, audiotape, 11 Mar. 1974, MA).

As this last anecdote reveals, Miriam believed in delegation. Marie
Chantal recalls that even if Ruth came to Miriam for information for
which the young secretary had been given responsibility, Miriam would
send the general superior directly to her. "It was her way of showing that
people really counted" (MCS, M of MR, audiotape, 11 Mar. 1974, MA).

A glimpse into her spirituality comes from Marie Chantal, who said
that whenever an important decision was at hand, Miriam could be found
in the chapel. "I'm wrestling with God," she would say (MCS, M of MR,
audiotape, 11 Mar. 1974, MA). Sister Marie Jeannette Boudreau, who sat
at Miriam's bedside a few days before her death, recounts: "Nothing
could be done for the pain and she seemed unsure someone was with
her. . . . Then sister rallied, caught my eye and spoke. 'No one, no one has
received more from God than me. No one at all, Sister, has received more
from God than me.' " [15]

## The Relationship Between Ruth and Miriam

The personal skills and qualities of Ruth and Miriam were especially
appropriate to the challenges that faced them in the building project.
They respected and relied upon each other's competencies and respective
roles, and they were close friends who were partners through a critical
period of community leadership. "We had it all," Miriam recalled when
she and Ruth later talked of that period with the youngest IHM sisters.
"There was nothing that you could name that we didn't have. And
Mother Ruth and myself travelled that route for twelve years together.
We never disagreed, did we! She was the best pal that anyone on earth
could have" (MR and RH, S of F, audiotape, 1962, MA).

Spiro Micallef—who drove the community's Buick during the years
before it was dreamed that sisters would drive cars themselves[16]—tells
of driving Ruth and Miriam to New York and to St. Paul, Minnesota, four
or five times each and to Chicago many times. Miriam would say as soon
as they left the motherhouse, "Now we can relax," and she would have
him stop at a gas station with a diner nearby and send him for hot dogs

15. Note from Sister Marie Jeannette, found in Sister Miriam's personal file (folder 1)
in MA.
16. The Council Minutes of 28 Oct. 1933 report the purchase of a Buick "because of its
durability" (MA).

and hamburgs for lunch (rather than bring along a bag lunch as some others did). The custom of the time prohibited their going into restaurants (SM, interviewed by FM, 26 June 1986, MA). This enjoyment of some privileges unusual for the time continued after they were out of office: It was an accepted fact that while Miriam was in charge of the farm in the 1950s, she had a little house in which she entertained the community on special occasions as well as her friends and the clergy.[17]

The most poignant and eloquent testimony to their relationship was given by Marie Chantal. She recalled an evening when she was working with Miriam just a few days before the balance sheet was to be audited by the Detroit Trust Company, holder of the congregation's debt. Suddenly, Miriam collapsed with a serious stroke—her second—and was rushed to the infirmary. The doctor ordered an ambulance but warned that she might not survive the necessary trip to Toledo. Marie Chantal was summoned to the infirmary. From her sickbed, Miriam, with halting speech, gave directions to her young secretary to finish the balance sheet. When Marie Chantal returned to Miriam's office, she found her general superior sitting alone. All of a sudden, "the valiant, the brave, the strong Mother Ruth broke down completely and sobbed and sobbed. She said: 'Sister, if anything happens to Sister Miriam, I can't, I can't bear this burden alone. I can't' " (MCS, autobiographical data in personal file, MRO, MA; MCS, M of MR, audiotape, 11 Mar. 1974, MA).

Ruth had the primary leadership role, and it was she who presented the options and recommendations to the rest of the council for decisions. It was she who wrote to the women of the congregation to inform and urge cooperation. Behind and beside her through all the plans and negotiations was Miriam, her friend and partner, thinking, researching, recommending, and providing the confidence that comes to a leader from knowing that the basis for decision-making and risk-taking is fully sound.

### Relationships with the Men Involved in the Project

Looking at this project as an accomplishment of the women of the IHM congregation, one is led to ask what role men played in all this. After all, multimillion dollar borrowings and the construction of large buildings were (and still are) considered to be men's work. From reading between the lines of the anecdotes, it appears that Miriam knew what she wanted from the men with whom she worked—and got it. It was a relationship of equals who respected one another's different competencies and responsibilities.

Ruth and Miriam relied upon the congregation's attorney, Oliver

17. The Motherhouse Chronicles tell of events planned by Sister Miram for the community at the farm; see entries for 27 May 1946 and 18 Aug. 1954 (MA).

Golden, to assist in preparation of contracts in the financing and refinancing arrangements (CM, 12 May 1931, MA; DJK to MR, 26 Oct. 1935,
MA). When Ruth wrote to inform the members of the congregation about
the successful refinancing, she mentioned that the decision was made
"after a very intensive study together with consultation with Mr. Golden"
(CL of RH, 27 Nov. 1936, MA). They did not always follow his advice,
however; initially at least, he opposed the refinancing (OG to RN, 14 and
17 June 1935, MA).

The architect, D. C. Bohlen, who had also done the planning of Marygrove College, was a continuing presence throughout the building project
and the financial negotiations. Bohlen accompanied Ruth, Miriam, and
Sister Francis Regis Reilly to St. Paul, Minnesota, to negotiate the refinancing of the Marygrove debt and the borrowing of the new money for
the project (SM, interviewed by FM, audiotape, 26 June 1986, MA). Bohlen's plans, like Golden's, were clearly subject to review; Miriam observed that the architect and the builder had considered many different
options before putting anything on paper, "but eventually they came up
with something that looked feasible for the community and after great
study, Mother Ruth, the Council, the Sisters—both junior and senior,—
friends, benefactors, clergy and hierarchy accepted it, thought it was very
fine" (MR, R from A, audiotape, 1963, MA).

The sisters' relationship with Henry Brennan of the W. E. Wood Company, contractors for the motherhouse complex, also spanned many
years. Apparently, his judgment carried great weight with the decision-
makers. The council minutes report the following about the selection of
the plumbing contractors: "Although Harrigan and Reid were not the
lowest bidders, all things considered—their integrity, their experience,
their open door policy in regard to the Union, their freedom from any
other large contracts at this time, Mr. H. Brennan's great confidence in
them, etc.—it was agreed to give them the contract, if they would reduce
the price" (CM, 12 May 1931, MA). When in 1935 it was decided to finish
a section of the infirmary wing, it was decided that it could be done by
the congregation's regular maintenance staff, "under the supervision of
Mr. Brennan" (CM, 25 Feb. 1935, MA).

Miriam told two anecdotes that show how she relied on these men
for information and for good judgment. When the statue from the old
motherhouse was being moved to the new one, it was discovered that it
was made of hammered zinc—which material, according to Brennan
and Bohlen, "who know these things," was "priceless" (MR, R from A,
audiotape, 1963, MA). In another context, Miriam described the interplay
between these three professionals in a meeting concerning the height of
the new chapel:

Mr. Brennan would just shake his head the least little bit if he wasn't
satisfied with what Mr. Bohlen was saying. The builder is never sup-

posed to question the architect, you know. But he'd just shake his head a little bit and then I'd know he wasn't satisfied. So I'd say to Mr. Bohlen, "It's got to go higher." And he'd say, "Sister, it can't go higher." When he got it up there where it is now I watched Mr. Brennan and he just gave me the least bit of a sign. "Well now, that's it," I said. (MR, R from A, audiotape, 1963, MA).

Miriam was clearly in control of the project and knew how to drive a hard bargain. For example, she wanted a pond in back of the mother-house. When the question of backfill—to bring the ground around the buildings up to the level of the entrances—came up, she proposed to Brennan, "You give us a pond . . . and you can have the dirt." He responded, with some surprise, that it would cost him about $10,000 to dig a lake. "I just suggested it," she replied, knowing that she would, indeed, get her lake—and two weeks later, they started digging (MR, R from A, audiotape, 1963, MA).

There must have been a good spirit among the men working on the construction project, because at Thanksgiving time in 1931, they had a "Feather Party" that yielded $625 for the benefit of the academy (CL of RH, 21 Dec. 1931, MA). Miriam noted, however, that at one point there was a three-week strike among the bricklayers, who were getting one dollar an hour and wanted a dollar-fifty. (She commented that they were having to kick back fifty cents to the contractor who hired them [MR, R from A, audiotape, 1963, MA]). With regard to Miriam's relationships with the men who were her direct employees, we have the testimony of Spiro, who said she was "like a Mother to him" (SM, interviewed by FM, 26 June 1986, MA), while Marie Chantal describes her as one who expected high standards of workmanship and productivity but who treated the workers with respect and without partiality (MCS, M of MR, audiotape, 11 Mar. 1974, MA).

Given the times, it is not surprising that the records show that Ruth and Miriam's relationships with ecclesiastical authority were quite different. Here, the women were all obedience and acquiescence. Detroit's bishop, Michael J. Gallagher, was clearly a friend of the IHM community (MJG to BCZ, 15 Sept. 1936, MA); however, in accord with the spirit of the times, the council minutes contain phrases such as "but nothing definite could be done [about withdrawing from a parish school] without consulting the wishes of the Right Reverend Bishop" (CM, 8 July 1932, MA) and "the Archbishop giving his approval [to building the new chapel]" (CM, 23 Sept. 1938, MA). When the bishop closed the schools early in 1933, causing a shortfall in salary revenues of $30,000, Ruth wrote to the community: "However we must accept it as God's Will and receive it in the spirit of obedience." She counseled the sisters not to talk about it to "outsiders" (CL of RH, 27 Feb. 1933, MA).

However, even though it was best to "acquiesce" to the archbishop's

1939 request that the congregation build a girls' high school in Detroit, the council felt free to tell him that they could not do it just then: "Just at present [while building the chapel] we are not in a position to build a school, but we are willing to do so as soon as possible even if we start with only a unit" (CM, 20 June 1939, MA). Moreover, Miriam revealed her knowledge of canon law and her attitude toward ecclesiastical authority in a letter to the underwriter for the 1936 refinancing regarding the congregation's legal status. After describing its legal incorporation in the State of Michigan, she went on to assure him that no further ecclesiastical permissions were needed: "Ecclesiastical authority does not function in this matter except in-so-far [sic] as it is better for a Community of religious to be in accord with Ecclesiastical authority" (MR to DJK, 11 Sept. 1936, MA).

In sum, partnership, collaboration, and mutual respect characterized the relationships of the IHM leadership with the architect, attorney, and builder, as well as with the male employees of the congregation. Within the church, however, such relationships between men and women did not exist. One can imagine a woman like Miriam cheering on today's Catholic feminists.

### Involvement of the Members of the Community

Although this essay is about an "enterprise of sisterhood," to this point the focus has been on the leaders. The women of the congregation, however, were also significantly involved in this building project.

According to Miriam's description (cited above with reference to the architect), the members of the congregation had some role in reviewing the plans (MR, R from A, audiotape, 1963, MA). Marie Chantal remembers that those living in Monroe at the time were involved in selecting the fixtures that would be used; when vendors came with samples of door frames or other accessories, they would be set out in one of the parlors in the old motherhouse, and the sisters cast their votes for what they thought would be the best (MCS, M of MR, audiotape, 11 Mar. 1974, MA).

Stories abound about the ways in which the sisters were involved in doing the final preparation of the buildings. In order to save money, they scrubbed the tiletex floors on hands and knees prior to the first waxing, a task that required many weeks of labor by many people. Volunteer squads were formed, including the general superior and the members of her council. The youngest members—novices and postulants—were drafted into service ([Kelly] 1948, 691–92). When the terrazzo floor of the chapel was being laid, it had to be kept continually wet for seven to ten days until it set; novices worked in twenty-four-hour shifts to do so (RMM, personal communication to author, 19 Jan. 1994).

In the years when the debt payments were most burdensome, all were involved in efforts to try to bring in extra revenue. Ruth's letters are full of both calls to and gratitude for such cooperation. Requests were made for needlework for the 1931 Autumn Festival (CL of RH, 12 Nov. 1931, MA), for participation in selling Christmas cards (CL of RH, 29 Sept. 1931, MA), for use in the schools of a history text and reading workbooks on which royalties and a profit could be realized (CL of RH, 3 Feb. 1932, MA), for purchasing first communion veils from the mother-house, and for selling the commemorative booklets from the dedication ceremonies of the new buildings (CL of RH, 14 Sept. 1932, MA). In May 1933, when the bishop's decision to close the schools early created a cash shortage of $30,000 and threatened the congregation's ability to make the July payment, Ruth sent an anxious letter requesting early estimates of end-of-the year surpluses. She also made a special request, asking if any sister knew of anyone—relative, friend, or parishioner—who could make a loan for a year of from one to five thousand dollars, "or almost any amount on which we are more than willing to pay interest and secure the amount to them by our note bearing the General Superior's and the Secretary's signature." In the same letter, it was noted that the Detroit missions who had transferred their "frozen Bank Balances" to the moth-erhouse would be notified as to whether the bank would allow them to be counted against the indebtedness of the congregation (CL of RH, 16 May 1933, MA).

Sisters remember doing many things to raise money to be sent to the motherhouse (as well as to pay their own expenses in the local houses). Candy received as gifts was sold by the piece to the students. Sisters gave extra music lessons and elocution lessons (at ten cents each) and tutored on Saturdays and after school. Movies were shown on Saturdays at the schools, and there were "raffles galore." Christmas gifts received from family and friends were sent in to be sold at the Academy or Marygrove gift shops—or to be used as furnishings in the new motherhouse. In addition, the congregation economized in countless ways. Sorghum was substituted for sugar at the table, milk for cream, chemises made from flour sacks for knit underwear. Butter was no longer served, and cakes were not iced. The congregation made its own soap. Though the custom of the time was for each sister to have three habits, the sisters in the infirmary were asked to relinquish all but one and the best were made over for the new members.[18] The rest of the sisters mended and patched and made their clothing do for even longer than usual ([Kelly] 1948, 692).

During the anxious spring of 1933, the general superior's letters re-flected the need for even more sacrifices. She wrote: "I know you have

---

18. This information comes from a report to the author by Sister Annunciata Grix of remembrances of Sisters Ann Margaret Hughes, Teresena Gallagher, Irene Mogg, Frances Rita Belenger, and herself as shared on 29 Dec. 1992.

all been making efforts to save in every way, still it may be that each one can find other little means of economizing. Just now every cent means much to us" (CL of RH, 27 Feb. 1933, MA). She asked that each sister try to bring a bar of soap with her when she came to the motherhouse for the summer and that extra medicine-cabinet supplies from the local communities be brought along also for summer use (CL of RH, 29 May and 12 Apr. 1933, MA).

The community never missed a payment during those difficult years. Ruth's letters continually expressed gratitude for the response to her requests.[19] In the centennial history, the congregation's historian observed: "Through thousands of small sacrifices made, with few exceptions, by the entire congregation, the depression was weathered" ([Kelly] 1948, 692). Sister Amadeus Dowd speaks of a sense of pride among the members of the community about how they were helping to pay "our" debt.[20]

Marie Chantal, in her recollections of trying to comfort Ruth on the night of Miriam's stroke, gives what is probably the most realistic picture of how it was among the members of the community:

> Helplessly, I tried to comfort Mother, to tell her that all of us understood what she was going through. But in my heart I knew that the Sisters didn't. I heard them complaining because some of them could not return to Notre Dame or Catholic University that summer, because there were not any professional magazines left in the community room, because we had to give up our knitted vests and make cotten [sic] chants out of sugar bags. I knew they meant well, that the great majority of Sisters were giving and sacrificing generously—but that they didn't realize how close, how very close the community was to bankruptcy. They did not realize the depths or the intensity of the courage needed to build a home for the Sisters in the middle of a depression. No, they didn't realize, and Mother Ruth knew they didn't—they couldn't know. (MCS, autobiographical data in personal file, MRO, MA).

At the same time, it is clear that without the involvement of the whole congregation, the financing of the building project could never have been achieved. According to Marie Chantal, who wrote of "the joy of all of us working together in something that we so badly needed at the time," that involvement was also a source of building a spirit of unity among the members: "It gave all of us a sense of belonging, a sense of being needed" (MCS, autobiographical data in personal file, MRO, MA). It was indeed an enterprise of sisterhood.

19. See, for example, CL of RH, 26 Oct. 1932, 29 May 1933, 6 Dec. 1933 (MA).
20. In several conversations with the author on various occasions.

Aerial view of the SSIHM Motherhouse complex.

# 10

## "Of Less-Than-Happy Memory"

### *A Reexamination of the Representative Assembly, 1972–1975*

### Maryfran Barber, I.H.M., and Mary M. McCann, I.H.M.

Between 1966 and 1972, amidst the energy and creativity that followed Vatican II and during the social unrest, protest, and civil disobedience that accompanied the ongoing civil-rights struggle and the antiwar movement in the United States, the IHM congregation in Michigan dramatically transformed its structures of authority and decision-making. In seven short, intense years, the community moved from a top-down organizational structure to one that involved the entire membership in making important corporate decisions. Two tangible fruits of this process of reorganization occurred in quick succession in 1972: Assembly '72 and the representative assembly.

Assembly '72 offered an entirely new approach to the congregational Chapter (the forum for electing the general superior and for planning and legislating for the congregation's life and mission). In a year-long, high-energy, collegial process involving educational sessions and personal retreats, every able and willing IHM sister helped build a consensus about corporate decisions and the choice of a new congregational leader. Still remembered as a vital and rewarding experience by most IHM members, the congregation continues to regard Assembly '72 as a high point and a touchstone experience of participatory government.

The participatory spirit of Assembly '72 was meant to be continued and sustained through a new general government plan that featured a representative assembly (RA) as its centerpiece (GP, 27 Mar. 1975, arts. 79–82, 7, MA; RAR, 3 Oct. 1972, MA).[1] Composed of seven ex officio members and twenty-five elected delegates (each of whom represented one or more local assembly groups), the RA was a collegial body with authority to make policy about major congregational matters. It also of-

---

1. For the spirit of the plan, see "Affirmations of Assembly '72," no. 35 (MA).

fered advice to the general superior and to the executive board[2] with which she shared "the unitive and directive function" of leadership as well as responsibility for the ongoing concerns of life and mission in the congregation (GP, 27 Mar. 1975, art. 63, 82, MA).

Chaired by the general superior, the RA ordinarily met quarterly. Its intended purpose was to enable the executive board and the general IHM membership to make *together* those decisions considered essential to the ongoing life and mission of the congregation (RAR, 3 Oct. 1972, MA). In particular, the RA was empowered to shape the policies and structures needed to ensure the proper ongoing implementation of the thirty-seven decisions of Assembly '72 (referred to as Affirmations).[3] Several adminis-trative staff members assisted the RA delegates in their work; appointed by the executive board, they attended RA meetings but were not voting members of the body (PDOD of 1972 GP, MA).[4]

The RA convened for the first time on 29 September 1972, amidst enthusiasm and great expectations. However, despite some important accomplishments, it sputtered to a premature end owing to persistent, unresolved conflict about its own authority and role and about the related authority and roles of the general superior, the executive board, and the administrative staff. The RA held its last meeting in October 1975, nearly a year before the official end of the delegates' elected terms of office. Twenty years later, participants characterized the RA experience vari-ously as "combat" (RAD, interviewed by MMcC, 6 Nov. 1992), "gridlock" (EBSM, interviewed by MMcC, 3 Dec. 1992), and "pure unadulterated pain" (EBM, interviewed by MMcC, 5 Nov. 1992). Some likened it to "two moods going bang" (RAO, in GI, 28 June 1992), or to "being backed into a corner" (RAD, interviewed by MMcC, 1 Dec. 1992), while others remember the anxiety they felt as meetings approached (EBM, inter-viewed by MMcC, 16 Jan. 1993).[5]

Although most of the participant IHMs interviewed for this essay echo one delegate's assessment of it as "the RA of less-than-happy mem-ory" (RAD, interviewed by MfB, 13 Aug. 1992), most insisted that the RA

2. The members of the executive board were the general superior, the assistant, four provincials, and the vice provincial (for overseas missions). For the board's role, see Legal Precepts of the Constitutions, no. 63, promulgated 27 Mar. 1975, MA. The board also func-tioned as the canonical council to the General Superior, i.e., they provided the advice or consent required in certain cases by canon law and by the IHM Constitutions.

3. See *Conclusion*, Assembly '72, referred to in "For the Love of God Do Not Sit Down," the title of the report of the General Superior to the Congregation ([1976], Part 1, 2, MA).

4. The role of key administrative staff was to carry out policies made by the RA in regard to specific areas of operation: apostolate, assemby implementation, communication, finance, and formation. In the general government structure prior to 1972, these roles were assigned to members of the Council, the predecessor of the executive board.

5. All interviews were taped; those interviewed were guaranteed anonymity. Quoted material is from verbatim transcripts (MA, restricted).

form of governance was a creative and promising approach to decision-making, which probably provoked growth even as it indisputably caused struggle and pain. In speaking of the RA's brevity, some conveyed a sense of sadness, grief, and lost opportunity; others spoke of the relief they felt when in 1976 the congregational Chapter replaced the RA with an advisory board, thus ending the gridlock and ineffectiveness experienced during the RA period.[6] For most everyone, however, there are lingering questions about the meaning of the RA experience in the congregation: What really happened and why? How could something sown in such a spirit of hope reap such frustration? What can we learn from this time that may help us in the present?

## The Ecclesial Context of the RA

Vatican II's universal call to holiness, with its image of the church as the one "People of God" who share a single mission in this struggling and suffering world, catalyzed a profound renewal in religious life beginning in 1965.[7] Most U.S. American women religious—including the IHM community in Monroe—were ready, willing, and able to respond because they were already involved in their own renewal process through the Sister Formation Movement[8] and the collaborative work of the Conference of Major Superiors of Women (CMSW, renamed the Leadership Conference of Women Religious in 1972). They now also moved swiftly to effect the participative "Special Chapters of Renewal" called for by the church.[9] Many took quite literally the call to examine the whole of their lives in light of the Gospels as the first rule of life, in accordance with the spirit of their founders and in response to contemporary needs. In

6. The advisory board was composed of the central administration (the president, vice president, and the coordinators of material resources, human resources, and ministry), six provincials, and representatives elected from each province. The central administration and provincials formed the governing board, which assumed the policy-making role of the RA. The central administration was the successor of the executive board.

7. See *Lumen Gentium,* Vatican Council II Dogmatic Constitution on the Church, 1964, chapters 2 and 5 (Abbott 1966, 24–37, 65–72), and *Perfectae Caritatis,* Vatican Council II Decree on the Appropriate Renewal of Religious Life, 1965, no. 2 (Abbott 1966, 468–69).

8. Begun as the Sister Formation Conference in 1953 by the National Catholic Education Association, the Sister Formation Movement addressed the professional preparation needs for U.S. sisters engaged in formal education at every level, transforming American sisters into the most highly educated group of nuns in the Roman Catholic Church and placing them among the most highly educated women in the U.S. A 1966–68 survey published in Quiñonez and Turner 1992, 44–47; 176n. 6 showed that 68.2 percent of the 139,691 sisters surveyed shared a strong preference for post–Vatican II ideals. (For further discussion of the Sister Formation Movement, see chaps. 11 and 12 of the present volume.)

9. Vatican norms for the implementation of *Perfectae Caritatis,* the Vatican II Decree on Religious Life, were issued *moto proprio* in the apostolic letter *Ecclesiae Sanctae* by Paul VI on 6 Aug. 1966.

numerous communities, the old paradigm featuring the dualistic separation of "sacred" and "secular" began to give way to the new Vatican II paradigm in which religious, as part of the people of God, were people with a mission in and to this world, particularly among the poor and afflicted. Those dimensions of religious life that had served to separate women religious "from the world"—the habit, cloister, rigid schedules, etc.—no longer seemed to serve the new call to mission in the world; many communities gave them up. In addition, national organizations emerged which brought together women religious from across the country, among them the activist National Association of Women Religious (later called the National Assembly of Religious Women and now defunct), the National Black Sisters Conference, *Las Hermanas*, and the Washington, D.C., national Catholic social justice lobby, NETWORK.

Traditional hierarchical authority patterns began to give way, although not without struggle and conflict. In the IHM community, for example, 362 women chose to leave between 1966 and 1976 (LW, 1966–76, MA).[10] Women religious of traditional, liberal, and more radical assumptions regarding authority were interpreting the Vatican documents and the call to renewal in substantially different ways. Members were challenging leaders; leaders were struggling both to understand their roles and to hold their congregations together in the midst of the fray. As Rome got wind of what women's congregations in the United States were doing in and through the Vatican Council–initiated renewal process— frequently in response to complaints from their own members—its male hierarchy often balked, blocked, and censured (Quiñonez and Turner 1992, 42).

The women religious did not back down, however. Painful confrontations between leaders of the Conference of Major Superiors of Women and Vatican officials can be documented. "We [the major superiors] were standing up against Rome the way our own were standing up against us . . . saying, 'You're not consulting us and you're just laying this on us; you're not asking our opinion,' " reflected the IHM general superior during this period. "The whole tenor of the time mirrored that authority struggle. It was just all around. The fever of it was everywhere" (EBM, interviewed by MMcC, 5 Nov. 1992).

## Conflicting IHM Views of Authority and Power

In placing certain policy-making authority in the hands of the representative and collegial RA that followed the well-received Assembly '72,

10. In Aug. 1966 there were 1633 members (RDC, 1966–67, MA); as of 1 July 1976 there were 1177 members (Mem. Stat. 1976–77, MA). The difference, 456, represents loss both by deaths and by withdrawals.

the IHM congregation was interpreting the call to collegiality as issued by Vatican II in progressive terms. However, the RA representatives themselves displayed a wide spectrum of beliefs about authority and power, and these differences were played out throughout the course of the RA.

Of considerable significance were the different understandings of the role of the congregation's general superior. Some believed that the new government structure "reduced the role of the general superior and her council to carrying out the decisions of the RA . . . [and] fundamentally contradicted the general experience of religious congregations worldwide . . . and our own long experience as a religious community (namely an experience of having strong and inspirational leadership that was supported by the membership) and . . . the principles of religious government that were in our Constitutions" (EBSM, written response to interview question, 24 July 1993). Others saw this same reality from a positive perspective: "[It was] a structure that would really take power away from the [few] elected leaders and put it in lots of elected leadership with the various groups" (RAF, interviewed by MMcC, 25 July 1992).

There were further differences in understandings of the role of the administrative staff: "[T]hese persons felt a very deep lack of clarity with regard to their own function and their own authority role because they were supposed to be in charge of something; on the other hand, the decisions which these persons were to move forward were not simply coming from the council [precursor of the executive board] anymore" (EBM, interviewed by MMcC, 5 Nov. 1992). Moreover, the role of the RA relative to the executive board was also debated. Those that thought the RA was the congregation's central decision-making body were perplexed by the sense "that everything that came before the RA, the executive board had already considered and had come up with a position" (EBM, interviewed by MMcC, 5 Nov. 1992). Those on the board, likewise, felt keenly their own responsibility to lead and to bring unity:

> To move forward . . . and to listen to the membership. . . . But then I think there was a fear or a hesitancy about how far to go or how to fast to go, whether what was proposed [in the RA] was good for us and also being tremendously aware of people who wanted for things to remain as they were at the time of their profession forever and who were experiencing huge changes that they didn't understand and were fearful about. . . . [In addition,] we had some rather significant feelings that Rome would be contacted in those years and some fears about a split happening in the congregation. (EBM, interviewed by MMcC, 16 Jan. 1993)

Still other delegates struggled with what they experienced as mutually exclusive roles: "Is this group advisory or is it decision-making?" (RAD, interviewed by MfB, 13 Aug. 1992).

There were also various attitudes about the political dynamic of the group and of the elections of the delegates. One delegate recalled her election: "It was very exciting because it was political. It was a political process that I hadn't been a part of before in the community. . . . [W]e [had been] saying things like political isn't a bad word; but it really was; but [now] we were saying it's okay to be political; it's okay to talk about who you want; a vote is a conscious choice" (RAD, interviewed by MfB, 26 Jan. 1993). Another's sense was quite the opposite: "I felt like I was in some kind of non-church-related political body—with people lobbying, strategizing, negatively criticizing leadership people and struggling for power to control" (EBSM, written response to interview question, 24 July 1993). Another participant named the struggle while withholding judgment: "I think people were on edge, they wanted more power, they wanted more say. . . . I think the RA was a reaction to that" (RAD, interviewed by MMcC, 24 Nov. 1992).

Difficulties also arose over the structure and content of RA meetings: "A turn could happen just by somebody's question and then if you stayed with the person's question, you could run into conflict because some people wanted to stick with the agenda and some people wanted to move with the question" (EBM, interviewed by MMcC, 16 Jan. 1993).

The confusions that plagued the RA can perhaps be summarized by the recollection of one delegate about the setting of the room (the old novitiate space) in which the assembly met: "It was like in a circle and then there was a stagelike space where the altar was in the novitiate. That's where some of the action was going on." When asked "Did the circle 'speak' to you"? the delegate answered: "Well, yes, the whole idea that we all had some authority; that we were all in a decision-making mode." However, she then corrected her image: "It was like a half-circle, not a complete circle" (RAD, interviewed by MMcC, 12 Jan. 1993).[11]

## The Search for Clarity about Roles and Functions

Given the dramatically different understandings that existed among the participants, it is not surprising that tremendous efforts were made to find some way to manage the confusion and disagreement. Most of the initial efforts addressed the situation in its "objective" face: role descriptions, arenas of decision-making, lines of accountability, and patterns of communication. Understanding and agreeing on the role and function of the RA, in fact, became a major theme, sometimes as an undercurrent but sometimes as an overt part of the agenda. At its first meeting in September 1972, using the official description of the RA for guidance, the

---

11. The stagelike space referred to was the place of the speaker's stand and the table at which the General Superior and facilitators sat.

RA members arrived at their own goal statement: "To personally involve all the members of the community in shaping and extending the life and mission of the congregation" (RAR, 3 Oct. 1972, MA). At the second meeting, "clarifications were reached regarding the relationship between the RA and the [administrative] staff":

> The Representative Assembly is the policy making organization in the co-munity [sic]. It makes decisions regarding the formation of policy in accord with the affirmations of Assembly '72.
> The [administrative] staff provides the preparation and research necessary to form the policy and administers the policy once it has been formed.
> The [administrative] staff can make decisions regarding the administration of policy.
> The collegiality on which our government operates presupposes the principle of subsidiarity on which the [administative] staff operates.[12] (RAR, 8 Nov. 1972, MA)

The same meeting also addressed the matter of the agenda (including how to handle proposals) and the function of the agenda committee and resulted in a decision for a tripartite agenda: administative staff reports, ongoing agenda, and "immediacies."

The RA's responsibility for dealing with matters that would affect the life and mission of the congregation was reiterated at the assembly's third meeting, at which a proposal suggesting that the RA engage in "discernment training" was also accepted. This discernment training occurred at the fourth meeting of the RA, in March 1973. At the conclusion of that meeting several questions were raised, among them:

1. What was the relationship of the RA delegate to the RA and to local assembly groups (LAGs)? That is, should a delegate present the thinking of her LAG and voice "her own thoughts after having discerned on the matter"?

2. How should LAGs be handled? It was pointed out in the minutes that "the assembly groups were not merely 'data reporters' but that they should be encouraged to share their experiences on the topics suggested. It was suggested that the individual assembly groups should be given adequate time for prayer, for sharing, and for really getting to know one another's experiences."

3. What is RA procedure? Should more time be spent in discernment? An entry in the minutes stated that "the atmosphere of the RA should be one of prayer and reflection and should not be concerned merely with business items handled in a short time span."

---

12. The fact that these clarifications were needed is evidence of conflict within the RA concerning both its own roles and those of the staff.

4. How should communal discernment be achieved? What kind of discernment assistance should be provided to individual assembly groups?

After asking these questions, however, the RA decided not to make any procedural changes, but did extend the length of the meetings (RAM, 16 Mar. 1973, 8–9, MA).

## Board Solutions:
### A Facilitator, Committees, and a Handbook

During that first year, the executive board decided to bring to the RA three ways to address the RA's operational problems—appointment of a facilitator, adoption of a committee structure, and preparation of an RA handbook. All three came out of the board's separate efforts to clarify its role with respect to the RA, one which it believed should be "active" (EBMin, 5 Apr. 1973, 4–5, MA). However, the handling of each only reinforced confusion about the role and function of the RA and its inter-relationships with the executive board, with the staff, and with LAGs.

Although the executive board's discussion of a facilitator had resulted in the decision to ask a particular person to serve in that capacity, this decision was not made known when the proposal was brought to the RA. As a result, the RA created its own search committee to seek a facilitator, which subsequently recommended two sisters for the job (to work as a team) who were then appointed by the general superior. Thus, while its initial instinct was to act independently, the board's subsequent actions clearly fostered a perception that the board supported the sharing of authority.

The board's idea of creating a new committee structure, however, came to the RA as a recommendation, not a proposal. This distinction was problematic to some RA delegates, who questioned why it was brought in finalized form (with committees determined and members assigned) without prior RA discussion. The minutes of the meeting indicate that "[t]wo answers were given: Most boards do not give the choice of a committee to the members but simply assign people to a committee. It would have taken too long a time to put the matter up for group discussion and choice of committee when already $3/4$ of the year has been spent in trying to organize the RA" (RAM, 11 May 1973, 9, MA). Although the RA delegates had challenged the board's assumption that it could exercise independent authority, in the end they reinforced that assumption by eventually unanimously adopting the board recommendation as presented.

Finally, the executive board suggested that a RA handbook be written. After discussion, a committee was appointed to flesh this out and to formulate a draft of operational guidelines to be brought back to the RA.

The committee worked during summer 1973 and presented their fourth draft to the RA at its October meeting, the first RA meeting of the second year. In their report, they highlighted three areas for specific attention of the RA body: first, the nature and function of the RA and the relation of the RA to the administrative staff; second, the role of RA members both in relation to LAGs and within the RA itself; and third, the functions of the RA's new standing committees (OGCR, 17 Sept. 1973, 1, MA).

Finally accepted at the RA's second meeting of its second year—but deemed to be only "provisional" and highly subject to future amendment —the new guidelines brought little clarity (RAM, 3 Dec. 1973, 2, MA). Based on the previous meeting, this could have been predicted. The general superior, in her role as RA chair, had made a potent attempt to address the underlying conflicts of assumptions and beliefs that created different expectations of leadership; because the RA "engages in a ministry of service in the congregation through participation in the ministry of authority and leadership," she "felt it necessary that the group reflect together on what each person understands by this ministry of authority" (RAM, 8 Oct. 1973, 1, MA). Little was resolved, however. Although the change in agenda was in large measure supported by the delegates, at least one wondered, "Why can we just dispense with the agenda we have sent out to the sisters? Is this not a breach of trust?" (RAD, private notes [8 Oct. 1973]).

The executive board, too, had been intensely self-reflective during this period, struggling (again independently) to reconcile board members' experiences with the concept of authority prevailing in the church before and after Vatican II. Some believed that what was needed was "a whole new approach to authority now as opposed to the past," using Jesus as the example. Discussions included the relationship between the RA and the executive board; delegates as leaders; and many other questions, among them, "In the absence of consensus, does the Board take action if the RA does not?" (EBMin, 4 Feb. 1974, 2–5, MA).

In February 1974, the executive board decided to schedule a summer workshop and training session (EBMin, 5 Feb. 1974, 4, MA). It would be conducted by Management Design Incorporated (MDI), "a group which helps value-based organizations to develop structures and processes which will enable them to best accomplish their purposes" (MDIR, 6 Sept. 1974, 1, MA). The board stressed the need for education and discussion on authority, obedience, and leadership, a need shown by "the lack of clarity re: lines of authority by sisters in the community" (EBMin, 4 Mar. 1974, 2, MA).

The RA began its third year in August 1974 by participating in the MDI workshop. The primary hope and expectation of the workshop was to clarify the roles of the RA, the executive board, the administrative staff, and the LAGs in the decision-making process. The workshop included an exercise that examined values and changes in values; explanation of how change occurs in value-based organizations; and a discussion of the members' personality types based on the Myers-Briggs Type Indicator to enable understanding of members' strengths. In its report on the results of the MDI workshop, the RA told the community that the members' "hopes [for the meeting] were well fulfilled." Clarity had at last been achieved about power and policy, roles, and a variety of governmental issues that had been a source of confusion (MDIR, 6 Sept. 1974, 2–3, MA; MB to "Sisters," 9 Sept. 1974, MA).

### Escalating Tension

All was now clear, but all was not well. Clarifying the "objective" face of the confusion did not dispel the discomfort; rather, it exacerbated it. This is evident in several respects, but particularly in the sequence of events that followed the MDI workshop.

The executive board was troubled when it reviewed the MDI report before its publication:

> What is the authority of the leader that comes from the fact that this religious congregation is a Church group—more than a value based organization? There is another level of existence of a religious group that is not the function of MDI to deal with. We might have some trouble with this at another time if we do not refer to it now. The major [general] superior receives a power from the Church. She has juridical power over their provinces, houses, etc. There is another source of her power that is not in the community but is from the Church. A religious group does not exist in itself—it is within the whole structure of the Church. (EBMin, 5 Sept. 1974, 6, MA)

In October 1974, in the process of setting long-range goals, the executive board made two decisions: it established a "government" committee separate from that of the RA (which had its own government committee) to draw up the general government plan for 1976, and it made plans for Chapter/Assembly 1976. In doing so, the executive board was clearly aware of the RA. Twice during the meeting, the executive board addressed how this would be communicated and received, discussing their feelings about it as well as strategy. "It is likely that the RA will surface issues and there will be a discussion," one board member said. "It might be tense when it is made clear that the Government Committee is an Ad Hoc Committee of the Board," another observed. Anxiety and discomfort prevailed, but another member pointed out that it was "necessary to say that the Board has this responsibility, therefore we have done this and we are appointing this committee. [It is] important to present this idea strongly" (EBMin, 7 Oct. 1974, 6, MA).

The question arose as to whether the government plan was in the area of major policy, and therefore properly the role of the RA. An MDI consultant, when phoned, replied that it was not major policy but rather an operation of the community that was the canonical responsibility of the board. Discussion ensued, with the conclusion that "it is important to stress to the RA that the Board as a ruling body is obliged to take charge of the Chapter and the government plan" (EBMin, 7 Oct. 1974, 6, MA). The call on hierarchical authority and on the canons had been intensified as a result of the clarity achieved by the MDI process, but the tension had also been pushed to a new level.

A similar struggle existed within the RA as well but manifested itself slightly differently. In mid to late November, after a reorganization of standing committees in October, a controversy arose (about the scheduled December RA and LAG meetings) that exposed differences in under-standings of the purpose of the RA meetings themselves. Several RA members, upon receiving the agenda,[13] wrote (some to the agenda committee, one to the entire RA) requesting the meeting be canceled for lack of adequate agenda (one suggested meeting once or twice per year). In addition to the "lightness" of the agenda, three points were raised as rationale for cancellation: the agenda did not call for a major policy decision; it did not justify the expense entailed; it would not give the LAGs insight into matters to be considered by the RA for major policy (EBM to AgC, 14 Nov. 1974, MA).

In response, two participants wrote letters (one to the writer of a prior letter, one to the entire RA) disagreeing. By meeting, one said, the RA would be able to look at why the agenda was slim and to strengthen the committee structure; the LAGs could generate their own agenda along with that which is sent, so that their concerns could be the basis of policy consideration; and not meeting would not address the already low level of communication (RAD to EBM, copy to RA, 24 Nov. 1974, MA). The other response, addressed to the RA member who had written to the entire RA requesting the meeting be canceled, questioned who had the power to cancel the meeting. This person noted that

> our last RA meeting finished on a very traumatic note for everyone. Is this the appropriate time then, to cancel the next meeting? Is it right to make such a decision between RA meetings? . . . Even though the agenda does not appear to be a crowded one, does not the RA find itself in a very crucial position, and is it not the responsibility of the RA

13. The agenda included prayer each day, LAG reports, facilitator evaluation and decision, salary committee report and clarifications, committee meetings, guidelines committee report, old and new business, process evaluation, executive board report, and general superior's report, closing with liturgy and supper (AgC memo to RA members, 11 Nov. 1974, MA).

to handle our smooth working together? Can this be accomplished by dodging the issue? (EBM to EBM, copy to AgC, 27 Nov. 1974, MA)

Tension escalated and the situation deteriorated. In January 1975, the executive board began to put a question mark on the future of the RA. In February, the executive board agreed to approve, if requested, the ongoing absence of the delegate from Puerto Rico (EBMin, 10 Feb. 1975, 5, MA). In March, the executive board discussed whether to have only one RA meeting during the next year. Further discussion presented the rationale that the RA could be replaced by meetings to prepare for the 1976 Chapter (EBMin, 3 Mar. 1975, 4, MA).

Clearly, conflict persisted beyond the objective and obvious reality, conflict that was challenging the roots upon which the RA's participative type of congregational governance had been based. The discernment training, the reflection and sharing on developing an understanding of leadership and authority that was introduced at the first meeting of the RA's second year, the MDI workshop, and time devoted at the February 1995 RA meeting to reflective discussion of diversity (potentially in beliefs and in values) had all failed to resolve the tension. The participation in LAGs had diminished from 1,006 in the first year to 664 in the third year. The delegate from Puerto Rico requested and was given permission to be absent from meetings, given "the cost of her travel and the small number of sisters represented" (EBMin, 10 Feb. 1975, 5, MA). The RA, having once committed to longer meetings in order to attend to the discernment "mode" of decision-making, reduced its last meeting of the third year to one day. The executive board first discussed the possibility of only one RA meeting per year, then that the RA might not meet during its last year due to involvement in Chapter preparations. And in May 1975, the RA scheduled only one one-day meeting for the next year, with tentative dates for three others if the agenda required. As the October 1975 meeting ended, "the Eucharist was celebrated as scheduled at 4:30 P.M. The meeting adjourned at 6 o'clock P.M." (RAM, 7 Oct. 1975, 3, MA) —"not with a bang, but a whimper" (Eliot 1930, 105). The RA never reconvened.

## Analyses

What might explain the enduring struggle experienced by the executive board members, elected delegates, and appointed staff members as the congregation implemented the collegial body of the RA? Several explanations suggest themselves.

Perhaps the most commonly accepted analysis is the one voiced by many members of the RA: "We simply weren't ready." Given the IHMs' long history of hierarchy, the change to collegial governance was too abrupt. They needed interim steps. They had no congregational experience in distinguishing between major policy and operational policy. The RA structure was not well integrated with the province structures initiated in 1968. The delegates lacked adequate communication skills; they had not yet learned to be in touch with and express their feelings, particularly anger; they did not know how to deal constructively with conflict. In summary, they were expecting too much of themselves.

A second possibility is that IHMs may have assumed that because both Assembly '72 and the representative assembly were collegial structures, both geared to the total participation of the members in congregational decisions, the preparation for the first had been a preparation for the second. However, the dynamics of the two structures were vastly different. Assembly '72 had the authority of a Chapter, meaning that while it was in session, the assembly—not the general superior—was the highest authority in the congregation. It was, in fact, a collegial body with ultimate authority. Its decisions had the stature and weight of Chapter enactments and thus were a mandate to all members and leaders. Also, Assembly '72 was of limited duration and had a well-defined focus and process, and its sessions were facilitated by persons trained in process dynamics.

The RA, on the other hand, existed in a substantially different congregational context. The 1972 governing structure gave ongoing decision-making authority both to the RA and to the executive board, particularly the general superior; thus, the lines of authority were continually unclear and subject to dispute.[14] RA members struggled to understand this structure and their respective roles within it through reference points in their own experiences. To some, the RA felt and acted like an ongoing Chapter; to others, the model of a school board or corporate board of directors was the point of reference; to still others, it was an exercise in democracy. Some delegates expected RA meetings to be marked by gut-level honesty, while others saw them as occasions for group discernment. Some RA members held two or more of these understandings. For the executive board leaders, particularly the general superior, the struggle was distressing, with everyday, lasting implications: What was the authority of this body? How did this authority affect and interact with their own ongoing authority in daily life and in canonical matters? How did all this relate to the exercise of religious and ecclesial leadership? The administra-

14. For example, the RA was challenged by the general superior's claim of authority: "Certain persons in the community are designated to represent the total Community"—local, provincial, or general—"by serving as unifiers in the collegial body and by exercising that authority which ecclesial authority and the total collegial body have assigned.... [I]n certain matter[s] reserved to her by the church, by the community she shall make decisions in the name of the Community" (MB to congregation, 13 Jan. 1972, enc. PGRL).

tive staff, full time and well qualified in their areas of responsibility, often felt impeded by the slow, laborious, and conflictual nature of the RA proceedings.

A third analysis is related to but different from the second. The IHM congregation may not have foreseen the difficulties involved in initiating the collegial RA structure while simultaneously retaining norms for elected leaders that were explicitly hierarchical. The executive board's minutes evidence these elected leaders' conviction that they possessed— and ought to exercise—a juridical and ecclesial authority by virtue of their office (EBMin, 8 Mar. 1973, 4 Feb., 5 Sept., and 7 Oct. 1974, MA). How to exercise that authority in the context of the collegial RA and whether its exercise would be acceptable were matters of ongoing, soul-searching, and sometimes soul-wrenching discussion. Both the conviction and the conflict were most poignantly felt by the general superior.

Why did the IHM congregation structure itself in this way—with a built-in tension between hierarchical and collegial forms of authority? Some would say that the congregation had no choice in this matter because of its ecclesial status in the Roman Catholic Church and because of the norms of canon law by which it is regulated. Canonically, the authority of the general superior was hierarchical in its nature and in its exercise (except during sessions of Chapter); the same was true of the provincials who sat on the executive board. The documents articulating the 1972 general government structure clearly reference canon law, demonstrating that the canons were a definite influence. However, there is no evidence that the role of the general superior as it came to be described (in hierarchical and collegial terms) was a matter of significant struggle during the planning and decision-making process. Rather, the emphasis was on the new, collegial RA structure and its potential for involving congregational members more fully in the ongoing decision-making and policy-making of the congregation. That this also altered the role of the general superior and how her authority would function seemed nonproblematic during the planning process. As the RA was implemented, however, this alteration was felt deeply and was a source of confusion and struggle in various ways.

Why was this change viewed as nonproblematic during the planning of the new RA-centered structure? We believe that this was because the changes were viewed as evolutionary more than as transformative. In the seven fast and intense years of change since Vatican II, the several governmental changes introduced by the congregation were driven by the principles of subsidiarity and collegiality. These principles had been subscribed to by the council and were adopted as guiding principles by the congregation at its renewal Chapter in 1969. The desire was for greater and more effective participation by the members in IHM life and mission. Of related importance, this movement was promoted and enabled by the general superior—an able and visionary leader, a woman with a doctorate in theology and steeped in the spirit and theology of Vatican II. Having led IHMs through the exciting and conflictual years of 1966–72, she was overwhelmingly reelected in 1972 and was also president-elect of the Leadership Conference of Women Religious in that same year. Thus, in 1972, the congregation was moving strongly in the direction of collegiality, led by a well-respected general superior; paradoxically, her position as the highest authority in the congregation was part of what had enabled it to move to a more collegial government. Practically speaking, the congregation was experiencing the value of both the hierarchical and the collegial approaches to authority.

Thus, the hierarchical-collegial tensions that were imbedded in the 1972 general government structures were more a manifestation of IHMs' own experience and consciousness at that time in history than a response to canonical norms or to pressure from Rome. This interpretation is strengthened when we acknowledge that this was the time of Vatican-authorized experimentation in religious life—a time when it was not necessary to get Vatican approval for changes in the Constitutions, such as the RA represented.

A fourth analysis may be derived from the literature on organizational change and transformation. The changes that the IHM congregation seemed to view as evolutionary were ones that organization theorists would tend to view as introducing an organizational transformation involving a paradigmatic shift (Levy and Merry 1986, 3–20). As the ongoing conflict in the RA revealed, the new structure was born of a new worldview and based on very different assumptions and values than a basically hierarchical model. It demanded of leaders and members a whole new way of understanding and exercising authority. It generated insecurity, anxiety, and highly charged conflict.

There is evidence that the IHM congregation underestimated the true nature of the change it introduced in 1972. According to studies in the field, an organizational paradigm shift normally takes three to ten years to plan, implement, and institutionalize, depending on the complexity of the system. Such a shift usually demands the devoted attention of a steering team over this whole time, an estimated 10 to 15 percent of this group's work time; in terms of money, the average cost is 5 percent of the annual budget (Levy and Merry 1986, 33–34). After the initial planning of the 1972–76 structure, the IHM congregation moved into implementation without any long-range plan about how to translate the new paradigm into operating concepts, procedures, and structures, none of which could be assumed as automatic in a change of this magnitude. Perhaps the strongest indication of the congregation's miscalculation was that the general superior, whose role and authority were substantially changed in this new model, chaired and facilitated the first year of meetings. Even though she supported the change, this placed her (and the body) in an untenable position.

The records of the RA indicate that the efforts to facilitate change or to intervene in the conflict that ensued were largely rational in their orientation. Some notable exceptions were biblically-based reflections introduced by the general superior in her capacity as leader and chair, and the effort around learning a discernment approach. The organizational change literature (Levy and Merry 1986, 4, 289–90) indicates that rational change techniques are not adequate or even appropriate to paradigm changes.

The literature also warns that power struggles are to be expected in the midst of such change. According to Levy and Merry (1986, 19), for example, "Once a new idea or procedure that represents a new worldview emerges and exists within the organization, the dominant coalition colludes to restrict its expansion and diffusion." The congregation seemed surprised by rather than prepared for the power struggles evident within and between the RA representatives, elected congregational leaders, and appointed staff. Hardly acknowledged were the inevitable tensions that the RA introduced for the IHM general superior, who by virtue of her leadership role in the Leadership Conference of Women Religious from 1972 to 1974 was continually moving back and forth between the congregation and the larger church context, negotiating very different, even contradictory understandings of authority.

Finally, the RA can be characterized as an experience of impasse in which there was no going back to what was—i.e., to the IHM's long tradition of purely hierarchical authority—and in which there was no satisfactory going forward into the new, preferred collegial model. The breakdown of communication of and effective functioning in the RA, the inability to right this situation despite good and well-intentioned efforts, the dwindling of hope and the rise of disillusionment, the obsession with the problem—all of these are giveaway signs of impasse (FitzGerald 1986, 288–89). Perhaps what the congregation was unable to see or to understand, however, was the potential for growth in the very experience of impasse itself. In trying so hard to solve or to escape the "problem(s)" posed by the RA struggle, which were very real and very painful, it may have failed to see and to embrace the transforming potential of the "darkness" of the RA experience. We say this not to criticize those who put so much energy into the struggle but rather to use the wisdom of hindsight to glean learning and meaning from this experience. We say this also knowing that the RA impasse was a large-group experience—a group darkness, so to speak—and that most of the commentary on impasse refers to an individual's experience of impasse. The dynamics of a group impasse are bound to be more complicated than in the case of an individual.

In her article "Impasse and Dark Night," Constance FitzGerald, a Carmelite, brings contemporary experiences of impasse—personal and societal—into dialogue with John of the Cross's rich reflections on the "dark night" experience. In doing so, she demonstrates the spiritual significance of these "no way out" experiences—how the Holy Spirit is educating and transforming one through what she calls these inescapable and uninvited impasse experiences. In this interpretative framework, what looks and feels like disintegration, meaninglessness, and even death at one's present level of perception and affectivity is, at a more profound but hidden level of faith, a process of purification leading to a resurrection experience.

From this perspective, the RA experience can be redescribed as full of potential for creative growth and transformation. What from 1972 to 1975 the IHM congregation viewed as signs of disintegration and unreadiness could instead have been viewed as signs of a spiritual growth process. Beyond rational understanding, control, and interventions, this growth process could have utilized even mistakes and limitations as it led the RA to a re-visioning of itself and of its functioning. However, such a growth process is a way of darkness and ambiguity that must be yielded to in deep faith—an act of tremendous trust for an individual and an even larger one for a group of thirty-five diverse persons intent on organizational tasks and a full agenda. Such a growth process is insecure, full of false starts and dark corners; it frustrates old assumptions and ways of doing things and resists a rational problem-solving approach; it pushes instead in the direction of intuition, imagination, contemplative reflection, and ongoing discernment.

To be true to the potential of this as an impasse or dark night experience would have entailed that several conditions be met (FitzGerald 1986, 290). First, the RA as a body as well as its individual members would have had to appropriate the impasse experience, in all its frustration, pain, and powerlessness—and to let go of further attempts to solve, explain, defend, lay blame, or convert others to one's own point of view. This step would have entailed facing, naming, sharing, and living into the suffering and brokenness of the impasse—letting it be what it was for one and all. Second, there would have had to have been a willingness to have sorrowed over and forgiven the results of individual, and group mistakes, culpability, and limitations as these seemed to have contributed to the impasse. Third, and very importantly, a willingness as an RA body to have surrendered in faith to the darkness, trusting that the Spirit was working imperceptibly in the darkness toward the birthing of a new and shared vision of authority not yet imagined by the RA members themselves, would have been needed. This third step would have grown out of the earlier steps and would have been most visibly evident in the RA bringing the impasse itself to prayer—to the God who desires to liberate us from all that imprisons us, to free our heart's deepest desires, and to reveal to us ways that are not yet our ways.

## Conclusion

Each of the above analyses contributes to an understanding of the rise and fall of the RA in the IHM congregation (1972–75) at the same time as they together enlighten the experience of impasse more completely. The congregation was not ready for the change from several practical vantage points. It did not appreciate the very real differences in assumptions and dynamics operative in the well-esteemed Assembly '72 and in the RA "of less-than-happy memory." It did not recognize the paradigm shift that the RA (more than Assembly '72) set in motion and the painful transition it inaugurated for everyone involved, nor did it adequately use the insights of organizational psychology to assist in the transition. Lastly, the congregation was unable to see and to choose the creative, spiritual potential of the impasse it experienced.

Of all the analyses we offer, we believe the last one is the most compelling for the IHMs as women religious. The RA was born of the IHM congregation's deep desire to be faithful to the spirit and the direction of Vatican II. In 1969, the special Chapter recognized the conciliar principles of hierarchical order, unifying leadership and collegiality, and subsidiarity as guidelines for the exercise of authority in the congregation (AC, pt. I, 7–13 Apr. 1969, 3–6, MA). Assembly '72 approved a new government plan featuring the RA as its collegial centerpiece (A of A '72, no. 33, MA). In actually implementing the RA, however, the congregation experienced impasse.

Although it is very human to interpret impasse in dysfunctional terms, in deeply spiritual terms impasse is a place in and through which the Spirit hovers over the chaos, breathing life into being where previously there was no life. The RA is history, but its legacy lives on. We believe that the RA "of less-than-happy-memory" challenges us to contemplate and to discern our experiences of communal darkness and struggle, knowing that the darkness may contain the new and authentic life for which our hearts long.

# PART FOUR

# The Ministry of Education

# The Context

## Margaret Susan Thompson

> The first purpose of the Sisters is to make saints of themselves. The second follows closely—the sanctification of others, chiefly through education of all types from kindergarten through college.
>
> —IHM Vocation Literature, 1952[1]

U nlike many American congregations, the Monroe IHMs historically have devoted themselves solely to work in education.[2] In a strictly quantitative sense, their record is undeniably impressive: from an initial membership of three in 1845, the IHMs evolved in less than a century into the largest family of teaching sisters with origins in the United States.[3] However, numbers alone do not determine the significance of this ministry to the IHMs' individual and collective experiences. It is almost impossible to separate the identity of the IHMs as sisters from their identity as educators. Until very recently, one entered the congregation in full awareness of the fact that profession almost inevitably would have two dimensions: the taking of vows and nearly lifelong pedagogical responsibilities.[4]

1. This citation is found in McCarthy 1952, 149.

2. The Scranton community has limited engagement in hospital work; neither the Monroe nor the Immaculata communities have ever maintained such institutions.

3. This reference to size includes all three congregations descended from Monroe (i.e., Monroe, Immaculata, and Scranton). As of 1930, there were 2,730 IHM sisters in the three communities. There were 5,100 School Sisters of Notre Dame in the United States, but this order was founded in Europe, and American sisters remained part of an international body. The total number of Ursuline Sisters—also, traditionally, teachers—that year was 3,000, but they came originally from several European nations and were split among nearly two dozen independent U.S. motherhouses.

4. According to the entry in McCarthy 1952, by midcentury Monroe had 1,100 sisters teaching and over 100 who "cooperate in cooking, nursing, sewing, and secretarial work" (149).

Thus, it is fitting that this book should conclude with three essays focused on this area. Collectively, they do not exhaust the topics that might have been included; indeed, given the thousands of vowed women who have taught in the United States alone, and the large number who have done research at the graduate and postgraduate levels, this remains a field that continues to cry out for further study.[5] Nonetheless, these essays delineate three important dimensions of the IHM educational experience. Josephine Sferrella investigates the training of the sisters themselves and the evolution of the IHMs' notable commitment to academic rigor and achievement. Ellen Clanon explores the life of a singular individual whose pioneering efforts had profound consequences for the IHMs, for sisters throughout the United States, and also—less happily—for herself. Finally, Barbara Johns uses the lens of a single institution to examine the contributions of the IHMs as teachers of young women, Catholic and non-Catholic, both in times of relative stability and certainty and in an era of change.

What emerges from these essays is an account that is at once specific to the community at Monroe and representative of what dozens of communities have experienced in the more than two-and-a-half centuries since sisters began to teach in places that are now part of the United States. Initially, like other sisters—and like most others who have taught, as well—the IHMs underwent no formal education before finding themselves in front of a classroom. Instead, their own literacy, a willingness to work hard, and the fortuitous (but not uncommon) presence of women with prior teaching experience who could mentor the others are factors that characterize the histories of most congregations of teaching nuns with origins in the same period as this one.

By the first part of the twentieth century, however, sisters as a group were better trained and more experienced teachers than those who staffed America's public schools. This was recognized and appreciated, albeit implicitly, by the nation's Catholic bishops as early as 1884, when (at the Third Plenary Council of Baltimore) they issued a declaration that every parish should have its own school. Traditionally, this has been cited as evidence of the bishops' concern for educating their rapidly expanding flocks, in a nation where at least some formal schooling was becoming the norm for most children and where the public schools not infrequently reflected an unapologetically Protestant (and sometimes blatantly anti-

5. Most early writing by sisters consisted merely of factual catalogues of their particular congregations' schools. In addition, much of what else was written prior to the 1960s consisted more of edifying piety or defensive justifications of separate Catholic schools than of serious analysis. Some works that stand as notable exceptions to this generalization include Durkin 1926 and Schmitz 1927. The best book on the history of teaching and teacher training within a single congregation is Maria Concepta 1965, which focuses on Indiana's Sisters of the Holy Cross.

Catholic) view. Thus, parish schools would be the church's first line of defense against wanderers from the fold, by preventing exposure to such hostile influences. However, the designation of schools to play this role looks inevitable only in hindsight. What it really signified was acknowledgment, however inexplicit, of the effectiveness of sisters' ministry. Public authorities were forced to recognize this, too; nuns, including the IHMs, compiled an impressive record in meeting secular certification standards in those places where such credentialing was required.

In time, the sisters' relative advantage over public school teachers was not to persist; as rules for public school faculties became more rigorous, religious began to fall behind, a development clearly noticeable by the 1940s. Several factors explain this: a rapidly growing Catholic population placing demands on an already overextended religious teaching force; sisters' lack of access to higher education (men's colleges, by and large, were reluctant to admit them, and many bishops prohibited sisters from attending public institutions); a piety that encouraged members to believe that God would not give them any job without the graces (i.e., competence) to carry it out; and an understanding that their value as religious lay in what they *were* rather than in what they *did* (or how well they did it).

As both Sferrella and Clanon describe, the Monroe IHMs were among the best-qualified teaching sisters in the United States at that point in history, but even they were haphazardly educated (mainly during the summers) and frequently undertrained for the tasks they were expected to perform. It is in that context that both the insights and the accomplishments of Mary Patrick Riley must be understood. Clanon details her contributions both to the IHMs and later—with her friend and colleague, IHM sister Mary Emil Penet—to sisters throughout the country as they played major roles in the creation and development of the Sister Formation Movement. As *Ave Maria* magazine first reported in 1960, quoting Annette Walters, C.S.J., "The 377 communities of sisters in the United States have established the Sister Formation Program . . . hoping 'to use all their resources for the enrichment of America, increasing vocations and extending the Church's work of mercy throughout the world. Our goal is excellence,' she says intently. 'Nothing short of it.' " (as cited in Lexau 1964, 196).

By the time their task was done, sisters once again comprised one of the most highly credentialed groups in America. Equipped with knowledge derived not only from pedagogy but from fields such as psychology, theology, and sociology, sisters not only became better-qualified as professionals but were led inevitably to reassess their roles in church and in society as well as in their own lives and in their congregations.

The work begun by Riley and Penet took on a life of its own—and neither of these women was able to appreciate or to accept the consequences that ensued. In chronicling Riley's later years, Clanon tells a story that could be told of religious congregations throughout the United States, a story of women who could move only so far and no farther and who ended up, sadly, resisting many of the changes that ensued, eventually doubting the value of their efforts and perhaps of themselves. Her essay is an honest and important reminder that "progress" has its casualties, even in an institution that is supposed to be a community.

In a sense, another casualty of the intellectual growth that resulted from Sister Formation was much of the pedagogical labor force that groups like the IHMs had supplied. With a new awareness of their potential and a greater willingness to reassess their lives, many women left religious life; of those who remained, large numbers moved into new and more individualized forms of ministry. However, as Barbara Johns reminds us, those who continued to teach—and the institutions in which they served—were changed profoundly, as well.

Not all of this was a result of developments in religious life, of course. The demographic evolution in the vicinity of Immaculata High School, for example, which at first transformed its student body and then led to its closing, had nothing to do with religious renewal. Indeed, what Johns implicitly suggests is that without the new insights and skills that the IHMs had acquired through the efforts of Riley, Penet, and Sister Formation, it is probable that Immaculata would have closed sooner than it did —or, at the very least, that it would have been far less equipped to respond to the needs of the young women who attended in its final years.

Two recent publications document the impact of the sort of education that, toward the end of its existence, Immaculata provided its primarily nonwhite, non-Catholic students. In *One Nation Under God,* Barry A. Kosmin and Seymour P. Lachman note that African-Americans comprise about five percent of the Catholic population, while about nine percent of the black population in the United States is Catholic. Many of these individuals (or their forbears) became Catholic specifically because of their experience in Catholic schools. Even non-Catholic black Americans tend to perceive these schools as superior to the public ones. The tangible results are impressive: More black Catholics are graduates from high school and college than are blacks in general. They are roughly equal in educational attainment to other Catholics and greater than the overall American average, regardless of race. Furthermore, proportionately fewer black Catholics drop out of high school compared either with the total black population or with the overall white population. It appears that black Catholics are 40 percent more likely to graduate from college than are other black Americans. An analysis of Catholic school enrollment by race suggests that a majority of black Catholics attended Catholic schools (Kosmin and Lachman 1993, 273 and especially chap. 7).

Meanwhile, the findings of a Harvard University–sponsored study of Catholic education suggests that, significant as the general statistics of Kosmin and Lachman might be, those for schools like Immaculata are even more impressive. Specifically, nonwhite students at all-female Catholic high schools often come from more disadvantaged backgrounds than the general minority population and yet achieve at higher levels than the population at large, whether or not the students themselves are Catholic. The Harvard study emphasizes the benefits of single-sex institutions, particularly for young women, who experience "salient" growth (substantially higher than that of young men) both in academic achievement and in educational/professional aspirations as a result of their attendance in such schools (Bryk, et al. 1993, see especially chap. 9).

Thus, Johns's case study of Immaculata High School illuminates an important phenomenon in American social and cultural history as well as in the history of the IHMs. Indeed, what all three essays in this section suggest is that even as the specific events recounted here move further into the past, their ramifications will continue to matter—in the lives of the IHMs and other sisters, in the lives of those to whom they have ministered, and in the lives of all Americans, as well.

Sister Mary Emil Penet, I.H.M., teaching novices.

# 11

# Preparing IHMs for the Educational Mission

*Infrastructures, Schooling, and Sister Formation*

Josephine M. Sferrella, I.H.M.

In 1844, as a group of Redemptorist priests under the leadership of the Reverend Louis Florent Gillet worked to establish a permanent mission in Monroe, Michigan, the need for a school arose. According to IHM historian Sister Rosalita Kelly, although the Redemptorists "could provide for the boys[,] a school for the girls was more difficult to achieve. Working quietly, Father Gillet succeeded in interesting four young women in his plan for founding a religious institute devoted to the education of youth" ([Kelly] 1948, 36).

Thus it was that the IHM congregation's missionary purpose was established. As the congregation's Constitutions specified, "The Congregation of the Sisters, Servants of the Immaculate Heart of Mary, has for its end: to secure the sanctification of each of its members and to extend Catholic Education" (Const. 1920, art. 1, MA). Moreover, "[a]s education is the principal work of the Congregation, the Sisters engaged in the care of children should be impressed with this great responsibility, and labor most earnestly to promote the glory of God and the salvation of souls by giving their pupils a thoroughly Christian training" (Const. 1920, art. 147, MA).[1]

The Monroe IHMs became known for their high standards of teacher preparation and of classroom performance, standards consistently up-

---

1. The 1920 edition of the Constitutions is cited because it was operative during the historical period addressed in this essay. However, every earlier version of the Rule states quite clearly that the second objective peculiar to the Institute of the Immaculate Heart of Mary is "the education of youth," and the 1966 Constitutions and the Superiors Guide also make clear the congregation's educational focus.

held throughout their history.[2] Leslie Woodcock Tentler speaks to this in her 1990 history of the Archdiocese of Detroit: "[M]ore than 80 percent of the teachers in the Catholic schools in 1887 were members of religious orders. The IHMs accounted for almost half the total, which presumably pleased their Bishop, for the order maintained notably high standards of training and pedagogy" (Tentler 1990, 91). In addition, Tentler notes that "the educational aspirations and achievement of the IHMs, unusually high from the order's beginning, meant that St. Mary's [the IHM-founded academy for girls located in Monroe] was in fact more rigorous and academic in its curriculum than the typical young ladies' academy of the period. By the 1890s, the school had largely shed its genteel image, boasting now of its strict academic standards and thorough instruction in the sciences" (96).

Although it is not possible to explore all of the factors that helped the Monroe IHM congregation develop this kind of reputation, I will examine two of the most significant: the infrastructures that the congregation developed to educate and to prepare the sisters for their teaching ministry and the impact of the Sister Formation Movement, a movement whose pioneer leader was an IHM.

### Educational Infrastructures:
### The Rule, Summer Schooling, and Supervisors

Organizational theory of systems and of institutions speaks of the institutional infrastructures designed to enhance an institution's power to control ideas, beliefs, and actions.[3] From its foundation in the nineteenth century until Vatican II, the IHM congregation had many infrastructures that supported its particular form of institutional life. Several were directly aimed at the educational preparation of the sisters and served to focus their attention on the work of teaching.

The IHM Rule or Constitutions, for example, laid out serious expectations for the conduct of a sister teacher. The sisters were to reflect earnestly on this written code of conduct, with specific times being set aside for this purpose.[4] The code of conduct was also the subject of spiritual conferences, the yearly retreat, the monthly day of recollection, the daily readings during meals, and the weekly "chapter of faults."[5]

---

2. In part 6 of her centennial history of the congregation, Kelly devotes three chapters to the educational mission of the congregation. These detail the sources of the IHM system of education, congregational support for the mission, and a description of the evolution of the methodology used in IHM schools (1948, 317–96).

3. Several documents that regulated IHM life were the Constitutions (or Rule), the Book of Customs, and the Superiors Guide.

4. This practice began with the 1911 printed version (pt. 2, chap. 14, art. 171, MA).

5. The chapter of faults was a public exercise where members gave public accounting of inappropriate behavior and in turn received a penance (some penitential task to perform) from the presiding superior, as a means of atonement for the infraction.

Other infrastructures were used by the governance to rally the sisters to reflect on their primary work for the purposes of improvement and of excellence. From its earliest days, the congregation saw its members coming "home" to Monroe for retreats and vacations. In 1876, a normal school was established at the motherhouse. Over the years, summer course offerings gradually came to include classes beyond the normal school level. Beginning with the academic year 1950–51, the motherhouse site became Marygrove College–Monroe campus (MgC, 19 Aug. 1950, MA).

In particular, summer school in Monroe was an important means of instilling among the sister teachers a commitment to educational excellence. Often, sister professors who during the school year taught at IHM-founded Marygrove College in Detroit would teach the classes. Seminars and conferences were also held. An entry in the Motherhouse Chronicles for 28 June 1937 reads: "Summer school opened this morning ... The teachers were about the same as of previous years, namely: Reverend Doctor George Cairns, members of the Marygrove [College] faculty, and sisters specialized in their fields. Reverend Carroll Deady, Superintendent of the Archdiocesan schools and Reverend John C. Ryan, Supervisor of Religion for the Archdiocese gave weekly lectures to the principals and teachers" (MA). A chronicle entry from six years later indicates the sheer magnitude of the endeavor: "On Wednesday, June 23, the 1943 Summer School opened with an enrollment of nearly 1000, to close on August 3. With the exception of two Sisters studying in Ann Arbor [Univ. of Michigan], four in Washington [DC, Catholic University], two in New York [Fordham University], and about fifty at Marygrove [Detroit], all were in class on the home campus" (MMC, SS 1943, MA).

In some instances, another position or layer of organization was created to insure that the sisters were exercising appropriate educational practices. The general superior, in consultation with her council, appointed congregational supervisors at both the elementary and the secondary levels. These individuals worked with local diocesan offices of education to ensure that IHM schools met both diocesan and congregational standards. The sister supervisor had input about a sister's work assignment; many times, supervisors suggested a sister for additional academic study according to a specific need in the schools. Supervisors often visited classrooms, evaluated teaching methods and class environment, and assisted teachers (AD, interviewed by author, 17 Feb. 1992, MA; DCr, interviewed by author, 19 Feb. 1992, MA).[6]

The congregation used the four IHM schools in Monroe, Michigan, for the student teaching practicum mandated by state requirements for certification. Hence, postulants, novices, and juniors could fulfill the student teaching requirement without leaving the city. Because, in Monroe, local convents were not established until the late 1950s, the sisters

---

6. Unless otherwise noted, citations from interviews are taken from audiotapes.

who staffed these local schools lived at the motherhouse. Often, they were recommended for their teaching positions by the congregation supervisors.

## The Local Mission:
## Peer Support, Study, and Guidance for Principals

Away from Monroe "on mission," sisters lived and worked together at the same convent and school, often for years at a time. This created a peer-to-peer ministry in which more experienced sisters could help less experienced teachers with lesson plans. Sisters with a higher level of academic training could also share new methods and techniques with their peers. A natural support group flourished; mentors became faithful, loyal friends throughout the years. In the words of one sister, "You find it easier in a large crowd to speak on a different level with those with whom you have lived and worked closely. You have experienced some joys and some frustrations together that do create a bond. With some you share in a special way" (MD, interviewed by telephone by author, 27 Jan. 1994, MA).

In larger schools, sisters who taught in the same department or the same grade worked together as a team—and team members often became friends. For many, the relationship continued even after team members' assignments changed: "You saw a side of the sister you had never experienced before; there was a mutual assistance and support. Even after you moved to another mission, you kept some kind of contact whenever and wherever it was possible" (AR, interviewed by telephone by author, 27 Jan. 1994, MA).

Beyond peer support, the very schedules of a local, school-based convent were designed to focus attention on the work of teaching. The horarium, or hourly schedule, assigned definite times for class preparation. Everyone studied from 5 P.M. to 6 P.M. in a common room. In addition, there were times and places where older or high school teachers enjoyed the privilege of studying in their bedrooms, away from the monitoring eyes of the superior or her assistant. Sisters could also use the time after dinner for study; those who had heavy schedules or were teaching an extra load could get permission to spend the first half hour of recreation in study.

From about 1863 until 1967, sisters who were the superiors and principals of local convents and schools had a "superiors guide" (with several variations in title over the years) to guide their administrative and supervisory duties.[7] Frequently, materials in the guide addressed the need

7. It should be noted that most principals of IHM schools were not only in charge of their schools but were also superiors of the local convent. The local superior was principal

for teacher preparation and suggested topics for well-planned faculty meetings. General superiors met regularly during the summer with principals to read and discuss items in the superiors guide. It was not unusual for the superintendent of the archdiocese to attend a general session of the principals meeting; Monsignor Carroll Deady used this platform to clarify his own goals or to ask the sisters to assist him in implementing a new method of instruction (MMC, SS 1943, MA).

## Councils, Committees, Associations, and Boards

The congregation also established educational councils and education committees, a principals' association, and boards of education to provide vehicles and occasions for reinvigorating and for maintaining the congregation's rich tradition of excellence in teaching. For example, in 1945—the congregation's centennial year—the Education Policies Council was established. According to Kelly, "The membership of the council includes a school supervisor, a board of consultants acting in an advisory capacity, and committees selected to work on special educational problems. The personnel of these committees is composed of specialists who are familiar with the trends in their fields" (1948, 747). Fifteen years later, in August 1960, the general superior and her council set up specific committees: adult education, Sister Formation, and a board of education (CM, 17 Aug. 1960, MA). Later in the same decade, an education fund was established to provide sisters with continuing education; in 1967, the administration established the IHM Principals Organization (GSR 1966–71, IV. B, VI. O, MA). Finally, on 2 November 1970, acting upon a proposal under consideration since the previous January, the central administration set up the Educational Board of the IHM Community Schools (EBICS)(GSR 1966–71, VI. N, MA).

These groups scheduled regular meetings and the various boards held educational institutes for all the sisters. Processes gathered the congregation's members into focus groups, which tapped their energies and

---

both of the high school and of the elementary school, if a parish had both. In 1960, this dual position was separated; elementary schools were given a principal, who had the title of assistant principal. The fact that the high school principal was retained as the superior of the house was viewed oftentimes as top administration approval of the myth that high school faculty members as a class were superior to their elementary school colleagues. When the principal made a decision, she made it with the additional authority of her position as superior. This also put the sisters in the sensitive position of employees living with their employer. One of the first experimentations after Vatican II separated the principal's task from the superior's role. In some cases, this placed additional tensions on the administrators; the employer at work was a subject at home, the superior of the house was an employee in the school, and both lived together under the same roof. After 1966, a school principal was permitted to live in another residence separate from the sisters who worked with her at school.

helped mobilize further reforms and changes to the congregation's educational mission.[8]

## Formal Teacher Training

Supportive infrastructures alone, however, were not responsible for the Monroe sisters' excellent reputation as teachers and as educators. The congregation's focus on teacher preparation, education, and formation was also a significant factor. As Kelly points out in her centennial history of the congregation, from the 1860s on "the full burden of teacher training was on the congregation" (1948, 746). In the very early years, sisters who had teaching experience assisted in the training of other members: "Even when the Monroe community numbered only a dozen in the early 1860s, it had at least two experienced teachers" ([Kelly] 1948, 354).[9]

In 1876, a normal or teacher training school was established at Monroe and teacher preparation classes were held for postulants and novices. The school's first director had been superior and principal of Holy Trinity, "the outstanding Immaculate Heart school of that time" ([Kelly] 1948, 355). Once this normal school was established, every sister could be state certified prior to receiving a teaching assignment. In many areas of the country in the years prior to 1920, state and regional requirements specified two years of normal school plus passage of the state teachers' examination as the basis for obtaining temporary certificates. After 1920, state and regional standards became more explicit and demanding. All had to have some successful teaching experience (five to fifteen years) and postsecondary professional training. Elementary school teachers had to work towards the completion of two additional years of college. Each high school faculty had to have at least one member who had a college degree and show that within a reasonable time all faculty members would possess a baccalaureate degree, with majors covering all subjects taught in the secondary curriculum ([Meyers] 1965, 28).

The sisters began teaching college courses at St. Mary's Academy in Monroe in 1905, and two years later, a college department was established with a full four-year course leading to the Bachelor of Arts degree (Kelly, HMg, 1–2, MA). The preparation of a college faculty was difficult at this time: No Catholic university in the United States accepted religious women for higher education. Faced with this dilemma, Mother Mechtildis McGrail, the congregation's general superior, and her advisors

---

8. For an analysis of how this process reflects the dynamics of social mobilization, see Etzioni 1968, 387–427.

9. Kelly cautions that teacher training in the IHM Congregation in the 1860s and in the succeeding decade should be viewed against the contemporary educational background of normal training in the United States. Very few normal schools existed at this time; most were "on a par with those of contemporary high schools" (1948, 354).

determined to send IHM postulants to the University of Michigan, a public institution, for their college education. This policy, which was inaugurated in the fall term of 1906 and continued until 1932, was without precedent—and perhaps unique—in Catholic higher education. In some instances, sisters also remained at the University of Michigan for their master of arts degrees (Kelly, HMg, 8–10, MA).

Once Catholic universities opened their programs to women religious, this policy was no longer needed. Between 1934 and 1950, the congregation sent two to four sisters each year to study full-time at reputable Catholic institutions; eight sisters were listed as studying during the 1946–47 academic year. From 1950 to 1960, the number of sisters on full-time study ran between five and nine per year (IHM mission lists, MA).

Still, the majority of the sisters earned their undergraduate degree at the Monroe campus of Marygrove College. "With the college transfer to Detroit," noted Kelly, "provision was made to continue a division of the College at Monroe for the young religious of the Congregation. . . . A program for the scholastic year, exclusively for the young sisters, and a Summer Session for all Sisters on the Monroe Campus, including the young sisters, was put in operation in the autumn of 1927" (Kelly, HMg, 42, MA).

Up until 1950, sisters were able to study full-time in Monroe only through the first two years of study. Many sisters would then spend the next ten to twenty years in attempting to finish their bachelor's degrees during their summer vacations in Monroe. However, the IHMs' involvement in the Sister Formation Movement brought a major change in this practice.

### The IHMs and the Sister Formation Movement

The grassroots movement of "Sister Formation," which had been brewing in surveys and discussions since the 1940s, crystallized in the founding of the Sister Formation Conference in 1954. The focus was on finding better ways to integrate the spiritual, social, intellectual, and professional preparation of sisters for their service in the church, which for many included teaching in Catholic schools ([Meyers] 1965, 105). According to historian Marjorie Noterman Beane, "With the forming of the Sister Formation Conference, a vehicle for institutional change was put into action. Now the voices of some far-seeing American women religious would be heard as they directed this organization toward planned change" (1993, 29).[10]

The movement was truly evolutionary. Beane's history clearly articu-

---

10. I would like to acknowledge in this essay the seminal work of Beane, *From Framework to Freedom,* which I perceive as capturing both the story and the spirit of the Sister Formation Movement.

lates this aspect of all the ideas, efforts, and events that blossomed into the Sister Formation Conference: "The story of the Sister Formation Conference tells of the evolution of an idea that reached its own time. That idea conceptualized the American woman religious as an integrated woman, as a prepared professional, and as an embodiment of Church . . . prepared for the work she sought to do in and for the Church" (1993, 1). At the same time, the movement was also revolutionary. The development of Sister Formation was a radical plan that demanded a high degree of courage on the part of those individuals who spared nothing in attempting to bring it into fruition. Beane's assessments of individuals, of their heroic contributions to the movement, and of the sociological history of the times leave no doubt that "the works and life-style of American women religious in recent years stand as a bold testimony to the energy and vision of the early pioneers of the Sister Formation Conference" (1993, 136).

What was the relationship between the IHMs and the Sister Formation Movement? Certainly, the IHM congregation participated in the movement. However, it was more than participation: In many respects, Sister Formation *was* the Monroe plan. Events that occurred at the national level either were preceded by a similar action in Monroe or were impacted by the involvement of those working in the IHM formation program at this time.

The two prime movers of Sister Formation within the congregation were Sister Mary Patrick Riley[11] and Sister Mary Emil Penet. Both had lived and worked together at St. Mary School, Akron, Ohio, where concern for the educational preparation of sisters crystallized at the local level: on Friday evenings, an hour before the recreation period, those sisters who did not have their degrees had classes. Penet taught them economics, Sister Frances Raphael Beaufait taught them apologetics, and Sister Frances Dumas took them for English. A laywoman, Mrs. Hammerkamer, taught speech. Even in Akron, teacher preparation became a challenge (MC, interviewed by author, 25 Sept. 1993, MA). Riley and Penet—one a religious superior and principal in her mid-forties and the other a young Latin and social science teacher in her late twenties, yet kindred souls intellectually and spiritually—would again work together in one of the most important movements in the history of women religious. Creatively, Penet's vision and leadership skills and Riley's administrative expertise and leadership position within the IHM congregation, combined with their unusual aptitude for risk-taking, would change forever sisters' education in the Monroe IHM congregation.

In August 1948, when the IHM sisters reelected Mother Teresa McGivney as their general superior, they also elected Riley as a member of McGivney's council. Her charge was to oversee the education of the sisters.

11. See chap. 12 of the present volume for more on Riley.

She began by focusing on making certain each sister in the congregation had the opportunity to acquire a college degree before beginning her teaching career. To do so, she set in motion a new plan for the education of the sisters—a plan discussed and developed with the assistance of Penet, who was only a phone call away (MPR, interviewed by FM, 14 Nov. 1979, MA).[12]

In January 1949, Riley established in Monroe the "junioriate" (an educational strategy that the Sister Formation Conference would not address until 1957).[13] All those sisters in the reception class of 1949 were to remain at the motherhouse so that they could complete their degrees at the Monroe campus of Marygrove College before being assigned to teach at a parish school. To facilitate the completion of degree studies begun prior to the juniorate plan, Riley had Sister Xaveria Barton assigned to Monroe to research and to reorganize the sisters' educational files so that assignments for summer schools and for study programs at other universities and colleges could be made more effectively (XB, interviewed by author, 7 Feb. 1993, MA). Classes were organized so that sisters could complete their studies in a more logical sequence.

In August 1950, Penet returned to the motherhouse as a faculty member on the Monroe campus of the college, a position she held until 1957. In 1949 and 1950, Penet, Riley, and the campus college staff developed a curriculum that integrated the spiritual, intellectual, and professional preparation of young sisters in formation. They focused on three objectives: to give the sisters an intellectual structure for their spiritual lives, to foster their appreciation of culture and of the intellectual life generally, and to develop their professional competence as teachers, in terms of both technique and content (MEP, 1954, MA).[14] The curriculum emphasized philosophy and theology, with a broad base in the humanities and the social sciences. These objectives and emphases would be reechoed by the Sister Formation Conference in 1956 at the Everett Curriculum workshop, "an assembly of educated women meeting with the blessing of the Catholic Church and financed by American industry for the purpose of planning the educational future of the American woman religious" (Beane 1993, 61).[15]

12. All citations from this audiotaped interview are taken from an edited transcript.

13. The Motherhouse Chronicles for the late 1950s and early 1960s has an addenda: "The beginning of the Junioriate seems to have been omitted in this book." Then follows a list of sisters who have been juniorate mistresses (MMC, 17 Oct. 1960, MA).

14. Penet, as a panelist at the 1954 Midwest Regional Meeting of NCEA (NCEA/SFC 5–7 Jan. 1954), summarized the Monroe plan in a paper entitled "Program of Formation, Sister Servants of the Immaculate Heart of Mary, Monroe, Michigan."

15. The report of this workshop recommended that each sister be given the opportunity to obtain "a strong background in theology and philosophy, a broad foundation in the humanities and the natural sciences, [a] mastery of the arts of communication, and a planned sequence in psychology and the social sciences" (RECW 1956, 23).

## "Sister Lucy," School Growth, and Pius XII

In 1948, the National Catholic Education Association (NCEA) finally approved a Teacher Education Section. Sister Madeleva Wolff, C.S.C., president of St. Mary College in South Bend, Indiana, was selected temporary chair. As an administrator of a Catholic women's college, Wolff had long been a part of collegial discussions about the necessity of improved education and formation for women religious. Thus, her appointment placed the educational needs of sisters in a public forum.

The initiatives in Monroe were reinforced by the tenor of the NCEA's annual meeting of 1949, where Wolff made two presentations. According to Beane, "In 'The Preparation of Teachers of Religion,' [Wolff] emphasized three areas that would be used . . . in speeches and as topics of research in the years ahead: that the religious habit did not automatically make the teacher, that there should be a conscious effort made to prepare lay people to teach religion, and that . . . the quality of [a sister's] education was important." However, it was Wolff's conference paper "The Education of Sister Lucy"

> that became known as a classic presentation, the "turning point" presentation in the early movement for sister formation. Sister Madeleva spoke clearly, precisely, and emotionally when she spoke of Lucy as the 1949 model of the religious teacher of the future. "Lucy" was the enthusiastic young person who outside of religious life would have worked for her degree and have been a successful educator, but who, now, when called by God, faced the difficulty of having to teach without a degree, with only partial preparation. Sister Madeleva challenged . . . "Because Lucy becomes a sister, does that mean she does not need to get her degree?" (Beane 1993, 7)

In July 1951, Riley invited Wolff (a personal friend) to give her two famous presentations to the entire IHM congregation (MMC, 8–9 July 1951, MA).

The growing interest in the tenets of Sister Formation did not come only from an interest in freeing Sister Lucy from unreasonable institutional expectations. With the end of World War II, Catholic schools in the United States had begun to enjoy phenomenal growth. Every pope called for unsurpassed excellence in Catholic education; every bishop and pastor reechoed the Baltimore Council's call for "every Catholic child in a Catholic school." Simultaneously, state departments of education began in the 1950s to demand professional certification of the teaching staff at Catholic schools.

Major superiors of women religious had been concerned about the quality of their teachers' preparation for years. Studies had been done to show the need for additional, focused formation of teaching sisters. Bertrande Meyers, D.C., had carried out a nationwide study of the higher education of sisters, visiting more than sixty communities from the Atlantic to the Pacific and from Wisconsin to Florida. The final results represented the educational practices of sixty communities, with a total of 46,585 religious teachers (approximately two-thirds of teaching sisters in the United States at the time). The study had been published in 1941, under the auspices of Chicago's Cardinal Stritch ([Meyers] 1941, xxxi).

This was also the era of Pius XII (1939–58), who in 1951 urged the Congress of Teaching Sisters to reconsider the way they had been preparing sisters for their work in the church, a message he reiterated in 1952 to the major superiors attending the Second International Congress.[16] His challenge exerted a profound effect on the major superiors from America. In Kansas City, at the 1952 NCEA convention, the Teacher Education Section sponsored a special panel to discuss the implementation of Pius XII's statement about teacher preparation for American teaching sisters.

### The 1952 NCEA Convention

The relationship between Sister Formation and the IHMs became more direct during the April 1952 NCEA convention. Riley was to be one of the panelists, speaking about the new IHM program of study for entering sisters; however, at the last moment, the death of one of her family members led Riley to ask a reluctant Penet to replace her. According to Beane, "The capstone of the panel presentation was the talk of Sister Mary Emil Penet, IHM" (1993, 12). Penet recalled the conclusions of the panel regarding "the major difficulties faced by the sisterhoods in maintaining satisfactory educational programs," naming a lack of "*time* required for the Sisters to complete the degree course . . . *resources* to cover the cost of protracted schooling," and a "generalized *understanding* of the needs and problems in the formation of teaching Sisters." The actions she recommended were: "supplementing the ranks of religious teachers with a definite ratio of lay teachers," a study "to determine to what extent such a lack [of resources] is impeding the carrying out of the Holy Father's directives," and that there be "some kind of institutionalized opportunity for an exchange of help and ideas among the motherhouses and colleges

16. Claudia Carlen, I.H.M., describes Pius XII as "a man of exceptional intelligence and training, of remarkable exactitude and energy" (1990, [4]). She also notes that his teachings, "in volume and scope . . . surpassed those of any of his predecessors. He contributed to the theological preparation for the Second Vatican Council especially by his positive expression of the doctrine on the Church, his liturgical reforms, a new impetus given to biblical studies, and the great attention he paid to the problems of the modern world (1990, [3]).

engaged in this kind of work" (Penet 1956, xvi). As a result of the discussion that followed Penet's talk, a decision was made to conduct a national study. A survey committee was established with Penet as the chair (Beane 1993, 13).

In August 1952, Riley also gave an influential address, "Share the Sisters," at the Major Superiors Conference.[17] She asked religious congregations, bishops, and pastors to add lay teachers to their faculties at a ratio of one to twenty. This plan would allow young sisters to remain in formation until their degree requirements had been completed. Her plan also spoke to the nationwide shortage of sisters, to the stewardship question of sharing resources, and to the fact that Catholic schools were a responsibility of the total church. Superintendents and bishops lauded the paper for its realistic approach to the problem and to the solution.[18]

Then, in March 1953, Penet, on behalf of her survey committee, submitted a proposal to the Teacher Education Section of NCEA asking the executive board to set up a separate commission on educational and professional standards for sisters. It would be an organization of sisters for sisters only. In October 1953, Penet appeared at the executive committee meeting to respond to questions regarding the setting up of this commission. The resolution passed. In 1954, at the Chicago NCEA meeting, the Sister Formation Conference officially came into being (Penet 1956, xix–xxi).

## A New Era: The Sister Formation Conference

A new era had begun, as Beane so aptly states:

New times were giving American women religious new challenges, and in an organized and systematic manner, sisters attempted to update educational and formational systems within a decade. The call of the Church had been given, the need for updating credentials was felt, and all the sisters went into action, some hesitantly and some in the vanguard. It was the SFC that provided avenues to research data that could be used for decision making and future planning. . . . American religious

17. The entire address was published in the Proceedings of the Sisters' Section of the First National Congress of Religious of the United States: *Religious Community Life in the United States.* (1952, 134–47).

18. Although a ratio of one to twenty was never realized, the IHM congregation did notify pastors that there were no more sisters to send to schools. In a letter to Cardinal Edward Mooney of Detroit, Mother Teresa McGivney notified the Cardinal of what she had told the pastors who had none or only one lay teachers: "We have missioned every available Sister in the community, have doubled and tripled the duties of some, and I find my chart still short of twenty-two Sisters, eighteen in the classroom and four in other duties. For these latter we will hire help, for the eighteen class-rooms, the pastors will have to engage teachers" (10 Aug. 1953, MA).

had begun to ask some serious questions about themselves and take some serious actions in the 1950s. In ten years, sisters had won the right to be educationally qualified before beginning their ministry. Sisters themselves questioned their conventual life style. Schedule, habit, and customs were being examined in the light of service to the Church in a modern age. (1993, 94–95)

In April 1954, Penet gave a paper on teacher training—a description of the Monroe plan of sister education—at the annual NCEA meeting. At this same convention, Penet was appointed chair of the Sister Formation Conference, in which office she served until 1957 (Penet 1956, xxi–xxii). From 1957 until 1960, she served as the conference's national executive secretary; during this period, Sister Anna Marie Grix, the IHM general superior, released Penet to do conference work full-time. As Meyers later wrote, "Into the promotion of Sister Formation, Sister Mary Emil poured all her rare talents: a keen and disciplined intellect, a grasp of psychological factors, a sense of timing, the gift of convincing speech, organizational ability and—unlimited devotion. . . . Through her untiring efforts, Sister Formation came to be known, understood and desired" ([Meyers] 1965, 108).

The Sister Formation Conference held national and regional conferences from 1954 to 1964.[19] In September 1961, after Penet finished her term as executive secretary, she was appointed president of Marygrove College. Penet was permitted by the IHM administration to maintain relations with Sister Formation insofar as her new duties would allow (CM, 14 and 28 July 1961, MA).

Although Penet had stepped down from the conference's national leadership, the Sister Formation Movement remained a force impacting the IHM congregation. With the reelection of Anna Marie Grix as superior general in 1960, the Chapter of Affairs recommended that a committee on undergraduate and graduate studies be established.[20] The Sister Formation plan continued, and increasing numbers of sisters assigned to Detroit schools remained at their local convents during the summer to attend Wayne State University and the University of Detroit. Anticipating a state requirement that teachers continue their education beyond the

19. Fordham University Press published five of the national proceedings; see Sister Formation Conference 1956, 1957, 1958, 1960, 1964.

20. The Council Minutes of 19 July 1957 summarized the educational status of IHMs: B.A., 497 (37 percent); M.A., 387 (29 percent); Ph.D., 20 (1.4 percent). The mission list of Aug. 1956 numbered 1,347 professed sisters and 74 novices, for a total of 1,421; this means that 65 percent of the IHM sisters had academic degrees. With 65 percent of the membership so prepared, the fact that a Chapter in 1960 would establish committees to continue higher education demonstrates the value that the congregation placed on the professional preparation of the sisters.

bachelors degree (either by obtaining a masters degree or completing thirty hours of additional classes), the community in 1961 increased considerably the number of sisters in master's programs. The General Superior's Report of 1960–66 indicated that 483 sisters were working on their master's degree in twenty-nine different subject areas and in seventy-seven different universities and colleges spanning the entire United States and Puerto Rico (35–37, MA).[21]

In 1961, the Dad's Club at Marygrove College initiated a study abroad education fund for the sisters who were faculty members of the college. As a result, by 1970—in addition to Sisters Anna Marie Grix, general superior, and Honora Jack, Marygrove president, who toured Europe for an overview of educational opportunities—forty of the Marygrove faculty sisters had studied abroad in countries such as Spain, England, Austria, Israel, Holland, Italy, Switzerland, Sweden, and Peru (Mg. Col. SAP MS, 1972, MA). During this period, with the availability of National Science Foundation grants and other funding, the number of sisters attending various universities and colleges across the country grew.[22] Nine sisters received Fulbright scholarships to study in India, France, Lebanon, Ethiopia, Mexico, Hawaii, and Italy; five sisters received other academic year grants to study and teach in Germany, Spain, India, and Iraq. As of the end of the 1965–66 academic year, over $165,000 had been received in grants during a six-year period (GSR 1960–66, 38–39, MA).

Some IHM sisters showed great ingenuity in finding opportunities for education. Sister Marie Ouellette, for example, was one of the many IHMs who took ten to twenty years to earn a bachelor's degree. From 1958 until 1975, while teaching physics, chemistry, and math to high school students, she used sixteen grants to improve her own background in those subjects. The grants took her to the University of Detroit, Wayne State, Purdue, St. Thomas College, Seton Hall, College of the Holy Cross, the University of Wisconsin, Kent State, St. Teresa College, and Notre Dame. She took classes in analytical physics, electronics, modern physics, optics, engineering concepts, solid state physics, and the chemistry of coordination compounds, with seminars in geometry and in high school mathematics.

The Sister Formation plan as outlined by Penet in 1954 continued in Monroe until the late 1960s. At the national level, "the Sister Formation

21. In 1985, a document titled *Education Facts—IHM Community* declared that as of June 1985, 82.3 percent of the IHM community had graduate degrees; 77.7 percent had master's degrees, 6.8 percent had two master's degrees, and 5.96 percent had doctoral degrees (EO, MM).

22. The 31 May 1963 Council Minutes record a letter from Reverend Mother Consolatrix, B.V.M. of the CMSW Secretariat asking that sisters receiving NSF grants be exact about the use of the funds and that they keep accurate records of all expenditures (MA).

Conference, as a semi-autonomous group, comprising all of the religious communities of women of the country, and having sectional status in the College and University Department of the NCEA," disappeared amidst controversy in August 1964 (AW open letter, Oct. 1964 cited in Beane 1993, 125, 157n. 49). Revised by-laws were enacted, and the conference officially became a committee of the Conference of Major Superiors of Women. Beane describes this change:

> The 1964 restructuring of SFC that resulted in its becoming a committee of the CMSW was to bring years of struggle and authoritative uncertainty to an end. It is confusing and difficult to document why this "take-over" happened and many who were witness to the restructuring said it was the result of conflicting interests, differing visions, and a fight for power. Misunderstanding between the two groups mounted as SFC diversified its activities and broadened its efforts to bring about a new type of formation for the American sister. . . . While the two leadership groups were trying to determine what authority each would have, a third group, the Congregation for Religious [in Rome], was there to make the final decision as to who was to have the greater power.
>
> The transfer of the SFC to the CMSW took the initiative of planning out of the hands of the sisters and put it back into the hands of leadership. What Archbishop Phillipe [representative from Rome] termed a step forward . . . would be judged by others as a return to the past. (Beane 1993, 119, 126)

## The Movement Continues

Despite the fact that the Sister Formation Conference had dissolved and that fewer women were now entering the congregation, the spirit of the Sister Formation Movement continued in Monroe.[23] Graduations took place on the Monroe campus until August 1969; that year, only five postulants had been accepted and only twelve novices were at the motherhouse (GSR 1966–71, VII. B, V. C, MA). Between 1966 and 1972, the congregation opened formation houses of studies in Chicago, Washington, D.C., St.

---

23. In a short essay such as this, it is impossible to mention all those who played major roles in the education of the Monroe IHM sisters. Kelly describes the work of early IHMs who were directresses of the sisters' education, such as Xaveria McHugh and Immaculata Heenan. The second century of IHM history needs to tell the untiring efforts of women in charge of sisters' education. Not the least of these individuals were Florence Louise Lahey and Frances Ellen Ryan, along with Juliana Bruin, Marie Isabel Murphy, Thomas Aquinas Walmsley, and Mary Mercy Geohegan, all of whom did much to continue the spirit of Sister Formation. Certainly, this list is by no means all-inclusive; each IHM sister can point to one or many sisters (superiors, supervisors, directresses, principals, mentors, and peers) who impacted her total educational background.

Louis, and Detroit, so that sisters could study at campuses in those cities. During this period, formation policy changed.[24] Young women had to have "some life experience beyond the high school years" (Info., Oct. 1973, C1, MA); this experience could be college classes or work experience prior to being accepted for entrance into the congregation. Thus, though the formation program changed and developed according to the circumstances of the time, the principles remained. In its education of all of its sisters, the congregation looked to the integration of the personal, the spiritual, and the professional development of the sister regardless of ministry.[25]

In the late 1960s, a unique program was established by Margaret Brennan (the IHM general superior from 1966 until 1976) to assist the congregation with theological resources. Ten sisters (about one for every hundred sisters then in the congregation) were sent to schools of theology in the United States and abroad in Belgium, in France, and in Rome to acquire doctorates and licentiates in various areas of theology and of scripture (GSR 1966–71, VII. C, MA). Further, an education fund established in 1960 continued to assist in the education of the sisters. Guidelines for its use were modified in 1970 so that sisters might take workshops and other noncredit courses that would update them in their particular ministry or prepare them to begin working in another new field.[26]

Thus, even without the SFC, the Sister Formation Movement has continued. With such well-prepared academic backgrounds, the IHMs have been able to serve in leadership positions in many offices of Catholic education and in many theological programs in universities across the

24. The formation program was not without its pain, misunderstanding, and frustration. Ebaugh 1977, 89–100, shows a correlation between education level, size of congregation, and the numbers of sisters who left religious life. IHM educational statistics show that between 1948 and 1959, six sisters who had no degrees left the congregation. From 1963 to 1993, the numbers leaving were: 278 with B.A. degrees; 173 with M.A. degrees; 1 D.M.; 1 R.N.; and 2 with Montessori diplomas. Two sisters with M.A. degrees and one with a Ph.D. transferred to the Immaculata IHMs and one Ph.D. transferred to a congregation in Germany (CWSED 1948–93, Sept. 1993, MA).

25. "The passage of Proposal C [in autumn, 1970] prohibiting all state aid to non-public schools forced the premature closing of many educational institutions [in Michigan]. As a result, many Sisters were led into new areas of apostolic service and new forms of community life" (GSR 1966–71, III. B, MA). At this time, a policy of "open placement" was initiated; a sister could choose her own ministry by consultation with (GSR 1966–71, VI. A, MA) and approval of (GSR 1972–76, II. 21, MA) a major superior.

26. The IHM Education Committee's annual report for 1 July 1992–30 June 1993 indicated that the congregation had two members in full-time doctoral programs, two in full-time master's programs, and two in full-time special programs (clinical psychology and music therapy). In part-time studies: one in a doctoral program, nine in master's programs, and one in a special program (diplomat in clinical social work). Education funds were used for the educational component of renewal programs for seventeen sisters (MA).

country. IHMs assist the marginally poor in prisons and in houses of hope for the battered and the abused. The IHM congregation has provided personnel for the direction and operation of NETWORK, a national Catholic social justice lobby. Members of the congregation publish widely on topics such as education, family life, scripture, church history, the papal encyclicals, the vows, religious life, science, and economics. IHMs are creative in the areas of poetry, music, literature, and the visual arts. IHM sisters give retreats, administer houses of prayer, run renewal centers for spirituality, and provide spiritual direction. IHM sisters are pastors where there are no priests. IHM sisters work with the poor in Brazil, Africa, Honduras, Puerto Rico, Mexico, and urban areas of the United States. IHM sisters are campus ministers and hospital chaplains as well as school teachers and school administrators. The IHM congregation traditionally has prepared its sisters well and continues to do so in the 1990s.

Sister Mary Patrick Riley, I.H.M.

# 12

# The Sacrament of a Life

## Ellen Clanon, I.H.M.

July 29, 1895.[1] It is midsummer in Estherville, Iowa, where the tall grasses clothe the prairies, where the wind sweeps over fertile farm lands, and where in a simple farm house Mary and Patrick Riley greet the birth of the seventh of their children, Kathleen Maureen, the daughter who would leave home as a young woman but who would take with her for the rest of her life the pioneering spirit of the West.[2]

In the richness of that summer day, Mary and Patrick Riley could not perceive the long and productive life of the child who lay in her cradle—that Kathleen would live her whole adult life far from home, that she would become a member of the Congregation of the Sisters, Servants of the Immaculate Heart of Mary in Monroe, Michigan, that she would be a remarkable teacher-leader-administrator, a woman of vision far too many years ahead of her time. However, when she died some eighty-eight years later, on 25 September 1983 in the convent infirmary, she died little appreciated, almost alone. A few friends would genuinely grieve. Many

1. The author's friendship with Mary Patrick Riley spanned a period of 62 years. This essay is a composite of information from the author's personal memories, interviews of Riley by Frances Manor, I.H.M., about five years before the former's death, interviews with and written remembrances of congregational members who knew Riley, and primary documents in the Monroe Archives. Where no citation is given, the author is the source of the information.

2. According to Elliott West, "Like all children, those in the West were both changing and being changed by what was around them. Of all the pioneers, they felt the frontier's shaping force most of all" (1989, xix). His book affords an understanding of how frontier children's "[b]eliefs and attitudes, the way they saw themselves—were formed partly through contact with surroundings that were different from those their elders had known. Work took them out into that environment—encouraging exchanges with it, helping them master their fears, and posing a variety of challenges and responsibilities. . . . [They] took on [the frontier's] aggressive, optimistic ways" (West 1989, 251–52). Throughout her life in the congregation, Riley would exhibit the strength and sweeping vision engendered by her prairie roots.

members of her IHM congregation would choose not to be present for the evening funeral liturgy; many chapel pews were vacant; many memorial booklets were still stacked in neat piles, unopened. Next morning at the gravesite, only a handful stood to say their last good-bye beside the white casket atop the open grave—the spot that would forever mark the burial place of the daughter of Mary and Patrick Riley, a remarkable woman leader of her time, a loyal member of the Sisters, Servants of the Immaculate Heart of Mary of Monroe, Michigan.

This essay is not about a single white headstone down the convent lane, not about death but about life, a life brimming over with doing and being—a life that leaped across the miles for half a century, ever the initiator, the implementor, darting from here to there, tripping over her own ideas as she raced along.

Kathleen Riley first met the IHM sisters in 1916. All through her high school years, she had longed to attend a Catholic college; by her senior year, she had filled a corner of the attic with catalogs. A simple newspaper clipping ended her search. It told of a visit of President Taft to St. Mary College in Monroe, Michigan;[3] if St. Mary's was good enough for the president, it was good enough for Riley. Patrick Riley sold a parcel of his farm land to finance his daughter's education. Alone by train, Riley traveled from her home in Sioux Falls, South Dakota, to Monroe. Riley later confided to me that as she walked through the front door of the college, something in her soul told her that Monroe would be her home forever. She loved every day of the two years she spent at the four-year college, but by the end of the school year in 1918, she knew that her student days at the college were over and that her life now lay just across the street in the old brick IHM convent on the banks of the River Raisin.

Like active religious communities elsewhere in the United States during the first years of the twentieth century, the aim of the IHM congregation was to somehow straddle the contemplative life and the active life, "to secure the sanctification of each of its members, and to extend Catholic education" (Const. 1920, art. 1, MA). In her first weeks in the novitiate, Riley listened intently to instructions about the hallmark virtues of the congregation—self-abnegation and the renouncement of self will—not knowing that in the weeks to come, in facing the death of her father, she herself would have to make a profound decision of self-abnegation. Patrick Riley died; so many miles from home, his daughter was transfixed with grief. Deep in her heart, however, she sensed that to return to Sioux Falls to say good-bye meant never to return to Monroe, and so she chose

3. Taft visited Monroe on 4 June 1910 to be present at the "unveiling of the Custer statue." The Motherhouse Chronicles record that "[t]hree hundred young ladies were arranged in tiers on the stage [of the college auditorium] and at his entrance rose to greet him with a song of welcome" (MMC, 4 June 1910, MA).

to stay.[4] Two months later, when she received the habit as a member of the IHM community, she received as her religious name the names of her mother and father—Sister Mary Patrick.

In mid-August 1921, fresh from her first vows and with her B.A. degree in hand, she traveled to the east side of Detroit to begin her professional life as an English teacher at St. Catherine High School. It was in this, her first assignment, that Riley initially put into practice the philosophy that was to guide her entire career in education—that the talents of each student should be fully developed, whether these talents be many or few.[5]

Riley and I first met on the first day of school that September.[6] I was a fifteen-year-old high school sophomore. From my two-seater desk (which accommodated three little girls), I sized up this tall, thin, hollow-chested young woman; even in her twenties, she was noticeably stooped. In a matter of months, she and I became friends, and our friendship endured with its peaks and valleys until her death six decades later.

### Nineteen Years Teaching High-School English

At age twenty-six, convent living for Riley meant being one of the youngest on the mission. It meant teaching seven class periods a day with minimal time for preparation. It meant cataloging a makeshift library in the school corridor during her lunch hour.[7] It meant rising at 4:30 A.M. on Saturdays in order to pour over steamy stationary tubs in the convent basement to do the weekly convent laundry and to be kneeling prim and proper

4. Both Mother Leocadia Delanty, the mistress of novices, and Mother Domitilla Donohue, the general superior, gave Riley permission to go home for the funeral. However, both also expressed their doubt that Riley, if she did so, would return, and she concurred. Riley's family always meant a great deal to her; four years before her death in 1983, she would say that for her, suffering "wasn't so much in the externals of everyday life and its duties but in an inexpressible loneliness for my own loved ones and the suffering in their lives" (MPR, interviewed by FM, 22 Oct. 1979, s.4, 7, MA). All material cited from this interview is taken from an edited transcript of the audiotape.

5. Riley expressed her philosophy thus: "What does the parable of the talents say? Jesus gave no value to the number of talents he gave each one but only to the use each one made of what she had been given. Jesus demands that whatever he gives should be doubled" (MPR, interviewed by FM, 22 Oct. 1979, s.2, 5, MA).

6. Riley herself described the situation: "I was there. The school was jammed with children . . . everywhere except on the hooks in the wardrobe. I had 67 ninth, tenth and eleventh graders in 48 seats. All rows were double. Each boy had the luxury of a whole seat but in the double rows of girls, there were three in the combined two seats" (MPR, interviewed by FM, 19 Mar. 1979, s.1, 8–9, MA).

7. The library at Saint Catherine in 1921 was a sparsely populated second floor corridor with mismatched bookcases but with the potential of holding books and more books—Riley worked to see that they were filled with good books and that the books circulated. Her love for libraries and for books would exhibit itself over and over again in her life.

with the other sisters by 5:30 A.M., ready for the half-hour daily meditation.[8] It meant depositing money at the local bank and, on Saturday afternoon, shopping "on Mack Avenue or going clear out to the East[ern]
Market for vegetables or almost anything that we could get cheaper than
in the stores" (MPR, interviewed by FM, 19 Mar. 1979, s.2, 1, MA).

The pastor of St. Catherine parish in 1921 exuded the hierarchical
church of this period. His word was law. He planned everything. Admonished by the general superior, the local superior of the convent knew her
major task was to get along with the pastor. All too often, getting along
meant giving in. Most pastors knew little about pedagogy. The sisters
were there to serve, whether there were fifty or eighty students in each
classroom or, if forced into half-day sessions, there were sixty or more
students in each "group."[9] Parish needs took precedence over lesson
plans and study times for class preparation. It was often understood that
the younger sisters would give their Sunday afternoons to counting the
Sunday collection and to recording contributions in the parish ledgers
(MPR, interviewed by FM, 19 Mar. 1979, s.2, 1, MA).

Within the confines of this system, Riley spent nineteen years as an
ordinary high school teacher in ordinary parochial high schools.[10] Against
all odds, she somehow survived, grew, and became a successful high
school English teacher. Whatever constraints the system imposed—and
these were many—they could not touch this teacher in her classroom.
Once she closed the door, walked to her desk, and began to teach, her
world knew no limits. Her whole person came alive as she exercised her
unique powers to inspire, to cajole, and to control. Dedicated as she was
to the development of the intellect, she was interested even more in the
individual as a whole person. Her heart reached out to so many of her
pupils, mentoring and encouraging them to reach beyond their grade
level, to compete for awards, and to enter contests.[11]

8. In describing this duty, Riley added: "We finished [the laundry] from 6:00 to 7:30,
ate breakfast and were on time for 8:00 Mass" (MPR, interviewed by FM, 19 Mar. 1979, s.2,
1, MA).

9. Riley described such situations in this fashion: "Few pastors were conscious that a
school was little more than a brick building that he had erected and that somehow the good
sisters could manage with little equipment such as labs, [a] library, or even cleanliness . . .
in many instances we were our own janitors. They seemed to have no idea that even the
best professionally prepared teachers needed time to fulfill their religious and professional
duties as well as [the time] necessary for the normal relaxation required for health and
living" (MPR, interviewed by FM, 22 Oct. 1979, s.3, 1, MA).

10. Riley served at three missions in Detroit: Saint Catherine for five years, Cathedral
Central for two years, and Saint Agnes for twelve years.

11. Riley's gift for "stretching" the minds of her students was legendary. One of her
former students said of her: "She was always trying to get us to reach beyond ourselves
and to look at the world situation, not just what was happening in this small city of Akron,
Ohio" (JS, remembrances of MPR, 4 May 1994, 5, MA). All material cited from this source
is taken from a verbatim transcript of the audiotape.

For Riley herself, the nineteen years of classroom teaching were years of accomplishment and of preparation—she had become "the" acknowledged high school English teacher in the Detroit archdiocese.[12] In 1935, at the invitation of Monsignor Carroll F. Deady, superintendent of Detroit's Catholic school system, she formed a committee of IHM high school English teachers (of which I was a member) to pilot a high school English course of study. The pilot was so successful that it served as a prototype for use in all Detroit archdiocesan high schools.

## St. Mary, Akron

In 1940, Riley became principal of the twelve-grade school and local superior in the convent at St. Mary parish in Akron, Ohio. Time would hurry along during the next six years; in the school were 750 minds to challenge and to help to grow. As one of her former students from Akron later said of her, "[S]he encouraged us to do the best we could and [told us] that the only yardstick that we [should] use to measure our progress was our own gifts" (JS, remembrances of MPR, 4 May 1994, 2, MA).

The sixteen teaching sisters in her charge were imbued with the IHM spiritual adage "Obedience will do everything." Riley, however, was not convinced this was true. She noted that some teachers were well prepared, were enthusiastic, and loved their five hours of daily teaching; others, however, lacked a background of organized knowledge and skills and seemed unhappy. In her own assessment, she said:

> "Certainly, it [obedience] did very much for decades and decades. But [a teacher's] feelings are reflected in the students. . . . [I]f [they] have a teacher in front of them who isn't happy in her work, who doesn't feel at ease, or who doesn't know it [the subject matter] well enough to feel she could present it with any kind of power, or any kind of enthusiasm, [then] that is going to be reflected in the results. (MPR, interviewed by FM, 19 Mar. 1979, s.2, 5, MA).

Always interested in the professional advancement of the sisters, she kept her eyes and ears open to cultural opportunities in the city for their enrichment. In an era when walls of distrust separated public from parochial teachers, Riley's own gift for friendship and her openness helped break down barriers. Teachers from both the public and the private sectors came together for pedagogy meetings, for lectures, and for sociability.

In her role as superior of the local convent, Riley focused on encouraging the personal development and the self-fulfillment of the sisters

---

12. Monsignor Carroll F. Deady regarded the IHM sisters as "the" outstanding educators of the diocese. For him, the best high school English teacher in the IHM congregation was "the" best in the diocese, and Riley was regarded as such in the congregation.

under her supervision, giving them freedom to correspond with relatives and with friends, to visit sick parents, to read good books—not in accord with common IHM practice. She examined staid community customs, separating the trivial from the worthwhile. For example, if a sister's parents came for a visit, an unwritten law decreed that they be served their meals in the convent parlor while the sister ate in the convent refectory. Riley made short shrift of such customs.[13]

## Ph.D. Studies in St. Louis

By 1946, IHM congregational leaders knew that they had a leader out there "on the missions" whose heart and soul possessed the magic for calling forth life wherever she saw it. They recognized her as a woman— as Henry Nash Smith says of the women of the West—"with energies [capable of] overpowering all obstacles" (1950, 41). They also knew that in the near future they would be called upon to name a new president for Marygrove College in Detroit.[14] Riley might be just the right person.[15] Thus, the time came for her to fashion the third piece of her professional life. At the direction of the IHM general superior, Mother Teresa McGivney, she registered for her doctorate in education at St. Louis University.

Riley was fifty-one when, on a winter's day in 1946, she arrived at the university and introduced herself to the dean of the graduate school. She had been engaged in no formal study since she completed her master's degree at the University of Detroit in 1933. In an interview, she recounted the main events of that first meeting:

> [The dean] looked up at me out of one eye and he said, "Sister, is your community trying to kill you off?" And I said, "Well, I wasn't aware of

13. Riley was unfailingly gracious to members of the sisters' families, and it was with rules and regulations involving relatives that she was most impatient. When faced with a stipulation that sisters' guests and family members not be given ginger ale and cookies when they came to visit, she said to the general superior: "Mother, I wish to tell you before anyone else comes that there's no way I can observe that rule. . . . I have certainly seen to it that the sisters' relatives have refreshment when they come and I shall continue to do that. . . . Our greatest endowments are the sisters who have been given to us by their families. So I shall not be able to follow that instruction" (JMB, interviewed by SF, 14 June 1994, 10, MA). All material cited from this source is taken from a verbatim transcript of the audiotape.

14. It was fairly common knowledge in the congregation that there were administrative tensions at Marygrove as in any institution. Honora Jack's tenure as president at that time spanned nine years, and some members of the congregation speculated that it was time for a change. As it turned out, Jack remained as president until 1961.

15. Before Riley left for St. Louis University in Jan. 1946, she confided to the author that she was being sent to get her doctoral degree so that she would be qualified to become president of Marygrove.

it father." And he said, "Well, here you are coming down here at fifty-one years of age. . . . We wouldn't think of sending a man who was past forty and the closer [they are] to thirty, the better. . . . How do you know you can learn?" I didn't answer him. I thought it was kind of an insolent question, to tell the truth. . . . I said, "Well, thank you, father; this is good news." . . . and I bowed and left. I got to the door and he said, "Sister, come back here. You stay around for a while until we see if you can [pass] the qualifying [tests]. The qualifying tests will tell us something. . . . [Y]ou sit down and I'll talk things over with you." And I said, "No father, thank you. I won't sit down this morning." (MPR, interviewed by FM, 19 Mar. 1979, s.2, 6, MA)

Her two years at St. Louis University opened a new world. Besides passing the qualifying tests, she gained the respect of the professors, class by class.[16] Because she recognized the value of a broad-based curriculum, she took as many courses as possible in philosophy and psychology.[17] Outside of classes, she learned from teachers and from other doctoral candidates of the stirrings that were happening in the church, in religious communities, and in the new worlds that were opening for women. She also "talked with sisters from all over the country" and found that they, too, worked with pastors who were not "convinced that the sisters were there to teach the children and not to take over parish duties at the expense of their primary obligations." These conditions "were more or less prevalent in most communities. All the Sisters regretted it, but no one [knew] how to correct it" (MPR, interviewed by FM, 19 Mar. 1979, s.3, 1, MA).

### Director of IHM Education

At the end of July 1948, with her course work completed, Riley returned to Monroe to participate as a delegate in the general elections of the IHM congregation. The delegates elected her second member of the council and general secretary of the congregation. Her autobiographical sketch records that her particular assignment as a council member was "Sisters' Education with all its ramifications" (MRO, MA). It was Mother

16. Riley must have been recognized by her professors and by her classmates as a gifted educator. She cites an interesting incident in which she was asked by one of her professors to take over his classes for a few days. Her response to his request was, "Could I burn the textbooks?" The outcome was that she took over for him and with the help of the rest of the students, reorganized the entire class for the remainder of the semester (MPR, interviewed by FM, 19 Mar. 1979, s.2, 8, MA).

17. Riley avoided education courses, partly because of her experience during the qualifying examinations with regard to knowledge of educational practices: "Really [answering the questions] was a matter of having had a little experience, and some common sense. That was my background knowledge" (MPR, interviewed by FM, 19 Mar. 1979, s.2, 7, MA).

Teresa McGivney's wish that Riley return to St. Louis University to complete her dissertation; however, because at that time canon law required council members to reside at the motherhouse, Cardinal Edward Mooney (the archbishop of Detroit) refused to grant permission.

Immediately following her election as a member of the council—"immediately" meaning within the hour—Riley sought out McGivney to share with her something she had learned in St. Louis, namely the importance of having a Chapter of Affairs in conjunction with the Chapter of Elections. Though the delegates did not respond favorably, McGivney called them to an unscheduled afternoon meeting to discuss major congregational objectives. The preparation of teachers and their continuing education became the crucial point of that meeting (MPR, interviewed by FM, 19 Mar. 1979, s.3, 2–3, MA).

The delegates were aware of the fine reputation that the community had enjoyed through many years, and they wondered about the need for change. The harvest in Catholic education was indeed ripe in 1948; pastors were asking for IHM teachers long before school buildings were completed. Riley appears to have taken the lead in the discussion. She later recalled "suggesting . . . that it seemed unjust to open more schools when those we already had were staffed with many sisters not sufficiently prepared for their assignments." Then, perhaps in recalling her later difficulties, she added, "This was not very well received, as some said that for over a hundred years we had been most successful in our schools and our graduates had proven the worth of our Catholic education." She also spoke with a touch of humor about requesting that the delegates consider the quality of education offered in the smaller schools staffed by IHMs: "This too got a wet blanket, but it wasn't comparable with the wet blankets I had later in the season" (MPR, interviewed by FM, 22 Oct. 1979, s.3, 3, MA).

The all-afternoon meeting signaled that the newly elected second member of the council was a woman of experience, a woman on the move. If the delegates were hesitant about Riley's dictum that "past achievements [in IHM schools] were not an excuse for present obligations," McGivney was not. A few days after the meeting, Riley recalled, McGivney sent for her and said, " 'Sister, I've had in mind that I wanted you to try to establish a plan for the education of the sisters.' . . . This is on Monday and [I was to come back to her] on Thursday" (MPR, interviewed by FM, 22 Oct. 1979, s.3, 3, MA).

On the day that Riley began her three-day planning session, in her solitude the years slipped away. Kathleen Riley reappeared. Once again she was like the 21-year-old free spirit flying along the rails to a new world in Monroe, Michigan. The winds blew no freer in Iowa or South Dakota than did the workings of her mind during those three days, as she dreamed dreams and planned plans for the professional lives of all the young women who would come knocking on the door of the motherhouse. She was again "a woman of the West who [fit] none of the stereotypes" (Armitage and Jameson 1987, 30). However, one thing had changed: she was now in a position to bring her vision and experience to bear on the future education of IHM sisters.

### The New Plan: College for Sisters in Formation

To McGivney and her council, Riley presented her nonnegotiable decision—sisters in formation would take a full four-year college program of studies so that they could begin their teaching careers with a college degree and Michigan state certification.[18] For her first objective, she explained, she would convert the entire first floor of the motherhouse into a fully furnished college department—classroom equipment, lecture-hall chairs, language laboratories, offices, a standard college library. For everything she touched and planned for, she would need money—lots of it. Community finances, however, had little to offer; Riley believed that there was no alternative but to appeal to the Detroit archdiocese, from which for more than a century the IHM congregation had received mea-ger compensation. Cardinal Edward Mooney headed the archdiocese, but McGivney chose to turn to the superintendent of schools, Monsignor Carroll F. Deady, for understanding and assistance.

Accordingly, McGivney invited Deady to Monroe and met him in the parlor. After explaining to him that the congregation was "planning for the future good of Catholic education in the Archdiocese, [and] that she had given [Riley] the responsibility of developing a program," McGivney sent for Riley and excused herself. As Riley later said, somewhat humor-ously, "At this point I might say, Exit, Mother Teresa—Enter, Sr. Mary Patrick" (MPR, interviewed by FM, 22 Oct. 1979, s.3, 5, MA).

Riley plunged immediately into the purpose of the meeting. She ex-plained to Deady that IHM sisters in formation needed a full four-year college program of studies before they began their teaching careers and that the small salaries the congregation received from its active teaching members were not sufficient to cover the cost of supporting the young sisters who would be educated at the motherhouse for four years. She also told him that in the past, only the sisters who were preparing to teach in college or to fill special community needs were freed from teaching to study full time. As she later related, in the pause that followed, Deady "looked around the parlor rather casually, coughed a couple of times and said, 'It seems to me, Sister, that you Sisters have done pretty well for yourselves.' That really burned me and my reaction was, '[Y]ou used

18. The program is described in the interview of MPR by FM of 14 Nov. 1979 (s.2, 2–3, MA).

the wrong preposition, Father. . . . I think you would have to say "BY" ourselves.' " She went on:

> There isn't an IHM Sister who has a pair of bedroom slippers, not one who has a bathrobe, not one who has a turkish [sic] towel . . . and for the most part, Father, we make our underclothing out of flour sacks. . . . There's no Sister who has a vacation in Florida or anywhere else except a few days at the beginning of the summer at our motherhouse and on the Marygrove campus. . . . I have been an IHM for thirty years and have not yet had a summer off for I was either in class or teaching classes. . . . Not that I regret any of this, father, I just think it's something that you should realize and maybe consider before you say again that we've done pretty well for ourselves. (MPR, interviewed by FM, 22 Oct. 1979, s.3, 5–6, MA)

After then describing to Deady the financial constraints under which the congregation operated (because of the indebtedness resulting from the building of Marygrove College, the motherhouse, and the academy), Riley stated,

> We have no resources, Father, except the salary [sic] of our Sisters and this will not permit us to carry out our plan to keep our Sisters home while they earn a B.A. degree before going into the parochial schools. . . . On the part of the Archdiocese, we [are requesting that the] salary . . . be raised to at least one hundred dollars a month per sister including the months of July and August as well as music money earned above [the music teacher's] salary or else return the music teacher to the classroom.[19] (MPR, interviewed by FM, 22 Oct. 1979, s.4, 1–2, MA)

The meeting ended politely but with no affirmative response; after declining to visit the college floor, Deady "said he would think over our discussion and get in touch again."[20]

Whatever the reluctance of the archdiocese, a host of lay friends and relatives graciously responded to this latest IHM crisis. By 11 November 1952, "a lay Board of Trustees [was formed] to assist the community" in its fundraising efforts (CM, 11 Nov. 1952, MA).[21]

19. In 1945, members of the congregation received $45 per month for the academic year only. For music teachers at that time, only one-fourth of the income they generated beyond earning their own salary was transferred to the congregation ([Kelly] 1948, 565–67).

20. Deady returned to the Archdiocesan offices saying, presumably to Mooney: "They ['ve] got a hard one down there in Monroe—she's a hard one" (JMB, interviewed by SF, 14 June 1994, 2, MA).

21. William Tenbusch, father of Loretta Mary Tenbusch, I.H.M. (now Sister Loretta Maria of Immaculata, Pa.), assumed the position as chair. Among his assistants was Henry Maher, father of Mary Jo Maher, I.H.M., and of Veronica Mary Maher, I.H.M. (CM, 11 Nov.

## Putting the Plan into Action

Transforming the first floor of the motherhouse into a college department meant building walls, pushing around desks, putting windows into
the cloister area to increase study space, and so on. However, dealing
with all kinds of people was another and greater challenge and called
for multiple conversions. The congregation was of two minds regarding
education: Its teachers were to be the best, but its superiors were wary of
"intellectualism" and were worried that bright sisters might become
proud or that one sister might receive recognition above another. Most
important, they feared that the "common life" might become less common.[22] Riley pushed her way into a culture in which some perceived that
"brooms had priority over books" (anonymous survey of twelve IHM
sisters, 24 Apr. 1994, MA).[23]

A full college program meant changing the daily schedule of the
approximately 180 students in the formation program to allow for sustained study time.[24] This drastic conversion called for all kinds of changes
on the part of everyone from the mistress of novices to a succession of
staff sisters responsible for the smooth operation of the motherhouse
(who, in a sense, controlled the daily lives of the novices from start to
finish). Before the conversion, novices reported three times a day for
kitchen duty to serve meals in the three convent dining rooms, the student triple dining room of the adjoining academy, and the workmen's
dining room in the basement. Novices carried trays three times a day to
the floors of the infirmary. Novices worked in the laundry, a separate
building. Novices cleaned the motherhouse chapel and the infirmary
chapel. Novices learned to sew, to make their own habits and undergarments. Novice life was synonymous with scrubbing bees, window washing, choir practice, occasionally helping out at the farm—and praying.

Transforming the novices from housekeepers to college students hap-

---

1952, MA). Riley said of the efforts of this group: "They not only promised, they carried out
beyond any of our expectations" (MPR, interviewed by FM, 14 Nov. 1979, s.6, 2, MA).

22. Riley would later say: "Now, when we began to plan or prepare the young sisters
for their ministry, we never dreamed of arousing any antagonism or fear of the intellectual
life. We had the highest respect for the ministry of teaching" (MPR, interviewed by FM, 19
Mar. 1979, s.1, 7, MA).

23. Hereafter cited as "survey."

24. It took five years to achieve this goal. By 7 Oct. 1953, sustained evening study time
was achieved by changing the evening supper from 6:00 P.M. to 5:00 and delaying the
beginning of the evening recreation from 7:00 to 7:30. This change was deemed so weighty
that it was discussed by the council itself and recorded in the minutes (CM, MA). Even the
congregational chaplain, Monsignor Walter Marron, resisted the change because he did not
want to eat that early.

pened slowly and with strong resistance, leading to ill-prepared students
and frustrated professors.[25] A novice might possibly succeed in analyzing
a poem as she swept down a stairway, but not solve a problem in calculus.
Over the years, the image of the novice doing housework had somehow
equated itself with "the ideal IHM sister." She was, as Riley used to say,
"wearing an apron, carrying a broom, or still better a mop, and always
had a duster tucked in her belt" (MPR, interviewed by FM, 19 Mar. 1979,
s.2, 4, MA).[26] Changing congregational attitudes about study would take
all of her energy, at times with minimal results, but this challenge would
not dim the vision of her mind, her very soul. She had glimpsed the
dawn of a new era in IHM education, not on any mountain top but in the
twenty-seven years of her own ordinary living with ordinary people in
the blue collar areas of Michigan and Ohio. The vision that they had for
their children's education stayed with her and gave her energy, hope, and
belief in her own convictions that planning the formal education of IHM
sisters served the greatest community need of the 1950s, the most enduring cause.

Riley needed to bring about another conversion as well. To grant
degrees, the new college in Monroe needed affiliation with an accredited
institution. The congregation had opened Marygrove College in Detroit
in 1927; Honora Jack, I.H.M., had been named president in 1937. Both
Riley and Jack were highly gifted, strong-willed women, outstanding
educators espousing a liberal arts program, but they were of different
molds. Well aware of their incompatibilities, Riley had thought that Marygrove might not want a Marygrove College/Monroe Campus affiliation
and considered seeking the sponsorship of St. Louis University or the
Catholic University of America. McGivney, however, "by this time saw
[Riley's] concern and said that the Sisters, she knew, would get their
degrees directly from Marygrove. This was her obligation" (MPR, interviewed by FM, 22 Oct. 1979, s.3, 4–5, MA).[27] In essence, the normal school

25. Even before the presentation of her plan to the council, Riley "spent some time
[finding out] the approximate number of hours they [the novices] spent in fruit picking,
potato bugging, scrubbing, serving meals, washing dishes, etc., etc." She did not minimize
the obstacles: "Primary among these, at least I felt . . . the greatest was the attitude of certain
sisters, especially those at the motherhouse of the previous administration and those in
charge of the general run of the house" (MPR, interviewed by FM, 22 Oct. 1979, s.3, 4, MA).
Thirty-six years later, one sister would give as a reason for antagonism toward Riley that
"[s]he reduced the novices' hours of manual labor (that affected the whole motherhouse
and academy) in order to afford them more time for study" (survey, 24 Apr. 1994, MA).

26. During the same interview (s.2, 4), Riley also relates that she once said to Mother
Teresa: "[I]f you walk[ed] through our college corridor . . . some morning and observed
everybody you'd be inclined to think that we are training our Sisters to be janitors rather
than teachers in our schools."

27. See written remembrances of MPR by Suzanne Fleming, I.H.M. (31 Mar. 1994, MA)
and by Rose Matthew Mangini, I.H.M. (3 May 1994, MA) for examples of the tension
between Monroe and Marygrove regarding the new program.

established at Monroe in 1876 was replaced in 1950–51 by Marygrove College/Monroe Campus ([Kelly] 1948, 355; MgC, 19 Sept. 1950, MA).[28]

It took more courage for Riley to attempt the conversion of the patriarchal church, in particular the pastors of all IHM parish schools in Michigan, Illinois, and Ohio. These men had the habit of arriving in Monroe each summer to visit the general superior, taking for granted that they would leave with the promise of one more teacher added to their parish school faculty. The new program in education would change all that. Riley personally visited the priests, knocking on rectory doors and advising pastors that they could not expect additional teachers for the next four years (until the sisters in formation had received their college degrees and Michigan state teacher certification). If the habit had never made the monk, she made clear to a host of surprised pastors that never again would the habit magically make a ready-made teacher-nun.

Slowly, the dream of a full college program changed to reality. Equipment was in place—even a college library[29]—and so were carefully selected IHM faculty members. Almost 200 IHM sister students comprised the student body. Those sisters teaching in the Monroe parochial schools who had not as yet completed their undergraduate studies would take classes after their school day had finished. In the evening, Riley offered cultural programs for interested Monroe adults (MPR, interviewed by FM, 22 Oct. 1979, s.4, 2–4, MA). The college floor stayed alive even on Saturdays for professed members in the Monroe area who were still working for their undergraduate degrees. Riley next concentrated her attention on IHMs teaching in parochial grade and high schools away from Monroe; many had spent a decade of summers working on their undergraduate degrees and still had not finished. She took action to speed up the summer progress toward achieving degrees and also enriched the summer program with frequent outside speakers—attendance required.[30]

## No "Ordinary" Sisters

During her twenty-five years as teacher and as principal, Riley came to believe there were no "ordinary" sisters. Each had her own gifts as a

28. When Marygrove was reaccredited by the North Central Association in 1957, the Monroe site was officially designated as a branch campus; this designation continued until the close of the program in Monroe. The 1977 accreditation renewal of Marygrove eliminated any designation of a branch campus (OAD).

29. The building of a college library in Monroe involved the moving of the postulate community room and sewing room from the first to the third floor and reorganization of the postulants' sleeping quarters (TMcG CL, Easter 1951, MA).

30. One famous example of "speeding up" the process occurred during summer 1950, when Riley brought together at Marygrove College a group of sisters who had not yet completed their language requirement. For most of these sisters, their first courses in French had been taken while they were postulants—often five or more years before. In one eight-

person, her own desire for fulfillment. The vow of poverty had to do with detachment from things, not the deprivation of a sister's personal development. Riley is remembered by many as a person who believed passionately that each sister was entitled to be educated in such a fashion as to make use of *all* her talents and abilities. For example, she once discovered a young sister sweeping crumbs from under the refectory tables and stopped long enough to say, "How much Latin do you have? See me in my office." That sister became the first IHM to receive her doctorate in theology and eventually became president of the Leadership Conference of Women Religious—Margaret Brennan, I.H.M. (MB, personal communication to author). She also recognized special potential in a young high school teacher, Mary Emil Penet, I.H.M., whom she recommended for doctoral studies. Penet became a crusader for the liberal education of all sisters preparing for the teaching profession through the Sister Formation Conference and, later, as president of Marygrove College.

As congregational leader for education, Riley also set out to destroy whatever built-in class distinctions existed. In convent and in school, the grade a sister taught often set the tone for how she was valued: the twelfth-grade teacher usually enjoyed a prestige denied the first-grade teacher; high school teachers in general had more status than grade school teachers; and Marygrove College faculty members stood on the very top rung of the ladder. It was to everybody's surprise, then, that Riley sent grade school teachers to study at the Catholic University of America and at Cardinal Stritch College in Chicago. Among grade school teachers, she also found women to study for their nursing degrees in order to serve in the motherhouse infirmary. Grade and high school teachers attended national education conventions, workshops, and seminars in their respective disciplines—privileges that had been previously restricted to college administrators and to department chairpersons. She sent the housekeeping sisters to take special courses in nutrition.

### "Sister Exchange Program" and "Share the Sisters"

Riley began the "Sister Exchange Program" to help members of the congregation to take graduate courses and to obtain degrees from a variety of Catholic universities. The plan enabled sisters from various congregations to take summer courses at Catholic colleges across the country, including in Monroe, where Riley had negotiated the offering of a five-summer master of education degree through collaboration with the University of Detroit. Sisters from other congregations would receive room

---

week period, these sisters completed two semesters—eight credit hours—of French (SF, remembrances of MPR, 31 Mar. 1994, 2, MA).

and board at the IHM convent in Monroe in exchange for providing room and board to IHMs taking classes in their locales.[31]

In the early 1950s, vocations to religious orders devoted to teaching increased, but there was also an increased demand for teachers. Faithful to the ideal of "every Catholic child in a Catholic school," letters poured in from pastors begging for sisters to staff newly built parochial schools.[32] Never one to want for solutions, Riley found one to this problem in the wider use of lay teachers, persons who up until this time had frequently received second-class treatment in parochial schools. When the Institute for Religious held its first meeting at the University of Notre Dame in 1952, Riley presented a paper entitled "Share the Sisters" to a capacity crowd of priests and sisters (MMC, 9–13 Aug. 1952, MA). The "sharing" meant that a faculty fully staffed with sister-teachers would give up one or two sisters, who would be replaced by lay teachers academically prepared and dedicated to the cause of Catholic education.[33] The one or two from one school added to the one or two from another school would enable teaching sisters to respond favorably to pastors' requests for opening new schools in many parts of the country. Riley had not yet left the stage when a "spirited young priest . . . mounted the platform to offer a vigorous handshake in enthusiastic congratulations" (IHMC, 1952–53, MA). He wanted to open a school himself, and this seemed to be the answer. As Sister Madeleva Wolff, president of St. Mary College in South Bend, Indiana, and a close friend of Riley's, said of the event, "We [are] coming at this late hour to the use of reason" ([Wolff] 1959, 113).[34]

31. Riley may have had a hunch that she would not be reelected in 1954. In speaking of the masters' program, she later indicated: "I wanted to begin it the following September, because it would take five years" (MPR, interviewed by FM, 14 Nov. 1979, MA). A copy of the offerings of the first summer of the joint program was sent to each mission by Mother Teresa McGivney on 9 Dec. 1951 (MA).

32. The move for the establishment of the Catholic school system was solidified at the First Plenary Council of Baltimore held in 1852. By this time, the public school system "was, in the opinion of many bishops, 'both heretical and infidel.' " A committee of theologians recommended that "if parents did not send their children to these schools they be 'denied the sacraments' " (Dolan 1992, 267–68).

33. Riley must have persuaded McGivney to implement "Share the Sisters" for the Monroe IHMs even before her presentation. McGivney had sent word to congregation members that the congregation had been requested to open a school for black children at Saint Peter Claver Parish in Mobile, Ala., in autumn 1950. She indicated that any sister wishing to go would need to receive a commitment from the pastor to replace her with a lay teacher (SF, remembrances of MPR, 31 Mar. 1994, MA; SPCC, 1950, MA).

34. In IHM schools, sisters began to be replaced by lay women who frequently were relatives and friends of the sisters and parents of children enrolled in or graduated from parish schools. Suzanne Fleming, I.H.M., cites three of these instances in her remembrances: her mother, Rose Fleming, taught at Christ the King and Epiphany schools in Detroit from 1953 through 1962; Edith Maloney, the mother of Father James Maloney, taught at Epiphany during the same period, as did Mary Brady, the mother of three children in attendance at Epiphany.

Riley touched so many individual lives with love during her six years of congregational leadership that at the time of her death, a friend would say: "There is probably no single person in the community who is not in some way indebted to Mary Patrick."[35]

## Riley's Term as Educational Director Ends

She continued to stay busy until 1948 changed to 1954, when her congregational leadership came to a sudden halt. On 29 July, she turned 59. Two days later, the fifty-seven members of the Chapter of Elections convened to name the new congregational leadership. They did not re-elect Riley.[36]

One likely reason for this was that from first to last, Riley had sent shock waves up and down the rank and file of the congregation. Intent on her goal, Riley "ruffled too many feathers" (survey, 24 Apr. 1994, MA), and "[f]or those who were unused to broad visions, or who needed detailed structure within which to work, [her] methods may well have created much stress" (RMM, Remembrances of MPR, 3 May 1994, MA). Many members were not ready to accept either the message or the messenger. They preferred the even tenor of quiet living and strict adherence to the daily horarium, their leisurely summertime afternoon conversations around the sewing room tables, cutting out habits and hemming veils. Riley made them nervous and kept them on edge with what they termed her "wild ideas," even though some of those ideas soon became standard practice. For example, one day amidst the clatter of doing dishes, she accosted a friend drying dishes with, "Do you think you could ever learn to drive a car?" (MB, personal communication to author). At this time, IHM sisters, with few exceptions, were forbidden to drive; they relied on public transportation and help from relatives and friends. The prohibition was dropped during Mary Patrick's tenure.

Riley also may have seemed too far ahead of her time. When she took office in 1948, the Catholic Church in the United States was only just experiencing the first stirrings of renewal. Devotional Catholicism was slowly yielding to liturgical reform, but in religious congregations, the European mindset prevailed. Women religious were warned to avoid all

35. Mary Patrick's vision of higher education and the programs she implemented also prepared many younger members of the Congregation for advanced studies in later years. Sometimes, the recipient of Mary Patrick's "love" saw it as a mixed blessing requiring an almost inhuman effort (SF, remembrances of MPR, 31 Mar. 1994, MA).

36. Twenty-five delegates were local superiors whose regular convent living was disrupted by many of Mary Patrick's actions; another twenty-five delegates were from the rank and file of the sisters, who found their free time or that of their colleagues intruded upon; and four delegates were from Marygrove, where there was considerable opposition to Riley's innovations.

that was worldly. Life outside the convent enclosure was full of snares and temptations; women religious needed to keep their eyes turned inward and to shun worldly pastimes such as reading daily newspapers and magazines, listening to radio programs, and attending public events —weddings were especially suspect. As dutiful daughters, IHMs followed rigidly the wishes of Rome, adding their own specific list of "do-nots"—including the "strictly forbidden" reading of novels (except for class purposes) and the ban on using fountain pens. Riley was always challenging such taboos.[37]

Finally, Riley herself may have been a major deterrent to her own reelection. She was a woman who espoused the cause of freedom and power for women religious everywhere, yet at times she wielded her own power in such an absolute fashion that these same women religious felt oppressed by her; at other times, her great-heartedness, tenderness, and generosity did not show but were overshadowed by her impatience and curtness with those who did not share her vision.[38] Defying categorization, "enigma" seems the word that best captures the waxing and waning of all the days of her professional life.[39]

### Holy Redeemer, Detroit

Following the 1954 election, Riley was assigned to Holy Redeemer, a large parish in southwest Detroit with both a grade school and a high school. She was appointed local superior of the convent of fifty-two sisters and the principal of the high school. All the enthusiasm and dedication to the education of youth that she had demonstrated in her past thirty-three years she carried with her intact to an area where brick,

37. It took some doing on Riley's part to convince her superior that fountain pens, like convent elevators, were both modern conveniences (JMB, interviewed by SF, 14 June 1994, 11, MA).

38. "Mary Patrick was a woman of vision, courage, and indomitable zeal—and [she] expected everyone to be equally that. She, therefore, challenged, upset, and frustrated the average IHM. . . . The congregation rebelled and showed it via the election process" (survey, 24 Apr. 1994, MA). "[S]he was only impatient . . . with people who squandered their time and their talents because she had a terrible sense of obligation to the young, whether they were young sisters [or] young students" (JMB, interviewed by SF, 14 June 1994, 9, MA).

39. Riley herself perhaps had in mind her reaction to the outcome of the Chapter when she was asked "How did you, through it all, carry on with zeal, and above all, how did you maintain a joyous disposition through all of the opposition and obstacles that you must have met?" She responded: "I wonder if you've ever read the essayist, Berdyaev. He says in his essay and I have read it quite young: that there is this by no means accidental connection between the geography of the soul and the plain geography in which one is reared. . . . I think that maybe the plains and the vast prairie of the west where one can ride horseback for hours without meeting any traffic signs gives one a freedom of spirit [that enables one not to] become tense or tied down by the clumps of bushes, tumbleweeds, or stony patches under foot" (MPR, interviewed by FM, 14 Nov. 1979, s.3, MA).

stone, cement, alley-ways, and nearby pool halls spoke no whisper of the intellectual life. No trees. No bushes. No bird songs. Just a quadrangular complex of frowning brick buildings. The whole place looked tired and forlorn. I myself taught there in the late 1940s.

For the next seven years, she would fill her days with eight hundred teenagers, including special courses for tutoring both gifted and slow learners. She would replace the machine shop on the first floor, full of roaring engines and shouting boys, with a large library, with counseling rooms nearby and an arts and crafts room around the corner. According to one sister, Riley "went at [the renovation of the school] with gusto." Needing new desks, she organized the sisters to dispose of the old ones: "[S]he opened the windows and [they] threw them out three floors. . . . [Two sisters] were engaged to keep the kids away [and] to see that there was order and that no one was killed by a falling desk" (JMB, interviewed by SF, 14 June 1994, 3, MA).

Riley also enriched the lives of Redeemer's sisters by taking them to Detroit events. When the first Auto Show following World War II opened in the newly constructed Cobo Hall, she made arrangements for her entire faculty to attend. When one sister expressed her doubts, Riley responded: "That's the biggest thing in this city so we will go." Her reputation as an educator spread throughout the area, until a professor at Wayne State University would exclaim: "What does that woman think she has over there, a junior college?" (JMB, interviewed by SF, 14 June 1994, 6, 5, MA).

### Immaculate Heart of Mary High School, Westchester, Illinois

Nineteen sixty-one. Was the retirement age 65? Not for Riley. In response to a community request, she gathered together the gifts of her whole life and lavished them on the development of a new congregational endeavor, Immaculate Heart of Mary High School in Westchester, Illinois. She had once said to a friend, "I, oh, I would wish that someday I could start a new school where no one else had shaped up the student body and I could do that with no interference" (JMB, interviewed by SF, 14 June 1994, 7, MA). In Westchester, she quite literally did just that, developing this school from the ground up.

The IHM administration had hoped that the school would demonstrate the finest, most progressive high school program for a girls' school. The inscription on a large mosaic that Riley had installed on one of the entry walls embodied her philosophy: "Every student has the need to become what she has the ability to become" (JMB, interviewed by SF, 14 June 1994, 8, MA). During the next nine years, Riley's achievements surpassed expectations. At a twentieth class reunion of IHM High School graduates, Mary Ann Hinsdale, I.H.M., recalled: "Mary Patrick pushed us to the limit. One year we started classes at 7:30 A.M. so we could fit more into the schedule. It was still dark outside. In our junior year, she decided we needed a more globally-aware curriculum. She hired a Chinese history teacher and a German lay theologian. In addition to Latin, French, German, and Spanish, we had language offerings in Chinese, Portuguese, and Italian—all taught by native speakers. Even the gym teacher was from the Philippines" (MAH, personal communication to author).

However, Riley's singleness of vision also sometimes left the teachers and pupils frustrated: "She was so full of ideas [that] we used to hate it when she got sick, because she would take all the magazines up to her room with her . . . [When she came down] life would be turned upside down" (JMB, interviewed by SF, 14 June 1994, 12, MA). On one of these occasions, she took to her bed, ill for three days, and emerged having abruptly rescheduled classes for the entire school—effective immediately. One French class ended up meeting in a broom closet because she had scheduled all rooms by room number rather than by room function (MVG, telephone conversation with SF, 27 June 1994).

Riley spent her final year of active ministry teaching in an inner-city Catholic high school in Chicago, rounding out her fifty years as an educator. She designed a curriculum of studies for students with special needs in reading and writing, and she spent her last teaching days working with these young men and women.

### Retirement: Prairie Night

Riley was seventy-six when she returned to Monroe to be one of more than two hundred retired sisters. The first years seemed peaceful with friends, an assortment of books, and busy letter writing with the extended Riley clan. Then, in a strange manner, her health failed—body and spirit. Her gifted mind traded vistas of clear vision for dark gullies. The "chasmed fears" (from Francis Thompson's *Hound of Heaven*) that she had written about for her masters thesis took on hideous shapes in her own life. She became a recluse in the IHM congregation, the greatest love of her life.

By this time, open placement had replaced the congregation's single ministry of teaching.[40] Proposal C to prohibit state funds for Catholic schools had passed overwhelmingly.[41] More and more sisters were leaving the Detroit area. The congregation's leaders were moving with the

40. Prior to the late 1960s, sisters were unilaterally assigned to their ministries by the general superior. With the advent of open placement, sisters were permitted to have a voice in their own ministries. It was a process by which each sister, her employer, and the religious superior entered into discernment about the qualifications of each (GSR 1966–71, VI. A, MA).

41. Proposal C was a Nov. 1970 ballot initiative in Michigan. Voters prohibited the appropriation of moneys for nonreligious education in parochial schools.

post–Vatican II times, and the times called for all kinds of adaptation and change. Everything Riley had lived for and cherished, she watched disappear. She who had boldly espoused change long before change was in fashion became a reactionary, longing for all that used to be. It was one thing for Riley to initiate community changes in the early 1950s, to stir the waters around the well-moored IHM boat, but quite another thing three decades later to hear from her sick bed about so many more changes that threatened the boat itself. Was the beloved 138-year-old IHM vessel itself about to founder?

She had once said that after her vocation, her greatest gift from God were her friends. Now, except for the Rileys and a few IHM friends, she saw her past as almost belonging to another lifetime. The darkness of her mind and spirit reflected the darkness of the life she lived in her corner infirmary room. Shades were drawn, the window closed and locked. Even the window's edge had its own cloth rolled up and stuffed against the ledge to keep any fresh air from coming in the cracks. Who was this dark, bundled-up, sad woman in her corner chair, deliberately withdrawn from so many friends? Why a repugnance for the great accomplishments of her life? Did she not remember that the tiny seeds of the Sister Formation Movement were very likely sown on the first floor of the motherhouse, and that those seeds had become a huge tree, its branches reaching from ocean to ocean? Like Rachel of the Old Testament, she would not be comforted even by the general superior herself, who tried to assuage her fears and to remind her of her life's good works. "It's not what you do in your life," Riley said, "but what you become in doing it" (MB, personal communication to author).

Time inched along; so did the last days, the last hours of her life when illness forced her from her corner chair to her bed. I stayed with her to the very end—my friend, my mentor of more than six decades. The curvature of her spine kept her from lying flat on the bed. Literally, her body and soul hung between life and death hour after hour, only the rhythmic quivering lips suggesting a flicker of life. Midnight came and went. So did the first hours of daybreak, until streams of the morning sun broke through the window pane and on the still body of Sister Mary Patrick Riley. The Sabbath day, 25 September 1983.

◆　◆　◆

"Wherever . . . the Good News is proclaimed, what she has done will be told also in remembrance of her" (Mark 14:9).

Immaculata's First Senior Class, October 1941.

# 13

# In Their Own Image

*Shaping Women's Education at Detroit's Immaculata High School*

Barbara Johns, I.H.M.

On the morning of 8 September 1941, when Sister Anna Marie Grix switched on the public address system and officially welcomed 529 students to the first day of classes at Detroit's Immaculata High School, she was launching not only a new academic year but also a new all-girls high school—only the second such institution in the ninety-six-year history of the IHM congregation (IHSMC, MA).

The girls Grix greeted that morning were mostly young white Catholic women from traditional, middle- to upper-middle-class families, most of whom lived in the residential neighborhoods of an expanding northwest Detroit. The city itself was almost fully recovered from the Great Depression; the auto companies were hiring, the migration of southern black and white workers to the city's factories was in full swing, housing was at a premium, and the conversion to a full defense economy was just months away.[1] In autumn 1941, the IHM community itself was attracting new members at a steadily advancing rate and had both the personnel and the financial resources to staff the new high school and to carry its $418,000 construction cost, in spite of the community's indebtedness for major construction projects from the 1920s and 1930s (HB to MR, 12 Feb. 1942, MA).[2]

The school closed permanently forty-two years later, at the end of the 1983 school year. The 145 students (GSR 1982–88, CS-6, MA) affected by the decision were predominantly young black women, many from nontraditional, non-Catholic, working-class families. Though they lived in the same neighborhoods as the original Immaculata student body, northwest Detroit by then was a bruised area of the city, with 25 percent

---

1. For a fuller discussion of Detroit during this period see Babson et al. 1986.
2. This letter details the final cost of the Immaculata building complex.

of its business structures vacant and many of the rest protected by steel gates or bricked-over windows (MgNCSS, Feb. 1987, 19; Dec. 1976, 48, OAD, Mg). Detroit was reeling from a 21 percent population decline and gripped by a life-threatening recession that would eventually close six hundred plants and remove 290,000 manufacturing jobs from the region's economy (GSR 1982–88, CS-6, MA; MgNCSS, Feb. 1987, 18–19, OAD, Mg).

The IHM community also had drastically diminished in size since the 1940s. Between 1966 and 1976, over 350 sisters had asked to be released from their vows, and in 1983, only three women had applied for membership (SLWY; ER, MA). The congregation had nonetheless subsidized or loaned Immaculata nearly $110,000 between 1979 and 1983, including $10,000 for a consulting firm to map strategies for the school's survival (GSR 1982–88, CS-5, MA). By 1983, however, neither the faculty nor the congregational leadership could revive the exhausted high school.

Although the beleaguered Immaculata of 1983 would seem to bear little resemblance to that of 1941, Immaculata in the late 1970s and early 1980s was, at its heart, what it had been from the very beginning: a mirror image of the IHM sisters' complex and evolving corporate identity, a reflection of the IHMs' attempt to define—for themselves and for their students—"women's place" and the role of women's institutions within changing ecclesiastical and social realities. The story of Immaculata is a story of how IHM women and the "spiritual daughters" who were their students sought together—often in ambiguous, difficult, and contradictory ways—to understand what it meant to be religiously-grounded, well-educated, and socially-conscious women in the world.

## The Decision to Build Immaculata

The impetus to build a new all-girls high school originated in an invitation issued by Archbishop—later Cardinal—Edward Mooney.[3] However, undertaking a new all-girls school was also an opportunity for the community to advance not only its educational mission but also its prestige and its hegemony in northwest Detroit. At the time, the IHMs had a strong institutional presence in newly developed northwest Detroit, where there was as yet no girls' high school. They staffed some of the largest parochial elementary schools built in the area in the 1920s and 1930s: St. Cecelia's, St. Gregory's, St. Francis de Sales, Epiphany, Christ the King, and Presentation. Gesu Parish and its IHM-run elementary school anchored one of the most fashionable neighborhoods at the inter-

3. The IHMs opened 23 new mission-schools, at a rate of more than one a year, between 1918 and 1939, all of them parish schools and all at the invitation of bishops or priests ([Kelly] 1948, 616–39).

section of McNichols and Livernois, and Gesu School had already become a jewel in the IHM crown. Built in 1925, by 1935 it enrolled 1,200 students, operated as a model school for teachers throughout the archdiocese, and served as a practice school for student teachers ([Kelly] 1948, 629–34). Just one mile west of Gesu on McNichols, the IHM congregation's Marygrove College occupied over sixty wooded acres that offered considerable room for new buildings, particularly on the edges of the campus. All of the IHM elementary schools in northwest Detroit were within fairly easy commuting distance for a new high school located on the congregational property at Marygrove, and each was a potentially rich source of students.

Ground was broken on 30 January 1941, although the congregation did not secure a loan with the National Bank of Detroit for $150,000 (at 3 percent interest) until 7 June 1941 (RMM, personal communication to author).[4] Three weeks before the laying of the cornerstone on 11 May 1941, Mother Ruth Hankerd and her council met in a special session to decide on the emblem to be used on the stone. They selected a title of Mary from the Litany of the Blessed Virgin Mary, *Rosa Mystica* or "Mystical Rose," and the words *Auspice Maria*—under the protection or auspices of Mary, in this case Mary Immaculate. At that same meeting, the council also approved an advertising folder describing the new high school (CM, 18 Apr. 1941, MA).

### The 1941 Prospectus

Remarkably muted in its description both of the purpose and of the curriculum of Immaculata, the brochure that was developed to advertise the IHMs' new educational venture stated only that the school was designed to meet an acute need for a Catholic high school for girls in northwest Detroit and that it aimed "to educate the girl in an atmosphere of Catholic culture." The course of studies was covered in a single sentence: "In addition to the regular academic courses Immaculata High School will offer opportunities to girls interested in cultivating the home arts and the fine arts." Far more detail was given to the building itself, to its "spacious and attractive classrooms, study and lecture halls, fully equipped laboratories, a modern commercial department, a complete home economics department—including dressing and fitting rooms to complement the sewing rooms—and a well-rounded library unit." The prospectus also called attention to the school's "beautiful chapel, removed from all the distracting elements common to a large school," and to the "community service wing," which housed music studios, practice rooms, a cafeteria, kitchen, private dining rooms, a lounge, large assem-

4. The Immaculata loan was paid off on 19 Jan. 1944.

bly rooms, showers, lockers, and a sixty-by-ninety-foot gymnasium "extending upward through two stories" (IHS Prosp., MA).[5]

The faculty was presented collectively as the "Community of the Sisters, Servants of the Immaculate Heart of Mary . . . founded in 1845 to answer the imperative need for religious education among the children of the diocese of Detroit," with no mention of their academic credentials or expertise.[6] The brochures stated with authority, however, that "Immaculata High School is another stone in the great monument erected to the glory of God by the Sisters, for the interests of Catholic education, under the auspices of Mary Immaculate." Appearing prominently in the brochure was the sketch of an attractive young girl wearing a dark, short-sleeved uniform—which, the reader was also informed, could be bought for $7.50 (including an extra collar) in the Girls' Department of Demery's, at the time one of Detroit's better department stores. The tuition for the new school was listed at fifty dollars per year; expenses connected with laboratory, home economics, gymnasium, library, and typing courses would cost from two dollars to twenty dollars in yearly fees. Weekly private music lessons could be arranged for an additional fifty dollars per year.

Although the brochure made little explicit mention of an IHM philosophy of women's education, the text communicated what the IHM community thought important in the education of young Catholic women in 1941. Immaculata's deepest purpose—and the sisters' motivation for all of their educational work—was "the glory of God," a belief resonant with meaning in the robust North American Catholicism of prewar Detroit. Faithful Catholics of this period understood that to live in "an atmosphere of Catholic culture" was to adhere to all the rich traditions of Catholic intellectual, spiritual, moral, and social practice. Their worldview included a role for women that was modeled after Mary, the Mother of God, who was understood to be a woman of pure heart receptive to hearing the will of God, to acting on it in faith, and to suffering pain and grief, if need be, in its service (Tentler 1990, 402–42). As educators whose very title dedicated them to Mary—and as founders of a school "under the auspices of Mary Immaculate"—the IHM sisters were

5. The brochure does not mention some features of Immaculata that were specifically highlighted in the architect's notes, features that in his mind were pertinent to a woman's school: the "spacious grounds . . . filled with trees, shrubs and flowers, which form a restful setting for the building and play an important part in arousing interest in the girls towards beauty and order," and the "soft-toned varegated [sic] textured brick . . . in very soft and feminine shades" (August Bohlen, "Has Quiet Setting Near Busy Streets," n.d., MA).

6. This silence may be because the IHMs' educational competency needed no justification in Detroit by 1941. Their schools often served as demonstration sites for new teaching techniques and curricular reforms, and many IHM educators were prominent in local and national chapters of professional organizations (see Tentler 1990, 251–52, 450–60; DMcC, T of E, 2–5 Aug. 1987, AsP, 9–34, MA).

implicitly promising to teach young girls a definition of womanhood derived from Mary's exemplary role.

The advertising flyer for Immaculata also reflected an understanding of women consistent with that of U.S. society at the time. In the early 1940s, women represented 40.2 percent of the nation's college enrollment, and the IHMs pledged to prepare them for higher education; indeed, Immaculata's college preparatory curriculum was consistent with the aspirations of the middle- and upper-class Catholic families living in relatively affluent northwest Detroit.[7] Even if a woman earned a college degree, however, both Catholic and American culture prescribed that her truest role was to marry and to raise children. To accommodate that belief, Immaculata offered opportunities to cultivate the "home arts" within the school's "complete home economics department." For students who needed or wanted to enter the work force immediately after high school, the sisters offered a "commercial curriculum," with its promise of access to good clerical and secretarial positions.

As presented in the brochure, then, the educational options for Immaculata girls were safely within the socially accepted parameters of the early 1940s. Despite all this, in the image of Immaculata as a stone in a "great monument erected to the glory of God *by the Sisters* " (emphasis added) and in the minute description of the new high school's state-of-the-art physical plant, the IHM community also signaled serious ambitions for its young women students that went beyond the purely academic. The special focus on the music rooms, large assembly rooms, and gymnasium served notice that the girls of Immaculata would be expected to actively exercise their artistic, intellectual, and physical gifts. In this sense, the 1941 prospectus sent mixed messages about the desired role of women, messages that reflected the IHMs' own sense of ambiguity about "women's proper place." At Immaculata, parents could be assured that their bright young daughters would be trained to become cultivated, accomplished, and faithful Catholic women, prepared for the university, the workplace, and the home, fit in mind, body, and spirit to take their places in Catholic culture. As the text also subtly made clear, however, their daughters would learn to assume these roles under the direction of women who knew their own strength and who took pride in it—women who had, in fact, been capable of undertaking monumental institution-building tasks for nearly a hundred years.

### "Ideals True and Lofty"

The Immaculata High School shaped and defined by its first faculty in the early 1940s remained relatively unchanged for the next twenty-five

---

7. Because of the depression, however, the proportion of women in the country's college enrollment had declined 3.5 percent from 1930 (Riley 1986, 215).

years. Like many other Catholic high schools of the time, it was "a total institution," one with a "consistent philosophy of education in which religion played the preeminent role" (Bryk et al. 1993, 6). However, because Immaculata was an autonomous women's school under the auspices and authority of a women's religious congregation, "religion" at Immaculata was often a balancing act comprised of roughly equal parts loyalty to the institutional Catholic church, loyalty to the IHM congregation's preferred understanding of the church, and loyalty to the congregation itself.

One of the most explicit statements of the Immaculata character was contained in the Immaculata High School Student Guide, handed out on the very first day of classes in 1941. The day began with homeroom at 8:30 A.M., preceded by an 8:25 warning bell that served as the signal to keep silence. During the two-minute exchange after each class, the girls were asked to move quickly and quietly and to keep to the right. At dismissal and at the lunch period, they were instructed that "all talking in the corridors and on the stairs should be in a whisper" and that silence was to reign in the auditorium at every assembly. The student guide said that "[e]very girl should strive for perfect attendance, as absence prevents good work" and that students ought to be prompt in getting to their study halls (where they should keep the definite places assigned them). "A few helpful regulations" regarding the uniform were also quite explicit, detailing everything from the correct shoes and stockings to prohibitions against fingernail polish and make-up (IHSSG [1941], MA).[8]

It is the introductory material to the handbook, however, that most captures the ethos of Immaculata, at least as the sisters envisioned it. "The Spirit of Immaculata" is an acrostic of the school's name, written by Grix and later set to music.[9] "Ideals," as it came to be called, would be sung lustily by Immaculata students at nearly every school event until at least the mid 1960s:

> Ideals—true and lofty
> Manners—sweet, sincere
> Modesty—like Mary's
> Aspirations—clear
> Charity—most Christ-like
> Unity—of mind
> Loyalty—to principle
> Actions—always kind
> Truth and honor always

8. The guide is undated, but internal evidence (a rehearsal schedule for the dedication mass) indicates that the document must have been given to the girls in autumn 1941.

9. "The Spirit of Immaculata" was set to music by Sister Mary Charboneau, a musician in the community and a faculty member at Immaculata beginning in 1942.

No matter what the odds
*A*ttractiveness of person
To draw others nearer God.[10]

These virtues—and the regulations described above—are a virtual compendium of the ideal behaviors for sisters that were spelled out in the IHM Constitutions and its accompanying Customs of the Congregation, behaviors that won the IHMs the reputation of being among the most ascetic of the American apostolic communities. Their days, for example, which began at 5:00 A.M., were punctuated by "signals" or bells that called them to strict periods of silence, prayer, study, household duties, and recreation, with the emphasis on silence and prayer. Article 66 of the 1920 Constitutions, for example, commanded: "Silence is observed the entire day, except during the hours of recreation; the Sisters speak only through necessity and give careful attention to silence of action as well as to recollection of spirit." If the IHMs valued silence in their own lives and asked some of it of Immaculata girls, the sisters were also committed to the good manners and modesty that ranked high in the list of Immaculata's "ideals true and lofty." Congregational leaders always required lessons in etiquette of the young sisters in formation and taught modesty as the necessary condition of chastity both to the novices and to the professed sisters. To preserve chastity, the Constitutions further cautioned that the sisters should "not only guard carefully purity of heart, but attend to exterior cleanliness, in their dress, their rooms, and in the house in general" (Const. 1920, art. 44, MA).

The IHM Constitutions also set the backdrop for Immaculata's ideals of "charity most Christ-like, unity of mind, loyalty to principle," and "actions always kind." In their relations with one another, the Rule instructed the sisters to "carefully avoid all disputes and whatever could give the least cause of dissension; they must not sustain their own opinion with obstinacy, endeavoring to take advantage of their learning or endowments; but . . . readily yield to the others in a spirit of humility and charity" (Const. 1920, art. 11, MA). In their training for the classroom, IHMs were taught: "If the teacher would gain and hold the interest of the . . . minds before her she must 'make her teaching attractive and *be so herself*' " ([Kelly] 1948, 343; emphasis added), a variation of Immaculata's "attractiveness of person to draw others nearer God." The Constitutions also instructed the sisters "to be models of meekness, piety, and charity" (Const. 1920, art. 147, MA).

In addition to "Ideals" and the list of regulations, the student guide contained a letter from the faculty that reiterated the conditions on which

10. Most Immaculata alumnae will recall the last lines of "Ideals" as "Attractiveness of person to draw souls near to God." The line was either mistyped in the first student guide or the words were soon changed.

young students would become "loyal and devoted children of Mary Immaculate": "Immaculata invites *you* to an interesting, fruitful, and happy school life. But you must pay in loyalty, helpfulness, and always in hard work, if you wish to enjoy its spirit" (IHSSG [1941], MA).

Certainly, the 1941 guide left few stones unturned in attempting to establish an atmosphere of strict discipline, womanly virtue, and religious decorum. The 1956 version was, if anything, more specific about what constituted a courteous, refined manner, probably in response to behaviors that were just the opposite of what the sisters wanted. "A student's conduct in the cafeteria as elsewhere is a reflection of her refinement," this updated guide noted.

> There should be no boisterous or unladylike conduct at any time. Only four students may sit at one table. Permission to sing on the occasion of a student's birthday may be obtained from the class teacher on duty. The record player is to be operated only by the student councelor [*sic*] appointed to do so. The cafeteria should be left as one would like to find it, i.e. tables clean; bottles, refuse, and dishes put in proper places, and no food or paper on the floor. (IHSSG 1956, MA)

Offcampus, the policies were just as strict: "Any boisterous, loud, disrespectful or unladylike conduct on buses, in stores or restaurants, on the street or elsewhere, will always be considered as a serious violation of loyalty not only to the school but also to the Church" (IHSSG 1956, MA).[11]

To reinforce their disciplinary concerns, the sisters printed in the 1956 guide a song titled "At Immaculata," sung to the tune of the "Hop Scotch Polka":

> We wear long-sleeved blouses / That are always so white, / With pleated skirts / That make a lovely sight. / Our matching saddle shoes / Must be just right / At Immaculata.
>
> Oh we take directions / So intelligently, / And fall in double lines accordingly. / We seldom fail in punctuality / At Immaculata.
>
> Oh, we take our turns / In forming clean-up corps, / And don't consider / Dusting floors a chore; / We wash the windows / And we do much more / At Immaculata.[12]

11. The Immaculata files in the Monroe Archives contain correspondence in which a homeowner on Greenlawn complained about the behavior of the Immaculata girls at dismissal. In another incident, Immaculata girls, like their Marygrove counterparts, were notorious at a Six Mile restaurant, Lou's Finer Deli, for lingering over their chips, cigarettes, and Cokes while better-tipping customers waited to be seated (see BJ, SFAATY, MgCC, summer 1989, 8–10).

12. As was true in most IHM-owned institutions, the sisters themselves did the major janitorial work in the building. In the 1950s, girls could work off their tuition by cleaning a

It's a female institution / Right straight through. / And what a blessing! / Always something new / To plan with girls / Who wear the
white and blue / At Immaculata.

"Truth and honor" notwithstanding odds; / Most attractive "to draw
souls to God." / Never forced to punish here with rod / At Immaculata.
(IHSSG 1956, MA)

From the very beginning, then, the sisters asked the Immaculata girls
to become women in the IHM mold and to be young disciples of the
sisters' own loyalty, service, discipline, refinement, hard work, and cleanliness—and they made no apologies for doing so.[13]

### The Informal Curriculum

Many of the in-school activities at Immaculata in the 1940s, 1950s,
and early 1960s—established within the first two years of the school's
opening—further emphasized traditional understandings of women's
place and were centered around Catholic culture, exactly as had been
promised in the first advertising brochure. Besides the typical high school
"secular" activities—dramatic presentations, choral concerts, music recit-
als, formal dances, class activities, basketball games, ticket drives to raise
money for the school, and honors assemblies—the Immaculata chronicles
consistently record a school year punctuated by liturgical processions,
First Friday Masses, priest and nun speakers on a variety of Catholic
topics, Christmas drives for the poor, student retreats, "vocation panels,"
and sodality assemblies.[14]

These activities reinforced a narrowly parochial view of Western culture, a sentimental and busy Marian piety, restricted career roles for
women, and a rather relentless emphasis on proper behavior. The Catho-

---

classroom after school, and Immaculata students were enlisted every spring to wash windows during their homeroom activity periods.

13. If the behaviors expected of Immaculata girls seemed a little constrained to them,
it struck a University of Michigan accreditation team evaluator the same way. In his letter
of 5 Mar. 1948 to the principal, Sister Frances Loretta Hackett, Dr. George E. Carrothers
wrote of his concern about "[t]he subdued, rather unnatural atmosphere pervading the
school. I was glad to see one girl running just a bit in the lower corridor as you and I were
examining the science room. It is true, she may have been doing a thing which is
forbidden. . . . but she exhibited the enthusiasm of youth which it was a delight to see in a
group of 700+ who march from class to class and who seemed not always to be responding
as individuals but as parts of a large, well-organized, efficiently moving army. Please do
not misunderstand me—the girls were grand and friendly and interested in their work, but
it did seem that there was a subdued, even suppressed, spirit in the school which is not
quite natural for teen-agers in these days" (cited in ARBEI, 1947, MA).

14. Except for periods when particular activities waxed and waned, Immaculata had
a full complement of extracurricular clubs and activities in which most students participated (see the IHSMCs, the IHSYBs, and the ARBEIs of the 1950s and 1960s).

lic Literature Committee of the Sodality, for instance, regularly sponsored a series of assemblies during Catholic Book Week and Catholic Press Month on such topics as "Catholic Authors of America," "Books on Trial," "Negro Catholic Authors," and "Catholic Authors of Other Countries" (IHSMC, 17 Nov. 1944, 25, 26, and 28 Feb. 1946, MA). To prepare for such presentations in 1945, the girls heard (according to the Immaculata chronicler) "a splendid lecture on Shakespeare given by Father Henry Courtney, a Holy Ghost priest. Father gave several reasons for believing that Shakespeare was a Catholic" (IHSMC, 25 Nov. 1945, MA).

The topics for the Vocation Week programs during the 1940s included "The Lab Technician," "Secretarial Work," "Social Work," "Journalism," "Nursing," "Married Life," "Home Life," "Religious Life," and "Motherhood."[15] Literally acting out these values and concerns, Immaculata students throughout the 1940s and 1950s either performed in or attended dramatic productions of "A Day With Mary," "Be a Little Cuckoo," "A Good Girl in the Kitchen," "Little Women," and "Career Angel" (IHSMC, 4–7 Dec., 7 Feb., and 21 Nov. 1945, 23 May 1947, 16 Nov. 1948, MA). Assemblies with titles such as "Postures on Parade" and "Courtesy Cues" and demonstrations of "the proper way to hold a clutch purse" punctuated each academic year well into the 1960s (IHSMC, 15 Nov. and 17 Sept. 1944; IHSYB 1964, MA). Not untypical was a 1949 cooperative venture in which Immaculata girls joined students from other IHM schools in presenting a panel on modesty, followed by a suitably modest style show (IHSMC, 13 Mar. 1949, MA).

Marian rituals abounded. In addition to an elaborate outdoor rosary procession at the beginning of October and the crowning of the Blessed Virgin Mary at the end of May, Immaculata girls honored Mary through pageants and programs. At an all-school assembly on the First Friday of May 1946, for instance, Our Lady's Committee of the Sodality "presented a tableaux of Our Lady under several of her titles," a pageant repeated throughout the 1950s (IHSMC, 3 May 1946; IHSYB 1954, 1955, MA). All of the yearbooks published in this decade—with the exception of one volume dedicated to "our parents" and two to Cardinal Edward Mooney —were inscribed to "Mary Immaculate, Queen of Our School." Often the yearbooks quoted from some portion of the retreat master's conferences during the school's annual three days of quiet and prayer, conferences that often dwelt on the "dignity of womanhood":

It is important for you to realize [the 1959 retreat director stressed] that a woman has by the gift of her nature the most powerful instrument in

15. Journalism, a fairly nontraditional role for women in the 1940s, probably appeared on the program because Marygrove offered it as a major and had produced some strong graduates who would be available for a "vocation" presentation.

the world. This power can be used for good, or it can be used for evil. Using it, a woman can raise man to his highest spiritual stature or drag him down to the depths of infamy. . . . When a woman fails to live up to her high calling; when she comes out of the depths and is bamboozled by the devil into leading a shallow, puny, artificial life—she becomes a miserable, cold, calculating, despicable, deplorable specimen of humanity. (IHSYB 1959, MA)

The "dignity of womanhood: received more positive—but no less apocalyptic—treatments in other yearbooks, but either way, the burdens on teen-aged girls to sacralize men must have seemed immense.

In one of the most stereotypical presentations of woman's place, the 1960 yearbook meditation on life choices, nearly the entire formal and informal curricula are presented in terms of how they might serve one of the three vocations that each girl must decide as her life's course: marriage and motherhood, a single life of service, or a religious vocation (IHSYB 1960, MA).[16] Each of the choices is itself narrowly described in the text, especially the "single life of service," which is presented as the opportunity "to fulfill a woman's role in one of the great occupational or professional fields best suited to women": nursing, teaching, or social service work.[17] This yearbook, in fact, seems constructed along the lines of an examination of conscience. "How are we accepting the responsibility to develop ourselves? to deepen our characters?" the text asks, followed by surgically precise questions aimed at the qualities a "good" Immaculata girl ought to possess: "Are we trying to practice self-control, to strengthen our moral convictions, and to enrich our spiritual lives in practical everyday ways? Are we making an effort to form in ourselves habits of industry, of accuracy, of thoroughness, of responsibility, of self-reliance, of self-direction, and of cooperation?" (IHSYB 1960, MA). Even the definition of school spirit—initially described in typical teen-aged terms as "shrieking and cheering at basketball games and swimming meets"—veers into descriptions of the perfect IHM novice: "Sometimes you will find School Spirit at out-of-the-way places—slipping around and turning light switches off and on, emptying wastebaskets, erasing boards; picking up that scrap of paper on the stairs and

16. Arts, sciences, and the humanities, but most especially "The Bride's Course"—the sequence of classes that included Clothing I and II, Home Economics, Christian Family Living, and Foods and Nutrition—are presented as particularly helpful for girls considering marriage. Business courses, too, had their relevance to the married state, as housewives would be able to "preserve television recipes through shorthand" (IHSYB, 1960, MA).

17. The traditional women's work matrix had long been in place at Immaculata. A 1947 graduate remembers her class getting "a sermon [from one of the sisters] on the evils of show business and to stay out of it, and if any of us did go into it, to never reveal the fact that we went to Immaculata" (IHSAS 1992, quest. 47D).

serving on clean-up committees, helping a fellow student with a tough math problem and lending a hand to the Sister in the cafeteria" (IHSYB 1960, MA).

In the discussion of the mathematics curriculum, which at the time included beginning and advanced algebra, plane and solid geometry, and trigonometry, the 1960 text likewise crashes upon the shoals of gender stereotyping: "Women, we know as a rule, are not naturally gifted with logical minds. They must struggle (as we do) to focus on important ideas, to concentrate on solutions, and such. The study of math will help us to become 'thinking women,' and this is why all of us labor through some of it; and the most zealous of us elect the higher courses" (IHSYB 1960, MA).

## The Intellectual Atmosphere

Such stereotyping aside, Immaculata, like other Catholic schools in the United States, espoused a strong academic curriculum for all of its students and offered few electives, even within the commercial or home arts curriculum (Bryk et al. 1993, 30–32). Also like the majority of Catholic women's high schools, it always presented itself primarily as a college-preparatory high school with such rigorous standards that the IHMs regarded it as an institution that buttressed their own reputation as excellent educators.[18] When school opened in 1946, Immaculata girls were offered four years of English, Latin, and religion; three years of math (two courses in algebra, one in geometry); three years of science (introductory science, chemistry, and biology); three years of social studies (world history, American history, and economics); typing and shorthand; home economics and sewing; French, art appreciation, and gymnasium.[19] By the next year, the history, art, and home economics offerings had expanded, and sixty students were enrolled in private music lessons; before the end of the decade, the music curriculum would include three separate chorale groups in addition to private study. By the late 1950s, trigonometry, physics, solid geometry, additional French courses, and other new classes would be in place, but in general, the curriculum established in the first years of the high school remained intact (with, of course, adjust-

18. Immaculata was open barely a month when the principal wrote to the Bureau of Educational Institutions of the University of Michigan to inquire about the process for accreditation and to invite the director for a conference. Dr. Edgar G. Johnston, the assistant director, visited the school on 30 Apr. 1942, and by 6 May had sent his praised-filled evaluation. On 1 June 1942, Immaculata received its coveted approval from the University of Michigan, an accreditation that would be renewed the whole of its institutional life.

19. Immaculata opened with 94 seniors, many of them transfers from the IHM-run Girls Catholic Central; 121 juniors; 154 sophomores; and 160 ninth graders (IHSMC, 8 Sept. 1941, MA).

ments in course content, textbooks, and teaching techniques) into the late 1960s.

Although the annual honors assemblies certainly recognized all of the "proper" behaviors expected of an Immaculata student, the ascending order of the awards—from perfect attendance, "cooperation," and athletics to scholastic honors—indicated their respective importance to the sisters. Young women, it was clear, should be rewarded for the traditional feminine virtues of steadfastness and courtesy, but most of all they should be recognized for the quality of their minds and for the power of their intellectual achievements. One of the Immaculata messages for women, then, was that no young woman should ever deliberately hide or diminish her own intelligence.[20]

Immaculata graduates of the 1940s, 1950s, and 1960s generally remember the academic atmosphere and their teachers as challenging and demanding, although they are quick to identify periods when the congregation apparently staffed Immaculata with a number of older sisters in the twilight of their careers or when some departments were noticeably weaker than others, particularly during the mid to late 1950s and early 1960s.[21] One 1956 graduate, for example, remembers an outstanding sister with a master's degree in mathematics who "taught with such clarity that I found the subject easy to master," but she also recalls an economics teacher who dozed while the student herself conducted the class. Other teachers were so "easily flustered by our 'shenanigans' . . . such as pencil tapping, coughing on cue, spilling perfume on the radiators, that they lost their effectiveness as teachers. The age of some, I'm sure, made it difficult to cope with us" (IHSAS 1992, quest. 56A).[22] Others remember rigidity, lack of creativity, inattention to less gifted students, rote learning,

20. The song "At Immaculata" also contained these lyrics: "Now, in scholarship you'll find / We really are apt. / Before our teachers / We are so enrapt! / In clever arguments / We can't be trapped / At Immaculata" (IHSSG 1956, MA).

21. In preparation for this essay, 800 IHS alumnae attending the school's 50th anniversary all-class reunion on 28 Nov. 1992 were asked to complete an eight-page survey about their perceptions of Immaculata and of the IHM sisters. One-hundred and fifty-two responded: 25 from the 1942–49 graduating classes, 39 from the 1950–59 classes, 67 of the 1960–69 graduates, and 21 of the 1970–83 graduates. I am grateful to Elizabeth Mary Larson, I.H.M., chair of the sociology program at Marygrove College, for her help in the preparation of the questionnaire (surveys and transcriptions of essay portions by author, MA).

22. The insights regarding the number of older sisters at Immaculata in the late 1950s are quite accurate. The decision to keep the young junior professed sisters in Monroe to complete their undergraduate degrees before entering the teaching ranks and the increased enrollment of sisters in full-time graduate study depleted the number of available teachers in the 1950s. In 1959 and again in 1960, the IHMs opened women's high schools and in each case sent some of the youngest, best, and brightest to serve as the first faculty—just as had been done at Immaculata in 1941. See chaps. 11 and 12 of the present volume.

strictness, perfectionism, favoritism and conformity (IHSAS 1992, quest. 50I, 56B, 57E, 57D, 58E, 63G, 64H, 64J, 65D, 67D).

Still, Immaculata alumnae overwhelmingly name as the academic trademarks of their education the challenges of the curriculum, the amount of homework assigned, the high expectations of their teachers, the seriousness of purpose that pervaded the classrooms, the intellectual discipline, and the excellent preparation they received for college work. One 1942 graduate, for example, recalled finding the University of Detroit "wonderfully liberating" after Immaculata, but the nightly homework and intellectual give and take of her high school education made her "as well equipped as any male to tackle all the serious and stimulating college subjects and bull sessions." Another summarized the academic expectations succinctly: "Much competition to be the best. High expectations by teachers. Much homework and studying. Many papers to write, many books to read." Similarly, a 1954 alumna wrote: "We were fortunate to have been taught by well-educated nuns who set high expectations for us in the classroom. They also seemed interested in us as individuals and prodded us to reach our potential." A 1958 graduate noted that "[i]n the late 1950s academics reigned supreme. Everything else was secondary. It was a Catholic *school* not a *Catholic* school." For the commercial graduates, too, the training seemed to pay off: "I took commercial courses, and was as well prepared, or more so, than had I been to business school to enter the work force. My education not only included the skills, but attitudes, which stood me well as a secretary for many years" (IHSAS 1992, quest. 42A, 47C, 54A, 58D, 44D).

The greatest enthusiasm for the intellectual atmosphere at Immaculata—with its emphasis on critical thinking, writing, and speaking skills—comes from graduates of the mid to late 1960s, when Immaculata became increasingly staffed by young nuns and laywomen, many of them fresh from summers of graduate work.[23] "I feel I received a superior education at Immaculata. I particularly benefited from the teaching of organizational skills, taking a position and logically supporting it," wrote one (IHSAS 1992, quest. 64B). "I generally spent three to five hours nightly [on homework] plus a lot of weekend time. We even had novels assigned to read over Christmas, Easter *and* summer vacation . . . always with a test waiting to 'prove' we had read them. . . . I remember the English program as being particularly demanding. I'm especially grateful for how it taught me to write," said another (IHSAS 1992, quest. 64C). Finally, another student of this period added:

23. Mary Jo. Maher, I.H.M. notes that 118 sisters received master's degrees and four received doctorates in 18 different fields of specialization between 1954 and 1960. The "big push" for graduate degrees, however, occurred in the 1960s, when "hundreds of IHMs enrolled in summer graduate programs at both Catholic and state universities" (IHM H/H, 2–5 Aug. 1987, AsP, 47, MA).

I found the school very exciting intellectually. The teachers were tolerant of questions and discussions and appeared to take pride in our minds when they were lively. The classrooms were clean, bright, quiet, and orderly. The general attitude was gentle and non-critical. One time my entire class got terrible grades in algebra. The teacher . . . said, "Don't worry, girls. Something must have gone wrong. I'll just repeat this chapter and we'll test again." This honesty in admitting things hadn't gone well and willingness to share in the responsibility was typical and was a lifelong example to me. (IHSAS 1992, quest. 64F)

Indeed, when asked what elements of their Immaculata education most helped them in adult life, a significant percentage of graduates from the first three decades named their academic preparation as crucial and could name an IHM teacher who had particularly influenced her.[24]

## Progressive Messages

The Catholic culture that permeated Immaculata from its first days did not take all of its cues from pious tradition or conservative past practice regarding women (Bryk et al. 1993, 41–46). In fact, the assembly speakers at Immaculata—even when they were a steady line of male clerics[25]—often represented organizations that in their day stood for a progressive version of Catholicism or, at least, something of a global perspective on church and society.

In the 1940s, 1950s, and early 1960s, Immaculata girls heard lecturers from nearly all of the home and foreign mission societies, including a number of women and leaders of the international mission movement who had traveled the world: the Reverend James Keller, author of *Men of Maryknoll;* the Reverend Leo DeBarry, the head of the Propagation of the Faith in Detroit, who was forthrightly critical on the issue of segregation in the American church;[26] and Malcolm Dooley, brother of the activist lay Catholic physician in Laos, Thomas Dooley (IHSMC 1941–49; IHSYB 1963, MA). The speakers probably did not see for themselves nor suggest to their audience a connection between missionary activity and colonialism, but their very presence on stage offered Immaculata girls glimpses of worlds far different from and far beyond Detroit (Tentler 1990, 416–19).

24. Of the 152 respondents, 96 (63 percent) cited their intellectual or academic preparation as influencing their adult life; 132 respondents (86 percent) named an IHM who had influenced her.

25. Priests did not dominate just the assemblies. All of the commencement speakers were priests until 1964, when a layman, Dr. Jorge Castellanos—a history professor at Marygrove and the father of one of the graduates—delivered the commencement address. The first woman commencement speaker was Marygrove's dean of women, Sister Jane Farrell, an Immaculata alumna and former faculty member who spoke to the 1968 graduates.

26. For information on Father Leo DeBarry, see Tentler 1990, 497.

The roster of speakers at Immaculata in its first twenty-five years also included a significant number who, in the categories of the time, addressed questions of race to Immaculata's overwhelmingly white audience.[27] These speakers, who appeared at least yearly and sometimes more frequently, were often home missioners raising money for their "colored parishes" in the South or in Detroit, but their topics occasionally addressed deeper questions of prejudice or injustice. In 1945, for instance, the chronicles noted: "A . . . lecture by Father Griffin, a Holy Ghost Father, who is on mission at Sacred Heart Colored Parish of Detroit. His theme: the Colored! His appeal: justice to a persecuted part of the Mystical Body" (IHSMC, 30 Nov. 1945, MA). Moreover, once the Catholic Interracial Council took shape in Detroit in 1942, their representatives made regular appearances at Immaculata.[28] The speakers apparently did not pursue the obvious segregation within the Catholic church and its institutions in Detroit, including Immaculata, but they at least extended to Immaculata girls some insight into their own white privilege and their obligation to act on the "race question" with charity or tolerance, if not with justice.[29]

Another source of more progressive Catholic thought came through the IHM congregation's leadership in liturgical reform. The liturgical movement campaigned for greater theological understanding of the eucharist, for congregational participation in the mass, and for musical and artistic improvements in church celebrations.[30] At Immaculata, the 1943 school year began with a *Missa Recitata* or "dialogue Mass" (in which the congregation recited the responses that were usually reserved for the altar boys or choir), and that form of eucharistic celebration was used

27. Immaculata enrolled its first African-American student in 1946, the school chronicles noting: "We received our first registration of a colored girl . . . Yvonne Wilson, from Our Lady of Victory Parish" (IHSMC, 24 Nov. 1946, MA).

28. On 16 Mar. 1945, for example, Mr. Droste spoke to the Immaculata girls on "interracial problems" and was, according to the IHM chronicler, "well received by the students" (IHSMC, 16 Mar. 1945, MA).

29. The *IHM School Bulletin*, a newsletter sent from the IHM school supervisors to all principals, notes in 1959 that "the IHM schools are represented in the newly formed junior division of the Catholic Interracial Council" (Jan. 1959, MA). The 1961 yearbook notes that "through apostolic activities [the Immaculata student] develops the spiritual strength necessary to fulfill the spiritual and corporal works of mercy, strength built on such virtues as unselfishness, sympathy for the unfortunate ones, tolerance toward those of other races, creeds, colors" (MA).

30. Through the work of Sister Mary Judith Connelly at Marygrove and then–General Superior Mother Domitilla Donohue, the IHMs offered what was probably the first college course on Catholic liturgy in the country in 1927. Every IHM mission in 1927 had a subscription to the liturgical magazine *Orate Fratres* and possessed all of the volumes of the *Popular Liturgical Library*. Beginning that same year, all IHM postulants were required to bring the liturgically sophisticated *St. Andrew Missal* with them on entrance day (see MJM, IHM H/ H 2–5 Aug. 1987, AsP, 52, MA).

whenever possible throughout the decades that followed. The Immaculata administration also actively endorsed the international laywomen's organization, the Grail, and its Detroit activities. They invited the Grail's Catholic Theatre to perform at the high school, took students to the Grail-sponsored "Liturgical Spring" conferences at Marygrove, and sent students to the Grailville Center in Loveland, Ohio (IHSMC, 23 May 1947, 20 Mar. 1948, 16 Sept. 1949, MA).

Speakers from the Catholic Worker movement—including its founder, Dorothy Day—also appeared at Immaculata assemblies, as did representatives of other Catholic action groups (IHSMC, 4 Oct. 1951, 9 Nov. 1962, MA). "Catholic Action," a popular umbrella term in the Catholic vocabulary from the 1930s to the 1960s, called "for a more fervent religious practice on the part of the laity, for careful study of Catholic doctrine and Catholic social principles, and for a deeper involvement of the laity in Catholic organizations and in defense of the Church" (Tentler 1990, 433). The IHMs took the invitation to Catholic action—and particularly its study of the social encyclicals—quite seriously, and in keeping with their position as professional educators, warmly embraced the principal techniques of Catholic action: first to see, then to judge, then to act.[31]

The congregation directed its institutional energies to the implementation of Catholic action by means of Sodality of Our Lady clubs. Although these societies always cited the personal holiness of their members as their chief purpose, they had been revitalized in the 1930s to emphasize "social action" (Tentler 1990, 434). The IHMs eagerly attended sodality training sessions, pushed sodality units in their schools, sent students to the Summer School of Catholic Action in Chicago and at Notre Dame, and published the monthly "IHM Sodality Bulletin" to inform sodality moderators about worthwhile activities. At the same time as the bulletins contained extensive information about how to increase vocations or to raise mission money, their suggestions also included "contacts with 'active Catholic groups and individuals,' " specifically, "visits to the Catholic Worker house, attendance at open meetings of the Catholic Interracial Council, and participation in basic training lectures of the Association of Catholic Trade Unionists" (MJM, IHM H/H, 25 Aug. 1987, AsP, 59, MA).

In the first two decades, the IHMs took the sodality at Immaculata so seriously that they practically structured student government around it; for many years, the positions of sodality prefect and chair of a sodality committee were elevated to a level that seemed more important—or at least as important—as those of class officers or student council represen-

---

31. This approach would eventually influence the development of liberation theology and of processes for theological reflection and for social analysis, two movements the IHMs would make their own from the 1960s and 1970s on.

tatives. In the 1940s and 1950s, it was the sodality officers who presided at many of the all-school assemblies and who organized and administered the students' fund-raising activities and volunteer efforts. Indeed, except for the purely social events, it was the rare student activity at Immaculata that existed for its own sake or for the pleasure of the students and that was not used to raise money for a good cause—an indication, perhaps, of how the IHMs arranged for the ideals of Catholic action to permeate the entire life of the school.

Although at one level nothing more than charitable enterprises that were long associated with women's societies or with women's work and that were made possible by the economic circumstances of their families (especially their fathers), the impetus for the Immaculata girls' generosity was not simply financial philanthropy. Urged on by their teachers and by the ethos of the IHMs and of Immaculata, many students experienced Catholic action as a cause, a movement, a spiritual drive, whose principal analytical techniques would influence them in direct and subtle ways for years to come.[32] As Leslie Tentler writes in her history of the archdiocese of Detroit,

> [The] very rhetoric of Catholic Action encouraged women to take on unaccustomed roles. Catholic Action flowed from faith, its advocates argued; the courage and militance of its practitioners was simply a measure of their spiritual vitality. It was not easy, under the circumstances, to insist that women be less militant than men, no matter how wedded most Catholics were to a conservative view of the female role. . . . A girl who admired the likes of Dorothy Day . . . was almost bound to imagine her own role as a laywoman in terms that went beyond the confines of the parish altar society. (1990, 440–41)

At the very least, even those Immaculata girls who were not interested in social action nevertheless saw and heard a singular message being driven home in all of the assemblies and mission drives: women had the skills—and the obligation—to make a difference in the world. In fact, all of the assemblies, panels, speakers, programs, and drives at Immaculata, even the ones that seemed to prescribe women's roles very narrowly, accomplished purposes other than conveying a particular content or message to the girls. Many students were heavily committed to the student organizations, to planning, financing, and orchestrating their various activities, and to presenting themselves to an auditorium of eight

---

32. When asked what elements of her Immaculata education had most influenced her adult life, for example, a 1967 alumna wrote: "The two areas that have stayed with me are the critical thinking that was encouraged constantly . . . and the social consciousness and responsibility that I attribute . . . to Sodality" (IHSAS 1992, quest. 67F).

hundred students to explain their causes. What is perhaps most important about many of the presentations is that they were written, arranged, directed, and given by the girls themselves. In one sense, when students addressed the student body, it didn't matter if their topic was the daily intentions of the Church Unity Octave or missionary work in Mexico; what did matter were the leadership skills they were learning and practicing, skills of importance to their teachers and of immense importance to women.

## In-groups

Immaculata girls discovered during their years at the high school a sense of belonging—to their school, to their class, and to each other—a feeling surely endorsed by their IHM teachers, who themselves knew the sustaining power of women's friendships and women's communities. The students' high school social life often began with their elementary school girlfriends (friendships that continued via the bus or car pools), but alumnae of the first twenty-five years report that they gradually made friends with girls from other parishes and from other parts of the city, based on mutual interests or shared classes. "My friends consisted of girls from my elementary school/parish as well as new friends met while in high school. For the most part we formed one group and still remain friends," wrote a 1946 graduate. Like a 1965 graduate who wrote, "the greatest gift of Immaculata was the depth of the relationships among friends," other graduates reported on the continuity of their relationships. "I still see about thirteen of the women on a monthly basis. I think that says something for relationships that were formed almost thirty-five years ago," wrote a 1958 graduate (IHSAS 1992, quest. 46A, 65H, 58C).

Not everyone, however, felt so good about their social relationships at Immaculata. Throughout the 1940s and 1950s, a number of graduates reported discomfort with the sheer number and with the economic status of the students who came to Immaculata from Gesu Elementary School. "Gesu Parish students dominated," a 1949 alumna reported. "The in-group on the whole were from Gesu Parish—the rich, 'in' parish. I was a Gesu product. Lucky me," said a 1950 graduate (IHSAS 1992, quest. 49A, 50H). Another recalled:

> Gesu Parish (upper-middle-class professional—attorneys) supplied the largest number of students. I came from a lower-middle-class factory worker parish. . . . Often we couldn't afford yearbooks, class rings, new books, new school uniforms each year. I was aware some girls from wealthy homes drove their own auto, had money for treats, dressed beautifully and I could never be on their level. The knowledge of the

difference may have been more on my part because I was keenly aware
of my family's sacrifice simply to send me to a private school and the
lack of funds for "extras." (IHSAS 1992, quest. 53E)

Sororities posed another difficulty for some girls. The origin of sororities at Immaculata is not entirely clear. In some cases, they seem to have
existed in the parishes as a means of maintaining friendships among
parish girls who went to different high schools. A 1945 graduate, for
example, reported that sororities—even when they included public
school students—exerted such peer pressure that they determined who
was "in" and who was "out" at Immaculata. Some sororities might have
originated in order to sustain former relationships or to create new "artistic," "sophisticated," or "intellectual" identities. A 1946 alumna stated:
"Some formed their own 'sororities' to counteract the 'in' group" (IHSAS
1992, quest. 45D, 46C).

The IHM mission chronicles make no mention of sororities until December 1945 and then in a complimentary sense, noting that the "some
of the sororities took care of the surplus [families]" not covered by home-
rooms in the annual Christmas drive for the poor (14 Dec. 1945, MA). By
the end of the 1947–48 school year, however, the superintendent of Catholic schools, Monsignor Deady, met with the principals of Immaculata,
Dominican, Mercy, and Blessed Sacrament high schools "to discuss sororities"; by September of the following school year, the principal of Immaculata called a meeting of sorority members "to inform them . . . that
no sorority member [could] be a class officer" (IHSMC, 27 May and 20
Sept. 1948, MA). The election of senior officers occurred two days later.
By the next week, the faculty, the officers of the sodality, and all of the
newly elected class officers were meeting to discuss the advisability of
a student council—in response, perhaps, to some sense of fragmentation
within the Immaculata student body, or to a directive from the archdiocese (IHSMC, 20, 22, 29 Sept. 1948, MA). In any case, to the degree to
which the sororities invited some girls to membership and excluded
others, they violated Immaculata's "ideals" and the IHM ethic of solidarity and uniformity.

The problem of sororities, to some extent, was coterminous with the
problem of Gesu, at least for the IHMs. Gesu girls and sorority girls were
often synonymous. Moreover, they were central to the school's functioning: their mothers were active in the Immaculata Mothers' Guild, the
school's principal fundraising group; Gesu families were major benefactors of the IHM congregation; and Gesu was, after all, an IHM school and
a source of pride to the sisters. Immaculata girls eventually circumvented
the sorority problem by forming "clubs with Greek names" that were
purportedly open to all, and the IHMs themselves encouraged and sched-

uled more class, interclass, all-school, and cocurricular activities.[33] The ban against sorority members as officers stayed in effect, however, until sororities themselves faded away in the late 1960s. At least on the policy level, the IHMs insisted on "charity most Christ-like" and "actions always kind" from their Immaculata students.

## Women's Place: Traditional Messages

Immaculata class lists and reports to the University of Michigan Bureau of Educational Institutions through 1970 indicate that the percentage of girls in a graduating class going on to college or to professional training went from a low of 51 percent in 1942 to a high of 95 percent in 1968. The majority of those graduates—fifty to sixty a year—went to the IHM-run Marygrove College or to the University of Detroit (two Catholic colleges in their immediate neighborhood), those attending Detroit generally slightly outnumbering those choosing Marygrove. Very few Immaculata graduates in the school's first thirty years went out of state to college, and those who did so for the most part selected Catholic women's liberal arts colleges (ARBEI 1942–70; IHSCL 1942–61, MA).

These graduates' choice of higher education, of course, verified the college-preparatory purpose of Immaculata and the belief of their IHM teachers that women ought to pursue further education. Certainly, the stress on academics was not lost on most alumnae, a number of whom, when asked what view of women's place they carried away from Immaculata, named a belief in their own intellectual power. "I derived the understanding that women were intellectually just as important as men,"

33. The club strategy is described by a 1956 alumna: "Immaculata High School during the . . . 50's was an eclectic school, one made of students from many parishes—wealthy ones such as Gesu, poorer ones such as St. Bridget, and far away ones such as St. Charles Borromeo. As in many schools, there was an 'in' crowd and an 'out' crowd. I was a member of the 'in between' crowd, a group of students who weren't the prettiest or the most popular with the U of D[etroit] and C-C [Catholic Central] boys, but who were interested in getting good grades, athletics, and student government. Because sororities were frowned on and because student officers could not be members of sororities, our group 'founded' a high school club, Greek name and all, but we did not consider ourselves a sorority because we did not pledge members. . . . Our club counted among its members students from many parishes and from many backgrounds, students who excelled academically and went on to undergraduate and graduate degrees, and others who married within weeks of high school graduation. We are all still very close, but our closeness did not prevent any of us from making friends with other students in the school, especially ones who shared our interests in student government or sports" (IHSAS 1992, quest. 56A). However, clubs could still be exclusive: "Unfortunately I remember a 'clique' type atmosphere due to the existence of 'clubs' (which were very similar to sororities, which were illegal). I was excluded from a club and remember the hurt it caused me and other girls who were excluded" (IHSAS 1992, quest. 63F).

a graduate of the first class said; echoing her, a graduate of twenty years later reported that "I certainly went into college believing that a woman's mind was as good as any man's and that I could do anything I wanted to if I worked hard enough." A 1964 alumna noted that her Immaculata education taught her that "a 'woman's place' was exactly wherever she chose to put herself, take herself, drive herself" (IHSAS 1992, quest. 42A, 62B, 64N).

Still, whether graduates of the 1940s or of the 1960s, the majority of alumnae of the first twenty-five years found their education marked by traditional messages about the role of women, in spite of the obvious respect for women's intelligence. "My understanding of 'women's place' in 1942 was either becoming a mother or joining a religious community," wrote an early graduate, a view reiterated throughout that decade (IHSAS 1992, quest. 42C). However, the options apparently broadened somewhat in the 1950s. "Immaculata's philosophy was one reflective of the times in which we lived," a 1956 graduate wrote:

> Students would fall into one of two categories—college prep or terminal. The college prep students would consider such traditionally female careers as teaching, nursing, and social work. The terminal students were expected to become secretaries or future homemakers and would flock to the cooking and sewing classes, and of course, the typing classes. Curiously enough, subliminally, we were all expected to be future homemakers because the above-mentioned professional careers were considered to be a stopgap means of making a living until the right man came along to support us financially for the rest of our days. Marriage, or certainly children, brought a stop to the aspirations of most career women, and not until their children were raised did they attempt to pick up where they had left off two decades earlier and start all over again. (IHSAS 1992, quest. 56A)

Graduates of the 1960s saw their options in similar terms. Three 1965 alumnae sound remarkably like the graduates of the 1940s:

> We were told a "woman's place" was "the heart of the home." . . . As a result, I personally felt totally responsible in relationships and believed I not only had the power, but the responsibility for everyone else.

> Women could be bright and competent but not authoritative, assertive, liberal.

> Women were [the] core of family life [but] . . . had contributions to make in all spheres of living. Women had several choices of careers in "traditional" roles (teacher, nurse, mother, sister). (IHSAS 1992, quest. 65H, 65D, 65G).

## Post–Vatican II: Radical Change

In 1965, Pope Paul VI officially closed Vatican II and sent the bishops home to implement the revolutionary work of church reform. In 1966, the IHM congregation elected new leadership and moved into the final stages of revising its Constitutions in the light of contemporary needs; in the same year, Betty Friedan organized the National Organization for Women. The next year, Detroit erupted in one of the worst urban rebellions of the decade. In 1968, assassinations and antiwar protests fueled the confrontational politics of a generation. In 1969, John Cardinal Dearden convoked "Synod '69," a diocesan-wide discussion of what it might mean for Detroit Catholics to call themselves "the pilgrim people of God," then took their advice and presided over a massive decentralization of archdiocesan offices and services (Tentler 1990, 523).

During this period of social change and unrest, Immaculata High School publicly communicated a strong sense of institutional mission and purpose and even a spirit of exhilaration. As early as 1963 and 1964, the Immaculata faculty had begun to put forward the church's changed theological thinking. By the mid-1960s, scripture services, religion classes emphasizing an activist church immersed in the world, increased all-school commitment to social action, and a new focus on personal growth and conscience-formation became part of the school's curriculum (IHSYB 1963–69, MA).

The new spirit of social and global awareness permeated Immaculata's academic offerings in every area. The English department, for example, began a course that introduced seniors to experimental drama and to African-American literature. Likewise, the history department introduced a course in Asian studies (with an emphasis on Japan, China, and India) and dispatched students to open housing meetings at Cobo Hall and to lectures by the national housing-rights activist James Groppi. Classroom activities in all disciplines emphasized discussions, student presentations, problem-solving group work, collaborative projects (including calculating the economic effect of the 1968 World Series on the Detroit economy), and simulation games (IHSYB 1968, 1969; KWL to HV, 14 Nov. 1968, MA). Throughout, expectations of intellectual commitment were high, a message made explicit in 1967 by the launching of a full-scale advanced honors program.

The clubs and volunteer activities showed comparable signs of vitality and increased sophistication. No longer performing in plays like "A Good Girl in the Kitchen," the Immaculata actresses put on "Rhinoceros" and "Skin of Our Teeth." Immaculata students participated annually in the Model United Nations program at the University of Detroit, and the student government reorganized itself into a coordinating council "based not so much on the idea of student government as on . . . student self-government" (IHSYB 1965, 43, MA). In 1973, Immaculata also held the first of its Free Education Weeks, a three-day period given to offcampus experiences in metropolitan Detroit and in other cities such as Chicago and Toronto; assemblies and movies; and in-school courses or workshops on such topics as car repair, banking, natural foods, self-defense, wine-tasting, and yoga (*Marq.*, 28 Feb. 1973, MA).

The shift in content during the late 1960s and 1970s at Immaculata reflected the same spirit of renewal and of change that the IHMs were experiencing in their own congregational life. In 1969, the order formally closed their formation college in Monroe and began sending their young nuns to study in Detroit, Chicago, St. Louis, and Washington, D.C. In 1970, the congregation initiated open placement, allowing sisters for the first time to choose their place of work and of residence in consultation with their superiors, even as Michigan citizens voted "yes" on Proposal C, a referendum amending the state constitution to prohibit any public funds from being spent on nonpublic schools—a vote that would eventually limit the future of parochial schools altogether. In 1972, meeting in a participative assembly of the whole for the first time, the IHM sisters voted to dedicate themselves to "eradicating the causes of injustice among men."

Immaculata's IHM faculty, like many of their sisters throughout the congregation, were now "out of uniform," often living offcampus in small group houses and apartments. The sisters no longer functioned strictly within the rule book that had disciplined their lives for decades but were instead electing their own courses of study and choosing their own ministries, friends, and spiritualities. In this intense period of renewal, many IHM administrators and teachers at Immaculata proposed to their young students personal freedom, individual responsibility, critical inquiry, solidarity, and action for justice as Immaculata's new "ideals true and lofty."

## Revised Code of Conduct

The *Marquee*, Immaculata's first all-school student newspaper, reported in 1971 on some features of the revised code of conduct for students, policies light years away from the first Immaculata High School Student Guide. The only uniform part of the school uniform was now a herringbone skirt, but if a girl had the permission of her parents not to wear the skirt, the choice would be respected. "Although wearing the uniform is advised and urged," the *Marquee* reported, "it is up to the girl and her parents to decide what is appropriate for school attire." Smoking —"allowed" but not "condoned"—was permitted on the school grounds, although suspension could still be imposed for smoking in school. Students could leave campus at any time during the day with permission of their parents, and any student finished with classes before 3:30 P.M. was free to leave entirely. Students could also bring visitors to class if they had received permission from their teachers and from the administration the day before. "All these policies . . . give the Immaculata girl much more responsibility," a *Marquee* writer noted. "College is the next step demanding maturity and responsibility of each student. Immaculata is trying to help its girls develop these qualities, but it is up to the girl to decide if she wants them or not" (*Marq.*, 13 Oct. 1971, MA).

As it turned out, some parents wondered whether these decisions should be left to the girls alone—or even to the suddenly liberal IHMs— and, accordingly, conducted a parents' survey in early 1972 that asked specifically about the dress code, offcampus privileges for freshmen and sophomores, the need for a visitor-control system, and whether students should have equal voice with faculty and parents on school decisions, as was then apparently the practice (IHSPPS, 21 Feb. 1972, MA).[34] By the next year, to prevent students from dressing like "house painters" or "garage mechanics," uniform regulations tightened up a bit and offcampus privileges were restricted to juniors and seniors (*Marq.*, 13 Oct. 1972, MA).[35] Other calls for order and for neatness during the decade came mostly from the students themselves.[36]

The 1972 parents' survey raised other issues, especially about academic standards and about the adequacy of the religion program, which now included courses in Eastern Thought and Counterculture, World Religions, Unanswered Questions, and Conscience and Social Concern (IHSPPS, 21 Feb. 1972, MA). One of the sources of concern among parents may have been the high school's shift to modular scheduling and to expanded electives, changes typical of both private and public high schools across the country in the 1970s. In any case, such changes— combined with Immaculata's rapid turnover of faculty (eighteen new faculty members in 1971 alone, several of them young, freshly trained IHMs just out of graduate school or with only two or three years of

34. Notes of 14 Mar. 1972 give preliminary results of the survey, based on 213 responses (of 750 possible).

35. In 1972, the IHM congregation appointed faculty member James P. Joyce as principal of the high school, the only male and non-IHM to serve in that capacity. Although the appointment of a male principal may have had to do with security and discipline concerns or with fundraising, it was not an unusual decision in Detroit in the 1970s: the IHMs also appointed a male principal of Marian High School, and the Dominicans did the same at Dominican High, both all-girl high schools.

36. See, for example, various articles in the *Marquee* (MA): "Give a Hoot; Don't Pollute IH" (13 Oct. 1971); "Assemblies: What's Lacking?" (13 Oct. 1972); "Graffiti: Right to Write?" (20 Dec. 1972); "Dance Policy Should Be Changed" (11 Nov. 1974); "What Happened to School Spirit?" (13 Feb. 1976); "The Cafe: a Mess!" (19 Dec. 1975); "The Issue: Changing An Image" (18 Nov. 1976); " 'Rapport' is Two-Way Street" (15 Feb. 1978).

teaching experience)—must have made the high school seem a very different place to parents who were themselves alumnae or who had educated older daughters at Immaculata (*Marq.*, 13 Oct. 1971, MA).

Although the curriculum revisions clearly changed the disciplined structure on which Immaculata's reputation had been built, parents had less to fear than they originally thought, as Immaculata's young women students continued to distinguish themselves academically. From 1970 to 1978, for example, Immaculata had at least six finalists, thirty semifinalists, and twenty-six commended students in the competition for scholarships from the National Merit Scholarship Program and from the National Achievement Program for Outstanding Negro Students (*Marq.*, vols. 1–8, MA).[37] In 1972–73, Immaculata ranked first in the state of Michigan among all-girls schools in the number of students named as semifinalists or as commended students in the National Merit competition, stood third among Michigan high schools in the National Achievement Program, and had the highest number of semifinalists of any IHM-operated high school in the country. In the 1974–75 school year alone, over fifty seniors won scholarships to such colleges as the University of Michigan, Northwestern, Vassar, and Spelman (*Marq.*, 22 Nov. 1972, 30 May 1975, MA).

Like their predecessors, Immaculata students of the 1970s regard their own education with pride. "I truly enjoyed my four years there and felt that some of the advanced courses I took in English and math were as challenging, if not more so, than classes I took in college," said a 1972 graduate. A 1973 alumna reported: "I had attended a co-ed high school for two years, then transferred to Immaculata for the junior term. During my senior year I received a scholarship to Wayne State University that required my taking college courses while still in high school. Immaculata faculty had an unmatched expectation of student preparation, participation and class involvement that I did not experience at the prior high school or at the college level." Similar sentiments persisted among graduates of the 1980s. Said a student who would have been in Immaculata's 1984 class had it remained open: "The atmosphere was extremely intellectual. To give an example, a regular or light amount of homework for my psychology class was considered by several of my public school peers as very heavy. I learned so much in my three years of French at IH, that my senior year at Marian High, I got an A in French IV, having attended only half the semester's worth of classes" (IHSAS 1992, quest. 72A, 73C, 84A).

37. See, for example, the following *Marquee* articles: "Joyce Hurley, Helen Ann Davis Win Top Awards" (18 Mar. 1971); "Twelve Students Receive NMSQT Recognition" (13 Oct. 1971); "NMSQT Results Boost School" (22 Nov. 1972); "NMS Winners Announced" (15 Nov. 1973); "Seniors Awarded Scholarships" (30 May 1975); "Ceremony Honors Seniors" (4 June 1976); "NMSQT Recognizes Eight IH Students" (18 Nov. 1976); "Four IHers Receive Recognition as National Merit Semifinalists" (18 Nov. 1977), all in MA.

The IHM tradition of bringing progressive speakers to the high school also continued in the 1970s and early 1980s. On the Immaculata stage from which Dorothy Day had espoused radical Catholicism in the 1950s, Jane Fonda, Tom Hayden, and Holly Near in 1972 advocated political revolution. In the gym where a white priest had asked for "justice for a persecuted part of the Mystical Body," the black activist attorney Kenneth Cockrel, known for his criticism of a Detroit police force he regarded as racist, discussed law enforcement with Immaculata students. In assemblies formerly given to missionary sisters discussing the medical needs of children in India, Bishop Thomas Gumbleton talked about hungry children in Africa and Mother Waddles spoke of her Perpetual Mission program, an effort to feed hungry families in Detroit (*Marq.*, 13 Oct. 1972, 28 Feb. 1973, 10 Oct. 1974, and 13 Dec. 1974, MA).

The Immaculata commitment to activism also remained high during this period, although now often tinged with protest. In 1971, for example, Immaculata's student government president, joined by classmates and by faculty members, led a protest march and testified in front of Detroit's Common Council against United States nuclear warhead testing; likewise, in 1973, in addition to the traditional Christmas Drive, Immaculata students sponsored a food drive for California farmworkers who were staying on the Marygrove campus while organizing grape boycotts (*Marq.*, 24 Nov. 1971, 11 Oct. 1973, MA). In addition to the newly formed Immaculata Volunteer Corps, the student government's CAM program (variously called the Christian or Community Action Movement) sent Immaculata volunteers to schools, soup kitchens, food prescription centers, hospitals, senior citizen homes, drug centers, and court-watching programs. Each year, under the direction of the religion faculty and of the committees of the United Students of Immaculata, IHS students participated in the multiple activities of Hunger Week and Human Rights Week (*Marq.*, vols. 1–8; IHSYB, 1970–79, MA). Although less confined to Catholic causes, the social action agenda of Immaculata did not abate during its last full decade.

## Women's Place Revisited

Given the IHMs' own departure from tradition during this period, it was perhaps inevitable that the 1970s also marked the advent of a less traditional message about women's place. "The IHM sisters and lay female teachers were all intelligent, highly motivated individuals who had strong convictions and opinions on life generally and what roles women [could] and should play," a 1972 graduate recalled. "I attended high school . . . [when] women were just beginning to enter non-traditional fields and become more career-oriented. My experience was that the IHM Sisters encouraged that movement and tried to cultivate an atmosphere that would give . . . young, impressionable girls the confidence to embark on the paths of self-fulfillment through education" (IHSAS 1992, quest. 72A).

"I Am Woman" was the motif of the 1973 yearbook, and the 1976 bicentennial volume was devoted to women in Detroit history. In 1974, a column on women's issues became a regular feature of the school newspaper; the same year, the IHM community sponsored an all-day woman's seminar at Immaculata, during which (the *Marquee* reported) women could select from among twenty-six workshop sessions ranging from a basic history of the women's movement to sex discrimination in insurance. Following IHM and Immaculata tradition, the keynote speaker was a Catholic nun, Sister Albertus Magnus McGrath, O.P., who told her audience that too many women were still bound by traditional notions that their "only objective in life was to snare a husband" or that they were "too frail to withstand the pressures of an executive position." The seminar concluded with a paraliturgical service because, the Immaculata reporter noted, "it seemed inconsistent with the views and goals of the seminar to have a mass where the central celebrant was a man" (*Marq.*, 21 May 1974, MA).

This antipatriarchal analysis carried over into the high school's last decade. As an alumna who was a junior when the high school closed observed, "I learned that a woman's place was the place where the woman wanted to be—successful physically, mentally, emotionally, and financially" (IHSAS 1992, quest. 84A).

## The Challenge of Racial Change

In September 1971, Immaculata enrolled 642 students; one year later, the number was 470 (ARBEI 1971, 1972, MA). In the face of such a sharp decline, the school's administrators were forced to reevaluate the school's future. The discussion inevitably took shape along racial as well as along financial lines. In 1960, the immediate Immaculata neighborhood had been 99 percent white; approximately 8 of 183 girls in Immaculata's 1965 freshman class were black. By 1971, 75 percent of the neighborhood was black, one of the highest rates of ethnic turnover in Detroit during the 1960s (MgNCSS, Dec. 1976, 48, OAD), and 122 of 187 students in that year's freshman class were black (IHSYB 1966–72; ARBEI 1965–71, MA).[38]

Comments from Immaculata's feeder schools (especially from parishes located west of the high school) in 1970–71 left no doubt as to the causes of the sudden decline in enrollment. "The area in which [Immaculata] is located is a factor which turns many girls away. Many girls are

---

38. The percentage of black students in the freshman class doubled from 7 to 14 percent from 1965 to 1969, then doubled again to 35 percent in 1970, and nearly doubled again in 1971 to 65 percent.

impressed with what the school offers, but hesitate to go out of fear," wrote one principal from a school just a short bus ride down McNichols. The principal of a school in Redford Township commented:

> Parents fear sending their girls into that area. I feel very sorry about this as I classify your school as a very fine educational institution. In the past and even now I have encouraged the girls to attend Immaculata but I'm meeting much more opposition which is based on fear. Some of the students have commented on the fact that many of the black students at Immaculata are militant and some feel the black students are favored. I realize stories are often exaggerated but . . . I'm mentioning it because I feel you should know some of the feedback. (IHSNCRM 1970–71, MA)

Immaculata's biggest and oldest feeder school reported that "among white students going to Immaculata . . . there is a growing feeling of frustration that the school caters to black demands and blackness is more important than qualification." The principal also noted that "a considerable number [of students] are being attracted to Mercy" (IHSNCRM 1970–71, MA). Indeed, in the early 1970s, Mercy High School, a suburban all-girls high school, began bus service from the Gesu area to Farmington Hills, even though at the time many suburbanites were arguing vehemently against impending court-ordered cross-district busing in metropolitan Detroit.

The Immaculata administration and IHM congregational leaders began to draw up pro and con arguments about the school's future. Finances, predictably, were essential to the discussion, for in the 1970–71 school year Immaculata was projected to use $50,000 in savings to meet operating costs, leaving it with a $30,000 deficit and with an obvious need to increase tuition and fees (KIO 1970, IHSF, MA). The bulk of the IHM discussion, however, centered on Immaculata's redefined place in the city. On her list of reasons for closing, the principal cited white fear of blacks, the prejudice of some of Immaculata's teachers (who were "sometimes the cause of race problems in the school"), the loss of enrollment from white flight and from diminished feeder schools, and a perception in the neighborhood that Immaculata was "an elite white school uninvolved in the community in which it exist[ed]" (AIC 1970, IHSF, MA). Other Immaculata administrators noted that declining enrollment had made it necessary to accept students who had difficulty following a college preparatory course; that the school's all-white faculty could never meet the needs of the rapidly growing black student population; and—surprisingly, coming from seasoned IHM administrators—that there was "little external evidence that Immaculata graduates [were] any better Christians than graduates of good public schools" (FACI 1970, IHSF, MA).

On the other hand, in their list of "pro" arguments, they noted that Immaculata contributed to maintaining integration in the civic community and was meeting the need for a college-preparatory school in what was now being called by some the "inner city" (FACI 1970, IHSF, MA). The principal's argument for continuing the school zeroed in on its social mission: "Perhaps the most valued reason I see at this time for keeping Immaculata open is the fact that racial integration is just beginning in a big way and the challenge to help the . . . white girl understand her black sister would be a unique contribution to our city . . . at this time" (KIO 1970, IHSF, MA). These justice considerations would characterize IHM discussions of Immaculata until it closed.

Although the archdiocese assisted Immaculata financially from 1972 through 1978, the IHM congregation absorbed a $80,000 deficit in school year 1979–80, then aggressively pursued several avenues for keeping Immaculata open (Marq., 4 Apr. 1978; GSR 1976–82, 1982–88, MA). These options included reorganizing it as an archdiocesan regional school, collaborating in an ecumenical venture with the Lutheran schools, developing new structures with Marygrove College, and consulting with the black community on the need for a women's high school. However, promising avenues turned into dead ends in the face of the archdiocese's demographic predictions, the Lutheran schools' concerns about security, Marygrove's own precarious financial situation, and preferences among parents for the Detroit Public Schools' excellent, co-ed Renaissance High School (newly opened in the former Catholic Central High School, just a few miles from Immaculata). As tuition went up and enrollment fell in the wake of Detroit's declining population and economic desperation, it became impossible to convert good will and community spirit into capital improvements and scholarship funds.[39]

Exaggerated white perceptions of "black militancy" no doubt caused Immaculata's period of genuine racial integration to be very brief—perhaps two or three years—and that period was often marked with tension.

---

39. The 1981–82 enrollment dropped by 25 percent from the previous year, leaving Immaculata with a student body of 200, the size of one class in the 1950s. On 13 Dec. 1982, the IHM Governing Board met in special session to review 1982 census data and the public schools' study of population trends, 1983–84 placement test results, projected enrollments for 1983–84, and proposals for collaborative planning mentioned earlier. Given the realities of an overworked faculty and staff at the high school, a reduced curriculum, escalating tuition, an underutilized building, and the community's own median age, decreasing membership, and declining numbers applying to teach at Immaculata, the Governing Board agreed that the high school should close with dignity. At the same time, the Governing Board noted that the decision was "painful and difficult" because Immaculata "embodied many cherished congregational values—service to the poor, commitment to the education of women, use of our resources in action on behalf of justice." The formal decision to close Immaculata occurred at the regular meeting of the Governing Board, 14 Jan. 1983 (GSR 1982–88, MA).

In autumn 1971, for instance, the *Marquee* reported that Immaculata, "an integrated school population-wise and trying hard to become one by conviction," had held two days of assemblies "in an attempt to repair some of the severed relationships between Blacks and Whites." From the discussions in large and small groups, the reporter concluded, "came the nucleus of mutual understanding which hopefully will develop in the months ahead" (*Marq.*, 24 Nov. 1971, MA).[40]

More often than not, the administration and faculty approached racial tensions as opportunities to practice Immaculata's ideals. Requests for a Black Student Association, for example, were regarded as signs of student leadership rather than as militant demands, and struggles over whether to play James Taylor or Sly and the Family Stone in the senior lounge were left to students themselves to work out, with faculty help as needed.[41] Often, the faculty encouraged students to use the structures already in place to resolve differences; for instance, when a *Marquee* article excoriated the church for never having been relevant to the needs of black Catholics or of the black community, a student letter to the editor in a later issue attempted a rebuttal but kept the issue in the public forum for debate (*Marq.*, 21 Dec. 1971, 7 Mar. 1972, MA). Offcampus class retreats, too, played their part in letting students meet one another on common ground.[42]

For Immaculata students of the 1970s, whether white or black, what constituted an "insider" or "outsider" was little different from what earlier alumnae reported: attendance at Gesu Elementary School, clothes, intelligence, participation in extracurriculars, boyfriends, being "fast." However, alumnae of that decade also report the benefits of crossing over barriers that earlier graduates did not face so directly. "There seemed to be a lot of camaraderie between students of varied backgrounds," wrote one veteran of the "black-white" assemblies. "It was my first experience of integration as I attended an all-white elementary and lived in a primarily Polish-Catholic neighborhood. [IHS] provided a foundation for my socially liberal attitude today." A 1973 alumna wrote: "The student popu-

40. A year later, when the principal called an assembly and asked the students "to be friends with each other, so that Immaculata would really be integrated, not just attended by blacks and whites," a *Marquee* editorial writer noted that some girls responded that they already were friends and "ran around in the cafeteria saying, 'Come on, let's integrate,' and passed it off as a joke." To the writer, however, "hassles" over bands for dances indicated that the principal might be right and "it's up to us to keep moving forward" (20 Dec. 1972, MA).

41. In fact, the *Marquee* reported that "the goals of the association are to promote better relations between blacks and whites at IH and in the community" (24 Nov. 1971, MA). See also *Marq.*, 7 Mar. 1972, MA.

42. In a description of an offcampus retreat for twenty-four juniors, the *Marquee* reported that "cliques, racial tensions, money, Christ, and personal hang-ups were just a few of the topics covered" (7 Mar. 1972, MA).

lation was diverse politically and racially. Broadly, the relationships reflected those outside in society. There were segregationist factions among
both whites and blacks, yet it seemed to me that the majority of students
crossed racial barriers in their friendships." Finally, a 1978 grad recalled:
"Aside from the established cliques, everyone was very open to new
friendships. I had the most ample opportunities at IH for making friends
of other ages and races and socio-economic backgrounds than I have
[had] at any other time in my life. I truly miss that, as the older I become,
the more distance I feel from my sisters out there in the world" (IHSAS
1992, quest. 72A, 73C, 78B).

## Conclusion

The women's education offered at Immaculata through its first
twenty-five years was, in many ways, a picture of ambivalence. On the
one hand, the IHMs kept the promises of the original prospectus: In the
name of dedication to Mary Immaculate, the sisters urged their students
to be self-disciplined, generous, obedient, refined, and self-sacrificing
models of ideal feminine behavior. Loyal to the church, the IHMs reinforced in their students the doctrines, rituals, and traditions of Roman
Catholicism. Believing in the place of a woman at the center of family
life, they cultivated in their pupils the "home arts," the virtues that would
serve husbands, sons, daughters, parents, parish priests, and bishops
competently and well. Moreover, convinced of the power of education,
the IHM sisters and their Immaculata students trained themselves in the
skills that would take them to the world of women's work—to teaching,
nursing, social work, secretarial support, and all of the traditional helping
professions.

However, the IHMs' most ardently espoused ideals often contained
within themselves contradictory impulses—oppositional subtexts or corrective interpretive instincts—that had the potential to subvert the very
way the IHMs and their students defined themselves as women. Publicly
identified as they were with the central woman in Christian iconography,
the Blessed Virgin Mary, the IHMs and their Immaculata students were
constantly drawing their religious strength not from a male model but
from a mother figure of great strength, whose powers hinted at their own
gifts and capacities. Though always regarded as loyal daughters of the
church, the IHMs and their students were, at the same time, equally
faithful to the *Ecclesia semper reformanda* dimension of the institutional
church and thus actively embraced the social encyclicals and lay movements that critiqued the traditional exercise of power. Never apparently
questioning the place of woman at the center of the family, the IHMs and
their Immaculata students nonetheless daily redefined home and family,
making the words conjure any place where strong women gathered in

friendship to do worthwhile work. Finally, never denying their intellectual gifts, the IHMs and their Immaculata students even explored worlds and entertained ideas that sometimes challenged—or at least questioned—the conventional pieties of their religion.

The Immaculata that emerged in the aftermath of Vatican II, the Detroit riots, and Proposal C was equally the offspring of this deep-rooted impulse towards redefining women's place; thus, the "new" school was no less the product of IHM corporate identity than was its 1941 foremother. In its last seventeen years, Immaculata was still a woman's high school, led by women instructors and women students and supported by women's organizations. It was an academic community where teachers and students put high demands on each other in a full range of courses. It was a religious community, rooted in Catholic tradition and ritual but also grounded in progressive Catholic social thought and service to the community.

As in 1941, Immaculata in 1983 was an extension of the IHM personality—organized, neat, and disciplined, but also innovative and occasionally daring. It was a place where teachers and students respected cultural taboos and carefully avoided some topics, but it was also a community where young women and their teachers tried to address together the life questions of young adults. Perhaps most consistently, it was a daily gathering of friends, where many young women forged lifetime relationships and often crossed ethnic, social, economic, and racial boundaries to do so.

Thus, the story of Immaculata is less an account of polarization than a record of a struggle for continuity, less a narrative of resignation than a glimpse of an effort to transform old categories into new relationships, all within a context in which one factor did not change. Immaculata remained, from beginning to end, an IHM enterprise, an institution of "sisters out there in the world."

# Afterword

Maryfran Barber, i.h.m., and Nancy Sylvester, i.h.m.

## The Beginning

Ten women gathered on Friday evening, 9 March 1990, to discuss how they could write a feminist, interdisciplinary IHM history. They knew implicitly that how the work was done would determine the shape and the impact of what was done. Thirteen months, seven meetings, and 250 hours of work later, the implicit became explicit as no. 11 of the "Working Assumptions for the Claiming Our Roots Project": "Believing that the *way* we do feminist history is crucial to what we discover as our history, we will design a feminist process for the history project that includes active participation, collaboration, and consciousness of our own biases" (see appendix).

Even a reading of the individual essays does not tell the whole story of Claiming Our Roots. The circle is completed only with an understanding of how this volume came to be.

Margaret Susan Thompson, in the Introduction, discusses the "concentric circles of sisterhood" that shaped the project and this volume. The circle is an appropriate metaphor: The dynamic of a circle is cyclic, and cycles are integral both to the COR project and to *Building Sisterhood*. The work took shape in three cycles—exploration and planning, writing, and publishing. This afterword will focus on the first two cycles.

## Exploration and Planning

The ten women who gathered on that Friday evening were an astonishing mix. Every decade of life was represented, from the thirties to the eighties. The group included theologians, chemists, a literature professor, a political activist, a sociologist, a psychologist, and a historian. There were radical feminists, there were women wary of feminism, there were women unaware of the feminist perspective, and there were those who were in between. They shared an interest in the history of their community, the Sisters, Servants of the Immaculate Heart of Mary, and they shared a willingness to listen and to learn.

As the discussion began, each person told the group why she had come and where she was coming from. Each shared her hopes and her concerns about what lay ahead. The patterns that emerged that evening energized and shaped the work of the next several years. COR became a circle of collegiality whose members concerned themselves with:

Attending to the emotional, intellectual, and spiritual aspects of the group and of the individuals within it;

Sharing perspectives, ideas, and visions;

Listening and responding to one another in order to achieve mutual understanding;

Studying together feminist perspectives and history;

Collectively defining the shape and scope of the project;

Participating inclusively in group tasks;

Appreciating (and nearly becoming addicted to) "trail mix," a seductive sweet/salt indulgence made of nuts, raisins, and M&Ms. It became a barometer of our intensity—the more gripping was the interaction, the more trail mix was consumed.

The first cycle moved through twenty months, from early March 1990 until November 1991. It was decided at that first meeting that the project would lead to a collection of essays, arranged by themes or by decisive events, approached with incisive questions, and infused with a feminist perspective.

The meetings took place in a circle. Thirteen women (ten of them consistent members) spent hundreds of hours working together and hundreds more hours laboring individually and in small circles, or subcommittees. The dynamic was cyclic, as well: A topic was approached, returned to later for animated discussion, reflected upon, and eventually settled by group assent. The effect was to create consensus and a group identity that had an organic texture to it.

The development of the document "Working Assumptions for the Claiming Our Roots Project" is a dramatic example. The group's initial conversations about feminist perspective and feminist history led to the suggestion in May 1990 that the group set forth assumptions. In July, after an extensive discussion, one person was asked to write them. That list of assumptions was reviewed and extensively discussed in September; a revised draft was discussed in December and again in February 1991. By April, the process had come full circle: the group embraced seventeen working assumptions about history, about feminist history, and about the COR process and product.

The consensus was created by the process. Each person spoke from her own perspective; everyone else listened. That provided a forum for those who were uncertain about the legitimacy of feminist history, who wondered whether facts and objective data would be used, who worried that criticism of patriarchy would be disrespectful. The process of identifying fears assuaged them. The process of discussing ideas helped to focus them. The result was a clear statement of beliefs and intentions; the group now "owned" a set of underlying assumptions.

Moreover, this process intensified the trust and respect members had for one another. Indeed, the lexicon changed from "you" to "we." The core group of ten women became a cohesive unit.

The circular dynamic was ratified by success. It then became possible to produce this book using a deliberative, inclusive method of decision making to work through all the steps associated with the creation and completion of a major anthology. The process was reinforced and enriched by socializing and by sharing IHM oral history.

The emphasis, however, stayed on the work, task by task. The selection of writers for the book is a good illustration of the process. After identifying nine topic areas and several potential subtopics, the ten women realized they needed more writers. So, in April 1991, a notice in the *Spinnaker* (the IHM community's newspaper) announced and explained the project and invited applications. There were forty-six responses. COR members set aside a full week—from Friday to Friday, 9 through 16 August 1991—to make decisions and to launch the research and writing phases. They met at the IHM motherhouse in Monroe, Michigan. They deferred final decisions until Thursday, allowing time for the process to work its magic.

The importance of ritual was also experienced during that week. On Sunday, the archivist for the IHM congregation cut a ribbon strung across the entrance to the archives and called each woman to enter. Once inside, all were seated in a circle, surrounded by a circle of poster-size photographs of several deceased IHMs. As the COR members celebrated the lives of these extraordinary women, they also gave voice to ordinary women prevented by historical circumstances from expressing their own voices during their lifetimes. COR became a circle within a circle of sisters.

During that week, the process of selecting the writers challenged the group process and affirmed it, even as it challenged and affirmed individual members. Each COR member rated the forty-six applications, and the scores were averaged. Applications were considered individually and were discussed until a consensus was reached. The emotions were strong and the ideas equally powerful as the process moved forward.

The intensity of the experience is captured in an excerpt from a COR member's presentation on 28 June 1992 to the History of Women Religious Conference at Tarrytown, New York:

I remember that August week as a slice of the possible. My sense of it was that the growth we had experienced together and the insight and the excitement that we had experienced all jelled in rather stunning ways for us. And it had to do, to a large extent, with the rhythm that we established. That's been a primary learning for us in terms of being together. There was a larger overall rhythm and then a more precise rhythm for decision-making.

We alternated tasks that week, and that kept our energy moving, because the sessions for choices of writers were very difficult for us. We came apprehensive about saying no to anyone—wondering who we were to say no to our friends, to each other possibly, and to some of the great women of the congregation. We had to articulate that apprehension and then move beyond it, asking always what would serve the project best and working from the criteria we had set out. We spent long sessions every day for the entire week before we completed the process.

Those sessions were intermingled with sessions of sitting at our computers in the archives in a sort of electric silence, then moving into meals and evenings where we could be together, just laughing and sharing stories. . . .

Finally, in terms of the more defined, tighter process of decision-making, we also established a rhythm. Our "grid" for selecting writers is a good example. We had our nine topic areas posted like a tic-tac-toe board. As we worked with the applications, we kept before us the priorities we'd set so that as we chose writers, we also slotted them in according to our topics and emphases. There were some very difficult times during that process, and we developed a habit of getting everything out onto the table—all feelings, everything we thought, all questions—grappling as long as we could with differences, and then "sleeping" on the whole issue. We would come back to a particular discussion sometimes for several days.

At one point in particular, we got gridlocked: it was evening, late in the week, and I remember crawling away from the table. Trail mix did not even bring us back to a sense of ourselves.

The next morning, someone snatched up a piece of chalk and began drawing arrows across some of those lines and recombining topic areas. There was a surge of energy and we were able to move forward. We came to a final schema that satisfied everybody. I think that where we have consistently stayed with a thing, put the conflict out there, not submerged differences, hammered at it, allowed that rhythm, we have been very creative and we've all owned the outcome.

COR's working patterns are evident in this narrative: the rhythm of looking at an issue, leaving it, and then returning later, and the pattern of addressing the work together emotionally as well as intellectually. What is less evident is that although the group attempted to deal with each application evenly and directly, at least one person considered the discussion of some applications to be much less probing than the discussion of others. Nonetheless, this work—done together and in an atmosphere of honesty and of confidentiality—was exhausting, challenging, and productive.

## The Writing Cycle Begins

During the thirty-one months from November 1991 to June 1994, the emphasis was on the product—the essays that would comprise this volume—and time became a new pressure. The project was commissioned by an administration that was to end (in the normal cycle of IHM leadership) in June 1994, so that date became the deadline. Within the frame of limited time and with a new task—writing—the work proceeded in the same rhythmic movement of cycles.

The group had to reshape itself to fit the new phase. The original ten became the COR Committee, overseeing the process and most of the project's administrative matters, planning meetings, and—except for the archivist—also working as writers. The original ten plus the new writers became the COR Writers Group. Fifteen women were now involved. Another person also joined the group at that time: once the project was well under way, the COR Committee had determined that an outside editor was needed. A national search turned up dozens of applications, and a subcommittee was put to work on the selection process. Several finalists were interviewed, and the names of two candidates were presented to the full committee, who made the final choice by consensus.

Julie Wortman, whose background included service on the communications staff of the national headquarters of the Episcopal Church and the managing editorship of a Detroit-based magazine, agreed to serve as editor to the COR collaborative project. She understood that unlike the editors of more traditional collections—where the editor frames the topics, selects the contributors, and writes the introductions and possibly an essay as well—the person serving as editor to the COR project had to be willing to enter into the group process, to believe in the operating assumptions, and to engage in the collaborative group critique. Wortman brought her skills to that part of the job as well as to the usual editorial tasks: offering suggestions on format and style, editing each essay, and working with each author on the revisions. However, final control—both artistic and intellectual—fell somewhere between the individual writer and the collective of writers (including the editor) rather than residing with the editor alone.

New faces required new alliances. The weekend of 15–17 November 1991 was a time for forging new ties with tried and true COR dynamics —a combination of ritual, sharing, relaxation, and a rhythm that allowed time to discuss and to clarify before final choices were made. For the original ten from the COR Committee, it was a difficult process of letting go of an experience that had transformed them and had bonded them one to another, but it was time to open the circle to include new sisters so that the body and the work could expand in a wider arc.

At first, the smoothness of the original COR process carried over, because the writing cycle phase was structured to reflect the rhythm that had been successful earlier. The COR Writers Group gave themselves eighteen months to refine topics, develop theses, prepare outlines, and write first drafts. In each meeting during this cycle, there was time for the authors to meet with others writing on similar topics, to present material, to receive feedback, and to respond.

However, looming deadlines—an August 1993 first draft, a February 1994 final revision, a June 1994 completion date—began to exert extraordinary pressures. The final deadline was tied to a singular event (the expiration of an administrative term) and not to the needs of a project that depended on a certain rhythm and on the time-consuming dynamic of participatory decision making. The COR Committee members, largely consumed with researching and writing their own essays, could hardly function as overseers as well. Moreover, the tight time frame did not allow for different working styles. During the August 1993 review of first drafts, tensions rose between those writers who made the deadlines and those whose creative processes demanded more flexibility. By February 1994, time pressures, missed deadlines, and less attentiveness to process demanded that the COR writers engage in critiques of final drafts in writing and by mail rather than in the sisterly collegiality of face-to-face discussions. This turned out to be a painful individual and collective experience; for some, it was the first time during the process that they had received significant critical feedback, and they felt surprised and blindsided.

When the COR Writers Group met in March 1994, ostensibly to sign off on the essays, significant time had to be given to what had been intended and what had been felt as a result of the written critiques. In the end the issues raised during this session and in the critiques served to make the final product better. Realizing that neither the essays nor the group process had come to genuine closure, the group agreed to meet again. In June 1994, tempered by the difficulties of the preceding months but trusting in their own resiliency, they ratified the essays and celebrated the talents of their individual members as well as the accomplishments of the group.

## Conclusion

COR was a positive, productive experience for the participants and for the IHM community. This is true in spite of—or perhaps because of —the tension, conflict, struggle, and pain. How could this be so? The process of circling, of establishing and then following a rhythm, allowed each person to express feelings and thoughts. The cycle allowed time to interact around those feelings and thoughts; just as important, it allowed time away from the discussion, and it made the most of the moment of return. When the cycle remained intact, it was possible to work through to a resounding consensus. When the cycle was broken due to time pressures or inattention to the process, the group was unable to reach consensus no matter how much work was done.

COR participants, like their sisters in the IHM community and their brothers and sisters in the human race, were (and are) all different. Their individuality was (and is) a source of strength as well as an occasion of struggle. What resulted from COR was growth, for the group and for the individuals.

It is too early to assess the legacy of COR, either its process or its product, in the historical sense. It is not too early to proclaim that it made a significant difference in the lives of those who participated. It demonstrated that people with diverse perspectives can work together in meaningful and fruitful ways for the sake of something they cherish and share. Finally, it provided for the readers of this volume an introspective look across one-and-a-half centuries of life in a religious community of women. In making the journey to tell the story, the COR Writers Group have widened their circle of sisterhood. They also have widened the circle of knowledge for all who care to join.

Appendix
Bibliography
Index

APPENDIX

# Working Assumptions for
# the Claiming Our Roots Project

### Working Assumptions about History

1. All history, including feminist history, is first of all grounded in factual data.

2. History in all its forms is interpretive.

3. Constructing history cannot be confined to formal written expression but should include the information and insights that come from oral, visual, and audio sources.

4. The construction of history can employ the educated guess and invention.

5. A hermeneutic of suspicion is essential to writing good history. The hermeneutic must be evenly applied to all elements of the task, i.e., to previously written accounts, to all sources old and new, to the authorities used to justify interpretations, and to the historian's own biases. A critical perspective attempts to be loyal to the truth, not disloyal to the past.

### Working Assumptions about Feminist History

6. Feminist history is an academically rooted school of history which takes as its focus the lives of women, reconstructing those lives where necessary, and giving particular attention to issues of gender in the shaping of women's lives.

7. In practice, a range of feminist ideologies exist, but feminist approaches to history accept as a starting point that patriarchy exists in society and in its institutions, including the churches.

8. Feminist history is done in a socio-economic, political, cultural context.

9. Feminist history assumes that it is necessary to examine both the private and the public lives of women, and feminist history values the ordinary as well as the extraordinary.

10. Feminist history recognizes that women have oppressed other women.

From the Claiming Our Roots Committee, Apr. 1991, SSIHM, Monroe Archive.

## Working Assumptions about the COR Process and Product

11. Believing that the *way* we do feminist history is crucial to what we discover as our history, we will design a feminist process for the history project that includes active participation, collaboration, and consciousness of our own biases.

12. Applying the process named above, we will produce a collection of feminist historical essays.

13. Based on our experience in the task force and the needs of our project, we will recommend additional questions to be incorporated into the process of gathering the oral histories of the members of the Congregation.

14. Based on our experience in the task force and the needs of our project, we will recommend additional guidelines for adding historical materials to the Congregational archives.

15. We assume that we will meet for extended, concentrated, collaborative working sessions throughout the life of the project.

16. We assume that resources, while limited, will be available to the committee from the Congregation and from the committee to the Congregation.

17. We assume that the material(s) produced will be well-researched and communally critiqued.

# Bibliography

## Archival Sources

Archivium Generale Redemptoristarum, Rome, Italy.
Detroit Archdiocesan Archives, Detroit, Michigan.
Hamilton, Ontario, Diocesan Archives.
Oblate Sisters of Providence Archives, Baltimore, Maryland.
St. Joseph's Society of the Sacred Heart Archives, Nazareth, Kentucky.
Sisters of Charity of Nazareth Archives, Nazareth, Kentucky.
Sisters of Divine Providence Archives, Melbourne, Kentucky.
Sisters of the Holy Cross Archives, Notre Dame, Indiana.
Sisters of St. Mary of Oregon Archives, Beaverton, Oregon.
Sisters, Servants of the Immaculate Heart of Mary Archives, Immaculata, Pennsylvania.
Sisters, Servants of the Immaculate Heart of Mary Archives, Monroe, Michigan.
Sisters, Servants of the Immaculate Heart of Mary Archives, Scranton, Pennsylvania.
University of Notre Dame Archives, Notre Dame, Indiana.

## References

Abbott, Walter M., ed. 1966. *The Documents of Vatican II.* New York: Crossroad.

Alphonsus Liguori, St. ca. 1732. *Primitive Rules and Constitutions of Saint Alphonsus Liguori.* 1906. Translated by W. G. Licking, C.SS.R. 1961. Reprinted with permission. Monroe, Michigan: SSIHM.

American Psychiatric Association. 1987. *Diagnostic and Statistical Manual of Mental Disorders.* 3rd ed. Washington, D.C.: American Psychiatric Association.

Armitage, Susan, and Elizabeth Jameson. 1987. *The Women's West.* Norman: Univ. of Oklahoma Press.

Armstrong, Karen. 1981. *Through the Narrow Gate.* New York: St. Martin's.

———. 1983. *Beginning the World.* New York: St. Martin's.

Armstrong, Regis J., and Ignatius Brady, trans. 1982. "The Testament of Saint Clare (c. 1350)." In *Francis and Clare: The Complete Works,* 226–32. New York: Paulist.

Babson, Steve, et al. 1986. *Working Detroit: The Making of a Union Town.* Detroit: Wayne State Univ. Press.

*Baltimore Town and Fells Point Directory*. 1796. 1st. ed. (Located at the Maryland Historical Society.)

Bateson, Mary Catherine. 1990. *Composing a Life*. New York: Plume Penguin.

Beane, Marjorie Noterman. 1993. *From Framework to Freedom: A History of the Sister Formation Conference*. New York: Univ. Press of America.

Benedict XV, Pope. 1949. *Codex Iuris Canonici*. Westminster, Md.: Newman. (Originally published in 1917.)

Bernstein, Marcella. 1976. *Nuns*. London: William Collins.

Bogel, Edwina M., and Jane Marie Brach. 1983. *In All Things Charity: A Biography of Mother M. Colette Hilbert, Franciscan Sister of St. Joseph*. Hamburg, N.Y.: Privately published.

Boo, Mary Richard. 1991. *House of Stone: The Duluth Benedictines*. Duluth, Minn.: St. Scholastica Priory Books.

Brady, M. Teresa. 1962. *The Fruit of His Compassion*. New York: Pageant.

Brennan, Peg. n.d. "Persistence of Vision." Unpublished biography of Mother Stanislaus Leary, founder of the Rochester Sisters of Saint Joseph.

Bryk, Anthony S., Valerie E. Lee, and Peter B. Holland. 1993. *Catholic Schools and the Common Good*. Cambridge, Mass.: Harvard Univ. Press.

Callahan, Mary Generose. 1954. *History of the Sisters of Divine Providence, San Antonio, Texas*. Milwaukee: Bruce.

Carlen, Claudia, [I.H.M.]. 1990. *The Papal Encyclicals 1937–1958*. Ann Arbor, Mich.: Perian.

Carr, Anne. 1988. *Transforming Grace*. San Francisco: Harper and Row.

Chafe, William. 1972. *The American Woman: Her Changing Social, Economic and Political Roles*. New York: Oxford Univ. Press.

Chesler, Phyllis. 1972. *Women and Madness*. New York: Doubleday.

Chinnici, Joseph P. 1989. *Living Stones: The History and Structure of Catholic Spiritual Life in the United States*. New York: Macmillan.

Chittister, Joan, O.S.B., et al. 1977. *Climb Along the Cutting Edge: An Analysis of Change in Religious Life*. New York: Paulist

Ciarrocchi, Joseph W. 1995. *The Doubting Disease: Help for Scrupulosity and Religious Compulsions*. New York: Paulist.

Cook, Blanche Wiesen. 1992. *Eleanor Roosevelt*. Vol. 1. New York: Viking.

Cotel, Peter, S.J. 1924. *A Catechism of Vows*, revised and harmonized by Emile Jobert, S.J. New York: Benziger.

Cruesen, Joseph, S.J. 1953. *Religious Men and Women in the Code*. [Milwaukee: Bruce].

Curley, Michael J., C.SS.R. 1952. *Venerable John Neumann: Fourth Bishop of Philadelphia*. Washington, D.C.: Catholic Univ. of America Press.

———. 1963. *The Provincial Story: A History of the Baltimore Province of the Congregation of the Most Holy Redeemer*. New York: The Redemptorist Fathers, Baltimore Province.

Curran, Patricia. 1989. *Grace Before Meals: Food, Ritual and Body Discipline in Convent Culture*. Urbana: Univ. of Illinois Press.

Curry, Catherine Ann. 1989. "Population Statistics, 1820–1900: Statistical Study of Women Religious in the United States." Unpublished paper.

Cusack, Margaret Anna. 1891. *The Nun of Kenmare: An Autobiography*. Boston: Houghton, Mifflin.

[Danforth], Sister Maria Del Rey, M.M. 1956. *Bernie Becomes a Nun.* New York: Farrar, Straus and Cudahy.

Dehey, Elinor Tong. 1930. *Religious Orders of Women in the United States.* Rev. ed. Hammond, Ind.: W. B. Conkey.

Dolan, Jay P. 1992. *The American Catholic Experience: A History from Colonial Times to the Present.* Notre Dame, Ind.: Notre Dame Univ. Press.

Dulles, Avery. 1974. *Models of the Church.* Garden City, N.Y.: Doubleday.

Durkin, Mary Antonio, B.V.M. 1926. *The Preparation of the Religious Teacher: A Foundational Study.* Washington, D.C.: Catholic Univ. of America Press.

Eagar, Irene Ffrench. 1979. *Margaret Anna Cusack.* Dublin: Women's Press.

Ebaugh, Helen Rose Fuchs. 1977. *Out of the Cloister.* Austin: Univ. of Texas Press.

Eliot, T. S. 1930. "The Hollow Men." In *Collected Poems 1909–1935,* 101–5. New York: Harcourt, Brace.

Ellis, Havelock, and John Addington Symonds. 1897. *Sexual Inversion.* Vol. 1 of *Studies in the Psychology of Sex.* London: Wilson and Macmillan.

Ellis, Janice Rider, and Cecelia Love Hartley. 1988. *Nursing in Today's World.* Philadelphia: Lippincott.

Etzioni, Amatai. 1968. *Active Society.* New York: Free Press.

Ewens, Mary. 1978. "Removing the Veil: The Liberated American Nun in the Nineteenth Century." *Cushwa Center Working Paper* no. 3. Spring.

————. 1989. "Women in the Convent." In *American Catholic Women: A Historical Exploration,* edited by Karen Kennelly, 17–47. New York: Macmillan.

Faderman, Lillian. 1981. *Surpassing the Love of Men: Romantic Friendship and Love Between Women from the Renaissance to the Present.* New York: William Morrow.

Fecher, Con J. 1959. "Health and Longevity of Today's Sisters." *Catholic School Journal* 59, Nov. 1959, 67–69.

Ferraro, Barbara, and Patricia Hussey. 1990. *No Turning Back: Two Nuns' Battle with the Vatican over Women's Right to Choose.* New York: Poseidon.

FitzGerald, Constance. 1986. "Impasse and Dark Night." In *Women and Spirituality: Resources for Christian Development,* edited by Joann Wolski Conn, 287–311. New York: Paulist.

Flaxman, Radegunde. 1991. *A Woman Styled Bold: The Life of Cornelia Connelly, 1809–1879.* London: Darton, Longman and Todd.

Foucault, Michel. 1977. *Discipline and Punish: The Birth of the Prison.* New York: Pantheon Books.

Gannon, Margaret, I.H.M., ed. 1992. *Paths of Daring, Deeds of Hope: Letters by and about Mother Theresa Maxis Duchemin.* Scranton, Pa.: SSIHM.

Gilbert, Sandra M., and Susan Gubar. 1979. *The Madwoman in the Attic: The Woman Writer and the Nineteenth-Century Literary Imagination.* New Haven: Yale Univ. Press.

[Gillespie, Immaculata, I.H.M.]. 1921. *The Sisters of the I.H.M.: The Story of the Founding of the Congregation of the Sisters, Servants of the Immaculate Heart of Mary and Their Work in the Scranton Diocese.* New York: P. J. Kenedy and Sons.

Goffman, Erving. 1961. *Asylums.* Garden City, N.Y.: Doubleday.

Goldman, Howard H., ed. 1988. *Review of General Psychiatry.* Norwalk, Conn.: Appleton and Lange.

[Greene, John H.] 1885. "A Scrap of Romantic History: Rev. Mother Noel." *St. Joseph's Advocate,* 3, no. 3: 106–7.

Healy, Kathleen, ed. 1992. *Sisters of Mercy: Spirituality in America 1843–1900*. New York: Paulist.

Heilbrun, Carolyn. 1988. *Writing a Woman's Life*. New York: W. W. Norton.

Henninger, Marie Gabriel. 1979. *Sisters of Saint Mary and Their Healing Mission*. St. Louis: Privately published.

Hochman, Anndee. 1994. *Everyday Acts and Small Subversions: Women Reinventing Family, Community and Home*. Portland, Ore.: Eighth Mountain.

Hoegerl, Carl, C.SS.R. 1976. "Redemptorists: Men from the Heart of St. Alphonsus." *Spiritus-Patris: The Mark of St. Alphonsus on His Sons* 2, no. 3 (Nov.): 5, 56–65.

———. 1979. "Presentation at Saint Peter's, Reading, Pa.", audiotape, 7 Apr., 2 cassettes, duplicate copy in SSIHM Monroe Archive.

Jackson, Glenna S. 1994. "Naomi, Ruth, and Orpah." *The Bible Today* 32, no. 2 (Mar.): 68.

*Jerusalem Bible*. 1968. Edited by Alexander Jones. New York: Doubleday.

Johnson, Elizabeth A. 1993. *Women, Earth, and Creator Spirit*. The Madeleva lecture in spirituality. New York: Paulist.

Joseph, Sister Catherine, S.P. 1958. "Someone to Live For." In *Melody in Your Hearts*, edited by George L. Kane, 32–42. Westminster, Md.: Newman.

Kelley, Shirley Dykes. 1978. *Love Is Not For Cowards: The Autobiography of Shirley Dykes Kelley*. as told to Elizabeth Gullander. Englewood Cliffs, N.J.: Prentice-Hall.

[Kelly], Rosalita, I.H.M. 1948. *No Greater Service: The History of the Congregation of the Sisters, Servants of the Immaculate Heart of Mary*. Monroe, Mich.: [SSIHM].

———. 1960. "The Apostolate: A Convent Profile." *Worship* 35, 36–43.

Koester, Mary Camilla. 1980. "Appendix Two: Poor Clares from Bruges." In *Into this Land: A Centennial History of the Cleveland Poor Clare Monastery of the Blessed Sacrament*, 155–69. Cleveland: Robert J. Liederbach.

Kosmin, Barry A., and Seymour P. Lachman. 1993. *One Nation under God: Religion in Contemporary American Society*. New York: Harmony.

Kraman, Carlan. 1990. *Odyssey of Faith: The Story of Mother Alfred Moes*. Rochester, Minn.: Privately published.

Lefebvre, Dom Gaspar, comp. 1954. *St. Andrew Daily Missal*. Bruges: Abbey of St.-André.

Leo XIII, Pope. 1890. *Quaemadmodum*.

———. 1900. *Conditae a Christo*.

Levy, Amir, and Uri Merry. 1986. *Organizational Transformation: Approaches, Strategies, Theories*. New York: Praeger.

Lexau, Joan M. 1964. *Convent Life: Roman Catholic Religious Orders for Women in North America*. New York: Dial.

Lieblich, Julia. 1992. *Sisters: Lives of Devotion and Defiance*. New York: Ballantine.

Londoño, Noel B., C.SS.R. 1995. "Is the Spirituality of St. Alphonsus Up to Date?" Translated by Ruskin Piedra, C.SS.R. *Spiritus Patris: The Mark of St. Alphonsus on His Sons* 21 (Aug.): 33–39.

Ludwig, M. Mileta. 1950. *A Chapter of Franciscan History, 1849–1949*. New York: Bookman.

Major, Ralph. 1954. *A History of Medicine*. Vol. 2. Springfield, Ill.: Charles C. Thomas.

Maria Concepta, C.S.C. 1965. *The Making of a Sister-Teacher.* Notre Dame, Ind.: Univ. of Notre Dame Press.

Marygrove. 1927. *Souvenir Volume: Dedication of Marygrove College.* Detroit: Marygrove College.

Maynard, Theodore. 1948. *A Fire Was Lighted.* Milwaukee: Bruce.

McCarthy, Thompson, comp. 1952. *Guide to the Catholic Sisterhoods in the United States.* Washington, D.C.: Catholic Univ. of America Press.

[McGrath], Mary, I.H.M. 1952. *Meet a Friend of Mine, Raphael, Angel of Happiness.* [Detroit]: Marygrove College.

[McHugh], M. Xaveria, [I.H.M.]. 1928. *Mother Mary Clotilda and Early Companions of the Sisters, Servants of the Immaculate Heart of Mary.* New York: P. J. Kenedy and Sons.

McNamara, Jo Ann Kay. 1996. *Sisters in Arms: Catholic Nuns Through Two Millennia.* Cambridge, Mass.: Harvard Univ. Press.

McQuaide, Rosalie. 1992. " 'My Dear Lord': Letters from Margaret Anna Cusack to Bishop Winand Michael Wigger." Paper presented at the June 28–30 meeting of the History of Women Religious Network, Tarrytown, N.Y.

Mettler, Cecelia C. 1947. *History of Medicine: A Correlative Text, Arranged According to Subject.* Edited by Fred A. Mettler. Philadelphia: Blakiston.

[Meyers], Bertrande, D.C. 1941. *The Education of Sisters.* New York: Sheed and Ward.

———. 1965. *Sisters for the Twenty-First Century.* New York: Sheed and Ward.

Miles, Agnes. 1988. *Women and Mental Illness: The Social Context of Female Neurosis.* Brighton, Eng.: Wheatsheaf.

Misner, Barbara. 1982. "Historiography of Women's Religious Communities in the 19th Century." Paper presented at the conference Perspectives on American Catholicism, Nov. 19–20. Univ. of Notre Dame, Notre Dame, Ind.

Mitchell, Broadus. 1947. *Depression Decade.* Vol. 9. *The Economic History of the United States.* New York: Holt, Rinehart, and Winston.

Murphy, Angelina. 1980. *Mother Florence, A Biographical History.* Smithtown, N.Y.: Exposition.

Neill, Thomas P., and Raymond H. Schmandt. 1957. *History of the Catholic Church.* Milwaukee: Bruce.

*New Catholic Encyclopedia.* 1967. Prepared by an editorial staff at the Catholic Univ. of America. New York: McGraw-Hill.

*Official Catholic Directory.* 1920, 1930, 1960. New York: P. J. Kenedy and Sons.

O'Neill, Margaret Rose. 1990. *The Life of Mother Clare: Out from the Shadow of the Upas Tree.* Seattle: Privately published.

Paul VI, Pope. 1966. *Ecclesiae Sanctae.* NCWC translation, printed in the U.S. by the Daughters of Charity.

[Penet], Mary Emil, I.H.M. 1956. "The Sister Formation Conferences of the National Catholic Educational Association." Introduction to *The Mind of the Church in the Formation of Sisters,* edited by Sister Ritamary [Bradley], C.H.M. xv–xxxi. New York: Fordham Univ. Press.

Philibert, Paul, ed. 1994. *Living in the Meantime: Concerning the Transformation of Religious Life.* New York: Paulist.

Posey, Thaddeus, O.F.M. 1994. "Praying in the Shadows: The Oblate Sisters of Providence, A Look at Nineteenth Century Black Spirituality." *U.S. Catholic Historian* 12, no. 1: 11–30.

Powers-Waters, Alma. 1962. *St. Catherine Labouré and the Miraculous Medal*. New York: Vision.

Proceedings of the Sisters' Section of the First National Congress of Religious of the United States: *Religious Community Life in the United States*. 1952. New York: Paulist.

Quiñonez, Lora Ann, C.D.P., and Mary Daniel Turner, S.N.D.deN. 1992. *The Transformation of American Catholic Sisters*. Philadelphia: Temple Univ. Press.

Radner, Joan Newlon, ed. 1993. *Feminist Messages: Coding in Women's Folk Culture*. Urbana: Univ. of Illinois Press.

Radner, Joan N., and Susan S. Lanser. 1993. "Strategies of Coding in Women's Cultures." In *Feminist Messages*, edited by Joan N. Radner, 1–29. Urbana: Univ. of Illinois Press.

Raymond, Janice G. 1986. *A Passion for Friends: Toward a Philosophy of Female Affection*. Boston: Beacon.

*Recueil de Prières a l'Usage des Commuautés et des Membres de la Congrégation du Très St. Rédempteur*. 1844. Wittem, Belgium: C.SS.R.

Reilly, L. W. 1900. "A Famous Convent of Colored Sisters." *The Messenger of the Sacred Heart*. 35 (Dec.). 1099–1105.

*Report to the Everett Curriculum Workshop*. 1956. Washington, D.C.: Heiden's Mailing Bureau.

Rich, Adrienne. 1979. "When We Dead Awaken: Writing as Revision." In *On Lies, Secrets, and Silence: Selected Prose 1966–1978*. 33–49. New York: W. W. Norton.

———. 1986. "Resisting Amnesia." In *Blood, Bread and Poetry: Selected Prose 1979–1985*, 136–55. London: Virago.

Rigney, Barbara Hill. 1978. *Madness and Sexual Politics in the Feminist Novel*. Madison: Univ. of Wisconsin Press.

Riley, Glenda. 1986. *Inventing the American Woman: A Perspective on Women's History*. Arlington Heights, Ill.: Harland Davidson.

Rizzuto, Ana-Maria. 1979. *The Birth of the Living God: A Pyschoanalytic Study*. Chicago: Univ. of Chicago Press.

Rodriguez, Alphonsus. 1929. *Practice of Perfection and Christian Virtues*, 3 vols. Chicago: Loyola Univ. Press.

Russell, Sandi. 1990. *Render Me My Song: African-American Women Writers from Slavery to the Present*. New York: St. Martin's.

[Ryan], Maria Alma, I.H.M. 1967. *Sisters, Servants of the Immaculate Heart of Mary: 1845–1967*. Lancaster, Pa.: Dolphin.

Sanders, Helen. 1982. *More Than a Renewal: Loretto before and after Vatican II, 1952–1977*. Nerix, Ky.: Privately published.

Schmitz, Sylvester, O.S.B. 1927. *The Adjustment of Teacher Training to Modern Educational Needs: A Comparative Study of the Professional Preparation of Teachers in the Public and Catholic Elementary and Secondary Schools in the United States, with a Proposed Plan for the Training of Teachers for American Catholic Schools*. Atchison, Kans.: Abbey Student Press.

Schneiders, Sandra, I.H.M. 1986. *New Wineskins: Re-imaging Religious Life Today*. New York: Paulist.

———. 1991. *Beyond Patching: Faith and Feminism in the Catholic Church*. New York: Paulist.

Schoenberg, Wilfred P. 1986. *These Valiant Women: History of the Sisters of St. Mary of Oregon, 1886–1986*. Portland, Ore.: Privately published.

[Shanley, Loyola, I.H.M.]. 1916. *A Retrospect: Three Score and Ten*. New York: Benziger.

Shea, Diane Edward, and Marita-Constance Supan. 1983. "Apostolate of the Archives: God's Mystery Through History." *The Josephite Harvest*. (Summer). 10–13.

Sherwood, Grace H. 1929. "The Oblate Sisters of Providence: America's First Negro Religious Order." Part 1 of 3. *The Voice of the Students and Alumni of St. Mary's* 7, no. 3: 14–15.

——. 1931. *The Oblates One Hundred and One Years*. New York: Macmillan.

Sister Formation Conference. 1956. *The Mind of the Church in the Formation of Sisters: Selections from Addresses given during the Six Regional Conferences and the First National Meeting of the Sister Formation Conference, 1954–1955*. Edited by Sister Ritamary [Bradley], C.H.M. New York: Fordham Univ. Press.

——. 1957. *Spiritual and Intellectual Elements in the Formation of Sisters: Selections from Addresses and communications on Discussion Tapes from the Six Regional Meetings of the Sister Formation Conference, 1955–1956*. Edited by Sister Ritamary [Bradley], C.H.M. New York: Fordham Univ. Press.

——. 1958. *Planning for the Formation of Sisters: Studies on the Teaching Apostolate and Selections from Addresses of the Sister Formation Conference, 1956–1957*. Edited by Sister Ritamary [Bradley], C.H.M. New York: Fordham Univ. Press.

——. 1960. *The Juniorate in Formation: Proceedings and Communications from the Fourth Series of Regional Meetings of the Sister Formation Conference, 1957–1958*. Edited by Sister Ritamary [Bradley], C.H.M. New York: Fordham Univ. Press.

——. 1964. *Religious-Apostolic Formation*. Edited by Sister Ritamary [Bradley], C.H.M. New York: Fordham Univ. Press.

Sisters, Servants of the Immaculate Heart of Mary. 1920, 1988. *Constitutions of the Congregation of the Sisters, Servants of the Immaculate Heart of Mary*. Monroe, Mich.: SSIHM.

——. [1920]. *Diamond Jubilee: Congregation of the Sisters, Servants of the Immaculate Heart of Mary*. Monroe, Mich.: SSIHM.

——. 1932. *St. Mary College and Academy, Monroe, Michigan: Commemorating the Dedication of the New Motherhouse of the Sisters, Servants of the Immaculate Heart of Mary and the New St. Mary Academy*. Monroe, Mich.: SSIHM.

——. 1948. *Customs of the Congregation of the Sisters, Servants of the Immaculate Heart of Mary*. Monroe, Mich.: SSIHM.

——. 1987. *A Collection of Prayers from Our Heritage*. Monroe, Mich.: SSIHM.

Smith, Henry Nash. 1950. *Virgin Land: The American West as Symbol and Myth*. New York: Vintage.

Smith-Rosenberg, Carroll. 1985. *Disorderly Conduct: Visons of Gender in Victorian America*. New York: Oxford Univ. Press.

Sullivan, Mary Christine. 1940. "Some Non-Permanent Foundations of Religious Orders and Congregations of Women in the United States, 1793–1850." *United States Catholic Historical Society, Historical Records and Studies*, 31:7–118.

Taves, Ann. 1986. *The Household of Faith: Roman Catholic Devotions in Mid-Nineteenth-Century America*. Notre Dame, Ind.: Univ. of Notre Dame Press.

Tentler, Leslie. 1990. *Seasons of Grace: A History of the Catholic Archdiocese of Detroit*. Detroit: Wayne State Univ. Press.

Thomas, M. Evangeline. 1948. *Footprints on the Frontier: A History of the Sisters of Saint Joseph of Concordia, Kansas, from 1883–1948*. Westminster, Md.: Newman.

―――. 1983. "Table of U.S. Founding Dates." In *Women Religious History Sources: A Guide to Repositories in the United States*, 169–76. New York: R. R. Bowker.

Thomas à Kempis. 1940. The *Imitation of Christ*. Translated by Aloysius Craft and Harold Bolton. Milwaukee: Bruce.

Thompson, Francis. 1922. *The Hound of Heaven*, with illustrations by Stella Langdale. New York: Dodd, Mead.

Thompson, Margaret Susan. 1985. "Philemon's Dilemma: Nuns and Blacks in Nineteenth-Century America—Some Findings." *Records of the American Catholic Historical Society* 96, 3–18.

―――. 1986a. "Discovering Foremothers: Sisters, Society, and the American Catholic Experience." *U.S. Catholic Historian* 5 (Summer / Autumn): 273–90.

―――. 1986b. "Loretto, The Vatican and Historical Irony." *NCAN News* (Dec.).

―――. 1987a. "To Serve the People of God: Nineteenth-Century Sisters and the Creation of an American Catholic Religious Life." *Cushwa Center Working Paper*. Series 18, no. 2.

―――. 1987b. " 'Father' Didn't Always Know Best: Sisters Versus Clerics in Nineteenth-Century American Catholicism." Paper presented at the 1987 symposium of the Social Science History Association, New Orleans.

―――. 1989a. "Sisterhood and Power: Class, Culture, and Ethnicity in the American Convent." *Colby Library Quarterly* (Autumn): 149–75.

―――. 1989b. "Women and American Catholicism, 1789–1989." In *Perspectives on the Catholic Church in America, 1789–1989*, edited by Virginia Geiger and Stephen Vicchio, 123–42. Westminster, Md.: Christian Classics.

―――. 1991. "Women, Feminism, and the New Religious History: Catholic Sisters as a Case Study." In *Belief and Behavior: Essays in the New Religious History*, edited by Philip VanderMeer and Robert Swierenga, 136–63. New Brunswick, N.J.: Rutgers Univ. Press.

―――. 1992. "Cultural Conundrum: Sisters, Ethnicity, and the Adaptation of American Catholicism." *Mid-America* 74:205–30.

―――. 1994. "The Validation of Sisterhood: Canonical Status and Liberation in the History of American Nuns." In *A Leaf of the Great Tree of God: Essays in Honour of Ritamary Bradley*, edited by Margot H. King, 38–78. Toronto, Ont.: Peregrina.

―――. Forthcoming. *The Yoke of Grace: American Nuns and Social Change, 1808–1917*. New York: Oxford Univ. Press.

Turner, Mary Xavier, I.H.M. 1984. "St. Mary Infirmary and Health Care Center." Unpublished manuscript.

Upton, Elizabeth. 1985. *Secrets of a Nun: My Own Story*. New York: William Morrow.

Valenti, Patricia D. 1991. *To Myself a Stranger: A Biography of Rose Hawthorne Lathrop*. Baton Rouge: Louisiana Univ. Press.

Vertinsky, Patricia. 1990. *The Eternally Wounded Woman: Women, Doctors and Exercise in the Late Nineteenth Century*. Manchester, Eng.: Manchester Univ. Press.

Vidulich, Dorothy. 1975. *Peace Pays a Price*. Teaneck, N.J.: Garden State.

Violet, Arlene (with Suda J. Prohaska). 1988. *Convictions: My Journey from the Convent to the Courtroom*. New York: Random House.

Waites, Elizabeth A. 1993. *Trauma and Survival: Post-Traumatic and Dissociative Disorders in Women*. New York: W. W. Norton.

Ware, Ann Patrick, ed. 1985. *Midwives of the Future. American Sisters Tell Their Story.* Kansas City, Mo.: Leaven.

————, ed. 1995. *Naming Our Truth: Stories of Loretto Women.* Inverness, Calif: Chardon.

Welter, Barbara. 1976. *Dimity Convictions: The American Woman in the Nineteenth Century.* Athens: Ohio Univ. Press.

West, Elliott. 1989. *Growing Up With The Country: Childhood on the Far Western Frontier.* Albuquerque: Univ. of New Mexico Press.

Westkott, Marcia. 1986. *The Feminist Legacy of Karen Horney.* New Haven, Conn.: Yale Univ. Press.

[Wilson, Harriet E.] 1983. *Our Nig; or, Sketches from the Life of a Free Black, In a Two-Story White House, North, Showing that Slavery's Shadows Fall Even Here.* 1859. Reprint. New York: Random House.

[Wolff], Madeleva, C.S.C. 1959. *My First Seventy Years.* New York: Macmillan.

Wolman, Benjamin B., ed. 1989. *Dictionary of Behavioral Science.* San Diego: Academic.

Wong, Mary Gilligan. 1983. *Nun: A Memoir.* New York: Harcourt Brace Jovanovich.

Wood, Ann Douglas. 1974. "The Fashionable Diseases: Women's Complaints and Their Treatment in Nineteenth Century America." In *Clio's Consciousness Raised: New Perspectives on the History of Women,* edited by Mary S. Hartman and Lois Banner, 1–23. New York: Harper Colophon.

Woodward, Carolyn. 1990. "Reclaiming Our Pasts." In *Changing Our Power: An Introduction to Women's Studies,* 2d ed. Dubuque, Iowa: Kendall/Hunt.

Wuest, Joseph, C.SS.R. 1899. *Annales Congregationis SS. Redemptoris, Provinciae Americanae.* III, 1. Ilchester, Md.: Privately published.

Yuhaus, Cassian J., ed. 1994. *The Challenge for Tomorrow.* New York: Paulist.

# Index

Italic page number denotes illustration.